Macroeconomics
Beyond the NAIRU

Macroeconomics Beyond the NAIRU

Servaas Storm and
C. W. M. Naastepad

Harvard University Press

Cambridge, Massachusetts, and London, England | 2012

Library of Congress Cataloging-in-Publication Data

Storm, Servaas.
    Macroeconomics beyond the NAIRU / Servaas Storm and
  C. W. M. Naastepad.
       p.   cm.
    Includes bibliographical references and index.
    ISBN 978-0-674-06227-6 (alk. paper)
    1. Natural rate of unemployment.   2. Macroeconomics.
  3. Monetary policy.   I. Naastepad, C. W. M., 1961–   II. Title.
  HD5706.S816   2011
  339—dc23   2011018741

Highly paid labour is generally efficient and therefore not dear labour; a fact which, though it is more full of hope for the future of the human race than any other that is known to us, will be found to exercise a very complicating influence on the theory of distribution.

ALFRED MARSHALL, *ELEMENTS OF ECONOMICS OF INDUSTRY*

Contents

Preface

This book grew out of our research on the macroeconomic causes of unemployment, rising inequality, and the rather lackluster growth and productivity performance in Western Europe, Australia, Japan, Canada, and the United States after 1980. It took a long time to write. Our main problem was how to put together, in one "artistic whole," the various bits and pieces of our work on OECD (Organisation for Economic Co-operation and Development) capitalism—it took time to find the right words to bring our message across.[1] As Mark Twain once wrote as advice to young beginners, "The difference between the *almost right* word and the *right* word is really a large matter—'tis the difference between the lightning-bug and the lightning."[2] We believe we finally managed to express our concerns about the mainstream macroeconomic view that persistent unemployment follows ineluctably from a more regulated labor market featuring protective, "rigid" labor market institutions. For many, this view has become even more compelling in recent times, as it is generally felt that if firms are to survive (and employment to be maintained), firms have to be able to adjust flexibly and efficiently to global market pressures and rapid technological change. The mainstream view further subscribes to what may be called Friedman's policy ineffectiveness theorem, which states that fiscal and monetary policies cannot have permanent impacts on (natural or structural) unemployment and growth.

To us, this view never seemed convincing, and in this book we explain why this is so. Our book is intended both to be a critique of the mainstream view, the NAIRU (non-accelerating inflation rate of unemployment) theory, and to provide an escape—a new theoretical approach to growth, distribution, unemployment, and technological progress—from the current "collective inability to imagine alternatives," as Tony Judt observed in his final essay in the *New York Review of Books*.[3]

We hope that the book will succeed in convincing readers that the conventional (NAIRU) wisdom is based on a faulty model, one that neglects the various positive contributions labor makes to economic performance, not least in the form of its contribution to technological progress and labor productivity growth. Highly paid labor is therefore not dear labor, as was also Alfred Marshall's view. Marshall got it right when he added that this fact is more full of hope for humanity than any other known to him. If these positive contributions are taken into account, as we do in this book, then it follows that a more regulated and coordinated industrial relations system, which offers strong legal protections to workers' rights and in which labor is organized so as to give workers an effective and safe say and stake in how they do their jobs and how their firms are run, can create the conditions for high growth, technological dynamism, and low unemployment. It also follows, and this is our second claim, that demand policies do affect the economy's long-run performance, including its structural rate of unemployment.

It is our hope that the book will be widely accessible to all those interested in the current debates on egalitarianism, unemployment, labor market reforms, and globalization. We offer the argument as an agenda for discussion, rather than as a completed piece of analysis—we feel it is worth the attempt to clear up some simple problems and confusion with respect to the NAIRU approach, in the hope that "our heads may grow stronger as we go on," as Joan Robinson (1979, x) remarked. The focus is on the rich OECD countries (see the Appendix for a complete list of the countries in the sample). We have used mathematics to illustrate and explain the standard theory as well as our preferred alternative. The level of mathematics, however, is not very demanding, and throughout we have tried to explain our algebraic conclusions.

Much of the material here draws on our earlier publications. Certain parts of the book have been adapted from essays published elsewhere. Chapter 3 has its origins in a paper published in the *Cambridge Journal of Economics* (Naastepad 2006) and in a chapter published in Mark Setterfield's *Handbook of Alternative Theories of Economic Growth* (Naastepad and Storm 2010). Chapter 4 is based on a paper published in *Industrial Relations* (Storm and Naastepad 2009b). Chapter 5 draws on and extends our paper in the *Journal of Post Keynesian Economics* (Naastepad and Storm 2007). An earlier version of Chapter 6 was first published in the *Eastern Economic Journal* (Storm and Naastepad 2009a) and also builds on a paper published in the *International Review of Applied Economics* (Storm and Naastepad 2008b). Some parts of Chapter 7 appeared in our article for *Challenge* (Storm and Naastepad 2009c) and an unpublished conference paper we wrote on the Nordic model.

Among the various friends and colleagues who helped us to understand NAIRU-based macroeconomics and develop essential building blocks for the alternative model, we would particularly like to thank Amit Bhaduri and Lance Taylor, whose ideas and advice over a long period helped shape and strengthen our argument. We are very grateful to the late Sukhamoy Chakravarty for emphasizing the relevance of classical political economy and distributional conflict for understanding contemporary economic problems. We received valuable comments on drafts from Jayati Ghosh, Andrew Glyn (whom we sadly miss), Trond Petersen, Malcolm Sawyer, Mark Setterfield, and anonymous publisher's readers. We are grateful to Michael Aronson and Kathleen Drummy at Harvard University Press for being very helpful and supportive. We also thank John Donohue and his team at Westchester Book Services for their excellent copyediting. Peter Auer and Malte Lübker of the International Labour Organization (ILO) provided invaluable help when we were writing an earlier version of Chapter 4. Chapter 5 (in embryonic form) was presented at the European Association for Evolutionary Political Economy conference in Maastricht in 2003, where Pascal Petit gave useful suggestions. We thank the participants in the April 2007 conference "Realistic Growth Policy for Our Times," organized by the Schwartz Center for Economic Policy Analysis at the New School for Social Research, where the core material was presented in a very rough form, as well as participants in the conference "The Long-Term Impact of Short Term Fluctuations—Theory, Evidence and Policy," Brookings Institution, Washington, D.C., November 5–6, 2009, where an earlier version of Chapter 7 was discussed. Errors, of course, remain our own responsibility.

**Macroeconomics
Beyond the NAIRU**

1

The Power of Ideas

> I must create a system, or be enslav'd by another man's.
> I will not reason and compare: my business is to create.
>
> WILLIAM BLAKE, *JERUSALEM*

Seventy-five years ago, in *The General Theory of Employment, Interest and Money*, John Maynard Keynes wrote:

> The ideas of economists and political philosophers, both when they are right and when they are wrong, are more powerful than is commonly understood. Indeed, the world is ruled by little else. Practical men, who believe themselves to be quite exempt from any intellectual influences, are usually the slaves of some defunct economist. Madmen in authority, who hear voices in the air, are distilling their frenzy from some academic scribbler of a few years back. (1973, 383)

Plus ça change, plus c'est la même chose. We argue in this book that while many things have changed since the mid-1930s, today's practical women and men are as much the slaves of defunct economic theories as were their predecessors, the macroeconomic policymakers of the early 1930s. Keynes attacked what he called classical economic theory (what we would now call neoclassical economics), arguing that its postulates are applicable only to a very special constellation of macroeconomic factors and not to the general case. Likewise, it is our objective to critically scrutinize the core of modern mainstream macroeconomics, the NAIRU model, which has been ruling macroeconomics textbooks and macro policy making for more than thirty years now and which continues to underlie and dominate national and international policy making (as will be obvious to anyone reading official publications by the IMF [International Monetary Fund], the OECD, and the European Union [EU]).[1] Our critique is similar to that of Keynes: the postulates of the NAIRU model are applicable, if at all, only to a special case—namely, the case of a profit-led economy, the special characteristics of which happen not to be those of the economic systems of most OECD countries.[2] And just like Keynes, we believe that "the matters at issue are of an importance which cannot be exaggerated" (Keynes 1973, xxi). Not only is the teaching of NAIRU-based macroeconomics misleading, but attempting to apply it to

1

practice is economically and socially disastrous—the costs of NAIRUvianist macroeconomic policy are very large and avoidable. It is our objective to persuade fellow economists to reexamine critically the basic assumptions of their core theory. In the attempt to distinguish our Keynesian approach as sharply as possible from the mainstream's NAIRU workhorse, it may seem we are being unduly controversial; perhaps this is true, in which case we must apologize, but, based on experience, we are convinced that clear-cut distinctions are needed if we are to have a chance of convincing fellow economists and policymakers, knowing that not many of them are open to "new theories after they are twenty-five or thirty years of age"—as Keynes himself was well aware (Keynes 1973, 383–384).

Keynes pointed his arrows at the second postulate of the classical theory of employment, which states that "the real wage of an employed person is that which is just sufficient . . . to induce the volume of labour actually employed to be forthcoming." Actual unemployment thus must be due at bottom to a refusal by unemployed workers to accept a lower money wage, which corresponds to their marginal productivity. Keynes argued that the second postulate excludes, a priori and unrealistically, the possibility of involuntary unemployment (Taylor 2010). In his view, there may be no forces tending to lower the real wage when there is an excess supply of labor. The only way workers could respond would be by cutting the money wage (since actual wage bargains are made in terms of money). Keynes argued that cuts in money wages cannot bring about a fall in the real wage, because money wages are such a large part of production costs; hence, prices will fall, keeping the real wage constant and leaving the economy with involuntary unemployment. Things can even get worse, because the deflation of wages and prices increases the real interest rate and the burden of servicing debts, which will discourage both investment and consumption.

Modern-day classical employment theory has buried Keynes's objections without actually resolving them, maintaining the "failed metaphor" of an "aggregative labor market" to conclude that actual unemployment, either voluntary or involuntary, is due to real wages that are too high and rigid (Galbraith 1997). High and downwardly rigid real wages, in turn, are caused by excessive labor market regulation, redistributive interventions, employment protection legislation, high taxation, and social welfare states, all of which are meant to reduce income inequalities and protect workers against uninsurable labor-market-related risk. However socially praiseworthy the intentions underlying these regulatory interventions, their sole macroeconomic impact is claimed to be a strengthened wage bargaining position for unions, higher real wage costs (relative to productivity), reduced real wage flexibility, and therefore higher unemployment (especially of the lower-skilled) and weaker overall macroeconomic performance.

The NAIRU model holds lessons not only for labor market policies but also for fiscal and monetary policy making. The key macro policy implication is that governments and central banks should not try to promote full employment, as efforts to push the unemployment rate below the critical threshold (the NAIRU) would generate accelerating inflation, essentially because the money printing required to create higher employment would be translated, by a rapid process of labor and product market adjustment, into higher money wages and higher prices. The model thus imagines that the economy exists on a knife edge and that even a small deviation toward low unemployment would generate hyperinflation. As James Galbraith (2008, 46) writes:

> The idea that low unemployment generates runaway inflation was an absurdity on its face. If it had been true, runaway hyperinflations should have been common in history, whereas in fact they are very rare. Yet the [NAIRU] model served the self-importance of central bankers and the perpetuation of conservative rule in monetary policy. . . . Over time, central bankers managed to persuade themselves, and many economists, of their indispensability to the anti-inflation struggle.

The key policy implication—that all attempts to promote full employment and more egalitarian growth are doomed to fail—lives on in many guises even today.

It follows from NAIRU theory that there exists a conflict, or trade-off, between growth and equity, especially now that market competition has become more intense as a result of globalization. It is on this doctrine—that egalitarian growth is not economically feasible—that most of us were brought up. It dominates the economic thought, both practical and theoretical, of the policy-making and academic classes of this generation—indeed, the macroeconomic world is ruled by little else (as we will illustrate in a few pages). We challenge this doctrine and argue that it is plain wrong, because it is based on a fundamental misunderstanding of how the economy in which we live actually works. Instead, it is our contention that the "nasty trade-off" between growth and equity, to use the words of Andrew Glyn (2006, 119–121), is man-made, created by the ways in which we organize and regulate our economic systems. It follows that egalitarian growth is absolutely feasible—even in open, globalized economies.

The Conventional Wisdom

As the starting point of our argument, we present our formulation of what Lawrence Ball (1999) has called "the conventional wisdom"—the standard mainstream NAIRU model, as it is usually presented in major macro textbooks. We are well aware that our characterization necessarily involves a subjective element; after all, it is our reading of the vast and differentiated macroeconomics literature and our attempt to extract a coherent core from this literature.[3] We often have been urged to recognize the variety within mainstream economics by using qualifications such as "monetarist" or "new Keynesian," but we think that, notwithstanding the variety, the core is essentially the same, irrespective of the precise label. In this view, the rate of inflation is seen as the outcome of a conflict over income distribution between workers (labor unions) and capitalists (firms). This follows from a wage bargaining process in which workers negotiate money wages designed to give them a certain standard of living, while firms set prices as an exogenous markup on expected variable costs that include labor costs. Wage setting depends positively on the expected price level and exogenous wage push factors (including employment protection legislation, social security provisions, unemployment benefits, and labor taxes) and negatively on the unemployment rate. Competing income claims by workers and capitalists are made consistent by means of variations in the equilibrium unemployment rate; in fact, it is the function of equilibrium unemployment to make workers accept the preordained wage share, for if they do not, the result will be accelerating and, ultimately, unsustainable inflation.[4]

The standard NAIRU model consists of a wage-setting (WS) curve and a price-setting (PS) curve. The WS curve is derived from the wage bargaining process, in which the bargaining power of workers over money wage growth $\hat{W}$ is assumed to depend on the rate of unemployment u, the exogenously given growth rate of labor productivity $\hat{\lambda}$ (a circumflex over a variable denotes its growth rate), expected future inflation $\hat{p}^e$, and z, which is a catchall variable that stands for all other institutional and regulatory variables that affect the outcome of wage setting.[5]

$$(1.1) \qquad \hat{W} - \hat{p}^e = \alpha_0 - \alpha_1 u + \alpha_2 \hat{\lambda} + \alpha_3 z \qquad \alpha_0, \alpha_1, \alpha_3 > 0; 0 \leq \alpha_2 \leq 1$$

Equation (1.1) states the following. First, lower unemployment will augment union bargaining power, and consequently wage demands by workers will be higher; hence coefficient α_1 has a negative sign. This relation between unemployment and expected real wage growth is drawn in Figure 1.1. Real wage growth is measured on the vertical axis. The unemployment rate is measured on the horizontal axis. The wage-setting relation is drawn as the downward-sloping WS curve: the higher the unemployment rate, the lower real wage growth will be. According to equation (1.1), wage setters are further assumed to build the underlying labor productivity growth into their real wage claims, with their share in productivity growth being dependent on the (perceived) state of the labor market and on the nature and extent of labor market regulation; coefficient α_2 represents the extent to which labor productivity growth is reflected in the real wage bargain, so if $\alpha_2 = 1$, productivity growth is fully reflected in real wage growth. Third, by convention, a higher z (meaning more extensive labor market regulation) reflects workers' strengthened bargaining position, which increases real wage growth demanded by workers at a given unemployment rate, hence $\alpha_3 > 0$. Finally, wage bargaining is based on the expected rate of inflation $\hat{p}^e$: higher expected prices will lead to higher nominal wage claims, as workers try to maintain the expected real wage.

The PS curve is assumed to reflect the rate of real wage growth, which is consistent with the price-setting behavior of firms—the latter is usually based on assuming oligopolistic competition in product markets. Specifically, firms set prices as a markup over unit labor cost. If we assume a constant markup rate, we get equation (1.2), expressed in growth rates:

(1.2) $\hat{p} = \hat{W} - \hat{\lambda}$

Rearranging equation (1.2), we obtain the PS curve (1.2'):

(1.2') $\hat{w} = \hat{W} - \hat{p} = \hat{\lambda}$

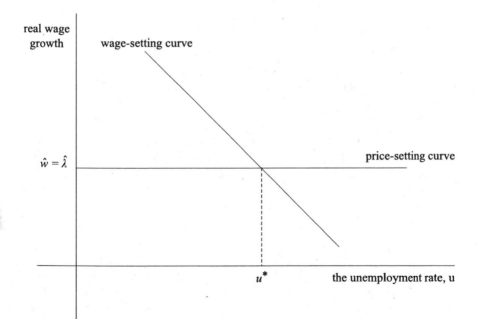

Figure 1.1. Wage-setting, price-setting, and the nonaccelerating inflation rate of unemployment (NAIRU).

Actual real wage growth, denoted by $\hat{w}$, thus has to equal labor productivity growth. This condition must hold in a long-run steady state, because it implies that inflation is constant (neither accelerating nor decelerating) while at the same time the distribution of income across wages and profits is constant. If labor productivity growth is exogenous, equation (1.2') implies that price-setting decisions determine the real wage growth paid by firms. This price-setting relation is drawn as the horizontal PS curve in Figure 1.1. The real wage growth implied by price setting is constant, equal to labor productivity, and therefore independent of the unemployment rate.

Equilibrium in the labor market requires that real wage growth demanded be equal to the real wage growth warranted by price setting. In Figure 1.1, equilibrium is given by the point of intersection between the WS curve and the PS curve, with equilibrium unemployment being u^*. We can also characterize the equilibrium unemployment or the NAIRU algebraically: if we assume that inflation expectations equal actual inflation or $\hat{p}^e = \hat{p}$, and next combine equations (1.1) and (1.2'), u^* is given by

$$(1.3) \qquad u^* = \frac{\alpha_0 - (1 - \alpha_2)\hat{\lambda} + \alpha_3 z}{\alpha_1}$$

Equation (1.3) represents the canonical formulation of how the NAIRU gets determined by institutions and policy (variable z) and by productivity growth $\hat{\lambda}$ (assuming that that $\alpha_1 > 0$, $\alpha_2 < 1$, and $\alpha_3 > 0$). In its essence, equilibrium unemployment is a macroeconomic disciplining device to curb workers' wage claims, bringing them back in line with exogenous labor productivity growth, so as to maintain firm profits. The concept of equilibrium unemployment is usually—and rather loosely—associated with Marx's reserve army of the unemployed (introduced in chapter 25 of *Capital* [1987]), which is "the pivot upon which the law of demand and supply of labour works." According to Marx, wage changes are determined "by the varying proportions in which the working-class is divided into active and reserve army." But Marx himself owes these ideas to Adam Smith, who wrote in *The Wealth of Nations* that normally there is always a scarcity of jobs relative to job seekers:

> There could seldom be any scarcity of hands nor could the masters be obliged to bid against one another in order to get them. The hands, on the contrary, would in this case naturally multiply beyond their employment. There would be a constant scarcity of employment and the labourers would be obliged to bid against one another in order to get it. If in such a country, the wages of labour had ever been more than sufficient to maintain the labourer and to enable him to bring up a family, the

competition of the labourers and the interest of the masters would soon reduce them to the lowest level which is consistent with common humanity. (Smith 1976, 80)

The conventional NAIRU equation (1.3) generates straightforward and powerful results. Consider the following two examples:

- *An increase in the extent of labor market regulation* (e.g., higher unemployment benefits, stricter employment protection legislation, or other pro-worker labor market interventions). An increase in regulation can be represented by an increase in our wage-push factor z: it increases the real wage growth demanded by workers at a given unemployment rate in equation (1.1). Graphically, this shifts up the wage-setting curve from WS to WS', as is shown in Figure 1.2. The equilibrium unemployment moves up from u^* to u_z^*. With more powerful unions, the system needs a higher structural rate of unemployment—to use the terminology of Edmund Phelps (1994)—to stabilize inflation and to bring the wage demanded back in line with the preordained wage share implied by firms' price setting. The powerful conclusion thus is that excessive labor market regulation (a high z) creates structural unemployment and, contrariwise, labor market deregulation will lower the steady inflation unemployment rate.

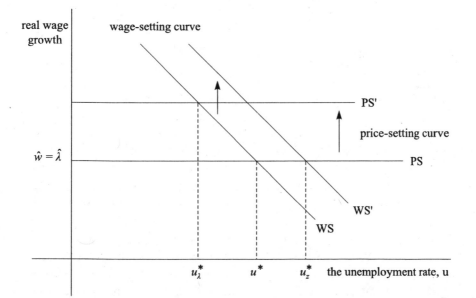

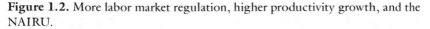

Figure 1.2. More labor market regulation, higher productivity growth, and the NAIRU.

- *A positive shock to exogenous labor productivity growth* (i.e., $\hat{\lambda}$ increases). As a result, firms can pay higher wages while maintaining their profit share and keeping their prices constant. Wage-push inflationary pressure declines at a given unemployment rate: now less unemployment is needed to keep inflation constant. In Figure 1.2, the increase in $\hat{\lambda}$ shifts up the price-setting curve from PS to PS', and the NAIRU comes down from u^* to u_λ^*. This is a second major finding: higher labor productivity growth is associated with lower structural unemployment—quite unlike popular and political Luddite worries that technological progress must lead to jobless growth and increased unemployment, and also unlike Marx's argument that productivity growth is instrumental to creating proletarian unemployment, needed to sustain capitalist profits.[6]

But the most powerful implication has not yet been mentioned. It follows from equation (1.3) that there is no role whatsoever for demand factors in determining equilibrium unemployment. Any attempt by fiscal or monetary policy to permanently move actual unemployment away from its equilibrium level u^* is doomed to failure. Macro policy may temporarily lower actual unemployment, but this will strengthen the bargaining power of wage setters, lead to higher wage claims, and set off a process of accelerating wage-push inflation (because firms raise prices to maintain profits). The inflation, in turn, will undermine demand (which is supposed to depend negatively on prices) and raise unemployment until the equilibrium rate of unemployment is reached again. Demand will adjust itself to the "natural" level of output, corresponding to the NAIRU, either passively through the so-called Pigou or real balance effect[7] or, alternatively, more actively through a policy-administered rise in interest rates by the central bank.[8] Hence, the implication of equation (1.3) is that employment policy should focus exclusively on the labor market (and not on aggregate demand and investment), above all on the behavior of labor unions and (mostly welfare-state-related) wage-push factors. To permanently reduce unemployment, labor markets have to be deregulated; employment protection, labor taxes, and unemployment benefits have to be reduced; wage bargaining has to be decentralized; and welfare states have to be scaled down. Why? Because egalitarian redistribution, employment protection, and social insurance (which are what most of labor market regulation is about) not only raise real wage costs for firms and hence reduce international cost competitiveness and profits but also reduce the capacity of firms to flexibly respond to global market and technological shocks—and this in an era in which globalization has sharply increased the range and intensity of competition, and more adaptable production systems and labor markets are essential to firm survival. Persistently high unemployment and weak growth performance thus do reflect a deliberate policy choice to maintain egalitarian institutional arrangements, which have the unintended effect of creating sclerotic labor markets, helping the "insiders" but hurting the unemployed "outsiders." This is what Milton Friedman meant when, to popularize his view, he commented that "there is no such thing as a free lunch." In the words of Paul Gregg and Alan Manning (1997, 395), this stance reflects the "touching faith that many economists have in the view that de-regulation of the labour market moves it towards the perfectly competitive ideal in which everyone who wants a job can find one at a wage equal to the value of their contribution to society"—a "touching faith," in other words, in the second postulate of the classical theory of employment, which persists, even after having been shown to be wrong by Keynes seventy-five years ago, as perhaps the clearest example of how defunct ideas continue to make the policy world go round.

The fundamental theoretical point here is that if one accepts the NAIRU approach to employment and growth, labor market outcomes cannot be improved upon by regulation or social planning. Things should be "left to the market," that is, left to the collective self-interest of individual agents (see Marglin 2008 for a critique). In practice, however, no serious mainstream macroeconomist would deny that labor markets need at least a modicum of regulation to function, because of problems of imperfect information and asymmetries in bargaining power.[9] Accordingly, the policy discussion has centered around questions concerning the nature and optimal extent of labor market regulation, on the implicit understanding that labor markets should not deviate "too much" from the ideal of a deregulated, perfectly competitive market. This led to a broad consensus (1) that the slow and inadequate growth of employment (and high unemployment) in many OECD countries is due not to interventions per se but to excessive labor market regulation and (2) that those countries that have more fully deregulated their labor markets are the best performers in terms of employment, innovation, and growth. Unsurprisingly, there has been endless, as well as fruitless, wrangling within the consensus view about which kind of labor market interventions are "excessive" and which are not, as we discuss in Chapter 2. In practice, this problem has been resolved by taking the U.S. economy and its deregulated labor market as the norm and considering any deviation from that norm as being "excessive."[10] What is not sufficiently recognized, however, is that no amount of econometric evidence will ever settle this issue— any more than evidence can settle whether a glass is half full or half empty. What is needed is a deeper analysis focusing on the hidden, implicit assumptions underlying the NAIRU model. But before going into this foundational critique, let us first turn to today's practical women and men who are (indirectly and directly) responsible for OECD macroeconomic and employment policy, "distilling their frenzy" from the—in our view—defunct NAIRU approach.

Voices in the Air

The NAIRU approach and its policy implications have been advocated with great rhetorical power, beginning with Friedman's formulation of the "natural rate of unemployment." They dominate today's textbooks, monopolize academic debate, and (almost) exclusively rule macroeconomic policy making in the OECD area, and are likely to continue to do so. It has become so self-evident that a leading scholar could recently claim that "evidence supports the traditional view that rigidities that reduce competition in labor markets are typically responsible for high unemployment" without actually citing any peer-reviewed evidence (Saint Paul 2004, 53). Princeton economist Paul Krugman compared people who challenged NAIRU doctrine to scientists who disputed evidence of damage to the earth's ozone layer; serious economists, Krugman himself included, were rightly offended by the "political reopening of what they regarded as a settled issue" (Baker 2002, 6).

Economists turned their eyes to the links between labor market regulation and unemployment in the early 1980s, as unemployment rates increased dramatically and persistently in the OECD countries, especially in Europe. This early research was firmly founded on the NAIRU approach and basically constituted attempts at explaining cross-country differences in unemployment in terms of differences in regulation (or institutions). The most influential early study has been *Unemployment: Macroeconomic Performance and the Labour Market*, authored by Richard Layard, Stephen Nickell, and Richard Jackman (1991). Their claim that excessive regulation was the primary cause of unemployment in the advanced countries was brought to the center of policy debate by the 1994 *OECD Jobs Study*. The *Jobs Study* provided an agenda for labor market deregulation, including increased flexibility of working time, making wage costs more flexible by removing restrictions, reducing employment security provisions, and scaling down unemployment benefit systems. The OECD has been consistently repeating this mantra in its annual *Employment Outlook* series. Spurred by the influence of Layard, Nickell, and Jackman and the *Jobs Study*, the NAIRU view rapidly became the consensus view. The title of a prominent paper in the *Journal of Economic Perspectives* summed it all up: "Labor Market Rigidities: At the Root of Unemployment in Europe." In an attempt to deride Marx and Engels, its author, German economist Horst Siebert, concludes that "the specter of unemployment that is haunting Europe will not be exorcised unless governments are prepared to undertake major reforms of the institutional setup of the labor market," that is, by drastic deregulation of labor markets (Siebert 1997, 53).

In particular, in-house OECD economists have played a leading role in the empirical research effort that has aimed to explain the variation in unemployment across the OECD countries mainly in terms of excessive labor market regulation (Scarpetta 1996; Elmeskov, Martin, and Scarpetta 1998; Nicoletti and Scarpetta 2003; Bassanini and Duval 2006). Elmeskov, Martin, and Scarpetta (1998, 242), for instance, write, in what almost looks like an advertisement for deregulation:

> [We] assign significant roles to unemployment benefits, collective bargaining structures, active labor market policies . . . and the tax wedge. . . . It requires strong political will and leadership to convince electorates that it is necessary to swallow all of the [deregulation] medicine and that it will take time before this treatment leads to improved labor market performance and falling unemployment. But the success stories show that it can be done!

Not only is the medicine bitter, it also has to be swallowed all in one go—piecemeal deregulation will not do. Nearly a decade after the *Jobs Study*, the IMF published a chapter in its *World Economic Outlook* (2003, 129) predicting that unemployment in Europe would fall massively below U.S. levels if the European countries deregulated their labor market and product markets (U.S. style); reductions in replacement rates, lower labor tax wedges, and much lower employment protection regulations "could produce output gains of about 5 percent and a fall in the [European] unemployment rate of about 3 percentage points." That inequality and job insecurity in Europe would rise (as the by-product of deregulation) is considered both inevitable and a lesser social evil than high structural joblessness. The same point—that inequality and unemployment are two sides of the same coin—has been made by a pair of leading liberal U.S. economists:

> The flexible U.S. labor market was able to accommodate these strains [shocks in the 1970s and 1980s] by letting absolute and relative real-wage levels adjust, thus permitting the unemployment rate to stay low. In contrast . . . in most other OECD countries, collective bargaining and other labor-market institutions and government regulations kept overall real wages rising and prevented the relative wages of unskilled workers from falling as fast as they did in the less-interventionist U.S.

labor market or, in some cases, preventing any decrease at all in the relative pay of low-skilled workers. (Blau and Kahn 2002, 255)

A recent and most prominent case for the NAIRU doctrine has been made by Stephen Nickell, Luca Nunziata, and Wolfgang Ochel in the *Economic Journal*. Without responding to critical commentary about the robustness of their results, these authors reiterate the claim that "broad movements in unemployment across the OECD can be explained by . . . labour market institutions"—"excessive" (vis-à-vis the United States) labor market regulation explains "around 55% of the rise in European unemployment from the 1960s to the first half of the 1990s."[11] In other words, the evidence that the bitter medicine of labor market deregulation will eventually cure the structural unemployment problem appears compelling—but, as Chapter 2 makes clear, this appearance is deceptive.

Our Foundational Critique: A First Pass

We are certainly not the first to criticize the NAIRU approach. There exists, for one, a sophisticated econometric literature that critically assesses the empirical evidence produced by the mainstream NAIRU literature; in Chapter 2 we present a review of these assessments. For another, there exists a theoretical literature criticizing the structural assumptions of the NAIRU model, including the absence of money illusion (implied by the assumption that $\hat{p}^e = \hat{p}$), the neglect of fundamental uncertainty about future events, the absence of information asymmetries (between workers and firms), a constant markup rate, the neglect of hysteresis, and the general absence of nonlinearities and multiple equilibria (Galbraith 1997; Ball 1999; Blanchard 2004). Without taking anything away from such structural critiques, we believe that a deeper critique can be made, one that focuses on the foundations of the NAIRU model. The starting point of this foundational critique is that we accept the NAIRU model and its assumptions, and next argue that even in such an idealized world, there is a good reason to be wary of the claims made by NAIRU-based economics.

The essence of our critique is that the NAIRU model's view of the roles played by (real) wages and labor in OECD capitalist countries is one-sided and neglects their major alternative role. In the conventional NAIRU model, real wages are seen as mere costs to producers; higher real wage claims (at unchanged labor productivity) necessarily reduce firms' profitability, so if firms want to protect profits (which are needed for investment and growth), higher wages must lead to higher prices. Workers want to work only in exchange for pay, as labor gives them disutility. Under these assumptions, any strengthening of organized labor's bargaining position leads to higher wage claims, higher prices (to maintain profits), a further increase in wage claims, and ultimately runaway inflation. The only way to stop this process is to increase equilibrium unemployment, which is the macroeconomic disciplining device to curb workers' wage claims, bringing them back into balance with exogenous productivity growth. What is missed here is that wages perform a second role, which is contradictory to their first role: wages also provide macroeconomic benefits, chiefly in terms of higher labor productivity growth and more rapid technological progress.

Let us for the moment accept the negativist assumption that workers work only for money (since work provides them straight disutility). Even then, higher wages will raise profitability because they stimulate demand by providing more purchasing power to workers. This can be seen directly from the standard definition of the profit rate ρ as the ratio of profits Π to (invested) capital $p_k K$:

$$(1.4) \qquad \rho = \frac{\Pi}{p_k K}$$

where Π = total profits, K = the capital stock, and p_k = price of the capital stock. Let us define X = real gross domestic product (GDP) and p = the general price level. Then if we multiply the right-hand side of equation (1.4) by the ratio (pX/pX), we get, after slight manipulation:

$$(1.5) \qquad \rho = \frac{\Pi}{p_k K} * \frac{pX}{pX} = \frac{\Pi}{pX} * \frac{p}{p_k} * \frac{X}{K} = \Phi * \frac{p}{p_k} * \Theta$$

where Φ = the profit share ($= \Pi/pX$) and Θ = the output-capital ratio (X/K), or the rate of capacity utilization. The profit rate therefore depends positively on the profit share and capacity utilization. Delving deeper, we look more closely at the profit share Φ. By definition, the profit share equals total profits divided by GDP. If we assume that total profits are equal to GDP minus wages, we get

$$(1.6) \qquad \Phi = \frac{\Pi}{pX} = \frac{pX - WL}{pX} = 1 - w \left[\frac{X}{L} \right]^{-1} = 1 - w\lambda^{-1}$$

where W = the money wage (per hour), L = the number of hours worked, and λ = hourly labor productivity. As equation (1.6) shows, the profit share depends on the real wage w and labor productivity λ. A higher real wage depresses the profit share, whereas higher productivity raises the profit share. Substituting (1.6) into (1.5), we obtain the following expression for ρ:

$$(1.7) \qquad \rho = (1 - w\lambda^{-1}) * \frac{p}{p_k} * \Theta$$

Profitability thus has three main determinants: the real wage, labor productivity, and capacity utilization (if we ignore p/p_k). Using equation (1.7), we can ask how higher real wages affect the profit rate. The answer is not straightforward, however. It is immediately clear from (1.7) that the profit rate declines in response to higher real wages, because unit labor costs increase and the profit share gets reduced. This, however, is just the direct impact. Higher wages also have significant offsetting indirect effects on profitability, which operate through capacity utilization Θ and labor productivity λ. Let us consider each of the two offsetting effects in more detail.

Capacity utilization Θ will increase in response to higher real wages if the latter lead to higher aggregate demand. This increase in Θ immediately raises profitability, which will, in turn, induce higher investments by firms. Capital accumulation also increases in response to the growth in aggregate demand (via the old-fashioned Keynesian accelerator effect). The result is a sequence of rounds of demand growth and increases in utilization. What this means in terms of equation (1.7) is that not only does the real wage w rise, but so does capacity utilization Θ. The higher real wage reduces the profit rate, but higher capacity utilization raises the profit rate. Hence the net impact on profitability is no longer unambiguously negative.

In addition, the new investments will result in a higher level of labor productivity λ for two reasons, highlighted most prominently by Cambridge economist Nicholas Kaldor (Kaldor 1957, 1966). First, newly installed equipment embodies the latest production technologies and is more productive than older vintages of capital stock; by modernizing the capital stock, higher investment will therefore increase average worker productivity. Second, the increase in aggregate demand, caused by higher wages, leads to an economy-wide deepening of the division of labor as well as more rapid learning by doing (in firms), processes that eventually get reflected in higher labor productivity growth. In both explanations, higher (investment and/or aggregate) demand growth is associated with higher labor productivity growth. This positive link is known in the literature as the Kaldor-Verdoorn relation; its existence is of central importance to our argument, as becomes clear in Chapter 3, where we present our growth model. As Kaldor (1966, 287) acknowledges, Adam Smith was the first to recognize that

> the *return* per unit of labour—what we now call productivity—depends on the division of labour: on the extent of specialisation and the division of production into so many different processes, as exemplified by his famous example of pin-making. As Smith explained, the division of labour depends on the extent of the market: the greater the market, the

greater the extent to which differentiation and specialisation is carried, the higher the productivity. . . . A greater division of labour is more productive, partly because it generates more skill and know-how; more expertise in turn yields more innovations and design improvements.

The bottom line, in terms of equation (1.7), is that higher wages simultaneously raise capacity utilization and labor productivity, thereby offsetting at least part of the negative impact of higher wages on the profit rate. As equation (1.3) shows, any endogenous change in labor productivity growth does affect the NAIRU if $0 < \alpha_2 < 1$; only if $\alpha_2 = 1$ and wages increase in tandem with productivity is there no impact—but this latter case is empirically not realistic, as we will see in Chapter 5.[12]

There is one more reason (in addition to the Kaldor-Verdoorn effect) why higher real wages are associated with higher labor productivity. This explanation goes back at least to Marx, who argued in *Capital* that high wages influence the bias of innovation and technological progress within the capitalist economic system. Marx claimed that there is an inherent tendency in capitalism for technological change to be biased toward labor-saving innovations—because only labor-saving technological progress, which he identifies with rising labor productivity, ensures the reproduction of both a positive economic surplus (profits) and a growing proletariat so that the basis of capitalist exploitation is sustained. He anticipated at various places in *Capital* the modern idea that the nature of technological change is conditioned by relative factor prices. He writes, for example, that

> between 1849 and 1859, a rise in wages practically insignificant, though accompanied by falling prices of corn, took place in the English agricultural districts. . . . What did the farmers do now? . . . They introduced more machinery and in a moment the labourers were redundant again in a proportion satisfactory even to the farmers. There was now "more capital" laid out in agriculture than before, and in more productive form. With this, the demand for labour fell, not only relatively but also absolutely. (Marx 1987, 638)

Marx's idea of wage-cost-induced technological progress has gone through various incarnations, including those of Hicks (1932), Kennedy (1964), and most recently Funk (2002). Duncan Foley and Thomas Michl (1999) present a model formulation to explain why more expensive labor induces firms (by means of higher research and development [R&D] investments) to intensify their search for and adoption of labor-productivity-raising techniques. The takeaway from all this is that higher wages may also directly lead to higher labor productivity.

Let us now reconsider equation (1.7). Clearly, the direct impact of a higher real wage on the profit rate is negative:[13]

$$(1.8) \qquad \frac{\partial \rho}{\partial w} = -\lambda^{-1} \frac{p}{p_k} \Theta < 0$$

But this direct impact—given by equation (1.8)—is only the partial effect of higher wages on profitability, not the complete impact. To determine the total effect, we must take into account the impacts of higher wages on (1) demand and capacity utilization Θ and (2) technological progress and labor productivity λ. Let us assume that capacity utilization depends positively on the real wage rate, or $\Theta = f(w)$; $f' > 0$. And higher wages raise labor productivity, because of higher demand (the Kaldor-Verdoorn effect) and Marx-biased technological progress, hence $\lambda = h(w)$; $h' > 0$. Substituting in equation (1.7) gives us the following more complicated expression for the profit rate:

$$(1.9) \qquad \rho = (1 - w\lambda^{-1}) * \frac{p}{p_k} * \Theta = \left(1 - \frac{w}{h(w)}\right) * \frac{p}{p_k} * f(w)$$

We can use equation (1.9) to determine the total impact on the profit rate of a higher real wage, as follows:

$$(1.10) \qquad \frac{d\rho}{dw} = \frac{p}{p_k}\left[(1 - w\lambda^{-1})f' + \frac{w\Theta}{\lambda^2}h' - \lambda^{-1}\Theta\right]$$

Whether the total impact is negative or positive is not clear. Sure enough, a higher real wage reduces the profit rate because it raises labor costs (at an unchanged level of labor productivity), as is indicated by the term $-\lambda^{-1}\Theta$ in equation (1.10), but at the same time the higher wage raises profitability because it raises capacity utilization and labor productivity. This is captured by the term

$$(1 - w\lambda^{-1})f' + \frac{w\Theta}{\lambda^2}h',$$

which is positive because $(1 - w\lambda^{-1})f' > 0$ and $h' > 0$. These effects are neglected in the conventional NAIRU theory. This error of omission (or commission?) could be forgiven if it turns out empirically that the impact of higher wages on productivity is negligibly small. However, our empirical investigation in Chapter 5 suggests that it is not small, and so the link must be included explicitly in the theoretical analysis.

We use Figure 1.3 to illustrate what may happen to the NAIRU if the real wage rate increases—for example, due to more extensive labor market regulation. As in the conventional NAIRU argument illustrated in Figure 1.2, the wage-setting curve will shift up from *WS* to *WS'*. But now, unlike what happens in Figure 1.2, the price-setting curve will also shift up because of the higher labor productivity growth, which comes about both directly and indirectly because of the increased wage rate. The crucial point is that the final outcome is not known a priori: if productivity growth rises very strongly (and the *PS* curve shifts up considerably), the NAIRU falls, as in panel (a); but if the productivity growth response is rather weak and the upward shift of the *PS* curve is limited, equilibrium unemployment increases, as shown in panel (b). If one accepts our argument so far, it follows that the conventional wisdom that more labor market regulation (leading to higher wage claims) must lead to higher equilibrium unemployment is false—as long as we do not know how strongly the higher real wage rate affects productivity, we don't know what will happen to structural unemployment. Steady-inflation unemployment may rise, fall, or remain roughly unchanged; in the last case, the conclusion must be that labor market interventions (causing higher wage demands) are not a cause of unemployment at all. What transpires from all this is that the NAIRU claim that unemployment is mostly due to regulation is not warranted on theoretical grounds and there must be other causes. Although we will analyze other possible causes in more detail in Chapter 3, we can say here that structural unemployment in the OECD is mostly determined by overly restrictive fiscal and monetary policies, which not only reduce aggregate demand but also reduce labor productivity growth (via the Kaldor-Verdoorn channel), thus raising the steady-inflation rate of unemployment.

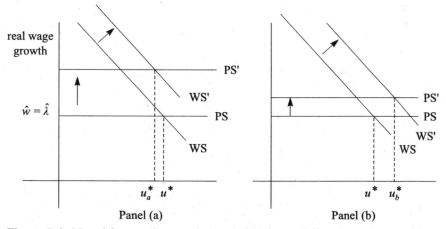

Panel (a)   Panel (b)

Figure 1.3. More labor market regulation and higher real wage growth may either reduce (panel [a]) or raise (panel [b]) the NAIRU.

A Second Pass

But this is not yet all. Standard NAIRU accounts treat labor productivity growth, $\hat{\lambda}$ in equation (1.3), as being exogenous to the nature of a country's system of industrial relations (which we assume gets reflected in our labor market regulation variable z). This is wrong, as we argue in Chapter 4: workers' motivation, work intensity, and hence labor productivity are all significantly influenced by the social relations of production, which mediate exchanges between workers and firms and within which notions of trust and fairness are defined.

It is true that the endogeneity of workers' motivation and labor productivity has been recognized in quite a few NAIRU models, especially those drawing from the efficiency-wage and labor-extraction literatures (Bowles 1985; Akerlof and Yellen 1986). In these models, work creates only disutility and hence work is endured only to secure an income, which is the means to derive utility from consumption. Being rational decision makers, workers behave opportunistically and either minimize work effort at a given wage or maximize the economic return at a given level of work effort. Firms view workers as a costly and noncooperative production factor, which must be used as effectively as possible to obtain maximum effort (and profit or surplus) at a given level of wage costs. To extract a maximum amount of effort (or labor productivity) while keeping total wage plus supervision costs constant, firms can either closely supervise their employees while paying them low wages or pay workers high wages and economize on the number of supervisors. The idea is that higher (efficiency) wages are a worker-disciplining device in an essentially conflictual employment relation, because higher wages mean that job loss is costlier for employees.

This efficiency-wage/labor-extraction take on the problem is very narrow and distorted, particularly in its view of the labor process and the worker. The worker is "distorted into a fragment of man," degraded "to a level of an appendage of a machine," alienated "from the intellectual potentialities of the labour process," and subjected "to a despotism the more hateful for its meanness," as Marx (1987, 799) famously wrote about the capitalist labor process. The worker is seen as being devoid of human spirit—a machine activated only by pecuniary stimulus—and labor is treated as being

> external to the worker, i.e., it does not belong to his intrinsic nature; that in his work, therefore, he does not affirm himself but denies himself, does not feel content but unhappy, does not develop freely his physical and mental energy but mortifies his body and his mind. The worker therefore only feels himself outside his work, and in his work he feels outside himself. (Marx 1844, 30)

What is missing is that workers' motivation is influenced by other intrinsic personal and social factors, including the social organization of the labor process. To drive home a simple point, more-intense supervision is likely to *demotivate* workers, causing a drop in productivity, because workers see this as a breach of trust and as being unfair, which induces them to turn to more instrumental patterns of behavior (Drago and Perlman 1989). The same may happen when firms pay workers above-market-clearing wages so that they fear the loss of their jobs, because the motivational force remains a threat. Hence, the major problem with this distorted approach to work and the worker is that (1) it denies the contribution of workers to increasing efficiency and productivity, basically assuming that workers are alienated from the intellectual potentialities of the labor process, while (2) it emphasizes the conflictual elements within the employment relation, thereby exacerbating the tendency for workers to behave instrumentally and opportunistically in their own narrow interests.

More generally, in an industrial relations system based on shared values, cooperation, and coordination (rather than conflict), "the logic of 'labor extraction' does not apply much at all—[because] worker productivity depends primarily on neither [efficiency wages] nor intensive supervision," as New School economist David Gordon (1994, 376) insightfully observed. Such a cooperative system, which relies on the carrot and not the stick, is conducive to labor productivity growth in two major ways. First, workers, who typically have more (tacit) knowledge of how the job is best done than do their supervisors or engineers, more easily accept and contribute to radical technological change, because they feel that their jobs are not at risk as a consequence of the resulting productivity growth and because they view the productivity gain sharing as being fair; as a consequence, they eschew their narrow self-interest in favor of a broader "public-spirited" form of behavior (see Lorenz 1992). Likewise, because significant employment security (in combination with a compressed wage structure) provides workers with insurance against ex ante wage risk (Agell 1999), workers will invest more in education, which has a strong positive impact on productivity growth. Second, as is argued in the firm-specific human capital model (Auer, Berg, and Coulibaly 2005), firms invest more in training, which further raises productivity growth, when employment protection is stricter, labor taxes are high, and average job tenure is long.

In sum, the more cooperative the social relations of production, the more strongly workers reciprocate by providing higher productivity—and the higher the rate of labor productivity growth. Both our evidence and findings by many other authors (reviewed in Chapter 4) suggest that, indeed, aggregate labor productivity growth is higher in economies having more regulated and coordinated industrial relations systems. In terms of this chapter's NAIRU model, this would mean that more labor market regulation (an increase in z)

not only raises wage growth claims—as is clear from equation (1.1)—but at the same time raises labor productivity growth $\hat{\lambda}$. As a result, the eventual impact of more regulation on the NAIRU is not clear a priori. We are back again to Figure 1.3: now, a higher z raises both the WS curve and the PS curve, and steady-inflation unemployment may either rise or fall. Both the dominant claim that excessive labor market regulation is at the root of (European) unemployment and the sweeping and unconditional prescriptions for labor market deregulation—the bitter medicine—lack firm foundations.

The Structure of the Book

In Chapter 2 we review the cross-country econometric evidence in support of the conventional NAIRU hypothesis. We argue that the evidence is weak and that the weaknesses are fatal; they cannot be resolved by improving the data or using more sophisticated econometric techniques. The problem simply is that many OECD countries do not perform according to what the NAIRU model predicts: many highly regulated countries (especially the Scandinavian ones) manage to combine growth, equity, and low unemployment. There are also highly deregulated countries that feature below-average growth and above-average unemployment. The mainstream's response has been to attribute these deviations from the NAIRU rule to country-specific idiosyncrasies or country-specific shocks. We do not think this is a convincing and productive approach, simply because the exceptions are dominating the rule. Hence, our conclusion is that the model should be modified.

As a first step, in Chapter 3 we present our more general growth model, which allows for variations in macroeconomic outcomes caused by similar labor market interventions. The crux of our argument is that economies can be either profit-led or wage-led, depending on how aggregate demand and output growth responds to an increase in real wage growth (and a consequent rise in the wage share). A higher wage share raises consumption (because the savings rate from wages is less than the savings rate from profits), but it reduces profits and investment as well as exports (because of higher unit labor costs). What is important is that an increase in real wage growth also affects the economy's supply side, especially the rate of labor productivity growth. Higher wage growth directly induces more rapid labor productivity growth along the lines suggested by Marx and Hicks. It indirectly induces productivity growth via the Kaldor-Verdoorn effect, but only if the economy is wage-led; if the economy is profit-led, higher wage growth will not only depress output growth but also slow down productivity growth (via Kaldor-Verdoorn). In determining the net impact on output growth of higher real wage growth, we take these impacts on productivity growth into account;

it is in this sense that our model is more comprehensive than more conventional models of demand-led growth (Setterfield 2010). If the net impact on output growth of higher real wage growth is positive, the economy is said to be wage-led; if the net effect is negative, the economy is labeled profit-led. The difference is crucial, because the same policy package (labor market deregulation leading to lower real wage growth) will raise growth and reduce unemployment if the economy is profit-led, but reduce output growth and possibly raise unemployment if the economy is strongly wage-led. Differences in the nature of the growth regime, in other words, determine the macro consequences of labor market policies.

In Chapter 4 we present empirical evidence on the productivity regime—the economy's supply side. We find empirical support for the Kaldor-Verdoorn effect as well as for the Marx-Hicks effect of higher real wage growth on productivity growth. We further find rather strong evidence of a positive association, at the aggregate level, between labor market regulation and labor productivity growth. It is therefore wrong to assume, as is done in the NAIRU approach, that labor productivity growth is not affected by labor market reform; it is, because changes in labor market interventions and institutions affect workers' motivation and work intensity. Figure 1.3 is empirically relevant, in other words.

Chapter 5 deals with OECD demand regimes, which can be either wage-led or profit-led. It addresses the core difference between our approach and the conventional NAIRU approach: we allow for the possibility that demand growth is wage-led rather than assuming that it is always profit-led. We investigate the nature of the demand regime for twelve OECD countries—Belgium, Denmark, Finland, France, Germany, Italy, Japan, the Netherlands, Spain, Sweden, the United Kingdom, and the United States—during the period from 1960 to 2000. What we find is that only Japan and the United States are profit-led; the other ten countries are wage-led. This clearly falsifies the unstated NAIRU assumption that profit-led systems are the norm. Finland and Sweden are strongly wage-led, which means (as we define in Chapter 3) that higher real wage growth not only raises GDP growth as well as productivity growth but at the same time reduces unemployment—in clear violation of NAIRU logic.

Chapter 5 investigates the issue of whether more openness to trade is likely to turn the demand regimes of OECD countries into becoming profit-led, but we conclude that this is not likely to happen for realistic increases in openness. Much more important to the nature of demand is the profit sensitivity of investment, which in turn is heavily influenced by the bank-based or stock-market-based nature of a country's financial system. Bank-based economies (such as Germany's) feature a significantly lower profit sensitivity of investment growth and therefore are more likely to have wage-led demand growth, whereas market-based economies (such as that of the United States) exhibit high profit sensitivity of investment growth and are more likely profit-led. Bank-based financial systems in turn are argued to be compatible with relatively strongly regulated labor markets and large welfare states, whereas market-based financial systems are argued to be consistent with deregulated labor markets and small government. Thus there exist important macroeconomic complementarities between the nature of the demand regime, the nature of the financial system, and the nature and extent of labor market regulation, complementarities that hold significant implications for labor market reform. For one, if Europe's wage-led economies want to maintain their labor market arrangements, this will require curbing their firms' increasing orientation toward the stock market and shareholders. Debates on unemployment and industrial relations often have been narrowed down to expert discussions on specific, isolated labor market interventions (e.g., employment protection or active labor market programs), which miss this central insight: if one wants to maintain Europe's protective labor market institutions and create economic security, equality, and stability, the agenda for action has to be significantly broadened beyond industrial relations issues per se to challenge stock market dominance and a single-minded orientation toward shareholders.

Chapter 6 combines productivity and demand regimes so as to determine the factors influencing structural unemployment in the OECD economies. The focus of this chapter is on long-run equilibrium—Joan Robinson's slippery eel—and we assume, as is done in the NAIRU approach, that income distribution (between wages and profits) is constant. We show that under realistic assumptions, steady-inflation unemployment is influenced by demand factors: structural unemployment is found to decline in response to expansionary fiscal policy and to rise as a result of higher real interest rates.[14] The reason is that demand policy affects productivity growth through the Kaldor-Verdoorn effect and through wage-cost-induced technological progress. Fiscal expansion is thus associated with more rapid productivity growth, which reduces inflationary pressure and allows unemployment to fall; a high real interest rate, in contrast, depresses investment and hence productivity, making the system more inflation prone, and unemployment must rise as a result. The NAIRU is therefore not an attractor, Friedman's "natural" constant, to which the system evolves after a long enough period of time. Far from this, it is a moving target, endogenous to policy, that shifts up and down in response to fiscal, monetary, and technology policies. No wonder that estimated NAIRUs in a variety of studies have closely tracked the actual unemployment rate. If we lack a theory of how demand policies affect productivity growth, wage bargaining, and unemployment, it is also no wonder that it remains a professionally troublesome mystery how big the NAIRU is, why it changes over time, and how it should be estimated.

Chapter 6 also looks into the various and conflicting impacts of labor market regulation on structural unemployment. We find, for our group of twenty OECD countries, that the net impact of regulation is to actually *reduce* unemployment. More heavily regulated economies, in other words, experience lower unemployment. The reason is that labor productivity growth is higher in these relatively more regulated economies, and this reduces inflationary pressures, allowing both real wage growth and employment growth to be higher. The rise in structural unemployment in the OECD countries therefore cannot be attributed to "excessive" regulation, but must be blamed on the slowdown of demand growth and structurally higher real interest rates. There is no need for bitter medicine, and there is no inherent conflict between growth and egalitarianism—the trade-off is fictitious, as it is a social construction, not a "natural state of affairs" that can be overcome.

To buttress this point, Chapter 7 is a case study of Europe's heavily regulated and open Nordic countries (Denmark, Finland, Norway, and Sweden), which manage to combine growth, technological dynamism, low unemployment, and income inequality. The Nordics manage all this by regulating markets, by coordinating macroeconomic decision making between unions, firms, and government, and through fair and macroeconomically responsible sharing of the gains and losses from globalization and technological progress. This Nordic approach is sometimes called the "visible handshake" (to differentiate it from the liberal "invisible hand" that rules the Anglo-Saxon economies), and we highlight here its deeply social-productivist foundations. Nordic cooperative capitalism testifies to the significant macroeconomic returns of "mutual aid": firms act against markets (asking for and accepting welfare provision and labor market regulation) because the ensuing higher productivity and stable work relations are in their interest; workers, on the other hand, accept some wage restraint and help promote productivity growth in exchange for full and stable employment, equal pay, and social protection. At a fundamental level, antagonism between workers and firms has been replaced by mutual responsibility (which does not at all imply harmony of interests), and the Nordics show that this foundational change in attitude pays off.

Our final chapter, Chapter 8, asks whether macroeconomics can live without the NAIRU. Our answer will not come as a surprise.

The Economic Crisis of 2008–2011

It is an understatement to say that not many mainstream macroeconomists foresaw the financial crisis that erupted in mid-2007 and the ensuing Great

Recession, the deepest global contraction since the 1930s. Nonmainstream macroeconomists did a better job, as many had been able to identify the fundamental instability of the processes well before the actual crash.[15] But as it concerns the pervasive and foolish complacency of mainstream economics, we concur with James Galbraith (2009, 95), who calls it a "Politburo for correct economic thinking" placed "on the wrong side of every important policy issue," predicting disaster where none occurs, denying the possibility of events that then happen, and not willing to reexamine ideas.

What the crisis has revealed is that the remarkable macroeconomic performance of the United States (and the United Kingdom) in the period from 1995 to 2006 was just a façade, hiding unnoticed behind it a growing mountain of unsecured credit and housing debt that was able to go on accumulating because a constantly extending network of secondary markets—the so-called New Wall Street System—seemed to be sharing the risk created by such debt, apparently diminishing the risk exposure of any one holder. How that debt mountain collapsed in 2008 and 2009 is well known and does not need to be explained here (see Palley 2009; Palma 2009; Wade 2009). As nature abhors a vacuum, so does society not long tolerate instability and the anomie that is its cause as well as its effect (Lowe 1988). Hence, given the loss of credibility of financial laissez-faire (Anglo-Saxon style), the legitimacy crisis of stock market capitalism, and the cynicism of Wall Street and the City, the global crisis *could* force a return of the state, of financial and labor market regulation and of more egalitarian labor-friendly policies. This is an open issue, although opinions are generally not optimistic.[16] But it is clear that monetarist macroeconomics is in a deep crisis—witness, for example, the harsh words about the state of mainstream macroeconomics uttered by Citigroup's chief economist, Willem Buiter, who earlier was at the London School of Economics: "The typical graduate macroeconomics and monetary economics training received at Anglo-American universities during the past 30 years or so, may have set back by decades serious investigations of aggregate economic behaviour and economic policy-relevant understanding. It was a privately and socially costly waste of time and other resources" (Buiter 2009). Princeton economist Paul Krugman said the same in the last of his Lionel Robbins Lectures at the London School of Economics on June 10, 2009, claiming that during much of the past thirty years mainstream macroeconomics was "spectacularly useless at best, and positively harmful at worst."[17]

We believe that the conventional NAIRU model, which belongs to the core of graduate macroeconomics and monetary economics, is seriously implicated in creating the economic crisis. It helped shape the broader macroeconomic conditions within which the spectacular macroeconomic imbalances could build up, eventually leading to collapse. The conventional NAIRU approach indeed has been "positively harmful" and must be discarded to provide space for "serious investigations of aggregate economic behaviour."

Why and how is the NAIRU model implicated? As Cambridge's Gabriel Palma (2009) compellingly argues, the process of financial deepening (the increase in the ratio of the value of financial assets [equity, public and private bonds, and bank deposits] to GDP) in the United States (and globally) has been closely related to the huge sustained increase in income inequality after 1980, in a process of simultaneous causation. NAIRU-based macroeconomics has created the deregulated labor markets and scaled-down welfare states within which the very sharp rise in inequality, especially in the United States, has occurred, and at the same time it has legitimized and justified high inequality as the unavoidable by-product of a low-unemployment economy based on global competition between autonomous individuals and firms. Palma's argument is broadly shared by other authors, including Andrew Glyn (2006), James Galbraith (2008), Thomas Palley (2009), and Lance Taylor (2010). Within NAIRU-based macroeconomics, rising inequality is a nonissue; Buiter was only being more explicit than most other mainstream economists when he declared in the *Financial Times*, "[Absolute] poverty bothers me. Inequality does not. I simply don't care" (Wade 2009, 1160).[18]

But, as Palma rightly insists, economists should care: not only because of reasons of equity or fairness, but because huge inequalities or "winner-take-all" distributions are likely to destabilize the system by making it more prone to financial fragility. This last fact is easily explained. One side of the increasing inequality in the United States has been stagnant average real incomes for the bottom 90 percent of U.S. households. This not only has led to a decline in personal savings but also has created a "captive market" for bank loans and sharp increases in household indebtedness (to sustain the "American dream" of material progress). The other side has been a truly dramatic rise in real incomes and wealth of the top 10 percent (or even 1 percent) of households (Dew-Becker and Gordon 2005). Ajay Kapur (2005), a former global strategist of Citibank, coined the term "plutonomy" to indicate this elite of multimillionaires or superconsumers and superinvestors searching for higher returns. The rise of the plutonomy created superabundant liquidity in U.S. financial markets, which transformed financial markets into unstable institutions, unable to self-correct. Income and wealth concentration in the hands of high-net-worth individuals (HNWIs) increased sharply. These HNWIs were the leading providers of finance to banks, the shadow banking system, and hedge funds, which in turn were the leading buyers of securitized mortgages. The HNWIs demanded above-average returns on their investments from the hedge funds, as they were also paying above-average fees and bonuses. As a result, banks and hedge funds found themselves in a dilemma, as Photis Lysandrou (2009) argues:

> On the one hand, more and more assets were placed under their management because other investors were finding it difficult to generate yield; on the other hand, the hedge funds were themselves finding it difficult to generate yield. It was hedge funds' need to resolve this dilemma that led them to search for alternative financial products that could give higher yields.

The result has been a demand-push process of virtual wealth creation on an unprecedented scale, marked by superabundant credit. But Robert Skidelsky (2009) explains that this credit "was not used to finance new [technical] inventions," as in earlier boom periods; "it was the invention. It was called securitized mortgages. It left no monuments to human invention, only piles of financial ruin." "Markets took their inevitable revenge," writes Palma (2009), once inequality-driven imbalances and instabilities became too large. Other Keynesian economists agree that rising inequality is a root cause of the financial crisis. For instance, Jean-Paul Fitoussi and Francesco Saraceno (2010, 3) provide the following succinct analysis of how the crisis came about:

> At the outset there is an increase in inequalities which depressed aggregate demand and prompted monetary policy to react by maintaining a low level of interest rate, which itself allowed private debt to increase beyond sustainable levels. On the other hand the search for high-return investment by those who benefited from the increase in inequalities led to the emergence of bubbles. Net wealth became overvalued, and high asset prices gave the false impression that high levels of debt were sustainable. The crisis revealed itself when the bubbles exploded. . . . So although the crisis may have emerged in the financial sector, its roots are much deeper and lie in a structural change in income distribution that had been going on for twenty-five years.

NAIRUvian macro and labor market policies must take a large part of the blame for unleashing and at the same time legitimizing an inegalitarian, unstable, and unsustainable growth process. According to Palma (2009), the key to preventing financial fragility and crisis is to impose "compulsions" and "restrictions" on the capitalist system, to discipline firms, investors, and financial markets; we believe that adequate labor market regulation could be one such systemic compulsion. More-egalitarian growth and low unemployment are crucial in order to avoid the excess financial liquidity that triggered the current crisis. That is why a serious rethinking of the NAIRU approach to macroeconomics is needed.

Further Reading

John Maynard Keynes's (1973) *The General Theory of Employment, Interest and Money* represents the turning point between the old economics and a new macroeconomics—it is perhaps the most provocative and inspiring book in economics of the twentieth century. Lance Taylor (2010) has written a masterly review of Keynesianism and post-Keynesianism, bringing out their relevance for today's economic problems. Taylor's final chapter applies essential Keynesian insights to the current financial crisis. Andrew Glyn (2006) presents a concise economic history of OECD capitalism since the end of World War II and in particular of the rise to dominance of "free market NAIRU-based economics" since the 1970s, showing that neoliberal policies after 1980 not only have failed to deliver faster economic growth but also have worsened inequality and undermined economic security. A more polemical analysis, but for the United States, is made by James K. Galbraith (2008), who argues that conventional macroeconomics is intellectually bankrupt and incapable of addressing today's pressing economic problems. Stephen Marglin (2008) provides a foundational critique of neoclassical welfare economics, arguing that it undermines community; translated to our context, the argument would be that it undermines work relations. The essays in David Howell's *Fighting Unemployment* (2005) are an in-depth empirical challenge to the received wisdom that excessive labor market regulation is to blame for poor employment performance. If our short exposition of the global financial crisis sounds like a fugue without the bass, the bass might come from the more systemic, longer-run analyses of J. Gabriel Palma (2009) and Robert Wade (2009), who highlight the key role played by rising inequality and the ways in which neoliberal policies (deregulation) were used to politically legitimize "the most remarkable dispossession feat" (Palma 2009) ever within a democracy.

2

The Weakness of the Evidence

The only man who behaved sensibly was my tailor;
he took my measure anew every time he saw me,
whilst all the rest went on with their old measurements
and expected them to fit me.

GEORGE BERNARD SHAW, *MAN AND SUPERMAN*

The empirical literature on the NAIRU is voluminous—beyond comprehensive reviewing. But even though the literature is large, opinion is uniform that "excessive" labor market regulation or "rigid" labor market institutions are the root cause of persistent high unemployment. The debate, accordingly, centers on which forms of regulation or which labor market institutions are most to blame, with the villains in the piece commonly being played by unemployment benefits, collective bargaining structures, and labor taxation (see Nickell and Layard 1999; Nickell, Nunziata, and Ochel 2005). However, labor economists Richard Freeman (2005) and David Howell (2006) have argued that the strong empirical consensus is merely appearance: it has come about because most researchers have been trying to confirm their own strong theoretical priors by letting their priors dictate their modeling choices and interpretation of empirical results and by forms of data snooping and regression-mongering. What has not been done is to confront these priors with the available data so as to try "to establish what is left after we put on our hat of scientific skepticism and put the prevailing wisdom through the wringer of challenging empirical tests that include comparing them to what alternative models would suggest."[1] According to Freeman, researchers often

> search the data for specifications/measures that support their priors, while barely noticing evidence that goes against them. If results are inconsistent with the priors, they assume that something is wrong with their empirical specification or measures, rather than question the validity of their case. If results fit their priors, they rarely look further to find weaknesses. (Freeman 2005, 10)

This happens "even when scholars try to be honest and not rig the cards in their favor," as social and political theorist Jon Elster (2009, 17) explains, because "they may unconsciously favor definitions and measurements that favor the hypothesis they want to be true." One underlying mechanism at work here is the sociological (peer) domination of the economics profession by neoclassical economics, which, in Elster's vocabulary, leads to "mind-binding" *("How could all these people, who are certainly smarter than I am, be so wrong?")* (ibid.). Elster approvingly quotes French philosopher Blaise Pascal ("Ordinary people have the power of not thinking of that about which they do not wish to think") (2009, 21) and concludes that economists are probably like ordinary people.

Of course, there are critical authors who have tried to shake the complacency of the economics profession and who did put on their "sceptical hats."[2] For example, more than a decade ago, Robert Eisner (1997) and James Galbraith (1997) presented trenchant briefs supporting their lack of confidence in the NAIRU model, arguing that the empirical evidence on the NAIRU is weak, econometric attempts to estimate the NAIRU are "a professional embarrassment" (because nothing resembling plausible or stable NAIRUs can be found), and adherence to the concept as a guide to policy has major costs and negligible benefits. Doubts about the NAIRU in the economics profession have grown further in recent years, following the publication of important studies that by reevaluating the robustness of the consensus-view findings discovered these results to be statistically fragile. We review in this chapter two major weaknesses of the empirical evidence in support of the claim that "excessive" labor market regulation "causes" structural unemployment. These weaknesses are fundamental and cannot be resolved by technical tinkering such as improving the quality of the data, combining macro data and micro data on how firms, workers, and unions operate in micro institutional settings, or using better econometric tools. The reason is that quite a few of the more regulated OECD economies feature very low rates of unemployment, and a complete and convincing analysis of the relationship between labor market regulation and unemployment must be able to explain the success of these countries as well. We think that the nonrobustness and the lack of uniformity of the empirical findings are related to a misspecification of the conventional NAIRU model, which underlies most econometric analyses. Hence we argue that the standard NAIRU model should be modified, and in Chapter 3 we highlight, using a more general model, the variety in labor market outcomes caused by labor market regulation.

The Disposable American: Underpaid, Overworked, Alienated

Before proceeding into a discussion of perhaps rather arcane econometric issues, let us pause for a moment and remind ourselves what is at stake. NAIRU wisdom holds that labor market deregulation is unconditionally good for growth and employment, because the employment costs of labor market regulation are argued to be higher than the potential benefits of regulation in terms of efficiency and equity. In more pedestrian terms, lower structural unemployment in combination with higher inequality (as in the United States) is taken to be preferable to a situation in which inequality is lower but unemployment higher (as in the European Union). In fact, the U.S. economy is setting the standard for rates of job creation and rates of unemployment in the OECD. But the United States is also renowned for its earnings inequality, which is higher than in Europe, with France being the exception (OECD 2007). More generally, the data show—as in Figure 2.1, which uses data for twenty OECD countries during the periods from 1984 to 1994 and from 1994 to 2004—that the higher the earnings inequality, the more deregulated a country's labor market. This is the bitter taste of the deregulation medicine: a more unequal society. But higher inequality may also have positive effects, the argument goes, because it motivates people to work harder, study more, and be more flexible and entrepreneurial. Unfettered firms would reward them over the longer run by providing them with employment and pay rises. The bitter medicine of labor market deregulation, U.S.-style, has to be taken for the long-run health of the economy (i.e., low unemployment, high profits and investment, rapid growth) (Elmeskov, Martin, and Scarpetta 1998).

However, what is not often stated clearly enough is that even in the United States, the estimated structural unemployment rate needed to stabilize inflation is as high as 6 percent of the labor force (Staiger, Stock, and Watson 1997; Pollin 2003)—which, as we may already point out, is higher than the inflation-safe unemployment rate in many European economies. One explanation holds that such a vast reserve army of the unemployed is needed to keep labor cost growth low (i.e., well below productivity growth) so as to maintain cost competitiveness in export and import markets, and to prevent firms from moving their operations to lower-wage economies such China or Mexico. The increasingly rapid pace of global capital mobility and the outsourcing, job dislocation, and corporate restructuring that follow in its wake have led to a climate of increased job insecurity among U.S. workers, which has served to hold down wage demands and pay increases even during periods of economic growth. Alan Greenspan openly talked about "the traumatized worker"—someone who felt job insecurity in the changing economy and so was accepting smaller wage increases—as being responsible for the dampening of inflationary pressures. Likewise, as noted by Robert Pollin (2003, 53):

> During her stint as a Federal Reserve Governor, Janet Yellen, co-author of *The Fabulous Decade*, reached similar conclusions . . . reporting [in 1996] . . . that "while the labor market is tight, job insecurity also seems alive and well. Real wage aspirations appear modest, and the bar-

gaining power of workers is surprisingly low." . . . [T]hese facts of declining bargaining power for workers did not deter Professor Yellen from nevertheless concluding that the overall macroeconomic performance in the 1990s was "fabulous."

Growing economic insecurity confronts not only the poorer segments of the population. "The movement of emerging economies such as those of China

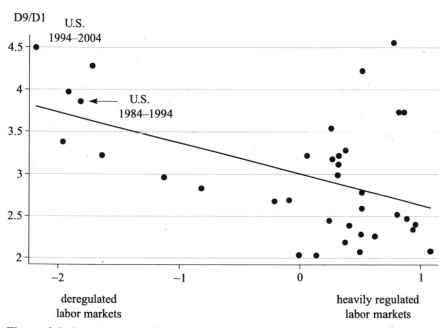

Figure 2.1. Earnings inequality (D9/D1) is higher in deregulated labor markets.

Notes:

a. Data are averages for twenty OECD countries for the periods from 1984 to 1994 and from 1994 to 2004.

b. Earnings inequality is defined as the ratio of top (10 percent) to bottom (10 percent) earnings. Our indicator of labor market regulation is a factor score for eighteen OECD countries for the periods from 1984 to 1994 and from 1994 to 2004; has a mean value (for the two periods combined) of 0; and loads highly on employment protection, the management ratio, earnings inequality, bargaining coordination, and collective bargaining coverage (for details, see Chapter 4). The higher the indicator, the more intensively regulated is a country's labor market.

c. The curve is based on the following OLS regression:

Earnings inequality = 3.0 − 0.37 labor market regulation
$(27.40)^{***}$ $(3.55)^{***}$ $\overline{R}^2 = 0.20$

d. *** = statistically significant at 1%.

and India into higher value-added activities has created new competition for the jobs of well-educated and highly experienced workers in the United States," writes William Lazonick (2009, 1). This has allowed capital to reduce the cost of control over labor, thus weakening the latter's countervailing power. Gabriel Palma (2009) has called this capitalism without the required compulsions for oligopolistic capital, without a critical mass of opposition, and with a compliant political class, while James Galbraith (2008) calls it predatory capitalism. As part of this capitalism unleashed, U.S. corporations transformed their business model into what Lazonick calls the "New Economy business model" (NEBM), which involves cutting costs by favoring the employment of lower-wage younger workers over older workers and by offshoring, which favors low-wage workers in developing nations over U.S. workers—often in the name of maximizing shareholder value. Lazonick documents in detail how corporations have been using their profits (including profits from employing a low-wage global labor force) to boost their stock price through massive stock buybacks, rather than invest these profits productively and keep U.S. workers employed. Lazonick (2009, 1) concludes:

> During the 2000s, even in growing high-tech industries, a college education has no longer offered assurance of stable and well-paid employment. If economic insecurity afflicts the best-positioned members of the US labor force in the most dynamic growth industries, what prospects are there for increasing the economic security of less educated workers in low-growth industries?

Increased job insecurity is therefore an integral part of the New Economy business model. Social critic Naomi Klein (2007, 359) uses a different label to describe the same transformation of the corporate world, talking about "hollow firms":

> During the 1990s, many companies that had traditionally manufactured their own products and maintained large, stable workforces embraced what became known as the Nike model: don't own any factories, produce your products through an intricate web of contractors and subcontractors, and pour your resources into design and marketing. . . . Some called the companies that underwent these radical restructurings "hollow corporations" because they were mostly form, with little tangible content left over.

Consequently, American workers saw their average hourly real wages stagnate after 1979, while productivity in the economy was increasing year by year, virtually without interruption (Boushey et al. 2006).[3] According to data compiled by Piketty and Sáez (2003), the average annual income (in US$ at 2006 values) of the bottom 90 percent of income earners actually fell during the period from 1973 to 2006—only the incomes of the top 10 percent increased, with the top 1 percent of income earners capturing about 60 percent of total income growth from 1993 to 2006. Gabriel Palma (2009) calls this extremely unequalizing distributive process "the most remarkable dispossession feat" ever within a democracy. While low-wage workers were experiencing a larger real wage fall than higher-wage workers, executive compensation exploded: for the largest 500 U.S. companies, the ratio of CEO pay to production worker earnings rose from 35:1 in 1979 to 300:1 in 2000 (Mishel, Bernstein, and Shierholz 2009).[4]

What is also not generally discussed is what it means for U.S. workers to have to operate in "flexible," deregulated labor markets. To get an idea, David Howell and Mamadou Diallo (2007) explored long-term aggregated evidence on U.S. labor market performance. Their data on quality of employment show that during the period from 1979 to 2006:

- As much as 30 percent of all U.S. workers were in low-wage employment, earning less than two-thirds of the median wage for full-time workers.
- The percentage of low-wage employment in total employment for young moderately educated male workers rose from 18.1 percent in 1979 to 37.6 percent in 2006 and from 43.5 percent to 52.4 percent for moderately educated female workers. Average real wages for young moderately educated men and women fell sharply relative to the overall median wage.
- The percentage of low-wage employment in total employment for young poorly educated male workers rose from 53 percent in 1979 to 72.4 percent in 2006 and from 85 percent to 91 percent for poorly educated female workers.

Howell and Diallo further find that low-wage employment is much more prevalent and increasing over time among native-born black workers and Hispanic workers than among native-born white workers. They conclude that the dramatic increase in low-wage employment (particularly for men) shows that "competitive forces have eroded the quality of many 'middle-class' jobs" in the United States. Howell and Diallo quote a *New York Times* article (Ramirez 2006) reporting that although official statistics indicated near-full employment, thousands of people—mostly young and black or Hispanic—showed up to apply for fewer than 200 positions at a New York candy store, out of which only sixty-five were full-time jobs, and which paid a meager US$10.75 an hour, just US$1.50 above the wage that marks the national poverty line. That this New York example is representative of U.S.-

wide trends has been shown by Juliet Schor (1992) and Barry Bluestone and Stephen Rose (1997): "flexible" American workers are both overworked and underemployed. Family members are found to work more, often as temporary workers, part-time workers, or independent contractors, to compensate for the increased job insecurity of breadwinners, and the poorly educated workforce is forced to work harder in response to stagnant real family incomes. In 1979, 4.9 percent of U.S. workers (mostly women) reported working more than one job during the same working week; in 1995 this had increased to 6.4 percent, and it is likely to have increased even further. "Flexible" workers are thus exposed to the triple coercion of low wages, employment insecurity, and overwork.

Howell and Diallo's main message is that the middle of the U.S. wage distribution has been hollowed out. Similarly, David Autor, Lawrence Katz, and Melissa Kearny (2006) and Heather Boushey et al. (2007) document how employment has been polarizing into high-wage and low-wage jobs— the latter also known as McJobs—at the expense of middle-skill jobs. Louis Uchitelle (2006, 6–7), who reports on economics for the *New York Times*, captured this polarization of the labor force in his book *The Disposable American*. He puts the blame on mainstream economic theory:

> Companies were freeing themselves from the many obligations to their employees that had accumulated over the years, and now mainstream economics blessed that endeavor. In the process, government was depicted as an obstacle to prosperity. Unfettered enterprises, the argument now went, would expand more rapidly and, over the long run, share their rising profits with their workers, doing so voluntarily through job creation and raises. If that did not happen . . . well, that was the fault of the job losers themselves. They had failed to acquire the necessary skills and education to qualify for the increasingly sophisticated jobs that were available. They lacked value as workers. . . . Layoffs, we were told, do not happen to people who improve their skills and are flexible, innovative, congenial, and hardworking. The layoff says that you have failed in these endeavors, no matter how hard you tried to follow the prescription. You are an inferior worker. The damage to self-esteem from this message is enduring. . . . Putting the laid-off back to work in new jobs [supposedly] solves the problem. There is income again and even prosperity, or the potential for it. But mental health is not easily restored.

Uchitelle documents the psychological costs of labor market flexibility or "disposability" in detail.[5] Low-wage jobs also mean few or no benefits, rigid schedules, late-night shifts, unsafe and unhealthy work conditions, and lack of respect. As Marx (1844) argued, by being reduced to "abstract labor," the worker is being regarded as a "horse" who "must get as much as will enable him to work. It does not consider him when he is not working, as a human being; but leaves such consideration to criminal law, to doctors, to religion, to the statistical tables, to politics, and to the poor-house overseer." In the present-day U.S. economy, most flexible low-wage jobs (mostly in the services sector) do not provide benefits that are typically associated with a "good job":

- About 75 percent of workers in the bottom wage quintile have no employer-provided health coverage (compared to 38 percent of workers in the middle quintile and 22 percent of workers in the top quintile). Employees in jobs with wages under US$15 per hour paid a greater share of employment-based health care premiums than employees working in higher-paying jobs. Only 17 percent of workers with wages under US$15 per hour had access to long-term disability insurance.
- Only 14 percent of workers in the bottom wage quintile have employer-provided pension coverage (compared with 48 percent in the middle quintile and 72 percent in the top quintile).
- Only 39 percent of these low-wage jobs offer any paid sick days for personal illness (compared to 79 percent of other jobs).
- Low-wage workers are less likely to receive employer-funded education and training than are better-educated workers (Boushey et al. 2006).

Inadequate wages, in other words, are only the beginning. But one can go further. Social critic and journalist Barbara Ehrenreich sought out work in low-wage jobs between spring 1998 and summer 2000. According to Ehrenreich (2001, 60), in the new version of the law of supply and demand, "jobs are so cheap—as measured by pay—that a worker is encouraged to take as many of them as she possibly can." Evaluating her experiences, she writes:

> If low-wage workers do not always behave in an economically rational way, that is, as free agents within a capitalist democracy, it is because they dwell in a place that is neither free nor in any way democratic. When you enter the low-wage workplace—and many of the medium-wage workplaces as well—you check your civil liberties at the door, leave America and all it supposedly stands for behind, and learn to zip your lips for the duration of the shift. The consequences of this routine surrender go beyond the issues of wages and poverty. We can hardly pride ourselves on being the world's preeminent democracy, after all, if large numbers of citizens spend half their waking hours in what amounts, in plain terms, to a dictatorship. (Ehrenreich 2001, 210)

David Gordon (1996), in his book *Fat and Mean*, called this particular approach to the employment relation, management, and production the "Stick

Strategy": squeezing and scolding workers, cheapening labor costs, trying to compete economically through intimidation and conflict in a deregulated labor market needing a NAIRU of 6 percent to keep inflation constant. He argued that

> stagnant or falling wages create the need for intensive managerial super-vision of frontline employees. If workers do not share in the fruits of the enterprise, if they are not provided a promise of job security and steady wage growth, what incentive do they have to work as hard as their bosses would like? So the corporations need to monitor the workers' effort and be able to threaten credible to punish them if they do not perform. The corporations must wield the Stick. Eventually the Stick requires millions of Stick-wielders. (Gordon 1996, 5)

This is the reason the intensity of supervision and monitoring by manage-ment is much higher in deregulated labor markets than in regulated, more cooperative ones, as we show in Figure 2.2. The heaviest supervision burden exists in the United States and other Anglo-Saxon economies, reaching al-most four times the scale of the lightest burdens (in Scandinavia and Swit-zerland). This conflictual character of the U.S. production system "spills over into conflicts in the broader society, helping erode whatever sense of community and cooperation we may once have shared," wrote Gordon (1996, 98; see also Marglin 2008). Workers in the United States "are more likely to live poorly in economic terms than are people living in nearly all other ad-vanced nations," note Boushey et al. (2007, 20). And the working poor are de facto subsidizing the rich through their underpaid labor:

> When someone works for less pay than she can live on—when, for example, she goes hungry so that you can eat more cheaply and conveniently—then she has made a great sacrifice for you, she has made you a gift of some part of her abilities, her health, and her life. The "working poor," as they are approvingly termed, are in fact the major philanthropists of our society. They neglect their own children so that the children of others will be cared for; they live in substandard hous-ing so that other homes will be shiny and perfect; they endure privation so that inflation will be low and stock prices high. To be a member of the working poor is to be an anonymous donor, a nameless benefactor, to everyone else. (Ehrenreich 2001, 221)

Abstractions and economic jargon aside, this is the benchmark model of flexible labor markets, which is unconditionally propagated by the conven-tional NAIRU view. It is useful to keep this in mind when turning to our review of the econometric studies on the impact of protective labor market regulation on unemployment.

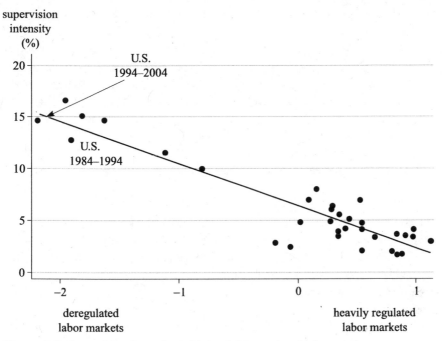

Figure 2.2. Supervision intensity is higher in deregulated labor markets.

Notes:

a. *Supervision intensity* is defined as the percentage of the (nonagricultural) labor force working in administrative and managerial occupations. It is used as an indicator of the intensity of supervision and monitoring by management (Gordon 1994, 1996; Buchele and Christiansen 1999). It is often interpreted as a negative indicator of the extent to which management trusts employees, and of the degree of autonomy that workers have in organizing and coordinating their work activities.

b. For our indicator of labor market regulation, see Figure 2.1.

c. The linear curve is based on the following OLS regression:

Supervision intensity = 6.32 − 4.07 labor market regulation
(24.6)*** (17.6)*** $\overline{R}^2 = 0.86$

d. *** = statistically significant at 1%.

Different Studies Produce Widely Varying Results

The empirical literature on the NAIRU is basically attempting to explain differences in unemployment rates across OECD countries by variations in labor market policies and institutions.[6] A general econometric (panel-data) specification that has been used is the following:

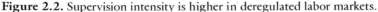

(2.1) $\qquad u_{it} = \alpha_{0i} + \sum_j \alpha_{3j} z_{ijt} + \beta_i \text{ control variables} + \varepsilon_{it}$

where i is a country index, t is a time index, and j an index of labor market interventions $j = 1, \ldots, n$. The dependent variable, u_{it}, is the unemployment rate in country i in period t; z_{ijt} is the value of the measure of labor-market intervention j in country i in period t; ε_{it} is the error term. Regression equation (2.1) can be extended by allowing for country-specific and time-period specific dummy variables as well as by introducing exogenous "shock variables," mostly some productivity shock or real interest rate shock. The main aim has been to obtain robust estimates of coefficient α_{3j}, which is the average impact of a change in intervention j on OECD unemployment.

Cross-country (panel-data) estimates of coefficient α_{3j} from nine prominent studies appear in Table 2.1. The table is based on comparisons by Baker et al. (2005a, 2005b) and Howell et al. (2007). As is evident from Table 2.1, the range of estimated impacts on unemployment of specified changes in each of the labor market interventions is disconcertingly wide. Only the coefficient for the unemployment benefit duration variable is significant in all the regressions in which it appears, although six of the nine studies did not include a duration measure. But even for this measure, the range of estimated coefficients is so large as to cause serious worries about the structure and reliability of the tests. In fact, the implied impact of a one-year increase in benefit duration ranges from an increase in unemployment of 0.17 percentage points (Nickell, Nunziata, and Ochel 2005) to an increase of 1.27 percentage points (IMF 2003). Differences are even more disturbing in the case of the other labor market regulations. For instance, six of the nine studies find no statistically significant effect of an increased employment protection legislation (EPL) variable on unemployment, while three studies report a positive and significant impact. Even when we only look at these three studies, the impact of a unitary increase in the EPL index ranges tremendously (by a factor of 4), from a 0.24 percentage point increase in the unemployment rate (Blanchard and Wolfers 2000) to a 0.91 percentage point increase (Nicoletti and Scarpetta 2003). While some of this difference can be explained by the different indices used in the regressions and perhaps by differences in time periods, there would still be a substantial range of estimates even after taking these into account.

Even more striking is the fact that there is serious disagreement about whether the impact on unemployment of the unemployment benefit replacement ratio is positive or negative. According to Michèle Belot and Jan van Ours (2001), the implied impact of a 10 percentage point increase in the replacement ratio is a *decline* in unemployment of 1.2 percentage points. In sharp contrast, the OECD (2006) reports that the implied impact of the same change is an *increase* in unemployment of 1.2 percentage points. A similar situation applies to the effect of labor taxation: the impact of an in-

Table 2.1. Implied impacts of differences in labor market regulation on structural unemployment: selected studies (1997–2008)

	Selected studies								
	1	2	3	4	5	6	7	8	9
EPL+1 unit	NE	NE	0.24	0.91	0.51	NE	NE	NE	NE
Replacement ratio+10 PP	0.88	1.29	0.70	0.30	0.53	0.96	NE	-1.20	1.20
Benefit duration+1 year	0.70		1.27			0.17			
Union density+10 PP	0.96	NE	0.84	1.00	1.50	0.30	1.02	1.50	NE
Bargaining coverage+10 PP	3.60		NE						
Coordination+1 unit	-3.68	-1.48	-1.13		-0.34	-3.92	NE	NE	-1.42
Taxes+10 PP	2.08	0.94	0.91	0.80	-0.69	NE	NE	NE	2.80
Period of study	1983–1994	1983–1995	1960–1995	1984–1988	1960–1998	1961–1995	1960–1998	1960–1995	1970–2003
Periodicity	6 years	annual	5 years	annual	annual	annual	annual	5 years	annual

Selected studies: (1) Nickell (1997); (2) Elmeskov, Martin, and Scarpetta (1998); (3) Blanchard and Wolfers (2000); (4) Nicoletti and Scarpetta (2003); (5) IMF (2003); (6) Nickell, Nunziata, and Ochel (2005); (7) Baccaro and Rei (2005); (8) Belot and Van Ours (2001); (9) OECD (2006).

Notes: The coefficients show the implied impacts in terms of a change in the unemployment rate of a given change in the labor market variable. NE = no effect (statistically insignificant at 5% level). PP = percentage point.

Sources: Baker et al. (2005a, 2005b); Howell et al. (2007).

crease in labor taxes varies between an increase in unemployment of 2.8 percentage points (OECD 2006) and a decline in unemployment of 0.69 percentage points (IMF 2003). A final point to note is that, contrary to the NAIRU equation (2.1), some labor market interventions are found to actually *lower* unemployment. In Table 2.1, for instance, the coefficient of the wage bargaining coordination variable is negative and significant in six of the studies shown, although the size of the effect varies too much to be plausible. All in all, Dean Baker et al. (2005b, 109) justifiably conclude that "the empirical case has not been made that could justify the sweeping and unconditional prescriptions for labor market deregulation that pervade much of the policy discussion."

Same Data, Opposite Findings

The first weakness of the empirical evidence in support of the NAIRU thesis concerns the embarrassingly wide range of estimated impacts of labor market interventions on unemployment. The second major weakness is perhaps worse: on closer inspection, the results in the NAIRU literature turn out to be nonrobust—meaning that, *while using the same data set*, the estimated coefficients on labor market interventions become zero or nearly so, become statistically insignificant, or even change sign when modest changes are made in the measures of institutions, the countries covered, and/or the time periods analyzed.

Maynard Keynes would not have been surprised had he learned about the extreme fragility of the findings in this literature. Keynes, as is well known, was not particularly impressed by econometrics—on profound technical, practical, and logical grounds—calling it a "brand of statistical alchemy" (Garrone and Marchionatti 2004). He questioned the logic of applying the method of multiple correlation to unanalyzed economic phenomena, stressing problems of interdependence and measurability, the constancy of the coefficients and the time lags involved, the problem of distinguishing correlation from causation, selection biases, and the problem of passing from statistical description to inductive generalization. Of particular importance to our argument here, Keynes insightfully noted that testing a theory is problematic when different econometric specifications can be derived from (or are consistent with) that theory. To drive home his point, he gave the following example: "The seventy translators of the Septuagint were shut up in seventy separate rooms with the Hebrew text and brought out with them, when they emerged, seventy identical translations. Would the same miracle be vouchsafed if seventy multiple correlators were shut up with the same statistical material?" (Keynes 1940, 155–156).

The answer is no, simply because the NAIRU theory does not specify the precise functional form of the relationship between unemployment and labor market interventions, the time lags involved, an exhaustive list of independent variables, the periodicity of the data, or the best estimation method. Much is inevitably left to the judgment and experience of the researchers—and this opens the door to data snooping (shopping around for independent data until one gets a good fit), curve fitting (shopping around for a functional form that gives a good fit), and arbitrariness in the measurement of dependent or independent variables and in the choice of the proper level of statistical significance and of diagnostic tests (Elster 2009). All of this makes it essential that researchers test for robustness of their results—and even then the number and variety of tests to run is a matter of judgment. Researchers "simply have to learn by trial and error until they know what tends to work," writes Elster (2009, 16), but the findings from econometric analyses still need to be "taken with enough grains of salt and applied with superlative common sense," as Keynes wrote in a 1939 letter to English statistician E. J. Broster (Garrone and Marchionatti 2004, 11n11).

In Table 2.2 appear the results from two major studies that have evaluated the statistical robustness of the empirical evidence in support of the NAIRU view. The first one, by International Labour Organization (ILO) economists Lucio Baccaro and Diego Rei, is exceptional in the attention it devotes to robustness issues. Baccaro and Rei test the NAIRU equation (2.1) in static and dynamic forms, compare the results when using annual data and five-year averaged data, and run regressions in levels and first differences. Their estimations provide "very little support for the view that one could reduce unemployment simply by getting rid of institutional rigidities," they write. "Changes in employment protection, benefit replacement rates, and [the] tax wedge seem negatively associated with changes in unemployment, even though the coefficients are (mostly but not always) insignificant" (Baccaro and Rei 2005, 43–44). Baccaro and Rei find just one labor market intervention—union density—to be statistically significantly different from zero (and positive) in their seventy-eight regressions.[7] Table 2.2 presents two of their estimations: one (in column 1) using the variables in levels, the other (in column 2) using variables in first differences (i.e., the change in the variable); the period of estimation (1960–1998), the number (eighteen) of OECD countries included in the analysis, and the periodicity of the data (five-year averages) are the same in both regressions. What is striking, when one compares the results, is that the coefficient for employment protection (EPL) is statistically insignificant in the level regression but statistically significant and negative in the first-differences regression. Same data, opposite results. We must note

Table 2.2. Determinants of the unemployment rate: a sensitivity analysis

	Selected studies				
	Baccaro and Rei (2005)		Baker et al. (2005b)		
	Model in levels	Model in first differences	1960–1999	1960–1984	1980–1999
	1	2	3	4	5
Employment protection	NE	−1.747**	NE	NE	−0.317**
Union density	0.083**	0.110**	NE	NE	NE
Benefit duration	NE	NE	−5.17***	−6.69***	NE
Replacement ratio	NE	NE	−0.61***	−0.06***	NE
Tax wedge	NE	NE	NE	0.185***	NE
Bargaining coordination	NE	NE	−4.79***	NE	−7.04***
Period	1960–1998	1960–1998	1960–1999	1960–1984	1980–1999
Periodicity	5-year data	5-year data	5-year data	5-year data	5-year data
No. of countries	18	18	20	20	20
No. of observation	121	103	156	96	80

Notes: ** and *** denote statistical significance at 5% and 1%, respectively. NE = no effect (statistically insignificant at 5%).

Sources: Column 1 is from table 9, and column 2 is from table 11, in Baccaro and Rei (2005); columns 3–5 are from table 3.6 in Baker et al. (2005b).

that the first-differences regression of column 2 is Baccaro and Rei's preferred model, which means that they accept that stricter employment protection legislation is associated with lower unemployment—in clear contradistinction to the NAIRU view.

The second major study appearing in Table 2.2 is that of Baker et al. (2005b), who tried to replicate findings by Nickell (1997) using Nickell's own improved data set. The results of estimating equation (2.1) for the whole period from 1960 to 1999 are reported in column 3. They provide no statistical support for the NAIRU thesis whatsoever: employment protection, union density, and the tax wedge have no systematic effects at all, and higher benefit replacement ratios, longer duration of benefits, and more coordination have significant effects in *reducing* unemployment. Column 4 presents the results when the period of estimation is restricted to the years 1960–1980. Now the coefficient for wage bargaining coordination is not significant and the coefficient for the tax wedge is significant and positive. The impact of the replacement ratio, while still significant, is much weaker than in column 3. In column 5, the results appear for the subperiod from 1984 to 1999. The effects of benefit duration, replacement ratio and the tax wedge disappear, and EPL now reduces unemployment (as with Baccaro and Rei). The impact of coordination is much stronger in the second period. Again: same data but different time periods, leading to contradictory outcomes. "If anything," Baker et al. (2005b, 107) conclude, "the results for the more recent period offer even weaker support for the de-regulationist position than does the 1960–1984 period." There exists therefore a "yawning gap between the confidence with which the case for labor market deregulation has been asserted and the evidence that the regulating institutions are the culprits" (ibid., 108). It is perhaps not saying too much to conclude that attempts to find an association between unemployment and labor market regulation have become "an embarrassment to the reputation of the profession" (Galbraith 1997, 101).

Such fragility of results may very well be an inevitable outcome of attempts to find uniform and reliable economic relationships with imperfectly measured labor market policies and institutions, shifting economic structures, macroeconomic shocks, and small numbers of country observations. The relevant model does not emerge automatically and unequivocally out of empirical study, as a result of what Keynes (1973, 297) called a "blind manipulation of the data." Econometric testing, while being of fundamental importance to "eliminate impressionism," is not a substitute for critical thinking and judgment of value concerning what part of economic reality to incorporate into a model (Garrone and Marchionatti 2004, 25). Hence, it may well be that the truly disturbing nonrobustness of empirical NAIRU findings reflects a deeper problem: a misspecification of the theory itself. This is the issue that will be taken up in Chapter 3.

Aesop's Fox

The weaknesses of the statistical evidence in support of the NAIRU view are so serious as to make one wonder how these studies managed to pass the peer review standards of leading economics journals. Indeed, one perhaps has to wonder about the quality of the field as a whole (Elster 2009). In more general terms, one may ask why mainstream macroeconomics ignores the outright fragility of the empirical evidence. Why are there so few skeptical economists? One answer, already mentioned in the introduction to this chapter, is that the strong (theoretical and/or ideological) prior that European unemployment was due to labor market regulation overwhelmed the empirics and the interpretation thereof. "The prosecuting attorney was committed to argue for conviction no matter what," as Freeman (2005, 17) writes. In our view, this is a clear case of what psychologists call cognitive dissonance. Cognitive dissonance occurs when a person perceives an inconsistency among his or her cognitions. The classic example is expressed in Aesop's fable of the fox and the grapes, in which a fox sees some high-hanging grapes and wishes to eat them. Unable to think of a way to reach them, the fox surmises that the grapes are not worth eating anyway because they are probably too sour. In this story, the desire for something unattainable is reduced by acquiescent sentience—by irrationally deciding that what is desired must be sour. Here follow two examples of how macroeconomists, knowingly or unknowingly, acquiesce in the inconsistency between NAIRU theory and reality.

The first example concerns the IMF, which in its *World Economic Outlook 2003* predicted that labor market deregulation in Europe (making European labor markets look more like those in the United States) would drastically reduce unemployment in the European Union. Remarkably, this claim does not follow from the IMF's own analysis:

> The most rigorous analysis in [IMF 2003] shows nothing like these effects. This analysis estimates a vector of "Institution-Adjusted Unemployment Rates" for OECD countries as unemployment rate minus the estimated impact of institutions on unemployment. Graphs in the article show that these rates closely track actual changes in unemployment rates, and the article informs the reader that this means that "institutions hardly account for the growing trends observed in most European countries and the dramatic fall in U.S. unemployment in the 1990s." . . . In particular, the article stressed that Germany had broadly unchanged

institutions while unemployment rose by about 6 percentage points. (Freeman 2005, 16)

But despite this finding, the IMF's message was that labor market deregulation would drastically reduce unemployment. How could they reach such a conclusion from such data? Only by ignoring or repressing this longitudinal evidence (which most analysts would regard as providing a more valid test of the claim) in favor of cross-country regressions showing that labor market interventions "alone explain a good deal of the cross-country differences in unemployment rates." Did not Sigmund Freud already show that unconscious repression of inconvenient experiences is a frequently used defense mechanism?

Our second example of cognitive dissonance in action concerns attempts to save the NAIRU approach by finding special—exogenous and idiosyncratic—factors that "might explain short-run deviations of unemployment from its equilibrium level" (Nickell, Nunziata, and Ochel 2005, 10). Special factors that have been identified are negative supply shocks (including energy price shocks), technology (that is, total factor productivity, or TFP) shocks, and real interest rate shocks, which all affect the feasible growth of real wages. It has been claimed that these special factors play a major role: as much as 40–45 percent of the rise in European unemployment during the last three decades has been attributed to such shocks (Nickell, Nunziata, and Ochel 2005). But can the effects of shocks on unemployment be permanent? Olivier Blanchard and Justin Wolfers (2000) suggest that the answer often is yes, because specific institutions inhibit the ability of economies to respond to adverse macroeconomic shocks, thereby leading to higher unemployment. Blanchard and Wolfers start off from two disturbing insights. First, they note that the standard NAIRU view runs into a major empirical problem: "Many of the institutions were already present when unemployment was low (and similar across countries), and, while many became less employment-friendly in the 1970s, the movement [in unemployment rates] since then has been mostly in the opposite direction." Second, they observe that the conventional results are "in part the result of research Darwinism. The measures used . . . have all been constructed *ex-post facto*, by researchers who were not unaware of unemployment developments. . . . [And] measures which do well in explaining unemployment have survived better than those that did not" (Blanchard and Wolfers 2000, C2, C22).

Therefore, Blanchard and Wolfers decide to focus not on labor market interventions per se but on the interaction of adverse economic shocks and labor market interventions. Their hypothesis is that "excessive" labor market regulation hinders the recovery of unemployment rates after the economy recovers from an adverse shock. But their statistical findings are disappointing, at least from the conventional viewpoint: the estimated impact coefficients are very sensitive to changes in measures used (e.g., when the measure of the benefit replacement ratio is changed, all coefficients for labor market interventions become insignificant). This nonrobustness of the Blanchard-Wolfers findings has been confirmed by the replication study of Baccaro and Rei (2007). Of course, the question of whether macroeconomic shocks (through their interaction with labor market interventions) do, in part, explain long-run unemployment is relevant. But the question is narrowly framed within the standard NAIRU approach and suppresses any possibility that these shocks are not exogenous but endogenous, caused by macro and/or labor market policies. This is where the existing cognitive dissonance has been reduced by denying—without investigation—that demand (and demand policy) can affect the NAIRU.

The Diversity of OECD Capitalism

The simple truth is that the empirical case to justify sweeping labor market deregulation cannot be rescued by attempts to improve the statistical explanation by introducing idiosyncratic shocks into the regression analysis. The real reason the evidence is weak is that the macro performance of many OECD countries does not conform to what the NAIRU model predicts.

NAIRU logic holds that redistributive interventions, high taxation, and generous social welfare states raise wage costs, reduce real wage flexibility, and strengthen the wage bargaining position of unions, thus leading to higher steady-inflation unemployment and weaker overall macroeconomic performance (Bowles 2002; Glyn 2006). Egalitarianism, it is therefore concluded in Hayekian fashion, must come at the cost of slow growth, high structural unemployment, and limited technological dynamism—especially now that competition has become more intense due to globalization. Figure 2.3 captures the ubiquitous trade-off between growth and equity inherent in the NAIRU approach.

This universalizing claim is belied, however, by the actual macroeconomic performance of the OECD countries, as we illustrate in Figure 2.4, where we present comparative empirical evidence on average real GDP growth and equity performance for four groups of OECD countries during the periods from 1984 to 1994 and from 1994 to 2004. The first group is the social-democratic Nordic economies of Denmark, Finland, Norway, and Sweden. The second group of countries includes the core European Continental (EC) countries: Austria, Belgium, France, Germany, the Netherlands, and Switzerland. The third group is the European Mediterranean

	low growth	high growth
egalitarian	corporatist, regulated, high-unemployment economies (Europe)	
unequal		liberal, deregulated, low-unemployment economies (United States)

Figure 2.3. The fundamental NAIRU assumption: a growth-equity trade-off.

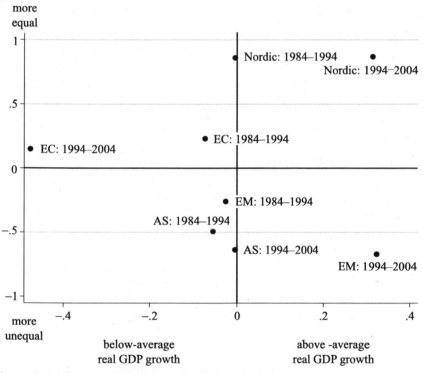

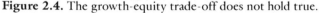

Figure 2.4. The growth-equity trade-off does not hold true.

Note: The taxonomy into four groups is explained in the text. The data on earnings inequality (D9/D1) and real GDP growth are averages for the periods from 1984 to 1994 and from 1994 to 2004. The horizontal axis measures the difference between average country group GDP growth and average GDP growth for all OECD countries; Ireland is excluded from the AS group because it is too much of an outlier in terms of growth (even in the AS group). The vertical axis measures (in absolute terms) the difference between average country group earnings inequality and average inequality for all OECD countries.

(EM) countries: Greece, Italy, Portugal, and Spain. The fourth group includes the liberal Anglo-Saxon (AS) countries: Australia, Canada, the United Kingdom, and the United States (Figure 2.4 does not include data on Ireland, which is too much of an outlier in the AS group in terms of GDP growth). It can be seen that actual performance of the country groupings does not, in general, conform to the diagonal pattern indicated in Figure 2.3. True, the group of relatively heavily regulated EC countries features below-average growth and below-average inequality, as NAIRU theory predicts. But the other groups deviate from the NAIRU norm. Specifically, we note the following:

1. The regulated and coordinated Nordic countries on average outperform the other countries of the OECD (including the AS ones) in terms of GDP growth and equity.
2. The corporatist EM countries did well in terms of growth, particularly in the period from 1994 to 2004, but feature high (that is, Anglo-Saxon-style) inequality.
3. The four AS countries (Australia, Canada, the United Kingdom, and the United States) experienced average GDP growth in combination with above-average inequality.

All this may be surprising to macroeconomists. But it is a commonplace conclusion in the varieties-of-capitalism literature that very different systems of labor market regulation, in conjunction with complementary institutions and policies in other (capital) markets, do yield equally good (or bad) employment outcomes (Hall and Soskice 2001; Boeri 2002; Sachs 2006a; Auer 2007).

Perhaps the pattern highlighted in Figure 2.4 is not yet convincing, as it deals with only two performance indicators (relative growth and earnings inequality). Therefore, Tables 2.3 and 2.4 present comparative evidence on various other indicators of labor market policy and macro performance for our four country groupings. All group averages are simple unweighted averages, and we test whether the differences in means between groups are statistically significantly different from zero.

Consider first Table 2.3, which presents a groupwise comparison of labor market policies in the OECD countries. Differences in regulation are most pronounced (in statistical terms) between the AS countries, on one hand, and the Nordic, EC, and EM countries, on the other hand. Labor markets in the freewheeling AS countries are regulated the least and feature the weakest levels of employment protection, lowest labor taxes, low levels of expenditure on active labor market policies, relatively little collective bargaining, and low levels of wage bargaining coordination (wage bargaining is highly decentralized); at the same time, non-health-related public social spending

Table 2.3. OECD policy models: labor market regulation

	Nordic Countries (N)	European Continental (EC)	European Mediterranean (EM)	Anglo-Saxon (AS)	Differences (statistically significant)					
					N–EC	N–EM	N–AS	EC–EM	EC–AS	EM–AS
Unemployment benefit replacement ratio, 1999	0.64	0.55	0.63	0.31			0.33***		0.24**	0.32***
Unemployment benefit duration index, 1999	0.56	0.61	0.29	0.67				0.32*		
Collective bargaining coverage index, 1994	0.81	0.86	0.77	0.50			0.31*		0.36**	
Wage bargaining coordination index, 1995–1999	2.13	2.08	2.17	1.50						
Wage bargaining coordination index without Ireland, 1995–1999	2.13	2.08	2.17	1.10			1.03***		0.98***	1.07***
Expenditure on active labor market policies (% of GDP), 1998	1.48	1.16	0.87	0.59		0.62*	0.89**		0.56*	
Total labor tax on average production worker, 1991–1999	45.2	45.2	39.2	32.2						

(continued)

Table 2.3. *(continued)*

	Nordic Countries (N)	European Continental (EC)	European Mediterranean (EM)	Anglo-Saxon (AS)	Differences (statistically significant)					
					N–EC	N–EM	N–AS	EC–EM	EC–AS	EM–AS
Total labor tax on average production worker, 2000–2004	43.4	44.8	38.0	29.1			14.28*		15.72**	
Index of strictness of employment protection legislation, 1999	2.0	2.1	3.4	0.6			1.38***		1.51***	2.81***
Index of strictness of employment protection legislation, 2003	2.1	2.1	2.8	0.9		−1.43***	1.21***	−1.29***	1.26***	1.97***
Non-health public social spending (% of GDP), 1990–99	27.70	24.17	19.80	17.12		7.91***	10.59***	4.37*	7.05***	2.68*
Non-health public social spending (% of GDP), 2000–2003	25.55	24.26	21.79	17.01		3.76*	8.54***		7.25***	16.78*

Notes: The division into four groups is explained in the text. We test whether the observed difference in the country group means is statistically significantly different from zero. We report only statistically significant differences. *, **, and *** denote that the differences in means are statistically significantly different from zero at less than a 10%, 5%, and 1% level, respectively.

Sources: Data sources are given in the Appendix in the backmatter.

Table 2.4. OECD policy models: performance

	Nordic Countries (N)	European Continental (EC)	European Mediterranean (EM)	Anglo-Saxon (AS)	Differences (statistically significant)					
					N–EC	N–EM	N–AS	EC–EM	EC–AS	EM–AS
Real GDP growth (%)										
1990–1999	2.26	2.19	2.24	3.63						
2000–2006	2.58	1.79	2.59	3.44	0.79**				−1.65**	−0.85
Labor productivity growth (%)										
1990–1999	2.41	1.84	1.57	2.53						
2000–2006	2.16	1.64	1.03	2.04	0.52*					
Standardized unemployment (% of labor force)										
1990–1999	7.80	6.60	10.20	8.79						
2000–2006	5.88	6.16	8.69	5.50		−2.81*				3.19**
Real wage growth (hourly)										
1990–1999	1.91	2.03	1.58	1.97						
2000–2006	2.09	1.37	1.00	1.53						
Earnings inequality (D9/D1)										
1984–1994	2.19	2.82	3.31	3.54	−0.62**	−1.12**	−1.35**		−0.73**	
1994–2004	2.18	2.90	3.72	3.69	−0.73***	−1.55***	−1.51***		−0.78**	
Income inequality (Gini coefficient)										
Mid-1990s	22.7	26.4	34.6	31.7	−3.7**	−11.9***	−9.0***	−8.2***	−5.4***	
2000	24.8	26.4	34.4	31.9		−9.7***	−7.1***	−8.0***	−5.5***	

Notes: The taxonomy into four groups is explained in the text. We test whether the observed difference in the country group means is statistically significantly different from zero. We report only statistically significant differences. *, **, and *** denote that the differences in means are statistically significantly different from zero at less than a 10%, 5%, and 1% level, respectively.

Sources: Data sources are given in the Appendix in the backmatter.

in the AS group is the lowest in the OECD. State involvement in labor markets of the Nordic, EC, and EM countries is significantly larger: they all feature more heavily regulated labor markets, substantial union presence in the workplace and involvement in wage setting, higher labor taxes, and higher levels of public social spending. These countries generally have legally mandated works councils, which are typically under a legal obligation to seek cooperation with the employer and to resolve disputes by negotiation rather than by conflict. Employers must consult with the council on matters of work reorganization, new technology, outsourcing, overtime scheduling, and health and safety issues. Wage bargaining is mostly centralized, which reduces employer resistance to wage increases, because these are equal for all firms and hence play no role in interfirm competition.[8] In addition to this, the Nordic countries stand out for the highest levels of social expenditures, the highest labor taxes, and the highest relative expenditures on activating labor market policies. The EC countries rely on high levels of social expenditure and high tax levels but lower expenditures on activating policies. In the EM countries, extensive labor market regulation takes the form of strict employment protection, high replacement ratios, and high collective bargaining coverage; both social spending and labor taxes are lower here than in the Nordic and EC countries.

Turning to Table 2.4, one sees immediately that the significant differences in regulation between our four country groupings do *not* show up in equally significant differences in performance. The AS countries, featuring the most flexible labor markets, do not experience statistically significantly lower average unemployment than the considerably more regulated Nordic countries, EC countries, and even EM countries—as one would expect from Figure 2.3. The relatively high 1990–2006 unemployment rates of "flexible" Australia (7.5 percent) and Canada (8.5 percent) are comparable to the unemployment rates experienced by "rigid" countries such as Belgium (8.2 percent), Germany (7.9 percent), and Sweden (6.7 percent). The relatively low unemployment rate of the United States (at 5.5 percent) during the same time frame is more than matched by the low unemployment rates of heavily regulated, coordinated countries such as Denmark (6 percent), Norway (4.7 percent), Austria (4.2 percent), the Netherlands (4.7 percent), and even Portugal (5.5 percent). Likewise, GDP and labor productivity growth rates for the period from 1990 to 2006 do not differ significantly between country groupings, notwithstanding the significant differences in labor market regulation, social spending, and taxation observed in Table 2.3. However, in one major dimension there is a statistically significant difference in group performance: income and earnings structures are significantly more egalitarian in the Nordic and EC countries than in the AS and EM countries.

Findings in Table 2.4 therefore reinforce the conclusion drawn on the basis of Figure 2.4 in two ways. First, the group of Nordic countries manages to escape the supposedly ubiquitous trade-off between growth and low unemployment, on one hand, and egalitarian outcomes, on the other. In violation of NAIRU logic, on average they outperform the other countries of the OECD on most measures of economic performance, notwithstanding the fact that they have the highest social expenditures, the highest taxes, and extensive labor market regulation, which ensures one of the most compressed wage structures in the world. The second anomaly concerns the liberal Anglo-Saxon countries Australia and Canada, which feature relatively high unemployment, below-average growth, and above-average inequality. In light of these findings, it is no wonder that the results from pooled-data regression analyses are fragile and easily perturbed.

Doing Better

Excessively strong priors—particularly the one that labor markets work perfectly absent policy interventions—are limiting our ability to increase our understanding of the causes of high and persistent unemployment, even when the statistical evidence is found to be weak and many OECD economies deviate from the NAIRU norm. What can we do to further our understanding of the unemployment problem? Definitely the solution is not "continued regression mongering of weak cross country data" (Freeman 2005). Our proposed strategy in this book is to develop more sophisticated priors about how labor market regulation affects macroeconomic performance and how macro performance interacts with labor markets. We do this by developing a Keynesian, demand-led growth model—featuring endogenous labor productivity growth—which we apply to the real world to explain the observed patterns of OECD growth, unemployment, and inequality. Based on this chapter's review of the empirical evidence, our model has to be able to explain two striking conclusions, which follow from a comparison of Tables 2.3 and 2.4 and which the NAIRU approach cannot explain. First, more or less similar labor market policies in the Nordic countries and the EC countries lead to rather different macroeconomic outcomes (in terms of growth and unemployment). Second, large differences in labor market regulation between the Nordic and the AS countries do not show up in diverging macro performance; their growth performance is broadly similar. We argue in Chapter 3 that macroeconomic performance depends on a country's macroeconomic growth regime. Similar labor market policies can have diverging macroeconomic impacts depending on the nature of the growth regime; alternatively, different labor market policies can produce similar macro consequences.[9]

Hence, it is not policy differences per se that matter; rather, regime differences mitigate and ultimately even determine the longer-run impacts of similar macro policy. The next chapter explains our notion of a "growth regime" in terms of our general Keynesian growth model.

Further Reading

Exceptionally careful and balanced replication studies of leading empirical analyses of the impact of regulation on OECD unemployment are Baker et al. (2005a, 2005b) and Howell et al. (2007). Baccaro and Rei (2005) is perhaps the best example of testing empirical findings for robustness. Hall and Soskice (2001) is a major contribution to the varieties-of-capitalism literature. Giovanna Garrone and Roberto Marchionatti (2004) have written a well-argued and readable reassessment of the 1938–1943 debate between Keynes and econometrician Jan Tinbergen; it is somewhat depressing to see how many of Keynes's criticisms are still relevant today. Jon Elster (2009), mincing no words, provides a sociological explanation of why we may be observing wasteful and spurious econometric research on a large scale. Richard Freeman (2005) offers a similar argument in the context of the debate over labor market flexibility. David Gordon (1996), Richard Sennett (1998), Barbara Ehrenreich (2001), and Louis Uchitelle (2006) give us passionate, well-founded accounts of the many downsides of labor market flexibility and low-wage work.

3

A Growth Model

> Too large a proportion of recent "mathematical" economics are merely
> concoctions, as imprecise as the initial assumptions they rest on, which
> allow the author to lose sight of the complexities and interdependencies
> of the real world in a maze of pretentious and unhelpful symbols.
>
> JOHN MAYNARD KEYNES,
> *THE GENERAL THEORY OF EMPLOYMENT, INTEREST AND MONEY*

The adequacy of any model meant to explain macroeconomic growth and
unemployment depends on the economist's ability to identify and include
the relevant factors. The decision of which variables to incorporate into a
model is what Keynes termed a "judgment of value." It involves a mixture
of intuitive selection and formal accounting principles. "The object of our
analysis," Keynes (1973, 297) wrote, "is to provide ourselves with an organ-
ised and orderly method of thinking about particular problems." Building
on Naastepad (2006) and Naastepad and Storm (2007), we have organized
our thinking on growth and employment in a demand-led growth model
that does allow for systemic diversity. Our growth model integrates neo-
Kaleckian growth theory (in which the interaction of growth and distribution assumes center stage, but technological progress is overlooked) and
neo-Kaldorian growth theory (in which long-run growth is accompanied by
endogenous technological progress, but there is no discussion of the impact
of distribution on growth). Our model does not deal with business cycles or
cyclical growth. Our focus, in contrast, is on differences in structural growth
paths, which in our view are related to structural, longer-term (not cyclical)
differences in OECD capitalism.[1]

The model can be reduced to a productivity regime, which specifies how
potential labor productivity gains are obtained, and a demand regime,
which specifies how productivity gains for a given real wage growth may
affect aggregate demand growth. We add a labor market regime, which de-
scribes how real wage growth is influenced by unemployment, productivity
growth, and extent of labor market regulation. We find that the observed
diversity in macroeconomic outcomes of similar labor market policies is in
large measure due to differences in demand regimes—aggregate demand being either profit-led or wage-led. The recognition of the variety in growth regimes, based on systemic differences between economies, leads us to conclude

that the trade-off between growth and unemployment, on the one hand, and egalitarian outcomes, on the other hand, does not apply universally and, accordingly, that the consequences of real wage restraint and labor market *de*regulation (both intended to raise profitability) are not unambiguously beneficial.

This chapter is theoretical in nature: we present and explain the growth model and use it to assess the effects on real GDP growth, labor productivity growth, and employment of labor market deregulation. Our model is linear (in annual growth rates), to "keep things as simple as possible, but not simpler."[2] The exercise brings out—we hope in an orderly and organized way—that similar (labor market) policies work out very differently in wage-led and profit-led systems. In Chapter 4, we present cross-country empirical evidence in support of our productivity regime, and Chapter 5 is an elaborate investigation into the (wage-led or profit-led) nature of OECD demand regimes. We must finally note that this chapter's model analysis deals with what must be regarded as a conditional or provisional equilibrium, as defined by Setterfield (2002, 4), and not long-run equilibrium in a classical or NAIRU sense; the reason is that we are not assuming that real wage growth must equal labor productivity growth (keeping income distribution constant). Long-run equilibrium, in this sense, is the subject matter of Chapter 6, where we use the growth model to identify the determinants of the steady-inflation unemployment rate.

The Productivity Regime

The supply side of the economy is modeled in terms of what we call a productivity regime—a description of how aggregate labor productivity growth $\hat{\lambda}$ is influenced by real GDP (or output) growth $\hat{x}$, real wage growth $\hat{w}$, and labor market policies z (a circumflex over a variable denotes its growth rate). As in Chapter 1, the essence of our critique of the conventional NAIRU approach is that it unrealistically assumes that labor productivity growth is *exogenous*, meaning that productivity does not change in response to demand growth, real wage growth, or shifts in the social relations of production (which depend on the extent and nature of labor market regulation). This is wrong. Labor productivity is likely to change in response to demand growth, especially capital accumulation, because investment embodies technological progress (Kaldor 1957, 1966). Productivity will change when real wages change, because of induced labor-saving technological change (Marx-biased technological change à la Foley and Michl 1999). And productivity will change when the social relations of production are altered—specifically, productivity growth may increase if the relationship between employee and firm becomes more cooperative and workers feel more secure and fairly treated (Gordon 1996; Buchele and Christiansen 1999). Chapter 4 provides more empirical detail as well as theoretical substance on these determinants of labor productivity growth. For the moment, let us assume that the productivity regime is given by:

$$(3.1) \qquad \hat{\lambda} = \beta_0 + \beta_1 \hat{x} + \beta_2 \hat{w} + \beta_3 z \qquad \beta_0, \beta_2, \beta_3 > 0; \ 0 < \beta_1 < 1.$$

We note that equation (3.1) can be derived from a neoclassical constant-elasticity-of-substitution (CES) production function (as we show in the Appendix to this chapter). But we do not need a production function to interpret the coefficients:

- β_1 is the Kaldor-Verdoorn coefficient. It measures the impact of demand-determined output growth on labor productivity growth, which may be due to the fact that aggregate production exhibits increasing returns to scale (Kaldor 1966; McCombie, Pugno, and Soro 2002). It may also be due to the fact that investment contributes simultaneously to aggregate demand, the capital stock, and average productivity, because it embodies new and more productive vintages of capital (Kaldor 1957).
- β_2 reflects the degree of wage-led technological progress. It reflects the extent to which more expensive labor induces firms to intensify their search for and adoption of labor-productivity-raising techniques (Foley and Michl 1999; Tavani 2009; Duménil and Lévy 2010b). For neoclassical economists, β_2 would be simply the elasticity of capital-labor substitution, as the Appendix explains.
- Coefficient β_3 indicates the extent to which the nature of the regulatory regime in the labor market (via the social relations of production) influences labor productivity growth. We assume—for reasons explained in Chapter 1—that $\beta_3 > 0$; that is, the more regulated the labor market, the higher the rate of labor productivity growth. Suffice it to state here that pro-worker (or protective) labor market regulation will improve labor productivity by promoting workers' motivation and by stimulating investment in human capital formation; supporting empirical evidence is provided in Chapter 4.

Figure 3.1 presents the productivity regime curve in the $(\hat{\lambda}, \hat{x})$ plane—note that output growth $\hat{x}$ is measured on the vertical axis and labor productivity growth $\hat{\lambda}$ on the horizontal axis. The curve is upward-sloping with a slope coefficient of $1/\beta_1$, thus reflecting the Kaldor-Verdoorn relation. A rise in real wage growth, or alternatively a shift to more extensive labor market regulation (a higher z), will shift the productivity regime curve downward to the right, as is illustrated in the graph. The same rate of output growth is now

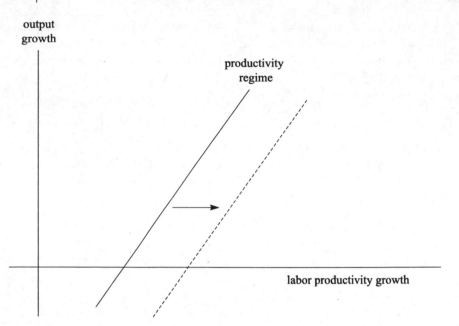

Figure 3.1. The productivity regime.

associated with a higher rate of labor productivity growth, the increase being due to induced technological progress. Contrariwise, a decline in real wage growth or a decline in z will shift the productivity regime upward to the left.

The Demand Regime

We now turn to aggregate demand. Following national accounting convention, aggregate production (or output) x is determined by effective demand as follows:

$$(3.2) \qquad x = c + g + i + e - m$$

where c is aggregate private consumption, g is public current expenditure, i is aggregate investment, e is exports, and m is imports; all variables are measured at constant prices. Before presenting the structural equations determining c, i, e, and m, it is convenient to define the real labor cost per unit of output or the real wage share as follows:

$$(3.3) \qquad v = (W/P)\lambda^{-1} = w\lambda^{-1}$$

where W is the nominal wage (per hour of work) and P is the aggregate price level. We assume that the real wage $w = (W/P)$ is fixed at any point in time, from institutions and a history of bargaining. For later use, we express equation (3.3) in growth rates as follows:

(3.4) $\hat{v} = \hat{w} - \hat{\lambda}$

It can be seen that the growth of unit labor cost depends (positively) on the growth of the real wage and (negatively) on the growth of labor productivity. From equation (3.3), and at a given level of labor productivity λ, it follows that there exists a negative relationship between the real wage rate and the profit share. To see this, note that, by definition, the real profit share π is equal to 1 minus the wage share:

(3.5) $\pi = 1 - \dfrac{W\lambda^{-1}}{P} = 1 - v$

Expressed in growth rates, this gives

(3.6) $\hat{\pi} = \dfrac{\Delta\pi}{\pi} = -\dfrac{v}{\pi}\dfrac{\Delta v}{v} = -\theta(\hat{w} - \hat{\lambda})$

where $\theta = (v/\pi) = v/(1-v) > 0$. Equation (3.6) shows that profit share growth will decline as a result of real wage growth in excess of labor productivity growth.

Consumption demand is a function of wage income and capital income; consumption behavior is income-class specific: denoting the savings propensity by σ and using the subscripts w and π to refer to wage income and profit income, respectively, wage earners consume $(1 - \sigma_w)$ of their income, while capitalists' average consumption propensity equals $(1 - \sigma_\pi)$. We assume further that wage earners save at a rate that is lower than the savings rate out of profits $(\sigma_w < \sigma_\pi)$ as a result of the retention of a significant portion of profits by corporations. Accordingly, the consumption function can be written as

(3.7) $c = (1 - \sigma_w)w\lambda^{-1}x + (1 - \sigma_\pi)\pi x - t = [(1 - \sigma_w)v + (1 - \sigma_\pi)(1 - v)]x - t$

where t is aggregate direct tax payments. Import demand is a linear function of output:

(3.8) $m = \zeta x$

where ζ is the average import propensity. Substituting equations (3.7) and (3.9) into (3.2) and rearranging, we get the following expression for x:

(3.9) $x = \dfrac{(g - t) + i + e}{[1 - (1 - \sigma_w)v - (1 - \sigma_\pi)(1 - v) + \zeta]} = \mu^{-1}(g^* + i + e).$

We define $g^* = g - t$ as government current expenditure minus direct tax payments (which is the government's current account deficit). Note that $\mu^{-1} = 1/[1 - (1 - \sigma_w)v - (1 - \sigma_\pi)(1 - v) + \zeta]$ is the Keynesian multiplier ($\mu^{-1} > 1$), the magnitude of which depends, via v, on the distribution of income and in particular on the real wage and labor productivity. Totally differentiating (3.9), dividing through by x, and rearranging, we get the following expression for demand-led output growth:

$$(3.10) \qquad \hat{x} = -\hat{\mu} + \frac{\mu^{-1}g^*}{x}\hat{g}^* + \frac{\mu^{-1}i}{x}\hat{i} + \frac{\mu^{-1}e}{x}\hat{e} = -\hat{\mu} + \psi_g\hat{g}^* + \psi_i\hat{i} + \psi_e\hat{e}$$

where ψ_g, ψ_i, and ψ_e are the multiplier-adjusted shares in GDP of net government current expenditure, investment, and exports, respectively. The multiplier is endogenous, because any change in real labor cost per unit of output will directly affect its denominator μ, which equals $[\sigma_\pi - v(\sigma_\pi - \sigma_w) + \zeta]$. Using this expression for μ, we can derive its growth rate as a function of unit labor cost growth as follows:

$$(3.11) \qquad \hat{\mu} = -\frac{v}{\mu}(\sigma_\pi - \sigma_w)\hat{v} = -\xi(\sigma_\pi - \sigma_w)(\hat{w} - \hat{\lambda})$$

where ξ is the positive fraction (v/μ). Hence, the denominator of the multiplier will decline (and the multiplier itself will become larger) when real unit labor costs rise.

With $\hat{\mu}$ being determined, we need to specify investment and export demand growth to complete the model. Following Bhaduri and Marglin (1990) and Taylor (1991, 2004), we assume that the growth rate of investment i depends positively on the growth rate of π and x and negatively on the real interest rate (or cost of capital) r_k:

$$(3.12) \qquad \hat{i} = \varphi_0\hat{b} + \varphi_1\hat{\pi} + \varphi_2\hat{x} - \varphi_3 r_k \qquad \varphi_0, \varphi_1, \varphi_2, \varphi_3 > 0$$

where $\hat{b}$ represents other, autonomous factors (mainly "animal spirits" of entrepreneurs) influencing investment decisions. Coefficient φ_1 is the elasticity of investment with respect to the profit share; the positive effect on investment of π can be justified by reference to the use of corporate retained profits for relieving financial constraint on investment, or else by thinking of π as the expected rate of return on new investment (assuming that expected profits equal actual profits for simplicity). Finally, φ_2 is the accelerator effect, that is, the effect of output growth on the demand for new capital equipment, and φ_3 is the elasticity of investment with respect to the real interest rate. Next we turn to exports e, which we assume to be a negative function of relative unit labor cost and a positive function of exogenous (or autonomous) exports e_0:

$$(3.13) \qquad e = e_0\left[\frac{v}{v_{row}}\right]^{-\varepsilon_1}$$

where v_{row} is the real labor cost (in domestic currency) associated with one unit of world exports, ε_0 is the elasticity of exports with respect to world demand, and ε_1 is the elasticity of export volume with respect to change in (relative) real unit labor cost. For simplicity and without loss of generality, we assume that $v_{row} = 1$; linearizing equation (3.13) in growth rates then gives

(3.14) $\qquad \hat{e} = \hat{e}_0 - \varepsilon_1 \hat{v}$

Substitution of equations (3.6), (3.11), (3.12), and (3.14) into (3.13) yields the following reduced-form equation for the demand regime:

(3.15)
$$\hat{x} = \frac{\psi_i \varphi_0 \hat{b} + \psi_g \hat{g}^* + \psi_e \hat{e} - \psi_i \varphi_3 r_k}{1 - \psi_i \varphi_2}$$
$$+ \frac{[\xi(\sigma_\pi - \sigma_w) - \psi_i \varphi_1 \theta - \psi_e \varepsilon_1]}{1 - \psi_i \varphi_2} [\hat{w} - \hat{\lambda}]$$

Note that for equation (3.15) to be economically meaningful, we must assume that $[1 - \psi_i \varphi_2] > 0$, that is, given that $0 < \psi_i < 1$, the accelerator elasticity has to fall within the range $0 \leq \varphi_2 < (1/\psi_2)$. Demand-led output growth thus depends on five factors:

(i) the growth of autonomous investment $\hat{b}$
(ii) the growth of net public current expenditure $\hat{g}^*$
(iii) the growth of autonomous exports $\hat{e}_0$
(iv) the real interest rate r_k
(v) the growth rate of real unit labor cost $\hat{v} = \hat{w} - \hat{\lambda}$

While the impact on output growth of (i) autonomous investment growth, (ii) government expenditure growth, and (iii) export growth is positive and that of the real interest rate (iv) is negative, the impact of (v) labor cost growth on output growth is ambiguous in sign. This is because any excess of real wage growth over labor productivity growth (i.e., $\hat{v} > 0$ or $\hat{w} > \hat{\lambda}$) has two opposing effects on output growth. On one hand, it will reduce investment growth (via the profit share elasticity φ_1) and export growth (via the export cost elasticity ε_1), and consequently lower output growth. But on the other hand, it will increase the size of the multiplier, because it entails a redistribution of income of income from profits toward wage income and a consequent decline in the aggregate savings propensity (because $\sigma_w < \sigma_\pi$). To derive the sign of the derivative of output growth with respect to unit labor cost growth $(d\hat{x}/d\hat{v})$ from equation (3.15), recall that $[1 - \psi_i \varphi_2] > 0$, $\xi = (v/\mu)$, $\psi_i = i/(\mu x)$, and $\psi_e = e/(\mu x)$. It then follows that $(d\hat{x}/d\hat{v})$ will be positive in the following circumstance:

(3.16)
$$\frac{d\hat{x}}{d\hat{v}} = \frac{[\xi(\sigma_\pi - \sigma_w) - \psi_i \varphi_1 \theta - \psi_e \varepsilon_1]}{1 - \psi_i \varphi_2} > 0$$
$$\text{if} \quad (\sigma_\pi - \sigma_w) > \left(\frac{i}{\pi x}\right) \varphi_1 + \left(\frac{e}{vx}\right) \varepsilon_1$$

If (3.16) is satisfied, real wage growth in excess of productivity growth will raise output growth—demand (and output) growth is then called *wage-led*. Let us use the symbol C for the impact of labor cost growth on output growth. If demand is wage-led, C will be strictly positive:

$$(3.17) \qquad C = \frac{d\hat{x}}{d\hat{v}} > 0$$

Alternatively, demand is *profit-led* if

$$(3.18) \qquad C = \frac{d\hat{x}}{d\hat{v}} < 0 \text{ if } (\sigma_\pi - \sigma_w) < \left(\frac{i}{\pi x}\right)\varphi_1 + \left(\frac{e}{vx}\right)\varepsilon_1$$

Now, higher labor cost growth reduces demand and output growth—because the consequent fall in profits and investments as well as exports is larger than the stimulus imparted to consumption.

Equation (3.15) is the demand regime, which can be wage-led (if $C > 0$) or profit-led ($C < 0$). Let us simplify its notation by assuming that Θ represents all autonomous influences on output growth (including the negative impact of a higher real interest rate):

$$(3.19) \qquad \Theta = \frac{\psi_i \varphi_0 \hat{b} + \psi_g \hat{g}^* + \psi_e \hat{e} - \psi_i \varphi_3 r_k}{1 - \psi_i \varphi_2}$$

The demand regime can then be expressed as the following function of real wage growth and productivity growth and autonomous demand growth:

$$(3.20) \qquad \hat{x} = \Theta + C[\hat{w} - \hat{\lambda}]$$

Figure 3.2 presents the demand regime curve in the $(\hat{\lambda}, \hat{x})$ plane—panel (a) shows wage-led demand and panel (b) shows profit-led demand. The wage-led demand regime curve is downward-sloping in the $(\hat{\lambda}, \hat{x})$ plane, with slope coefficient $-C$. Why is it downward-sloping? The reason is that faster labor productivity (at a given rate of real wage growth) redistributes income from wages, which have a lower savings rate, to profits, which have a higher savings rate (see equation (3.6)); in other words, it raises the profit share. This reduces consumption growth, and the fall in consumption growth is larger in absolute terms than the rise in investment and export growth induced by higher profits and lower unit labor costs. Output growth consequently declines. The profit-led demand regime curve is upward-sloping because faster productivity growth stimulates output expansion (mainly because higher productivity reduces unit labor costs and thus stimulates investment and exports). Figure 3.2 also illustrates what happens when there is a rise in real wage growth, or alternatively a shift to more extensive labor market regulation (a higher z). The wage-led demand regime will shift upward, reflecting the fact

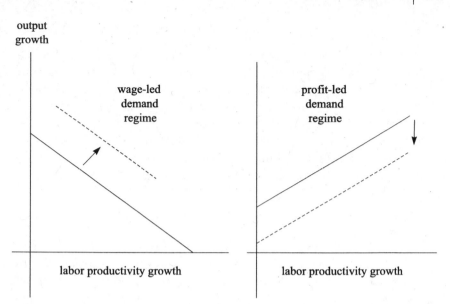

Figure 3.2. The demand regime.

that the same rate of labor productivity growth is now associated with higher wage-led output growth. The profit-led demand regime, in contrast, will shift down: higher real wage growth reduces profit-led output growth at a constant pace of productivity advance.

The Employment Regime

By definition, employment growth (i.e., labor demand growth) $\hat{\ell}$ is equal to

(3.21) $\qquad \hat{\ell} = \hat{x} - \hat{\lambda}$

Using the productivity regime equation (3.1), we can express $\hat{\ell}$ as a function of only output growth:

(3.22) $\qquad \hat{\ell} = (1 - \beta_1)\,\hat{x} - \beta_0 - \beta_2\,\hat{w} - \beta_3\,z$

(This is the relationship underlying the employment regime curve in Figures 3.3, 3.4, and 3.5, below.) Unemployment u, in turn, is a negative function of employment growth (assuming that labor supply growth is exogenous):

(3.23) $\qquad u = f(\hat{\ell}) = \Omega - \gamma\hat{\ell}$

Finally, in line with the standard NAIRU approach to wage bargaining, we assume that

(3.24) $\hat{w} = \alpha_0 - \alpha_1 u + \alpha_2 \hat{\lambda} + \alpha_3 z$ $\alpha_0, \alpha_2, \alpha_3 > 0.$

Coefficient α_1 reflects the negative impact on the real wage of a rise in unemployment: because higher unemployment weakens workers' bargaining power, they are forced to accept a lower real wage. Coefficient α_2 represents the extent to which labor productivity growth is reflected in the real wage bargain. We assume, in line with recent econometric evidence (see Chapter 6), that α_2 is statistically significantly smaller than unity. A higher z reflects workers' strengthened bargaining position, which increases the real wage growth demanded by workers at a given unemployment rate, hence $\alpha_3 > 0$.

Equilibrium Growth: The Wage-Led Case

Let us for the moment ignore equation (3.24), however, and assume that real wage growth is exogenously given as the outcome of institutionalized negotiation and bargaining between unions and employers' associations.[3] Combining equations (3.1) and (3.20), we solve for the equilibrium rates of output and labor productivity growth $\hat{x}$ and $\hat{\lambda}$ and equilibrium employment growth $\hat{\ell}$:

(3.25) $\hat{x} = \dfrac{\Theta - \beta_0 C}{1 + \beta_1 C} + \dfrac{(1 - \beta_2) C}{1 + \beta_1 C} \hat{w} - \dfrac{\beta_3 C}{1 + \beta_1 C} z = \overline{\Theta} + \Xi \hat{w} - \Phi_z$

(3.26) $\hat{\lambda} = \beta_0 + \beta_1 \overline{\Theta} + [\beta_2 + \beta_1 \Xi]\hat{w} + [\beta_3 + \beta_1 \Phi]z$

(3.27) $\hat{\ell} = -\beta_0 + (1 - \beta_1)\overline{\Theta} + [(1 - \beta_1)\Xi - \beta_2]\hat{w} - [\beta_3 + (\hat{\ell} - \beta_1)\Phi]z$

where

$$\overline{\Theta} = \dfrac{\Theta - \beta_0 C}{1 + \beta_1 C}; \ \Xi = \dfrac{(1 - \beta_2) C}{1 + \beta_1 C}; \ \text{and} \ \Phi = \dfrac{\beta_3 C}{1 + \beta_1 C}.$$

These equilibrium expressions can be used to analyze how output, productivity, and employment growth are affected by changes in real wage growth ($\Delta\hat{w}$) and by changes in the extent of labor market regulation (Δz). Let us consider the effects of real wage restraint, operationalized as a reduction of real wage growth ($\Delta\hat{w} < 0$). It is useful to recall here that the main implication of the NAIRU approach is that a restoration of profitability is necessary for a revival of growth and a reduction of unemployment and that this can be achieved by a policy of real wage growth restraint in combination with a more general policy of labor market deregulation. As Alan Greenspan remarked, subdued wages, caused by heightened job insecurity and "traumatized workers," were a major factor in the extraordinary macro performance of the U.S. economy in the late 1990s (Pollin 2003, 53). What are the effects of lower real wage growth according to our model?

From equation (3.25), we derive the total impact of the decline in real wage growth on equilibrium output growth as follows:

$$(3.28) \qquad \frac{d\hat{x}}{d\hat{w}} = \frac{(1 - \beta_2) C}{1 + \beta_1 C} = \Xi$$

We note that $1/1 + \beta_1 C$ represents an endogenous technology multiplier that captures the process of cumulative causation implied by the Kaldor-Verdoorn relationship; if the Kaldor-Verdoorn coefficient $\beta_1 = 0$, the endogenous technology multiplier vanishes. It follows from the model's stability conditions that the denominator $1 + \beta_1 C$ of equation (3.28) is positive (Naastepad 2006). Accordingly, the sign of $(d\hat{x}/d\hat{w})$ depends on whether the numerator $(1 - \beta_2) C$ is positive or negative.

Let us first consider the case of wage-led demand $(C > 0)$. When the demand regime is wage-led, the numerator will be positive only if $0 \le \beta_2 < 1$, that is, the elasticity of productivity growth with respect to real wage growth (the wage-cost-induced technological progress effect) is smaller than unity. In this case, lower real wage growth unequivocally lowers output growth—quite unlike Greenspan's hypothesis. Traumatizing workers and reducing wage growth does not raise the structural rate of output growth in a wage-led system (and assuming that $0 \le \beta_2 < 1$). Bhaduri and Marglin (1990) call this the *stagnationist* regime, in which there is no inverse relation between output and the real wage rate (as Keynes argued). It must be noted, however, that if $\beta_2 \to 1$, $(d\hat{x}/d\hat{w}) \to 0$, that is, the impact on output growth of reduced real wage growth becomes smaller (in absolute terms) and eventually vanishes the more β_2 approaches a value of 1. The reason is simple: if wage growth declines, and if, as a result, labor productivity growth declines almost in the same proportion (which is what happens when β_2 is close to unity), then—from equation (3.4)—unit labor cost growth $\hat{v}$ does not change much, and hence output growth does not change much. This leads us to an important qualification: a higher sensitivity of labor productivity growth to real wage growth reduces the strength of the wage-led nature of aggregate demand.[4] This impact of a decline in wage growth on productivity growth is generally ignored in models of demand-led growth; in our more general model, we can see that this omission will be serious, leading to the overestimation of the impact of a change in wage growth on demand growth $(d\hat{x}/d\hat{w})$ the higher the value of β_2.

Turning to equation (3.26), what can we say about the impact of reduced real wage growth on equilibrium productivity growth when demand is wage-led? From (3.26), it follows that

$$(3.29) \quad \frac{d\hat{\lambda}}{d\hat{w}} = \beta_2 + \beta_1 \frac{d\hat{x}}{d\hat{w}} = \beta_2 + \frac{\beta_1(1-\beta_2)C}{1+\beta_1 C} = \frac{\beta_2 + \beta_1 C}{1+\beta_1 C}$$

A reduction in real wage growth has both direct and indirect effects on productivity growth. The direct effect is a decline in productivity growth by $\beta_2 \Delta\hat{w}$; a permanently lower rate of wage growth reduces the incentive for firms to invest in labor-saving technological progress. The indirect effect is equal to the change in long-run demand growth, caused by the decrease in real wage growth $(d\hat{x}/d\hat{w})$ multiplied by the Kaldor-Verdoorn elasticity β_1. If the economy is wage-led, $(d\hat{\lambda}/d\hat{w})$ is always positive, because $C > 0$; consequently, reduced real wage growth always depresses long-run productivity growth both directly (providing less inducement to improve technology) and indirectly (by reducing demand, which reduces productivity growth via the Kaldor-Verdoorn channel). Hence we arrive at a paradoxical result: any attempt to restore firms' profitability by cuts in real wage growth is self-defeating if the economy's demand regime is wage-led, because it ends up in a fall of both output growth and labor productivity growth, and ultimately declining profits. It follows, contrariwise, that higher real wage growth may raise growth, productivity, and total profits. As Amit Bhaduri and Stephen Marglin (1990, 382) write:

> Capitalism is not necessarily a zero-sum game. Despite a higher real wage rate and lower profit margin/share, capitalists may continue to make a higher total profit in the stagnationist [wage-led] regime as long as they recoup on the volume of sales what they lose on profit margin per unit of sale.

What happens to employment growth (and unemployment)? From equations (3.28) and (3.29), we derive the following employment growth effect of reduced real wage growth:

$$(3.30) \quad \frac{d\hat{\ell}}{d\hat{w}} = \frac{d\hat{x}}{d\hat{w}} - \frac{d\hat{\lambda}}{d\hat{w}} = (1-\beta_1)\frac{d\hat{x}}{d\hat{w}} - \beta_2 = \frac{(1-\beta_1-\beta_2)C - \beta_2}{1+\beta_1 C}$$

It can be seen that the total impact on employment growth is the net result of three separate (and opposing) effects of reduced real wage growth:

 (i) Employment growth declines due to a decrease in output growth because demand is wage-led $(d\hat{x}/d\omega) > 0$.
 (ii) Employment growth increases due to the direct decline in labor productivity growth via β_2.

(iii) Employment growth increases because labor productivity growth falls via the Kaldor-Verdoorn coefficient β_1.

The sign of $d\hat{\ell}/d\hat{w}$ depends on the magnitude of each of these effects; hence, employment growth may rise or fall in response to the fall in real wage growth. Formally, if $d\hat{\ell}/d\hat{w} > 0$, then

$$C > \frac{\beta_2}{1 - \beta_1 - \beta_2}$$

because the decline in employment induced by lower wage growth is larger in absolute terms than the rise in employment caused by slower productivity growth (also the result of lower real wage growth). Under wage-led demand ($C > 0$), this condition is always met if we assume that $\beta_2 = 0$; hence, absent wage-cost-induced technological progress, *lower* real wage growth results in *lower* employment growth—in clear violation of what Keynes called the second postulate of classical employment theory. The picture changes and becomes more neoclassical when $\beta_2 > 0$. For high values of β_1 and especially β_2, the sign of $d\hat{\ell}/d\hat{w}$ becomes negative; in other words, a decline in real wage growth may then lead to a rise in employment growth, mainly because of its negative impact on induced labor-saving technological progress and productivity growth and the consequent positive effect on the growth of demand. To conclude, as equation (3.30) shows, in a wage-led system the employment effect of increased real wage growth is ambiguous—and it could as well be about zero (i.e., $d\hat{\ell}/d\hat{w} \approx 0$) if effect (i) and effects (ii) plus (iii) cancel each other out. The upshot of our discussion of a wage-led economy is that real wage restraint is not a necessary condition for adequate long-run macroeconomic performance. Subdued wage growth leads to subdued output growth while at the same time hampering labor productivity growth. The outcome in that case may well be increased employment growth and lower unemployment, but this is achieved by depressing productivity growth rather than by raising profitability, investment, and export and output growth). Lower unemployment, in other words, compromises welfare and the overall technological dynamism of the wage-led system.

Equilibrium Growth: The Profit-Led Case

Let us now consider the case of profit-led demand ($C < 0$). The impact on output growth of a decline in real wage growth is given by the equation (3.28). The numerator of (3.28) will be negative if $0 \leq \beta_2 < 1$. Hence, a fall in real wage growth increases output growth (as in the standard NAIRU model). Bhaduri and Marglin (1990) call this the *exhilarationist* regime—

the antithesis of the wage-led/stagnationist regime. But we note again that if $\beta_2 \to 1$, $(d\hat{x}/d\hat{w}) \to 0$, that is, the growth-promoting impact of lower real wage growth becomes smaller the more β_2 approaches unity. Hence, aggregate demand growth becomes less profit-led when productivity growth becomes more sensitive to real wage growth.[5] What happens to productivity growth in the profit-led case? Going back to equation (3.29), we note that—given that $C < 0$—the numerator can be positive, zero, or negative, depending on the size of the coefficients. If $0 \leq \beta_2 < -\beta_1 C$, the numerator is negative and a decline in real wage growth raises productivity growth, because the wage-cost-induced productivity growth decline is more than offset by the increase in productivity growth due to higher (profit-led) demand growth (the Kaldor-Verdoorn effect). This would be a case in which real wage growth restraint raises both output and productivity growth. We're now in Alan Greenspan's world, in which subdued wages lead to "outstanding [macroeconomic] achievement." But if $\beta_2 > -\beta_1 C$, then $(d\hat{\lambda}/d\hat{w})$ is positive and lower wage growth leads to reduced productivity growth, even though output growth increases. Employment growth in a profit-led system will most likely increase due to lower real wage growth, because

$$C < \frac{\beta_2}{1 - \beta_1 - \beta_2}.^6$$

The profit-led case thus resembles the workings of the NAIRU model: in equation (3.23), real wage restraint is necessary to raise employment growth and reduce unemployment. But the effect of wage restraint on productivity growth and technological dynamism is unclear, and may very well be negative if coefficient C is small and coefficient β_2 is large. In that case, unemployment declines mainly because of declining productivity growth, while output growth remains more or less stagnant.

The Macroeconomic Effects of Labor Market Deregulation

We are now in a position to highlight two theoretical flaws built into the NAIRU approach: (1) it presupposes that all OECD economies are profit-led, which is not the case (labor market regulation works out differently in wage-led economies), and (2) it rather one-sidedly ignores potential beneficial effects of regulation, such as that more regulation may induce more rapid labor-saving technological change and more rapid productivity growth. What are the effects on growth, productivity, and employment of labor market deregulation in our (arguably more general and realistic) growth model? To explore the macro effects of labor market regulation and to illustrate our two main points, while keeping the derivations tractable, we assume (without loss of generality) that $\alpha_0 = \alpha_1 = \alpha_2 = 0$ in equation (3.24). Real wage growth thus becomes a function of regulation only:

(3.31) $\hat{w} = \alpha_3 z$

Labor market deregulation is operationalized by a decline in our variable z. This has two effects. First, real wage growth will decline from equation (3.31). Second, from equation (3.1), we can see that less regulation reduces pressures to economize on labor cost, and hence productivity growth declines—via coefficient β_3. To determine the impact of a decline in z on output growth, we substitute (3.31) into equation (3.25) and totally differentiate the resulting equation with respect to z as follows:

(3.32) $\dfrac{d\hat{x}}{dz} = \dfrac{\alpha_3(1 - \beta_2)C - \beta_3 C}{1 + \beta_1 C}$

The sign of $\dfrac{d\hat{x}}{dz}$ is ambiguous and depends on the nature of the demand regime. If demand is wage-led $(C>0)$, $\dfrac{d\hat{x}}{dz} > 0$ if $\alpha_3 > \alpha_3 \beta_2 + \beta_3$, that is, the decline in real wage growth due to a decline in z is larger in absolute terms than the corresponding decline in labor productivity growth. When real wage growth declines by more than productivity growth, unit labor cost growth, or wage share growth, declines as in equation (3.4). The perhaps unexpected result is that output growth declines if z is reduced. Deregulation, in other words, is not good for wage-led growth, because it reduces the wage share or, equivalently, raises the profit share—mainly by (directly and indirectly) depressing labor productivity growth. In contrast, if $\alpha_3 < \alpha_3 \beta_2 + \beta_3$, a reduction of z will raise output growth even in a wage-led economy. This happens because now the decline in z raises the wage share and reduces the profit share, which is good for growth, since wage growth declines less than productivity growth. This shows that it is crucial to carefully distinguish how the two separate components of the wage (profit) share, the real wage rate and labor productivity, get determined and how the wage (profit) share changes as a result. Alternatively, let us consider profit-led demand $(C<0)$. Then from equation (3.32), $\dfrac{d\hat{x}}{dz} < 0$ if $\alpha_3 > \alpha_3 \beta_2 + \beta_3$, that is, output growth will now rise if z is reduced, because real wage growth declines more than productivity growth, which means that income is being redistributed from wages to profits; the consequent increase in the profit share raises output. This vindicates the standard NAIRU argument that overall performance improves in response to deregulation. But it is a conditional result, not a general one, because if $\alpha_3 < \alpha_3 \beta_2 + \beta_3$, a reduction of z reduces output growth in a profit-led system (since now the profit share declines due to the deregulation).

This shows that the same policy change (a decline in z) may provoke very diverse output responses—even under the same demand regime.

The same holds true for the productivity growth effects. The impact of a decline in z on productivity growth can be determined by substituting equation (3.31) into equation (3.26) and totally differentiating with respect to z:

$$(3.33) \qquad \frac{d\hat{\lambda}}{dz} = \frac{\alpha_3 \beta_2 + \alpha_3 \beta_1 C + \beta_3}{1 + \beta_1 C}$$

Because the denominator is positive (by assumption), the sign of $(d\hat{\lambda}/dz)$ depends on the sign of the numerator. If the economy is wage-led, the numerator is positive; as a result, productivity growth *always* declines due to labor market deregulation, because (by depressing wage growth) this leads to less rapid induced technological change and negative Kaldor-Verdoorn effects. However, if the demand regime is profit-led, the sign of $(d\hat{\lambda}/dz)$ becomes ambiguous. We can see that the numerator is positive only if $\alpha_3 \beta_2 + \beta_3 > -\alpha_3 \beta_1 C$; in this case, the decline in z reduces productivity growth, because the productivity-growth-augmenting (Kaldor-Verdoorn) effect of higher output growth due to lower real wage growth $(-\alpha_3 \beta_1 C)$ is more than offset by the productivity-growth-depressing effect of the reduced rate of technological progress $(\alpha_3 \beta_2 + \beta_3)$. But if, in contrast, $\alpha_3 \beta_2 + \beta_3 < -\alpha_3 \beta_1 C$, the decline in z raises labor productivity growth. Accordingly, the impact on productivity growth of labor market deregulation can be positive or negative when demand is profit-led.

In view of the diversity in output and productivity growth responses, it must come as no surprise that the impact of deregulation (a lower z) on employment growth $\hat{\ell}$ is equally ambiguous and contingent upon the nature of the demand regime. From equation (3.22), it follows that

$$\frac{d\hat{\ell}}{dz} > 0 \quad \text{if} \quad \frac{d\hat{x}}{dz} > \frac{d\hat{\lambda}}{dz}:$$

if the decline in output growth due to a lower z is larger than the decline in labor productivity growth, the growth rate of employment will fall. Using equations (3.32) and (3.33), we can derive the following condition for $d\hat{\ell}/dz > 0$:

$$(3.34) \qquad C[\alpha_3 - \beta_2 \alpha_3 - \beta_3] > \alpha_3 \beta_2 + \alpha_3 \beta_1 C + \beta_3$$

The left-hand side of (3.34) gives the impact of a change in z on output growth; the right-hand side equals the corresponding change in productivity growth.

Consider first the case of wage-led demand. If $C > 0$, the right-hand side is positive, indicating that productivity growth will fall in response to a decline in z. The left-hand side can be positive or negative. If $\alpha_3 > \alpha_3 \beta_2 + \beta_3$, the left-hand side is positive, meaning $d\hat{x}/dz > 0$, hence a decline in z reduces $\hat{x}$. If the decline in $\hat{x}$ is larger than the decline in $\hat{\lambda}$ (condition (3.34) is met), employment growth will fall in response to deregulation—and unemployment will rise (from equation (3.23)) due to the deregulation, which is quite unlike NAIRU predictions. Condition (3.34) need not be satisfied, however, even if $\alpha_3 > \alpha_3\beta_2 + \beta_3$; in that case, employment growth under wage-led demand rises due to a reduced z (and unemployment falls), because productivity growth declines more than output growth (Naastepad 2006; Dew-Becker and Gordon 2008). We note that employment growth must rise if $\alpha_3 < \alpha_3\beta_2 + \beta_3$, because output growth increases while productivity growth declines in the wake of labor market deregulation. On the face of it, this is a NAIRUvian outcome (less regulation being associated with higher employment growth and lower unemployment), but we emphasize that the employment growth is the result more of technological stagnation than of economic dynamism.

Likewise, a decline in z provokes a similar multitude of outcomes when the demand regime is profit-led ($C > 0$). In Table 3.1 appears a complete

Table 3.1. Classification of macro responses to labor market deregulation (a decline in z)

Labor market deregulation leads to:	Macro impacts in a wage-led regime	Macro impacts in a profit-led regime:	
		When the decline in z reduces productivity growth (if $\alpha_3\beta_2 + \beta_3 > -\alpha_3\beta_1 C$)	When the decline in z raises productivity growth (if $\alpha_3\beta_2 + \beta_3 < -\alpha_3\beta_1 C$)
A decline in the wage share if $\alpha_3 > \alpha_3\beta_2 + \beta_3$	(W1) $\hat{x}\downarrow$; $\hat{\lambda}\downarrow$; $\hat{\ell}$?	(P1) $\hat{x}\uparrow$; $\hat{\lambda}\downarrow$; $\hat{\ell}\uparrow$	(P3) $\hat{x}\uparrow$; $\hat{\lambda}\uparrow$; $\hat{\ell}$?
An increase in the wage share if $\alpha_3 < \alpha_3\beta_2 + \beta_3$	(W2) $\hat{x}\uparrow$; $\hat{\lambda}\downarrow$; $\hat{\ell}\uparrow$	(P2) $\hat{x}\downarrow$; $\hat{\lambda}\downarrow$; $\hat{\ell}$?	(P4) $\hat{x}\downarrow$; $\hat{\lambda}\uparrow$; $\hat{\ell}\downarrow$

Notes:

(a) $\uparrow$ = increase in growth rate; $\downarrow$ = decline in growth rate; ? = ambiguous response.

(b) If $\alpha_3 > \alpha_3\beta_2 + \beta_3$, a decline in z causes a larger decline in real wage growth than in labor productivity growth; if $\alpha_3 < \alpha_3\beta_2 + \beta_3$, wage growth declines less than productivity growth in reaction to a fall in z.

(c) Scenario W1 is the paradigm wage-led case in which both output and productivity growth decline in response to a lower wage share; employment growth could go up if productivity growth declines more than output growth. Wage-led scenario W2 is counterintuitive, because output and employment growth increase even though real wage growth falls (but productivity growth declines even more). P1 and P3 are clear-cut profit-led cases, as output growth increases in response to a lower wage share. Because employment growth also increases in P1, it resembles the NAIRU outcome (but at the cost of deteriorating productivity growth). The employment outcome in P3 is ambiguous. Profit-led cases P2 and P4 have counterintuitive outcomes, because output growth falls while wage growth declines (note that productivity growth declines more). P4 features a decline in employment growth and a rise in unemployment as well, in sharp deviation from the NAIRU outcome.

classification of macroeconomic responses to labor market deregulation. Let us look at two sharply contrasting trajectories. First, we know from equation (3.32) that output growth will decline in response to a decline in z if $\alpha_3 > \alpha_3 \beta_2 + \beta_3$. This output growth decline coincides with an increase in productivity growth if (at the same time) $\alpha_3 \beta_2 + \beta_3 > -\alpha_3 \beta_1 C$; as a consequence, employment growth $\hat{\ell}$ must decline. Accordingly, under the stipulated conditions, labor market deregulation reduces employment growth and increases unemployment, even though the system is profit-led—a finding that squarely contradicts the standard NAIRU claim. Second, the opposite outcome— higher output growth, lower productivity growth, and consequently higher employment growth—will come about if $\alpha_3 < \alpha_3 \beta_2 + \beta_3$ and simultaneously $\alpha_3 \beta_2 + \beta_3 < -\alpha_3 \beta_1 C$. Unemployment will fall in reaction to deregulation, as in the NAIRU approach, but again the underlying cause is a significant slowdown of productivity growth (due to technological regression). Thus, unlike the NAIRU approach, our demand-led growth model not only realistically allows for a variety of macro responses to labor market deregulation but also—by uncovering the mechanisms through which a decline in z affects demand growth as well as productive capacity and productivity— highlights the often substantial opportunity costs of deregulation in terms of productivity growth foregone. Clearly, deregulation, to paraphrase Milton Friedman, is no free lunch.

Same Policy, Different Macroeconomic Effects

The great diversity in macroeconomic outcomes to a policy of labor market deregulation highlighted in Table 3.1 may, at first sight, appear disheartening: how to see the forest for the trees? One way is "to go back on ourselves and allow, as well as we can, for the probable interactions of the factors amongst themselves," as Keynes (1973, 297) wrote. Hence, with reference to the OECD economies, which of the configurations appearing in Table 3.1 are probable? Chapters 4, 5, and 7 shed light on this issue, presenting empirical evidence on OECD productivity and demand regimes, respectively. Getting ahead of these chapters, we now graphically analyze three probable interactions between productivity and demand regimes, relevant for three classes of OECD countries: the profit-led U.S. economy, the strongly wage-led Scandinavian countries (Denmark, Finland, Norway, and Sweden) and the weakly wage-led European Continental countries (France, Germany, and the Netherlands). The productivity regime, demand regime, and employment regime curves are given in Figure 3.3 (for a profit-led economy) and Figures 3.4 and 3.5 (for strongly wage-led and marginally wage-led economies, respectively). Employment growth is presented as a function of output growth, as in equation (3.22). The intersection of the productivity regime and demand regime curves determines the equilibrium rates of labor productivity growth $\hat{\lambda}_0$ and output growth $\hat{x}_0$.[7] The (dynamic) stability conditions require that the slope of the productivity regime curve exceed the slope of the demand regime curve. Figures 3.3, 3.4, and 3.5 show what happens to growth, productivity, and (un)employment when labor markets are deregulated, that is, when z is reduced and real wage growth declines.

Consider first the case of profit-led demand (case P1 in Table 3.1), illustrated in Figure 3.3. We will argue in Chapters 4 and 5 that the United States is a prominent example of such a profit-led economy, so one might wish to think that Figure 3.3 illustrates the impacts of further labor market flexibility in the United States. Due to the decline in z and the consequent

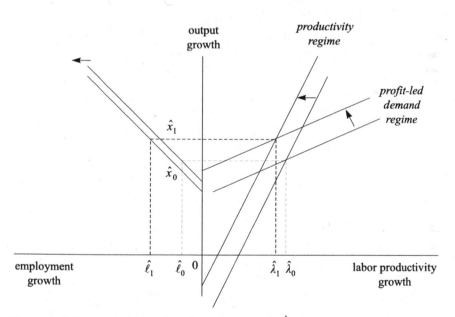

Figure 3.3. Determination of productivity growth ($\hat{\lambda}$), output growth ($\hat{x}$), and employment growth ($\hat{\ell}$): profit-led demand.

Note: The arrows indicate shifts in the demand, productivity, and employment regime curves caused by a decline in real wage growth, which is in turn due to a weakening of the bargaining power of workers caused by labor market deregulation (a decline in z). In this profit-led economy, labor market *deregulation* will lead to a rise in employment growth. Unemployment will fall as a result, which is a NAIRUvian outcome, but brought about by a long-run increase in profit-led output growth. This is scenario P1 in Table 3.1.

decline in real wage growth, the productivity regime shifts upward toward the left, which means that the initial rate of output growth $\hat{x}_0$ now warrants a lower rate of labor productivity growth. At the same time, the profit-led demand regime shifts upward, because the decline in wage growth—given $\hat{\lambda}_0$ and given that $C<0$—leads to an increased profit share and hence to higher output growth. The eventual result is an *increase* in equilibrium output growth (from $\hat{x}_0$ to $\hat{x}_1$) but a *fall* in labor productivity growth (from $\hat{\lambda}_0$ to $\hat{\lambda}_1$). Employment growth must rise (and rather strongly so) as a consequence, as is illustrated in Figure 3.3, and unemployment declines (from equation (3.23)). Hence, in the profit-led case P1, labor market deregulation leads to lower unemployment, as is also predicted by the NAIRU model, but one must note that this particularly strong decline in unemployment is the result of rising output growth and declining labor productivity growth. There is a cost to deregulation not recognized in standard NAIRU models, however—namely, a slowdown of productivity growth and a concomitant rise in lower-productivity and low-wage employment. New School economist David Gordon is one of the few to make this cost of deregulation explicit for the U.S. economy, writing:

> I would argue that in economies governed by the Stick Strategy there is a kind of macroeconomic tension between "full" employment and rapid productivity growth. With unemployment rates very low, productivity growth may sputter—as the discipline threat attenuates. When unemployment rates drift back up during and after a recession and the immediacy of the discipline threat is reinstated, productivity growth may accelerate. What's good for growth in the short run may be bad for long-term prosperity. (Gordon 1996, 151)[8]

All this does mean that the NAIRU approach appears relevant to a profit-led economy (such as that of the United States). Hence, in a profit-led system, deregulated labor markets make sense—they underpin a relatively high profit share, relatively high investment and output growth, and low unemployment. "Traumatized workers" and high inequality are included in the NAIRU bargain. We emphasize that the macro behavior of the profit-led system will resemble that of the standard NAIRU model somewhat less once we assume that $\alpha_1 \neq 0$ in equation (3.24), meaning that lower unemployment leads to higher real wage growth. In this case, real wage growth will not decline as much as in Figure 3.3, since there is upward wage pressure because of lower unemployment; in terms of Figure 3.3 (but not illustrated in the figure), shifts in the positions of all curves will be smaller, though still in the same direction.

Figure 3.4 illustrates the opposite case of an economy in which demand growth is strongly wage-led (the demand regime curve is strongly downward-sloping). This case is exemplified by Europe's Nordic economies, as we will see in later chapters. As in Figure 3.3, the productivity regime curve shifts upward (to the left) due to a decline in z. But now the demand regime shifts downward because of the decline in real wage growth (since $C > 0$). This reflects the fact that the decline in the wage share (caused by the decline in wage growth at the initial rate of productivity growth $\hat{\lambda}_0$) forces down equilibrium output growth in a wage-led system. The result of these shifts in productivity and demand regimes is a *decline* in output growth (from $\hat{x}_0$ to $\hat{x}_1$) and a *decline* in labor productivity growth (from $\hat{\lambda}_0$ to $\hat{\lambda}_1$). We assume in Figure 3.4 that the output growth decline (in absolute terms) is of about the same size as the productivity growth decline; hence, employment growth and the unemployment rate (from equation (3.23)) remain unchanged. This

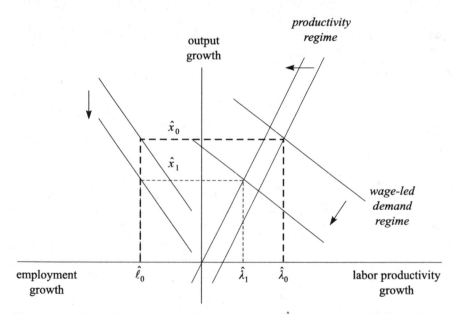

Figure 3.4. Determination of productivity growth ($\hat{\lambda}$), output growth ($\hat{x}$), and employment growth ($\hat{\ell}$): wage-led demand (strong).

Note: The arrows indicate shifts in the demand, productivity, and employment regime curves caused by a decline in real wage growth, which is in turn due to a weakening of the bargaining power of workers caused by labor market deregulation (a decline in z). In this wage-led economy, labor market deregulation has no impact on employment growth and hence unemployment remains constant—a non-NAIRUvian outcome. This case falls under scenario W1 in Table 3.1.

is, in fact, the essence of our definition of a strongly wage-led economy: it is an economy in which output growth and productivity growth respond equally strongly to changes in labor market regulation and in the real wage rate, so unemployment remains more or less unaffected. Regulation, as in Europe's Nordic economies, is equally good for growth and technological advance in strongly wage-led systems, because it keeps up aggregate demand growth as well as productivity growth, and this in turn helps to maintain firms' profitability and investment, stimulating growth and keeping a check on structural unemployment. Samuel Bowles, Richard Edwards, and Frank Roosevelt (2005, 243) call this the "visible handshake solution" to the problem of unemployment—more on this in Chapters 6 and 7. Finally, we point out that the negative macroeconomic effects of a reduction of z are augmented if we assume that $\alpha_1 \neq 0$ in equation (3.24) (higher unemployment leads to lower real wage growth).[9] The reason is that under wage-led demand, lower employment growth and the consequent rise in unemployment depress real wage growth even further—which again reduces output growth more than productivity growth, in turn raising unemployment even more. It will be evident that the macro responses to reduced z of this strongly wage-led system are diametrically opposed to the reactions implied by the standard NAIRU model.

Figure 3.5 illustrates what happens in a marginally wage-led economy (i.e., C is close to zero) when z is reduced. The downward shift of the demand regime is now small compared to the leftward shift of the productivity regime—which means that productivity growth now declines considerably more than output growth, due to deregulation. The result is an increase in employment growth from $\hat{\ell}_0$ to $\hat{\ell}_1$. Clearly, unemployment is reduced due to the deregulation of the labor market, even though the economy is wage-led. This shows that a weakly wage-led economy (unlike the strongly wage-led case) may exhibit unemployment responses to policies of labor market deregulation that are in accordance with the outcomes of similar changes in the NAIRU model. But the underlying mechanisms are very different: here it is the larger slowdown of labor productivity growth (compared to demand and output growth) that brings about more job growth and reduced unemployment. Technological stagnation and a productivity growth crisis are therefore the flip side of low unemployment in this system. The Netherlands has been found to be a weakly wage-led economy by Naastepad (2006) as well as by Tavani, Flaschel, and Taylor (2011). Dutch aggregate demand growth is relatively insensitive to changes in real wage growth, but Dutch labor productivity, in contrast, is significantly affected by changes in real wage growth. Accordingly, the decline in real wage growth, due to labor market deregulation and voluntary real wage restraint by the Dutch trade unions, led to only a very small decline in output growth but a much larger drop in productivity growth. In effect, Dutch employment growth increased tremendously. We believe, and provide evidence of this in Chapter 5, that other European Continental economies, including Germany and France, are also weakly wage-led and exhibit the same pattern of responses to deregulation as the Dutch economy.

One final configuration of productivity and demand regimes needs to be mentioned: an economy may empirically turn out to be neither wage-led or profit-led, meaning that the empirical estimate of $C=0$. Changes in income distribution then do not affect aggregate growth, because the various positive and negative impacts (on consumption, investment, and exports) cancel each other out. This case is illustrated in Figure 3.6, showing a horizontal demand growth curve (meaning that changes in productivity or real wages do not affect output growth). Labor market deregulation reduces productivity growth directly via β_3 and indirectly through lower real wage growth.

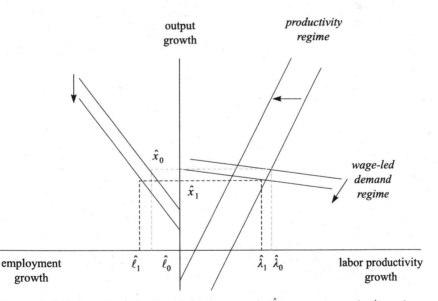

Figure 3.5. Determination of productivity growth ($\hat{\lambda}$), output growth ($\hat{x}$), and employment growth ($\hat{\ell}$): wage-led demand (weak).

Note: The arrows indicate shifts in the demand, productivity, and employment regime curves caused by a reduction in real wage growth, which is in turn due to labor market deregulation. In this (marginally) wage-led economy, labor market deregulation leads to a rise in employment growth and lower unemployment—which is in line with NAIRU theory—because productivity growth declines more than output growth. This case also falls under scenario W1 in Table 3.1.

Hence, the productivity regime shifts upward, and, with unchanged output growth, equilibrium labor productivity declines (from $\hat{\lambda}_0$ to $\hat{\lambda}_1$). Employment growth, being equal to the difference between constant output growth and lower productivity growth, must rise, as is illustrated in the graph. Clearly, what we observe here is a strong negative association between unemployment and regulation, as in the NAIRU model. But the unemployment decline (and higher employment growth) is due solely to a change in the nature— not the pace—of economic growth; the same output is now being produced using more labor (working hours), especially lower-paid workers, than be-

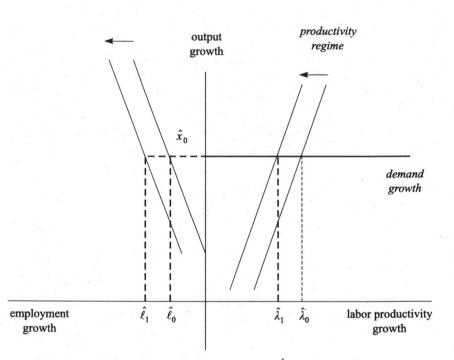

Figure 3.6. Determination of productivity growth ($\hat{\lambda}$), output growth ($\hat{x}$), and employment growth ($\hat{\ell}$): $C=0$.

Note: The arrows indicate shifts in the productivity and employment regime curves caused by a reduction in real wage growth, which is in turn due to labor market deregulation. This economy is neither wage-led or profit-led. Labor market deregulation leads to a drop in productivity growth and a rise in employment growth and lower unemployment—which is in line with NAIRU theory. But note that because aggregate growth of the system does *not* increase, the favorable unemployment outcome is the result of more labor-intensive (low-wage) and less productive growth. This case comes close to scenario W2 in Table 3.1.

fore. This does not look too attractive: rather than working more hours to produce the same income, the other option would have been to keep up high productivity growth and have a system of employment sharing to equally distribute working hours across the labor force and keep unemployment down. This latter option obviously involves more regulation and coordination, not less, and as such, it goes against the grain of the NAIRU approach. But it would have received the approval of Keynes, who felt that capitalism needed some patching up to make it work tolerably well:

> I think that Capitalism, wisely managed, can probably be made more efficient for attaining economic ends than any alternative system yet in sight, but that in itself it is in many ways extremely objectionable. Our problem is to work out a social organisation which shall be as efficient as possible without offending our notions of a satisfactory way of life. (Keynes 1931b, 321)

This chapter has identified, with the help of our model, different forms of social organization, varying between profit-led and strongly wage-led. In the next two chapters, we empirically investigate the nature of demand and productivity regimes in the OECD economies.

Further Reading

Bhaduri and Marglin (1990) is the classic paper on wage-led versus profit-led demand; earlier formulations of the same are Rowthorn (1977), Dutt (1984), and Taylor (1990, 1991). Taylor (2004) is a good review of structuralist (Keynesian/Kaldorian/Kaleckian/Marxian) macroeconomic theories. Our formulation draws heavily on Naastepad (2006), where the productivity and demand regimes are introduced. Setterfield (2010) is a rich collection of papers presenting heterodox models of growth, including Gérard Duménil and Dominique Lévy's (2010b) engaging piece on Marxian technical progress.

Appendix: Derivation of the Productivity Regime

Consider the following increasing-returns-to-scale CES production function:

(A.1) $x = a[\,\delta l^{-\rho} + (1 - \delta)\,k^{-\rho}\,]^{-(h/\rho)}$, with $-1 < \rho < \infty,\ \rho \neq 0,\ 0 < \delta < 1,\ h, \gamma > 0$

where $x =$ GDP measured at constant prices, $k =$ the economy's fixed capital stock (at constant prices), $l =$ the number of hours worked (in a year) by the labor force, $a =$ an efficiency parameter, $\delta =$ the distribution parameter,

ρ=the substitution parameter, and h=the returns-to-scale parameter ($h>1$ corresponding with increasing returns to scale). Denoting the price of capital by Π, the elasticity of capital-labor substitution σ is defined as

$$(A.2) \qquad \sigma = \frac{\partial(k/l)/(k/l)}{\partial(W/\Pi)/(W/\Pi)} = \frac{1}{1+\rho}$$

From the first-order condition $\partial x/\partial l = W/P$ where W=the (nominal) wage rate and P=the GDP deflator, and using definition (A.2), it follows that labor productivity λ is equal to

$$(A.3) \qquad \lambda = \left[\frac{x}{l}\right] = (h\delta)^{-\sigma} a^{\frac{\sigma\rho}{h}} \left[\frac{W}{P}\right]^{\sigma} x^{\frac{(h-1)\rho}{h(\rho+1)}}$$

Log-differentiating (A.3) and dividing through by λ gives us an expression for the proportional growth rate of labor productivity:

$$(A.4) \qquad \hat{\lambda} = \left[\frac{\sigma\rho}{h}\right]\hat{a} + \sigma\left[\frac{\hat{W}}{P}\right] + \left[\frac{(h-1)\rho}{h(\rho+1)}\right]\hat{x}$$

If we assume that

$$(A.5) \qquad \hat{a} = \alpha_0 + \alpha_1 z$$

and if we substitute (A.5) into (A.4), we obtain

$$(A.6) \qquad \hat{\lambda} = \left[\frac{\sigma\rho}{h}\right]\alpha_0 + \left[\frac{(h-1)\rho}{h(\rho+1)}\right]x + \sigma\hat{w} + \left[\frac{\sigma\rho}{h}\right]\alpha_1 z$$

where $w = W/P$. (A.6) is the productivity regime equation (3.1) used in the main text.

Note that (1) $\beta_1 = \frac{(h-1)\rho}{h(\rho+1)}$ is the Kaldor-Verdoorn elasticity, which is economically meaningful only if $h>1$ (there exist increasing returns to scale); (2) $\beta_2 = \sigma$ is the coefficient of wage-led technological change, and (3) $\beta_3 = \frac{\sigma\rho}{h}\alpha_1$ is the coefficient giving the impact of the degree of labor market regulation on productivity growth.

4

The OECD Productivity Regime

Within the capitalist firm it is the social forms that dominate technology, rather than the other way around.

HARRY BRAVERMAN, *LABOUR AND MONOPOLY CAPITAL*

Nicholas Kaldor argued that theory construction should begin with a summary of relevant facts, but because the "facts, as recorded by statisticians, are always subject to numerous snags and qualifications, and for that reason are incapable of being summarized," he suggested that theorists "should be free to start off with a stylised view of the facts—i.e. concentrate on broad tendencies, ignoring individual detail" (Kaldor 1965, 178). Although many have scoffed at Kaldor's notion of stylized facts, it is clear that these can provide a useful initial discipline in the construction of economic theory and inform the formulation of statistically testable hypotheses.[1] This chapter investigates three broad stylized facts concerning aggregate labor productivity growth. The crux of our argument is that in capitalist economies, labor productivity growth is influenced by income distribution, by aggregate demand, and by the social relations of production.[2] Any change in the wage rate or profit rate, any change in aggregate demand or capacity utilization, or any reform of labor market regulation affects productivity, and this, in turn, necessarily influences unemployment. These stylized facts are expressed in our productivity regime as follows:

$$(4.1) \qquad \hat{\lambda} = \beta_0 + \beta_1 \, \hat{x} + \beta_2 \, \hat{w} + \beta_3 \, z \qquad \beta_0, \beta_2, \beta_3 > 0; \, 0 < \beta_1 < 1$$

where $\hat{x}$ is real GDP (or output) growth, $\hat{w}$ is real wage growth, and z is an indicator of labor market regulation, as in Chapter 3. Our hypothesis, to be empirically scrutinized in this chapter, is that the coefficients are positive and statistically significantly so, that is, $\beta_1, \beta_2, \beta_3 > 0$. Before going into the empirics, we look into the three determinants of the productivity regime in more theoretical detail.[3] We then present empirical evidence on the productivity regime for a cross section of twenty OECD countries (1984–2004).

The Kaldor-Verdoorn Effect

Higher output growth raises labor productivity growth by a factor of β_1 in equation (4.1). This effect is known in the literature as the Kaldor-Verdoorn effect, after the two economists, P. J. Verdoorn (1949) and Nicholas Kaldor (1966), who observed and theorized this positive association between output and productivity growth. Verdoorn first observed the association, finding a coefficient β_1 of about 0.45, meaning that in the long run a change in output by 10 percent is associated with an average increase in labor productivity of 4.5 percent. Kaldor (1966) reports a coefficient of about 0.5. John McCombie, Maurizio Pugno, and Bruno Soro (2002) have reviewed more than eighty empirical studies on the Kaldor-Verdoorn effect from 1949 (the year when Verdoorn published his work) and 2001. They find that the Kaldor-Verdoorn effect has been confirmed in the overwhelming majority of these studies, irrespective of the differences in econometric methods and data employed. The effect is found statistically significant for cross-section estimations across countries or regions and for specific industries, but also for time-series econometric studies for single countries or regions. John McCombie (2002, 106) confidently concludes: "The picture that emerges is . . . that the Verdoorn Law estimates are particularly robust with the values of the Verdoorn coefficient in the range of 0.3 to 0.6 and statistically significant." This stylized fact—the Kaldor-Verdoorn coefficient β_1 taking a value of 0.3 to 0.6—is confirmed by more recent studies, as can be seen from Table 4.1.

Theoretically, the main reason this association arises at the level of the aggregate economy is that firms can reap economies of scale when demand and output grow by exploiting new divisions of labor, or new forms of specialization, which lead to improved productivity. As Allyn Young explained some eighty years ago:

> The important thing . . . is that with the division of labour a group of complex processes is transformed into a succession of simpler processes, some of which, at least, lend themselves to the use of machinery. In the use of machinery and the adoption of indirect processes there is a further division of labour, the economies of which are again limited by the extent of the market. It would be wasteful to make a hammer to drive a single nail. . . . It would be wasteful to furnish a factory with an elaborate equipment of specially constructed jigs, gauges, lathes, drills, presses and conveyors to build a hundred automobiles. . . . Mr. Ford's methods would be absurdly uneconomical if his output were very small, and would be unprofitable even if his output were what many other manufacturers of automobiles would call large. (Young 1928, 530)

In addition, as Young emphasized, increasing returns are a truly macro phenomenon—because so many of the economies of scale come about as a result of increased differentiation, the emergence of new processes and new subsidiary industries, they cannot be "discerned adequately by observing the effects of variations in the size of an individual firm or of a particular industry."

Table 4.1. Empirical evidence on the productivity regime coefficients

	France	Germany	The Netherlands	United Kingdom	United States	The Nordics	All OECD countries
Kaldor-Verdoorn coefficient β_1							
McCombie, Pugno, and Soro (2002)							0.3–0.6
Cornwall and Cornwall (2002)							0.5
Leon-Ledesma (2002)							0.64–0.67
Naastepad (2006)			0.63				
Angeriz, McCombie, and Roberts (2008)							0.50–0.67
Hein and Tarassow (2009)	0.54	0.43	0.45	0.23	0.11		
Alexiadis and Tsagdis (2010)							0.43–0.49
Real wage-productivity growth coefficient β_2							
Rowthorn (1999)	0.11–0.24	0.33–0.87	0.24–0.44	0.25–0.60	0.13–0.28	0.10–0.54	0.24–0.30
Nymoen and Rødseth (2003)						0.50	
Naastepad (2006)			0.52				
Carter (2007)							0.50–0.67
Hein and Tarassow (2009)	0.31	0.32	0.33	0.25	0.36		

Notes: McCombie, Pugno, and Soro (2002): average of 80 empirical studies; Cornwall and Cornwall (2002): based on data for 16 OECD countries (1960–1989); Leon-Ledesma (2002): for 18 OECD countries (1965–1994); Angeriz, McCombie, and Roberts (2008): for European regions (1986–2002); Alexiadis and Tsagdis (2010): based on data (1977–2005) for 109 EU12 regions; Rowthorn (1999): data are from his table 2, panel (b); Nymoen and Rødseth (2003): for the four Nordic countries (1965–1994); Carter (2007), based on data for 15 OECD countries (1980–1996).

At any one time, there are industries in which economies of scale may have ceased to be important. They may nevertheless benefit from a general industrial expansion, which should be seen as an interrelated whole. Kaldor (1957) added a complementary explanation of the positive association between demand growth (as the cause) and productivity growth (as the consequence). This has to do with the fact that new investments generally embody the latest, most modern technology, making the newly installed machines more productive than the older vintages of capital stock. If demand growth leads to investment growth, this will modernize a country's capital stock (at the margin) and raise average worker productivity.

Of course there are economists who, while admitting the statistical relationship between productivity growth and production growth, argue that it says nothing about cause and effect. The Kaldor-Verdoorn effect, in their view, may simply reflect the fact that faster growth rates in productivity induce, via their effects on relative costs and prices, a faster rate of growth of demand, and not the other way round; here productivity growth is seen as being an exogenous or autonomous factor. But the criticism of the Kaldor-Verdoorn effect is not at all convincing. As Kaldor himself explains, the alternative hypothesis is not specified—if it were, its logical shortcomings would at once be apparent.

> If the rate of growth of productivity in each industry and in each country was a fully autonomous factor, we need some hypothesis to explain it. The usual hypothesis is that the growth of productivity is mainly to be explained by the progress of knowledge in science and technology. But in that case how is one to explain the large differences in the *same* industry over the *same* period in different countries? . . . This alternative hypothesis is tantamount to a denial of the existence of increasing returns which are known to be an important feature of manufacturing industry. . . .
>
> Moreover, to establish this alternative hypothesis, it is not enough to postulate that productivity growth rates are autonomous. It is also necessary to assume that differences in productivity growth rates between different industries and sectors are fully reflected in the movement of relative prices . . . and further that the price-elasticity of demand for the products of any one industry, or for the products of manufacturing industry as a whole, is always greater than unity: none of this, as far as I know, has been submitted to econometric verification. (Kaldor 1966, 290–291)

Not much has changed since 1966; hence Kaldor's defense of the Kaldor-Verdoorn effect is as valid today as it was back then.

Induced Labor-Saving Technological Progress

Our second stylized fact is that changes in relative factor prices influence the type of technological progress; in particular, high real wages induce labor-saving innovations and higher labor productivity growth, that is, $\beta_2 > 0$. The idea is generally credited to John Hicks, who wrote in his *Theory of Wages* (1932, 124–125) that "a change in the relative prices of factors of production is itself a spur to innovation and to inventions of a particular kind—directed at economising the use of a factor which has become relatively expensive."

But the concept of wage-cost-induced technological change has a longer pedigree, going back to at least Karl Marx, who believed that a bias toward labor-saving innovations is an inherent feature of capitalism (Duménil and Lévy 2010b). Labor-saving technological change ensures the reproduction of both a positive economic surplus and a growing reserve army of the unemployed (necessary to keep real wages constant in a growing system), so that the basis of capitalist exploitation is sustained. Marx anticipated the modern idea of induced labor-saving technological progress, arguing that in periods of excess demand for labor and declining profit rates, the application of labor-saving innovations will be accelerated, thus reducing the bargaining power of workers.[4] Hicks's suggestion, with its Marxian roots, initially received implicit assent but little attention. In the 1960s and 1970s, however, it did stir up a major debate, which addressed possible reasons for the apparent stability of the wage share (and profit share) in the presence of rapidly rising real wages.[5] This debate helped focus empirical attention on the implications of changes in relative factor prices for the rate and direction of technological change, particularly at the sectoral level (Ruttan 1997). But the debate was left floundering, to be revived only in the late 1990s as part of the renewed interest in economic growth ("new growth theory") and endogenous technological change. For example, Duncan Foley and Thomas R. Michl (1999, 275–278) develop a microeconomic model of induced technological change in which labor productivity growth is a positive function of the wage share. Firms are assumed to minimize unit production costs, subject to a technological trade-off between labor productivity and capital productivity growth. A higher real wage, in their model, induces more investment in research and development; this leads to labor-saving innovation, eventually resulting in higher labor productivity growth. Likewise, Peter Funk (2002), Amit Bhaduri (2006), and Daniele Tavani (2009) provide micro foundations for Hicks's hypothesis of induced innovation.

Empirically, there is strong evidence that real wage growth and labor productivity growth are statistically significantly associated with each other in the long run (in jargon, the two variables are cointegrated). Adalmir Marquetti

(2004), for instance, finds a one-to-one relationship between wage and productivity growth for the U.S. economy over the 130-year period from 1869 to 1999, which in terms of our equation (4.1) would mean that $\beta_2 = 1$ and that the wage share is constant. Marquetti also tests for Granger causality, with the important finding of unidirectional Granger causality from the real wage to labor productivity. Real wage change therefore is found to lead movements in labor productivity, which supports the idea of both Marx and Hicks that real wage pressures drive profit-seeking capitalists to increase labor productivity by means of labor-saving technological progress in order to maintain their profitability. But over shorter periods of time, the association between real wage growth and labor productivity growth is significantly less strong. Using evidence for fifteen OECD countries for the period from 1980 to 1996, Scott Carter (2007) finds that β_2 takes a value of about 0.4–0.5, meaning that an increase in real wage growth of 1 percentage point will lead to an increase in productivity growth of 0.4–0.5 percentage points. Evidence for nineteen OECD economies provided by Robert Rowthorn suggests that β_2 may even be lower, varying between 0.2 and 0.3. "It is possible that [my] estimates are biased downwards," he writes, "but the error would have to be truly gigantic to justify the assumption that $[\beta_2]$ is equal to unity" (Rowthorn 1999, 416). Country evidence supports this conclusion, as is shown by the findings appearing in Table 4.1. Hence, we expect that β_2 is positive but well below unity for our sample of countries during the period from 1984 to 2004.

The Social Relations of Production

We hypothesize that $\beta_3 > 0$, which, if true, would mean that labor productivity growth, on average, is higher in economies having relatively regulated, coordinated labor markets than in countries featuring deregulated, flexible labor markets. This probably is the most controversial of our three stylized facts incorporated in the productivity growth equation (4.1). One reason for the controversy lies in the view, characteristic of much of the macroeconomics research, that the social organization of production—and labor relations in particular—can affect technology only through its directly measurable impacts on production costs to firms, not through workers' motivation and effort, which supposedly depend solely on pecuniary stimulus as a compensation for the disutility of work. Accordingly, workers are assumed not to care about the non-wage-related dimensions of the industrial relations system—they supposedly maintain work intensity in the face of whatever technological changes are being introduced in the workplace and whatever changes in work effort and work organization accompany the technological change, as long as their real wages do not fall. The "selfish" worker is seen as an automaton, a cog in the wheel—rather unlike the iconic, all-too-human factory worker portrayed by Charlie Chaplin in the 1936 film *Modern Times*. "At a certain point, routine becomes self-destructive, because human beings lose control over their own efforts; lack of control over work time means people go dead mentally," writes Richard Sennett (1998, 37). One of the grimmest passages of *The Wealth of Nations* argues:

In the progress of the division of labour, the employment of the far greater part of those who live by labour . . . comes to be confined to a few very simple operations; frequently to one or two. . . . The man whose whole life is spent in performing a few simple operations . . . has no occasion to exert his understanding, or to exercise his invention in finding out expedients for removing difficulties which never occur. He naturally loses, therefore, the habit of such exertion, and generally becomes as stupid and ignorant as it is possible for a human creature to become. (Smith 1976, 302–303)

We note an important discrepancy here, or perhaps we can even talk about a bias. Standard macro theory acknowledges only that labor market regulation is a *cost* to firms or firm management, because it raises labor costs (and profits) and reduces the flexibility of firms to adjust their workforce, which is argued to be often needed after innovations have been introduced. Regulation may lead to increased wage pressure from (and higher wages for) employed "insiders" whose bargaining position is strengthened by the interventions. What is not recognized, however, is that regulation may actually have benefits for firms, mainly because of its impact on workers' motivation, effort, and work intensity.

Perhaps remarkably, very few studies of productivity growth pay attention to the effects of labor relations. As a recent OECD *Employment Outlook* study (2007) concludes after reviewing the literature, "Evidence on the [productivity] growth effects of labor market reforms does not loom large in the existing empirical literature" and hence "more research is needed." Characteristically, the OECD ignores the few relevant studies that have actually been done on the issue and which reveal that if other factors are constant, regulation has a positive and statistically significant impact on productivity growth (more on these studies follows below; see Table 4.2). Its own analysis suggests that the net effect of labor market regulation on productivity growth is negative but relatively small. This finding is explained by pointing out two contradictory effects of regulation on productivity growth. On one hand, labor market regulation (and especially strict employment protection legislation) raises labor costs, as explained above. Labor cost increases, in turn, *raise* labor productivity growth, because these stimulate capital deepening (that is, growth in capital intensity), increase the proportion of high-skilled workers in the labor force, encourage capital-intensive industries, and promote labor-saving technological progress (Autor, Kerr, and Kugler 2007; OECD 2007). This conclusion echoes back to the Swedish debate over solidaristic bargaining (Rehn 1952), in which it was argued that nationwide wage settlements, characterized by a high degree of wage equality, drive inefficient firms off the market and expedite structural change, thereby fostering productivity growth. On the other hand, however, because higher labor costs reduce the expected returns on innovation and technological progress, they may slow down innovation investments and thus *reduce* total-factor-productivity (TFP) growth and labor productivity growth (Malcomson 1997). These two opposing effects presumably cancel each other out, in which case productivity growth is, on balance, not strongly affected by changes in labor market interventions. Hence, the consensus view is that productivity growth is not affected by the non-wage-related dimensions of its industrial relations system. In terms of equation (4.1), this would mean that β_3 is zero or negligibly small indeed and that it is not unrealistic to ignore the possible impact of regulation and of the social relations of production on productivity growth.

Common sense might lead us to expect otherwise, however. Let us follow the example given by David Gordon:

> Imagine two workers in the same industry, working in firms with more or less comparable machinery. One works in a firm with massive, top-down management, little job security, stagnant wages, no chance to participate in organizing or planning production. The other works in a firm with a much less obtrusive bureaucratic structure, substantial job security, rapid wage growth—particularly if and when productivity itself improves—and the opportunity to participate in decisions about the organization of work. It seems likely that the [second] worker . . . will make a much more substantial commitment to the progress and future of the enterprise. (Gordon 2006, 146)

But we do not need to rely on common sense alone. A mountain of studies is available reviewing the effects of work organization on productivity. The principal conclusion of this industrial relations literature is unambiguous: if all other things are equal, productivity is higher in enterprises that feature relatively more substantive worker involvement in production, participation in decision making, and profit sharing.[6] Gordon's example is telling: with similar technology, productivity will be higher in the firm having the more cooperative organization of production. The social organization of production has a strong, perhaps even dominant impact on the way in which a given technology is being used and, as a result, on the productivity of labor. The key insight here stems from Karl Marx (again), who was occupied with analyzing the interplay between technology (the productive forces) and the social relations of production in almost all his historical writing. Marx's conclusion in the first volume of *Capital* is that technology gets determined within and transformed by the system of social relations—until it outgrows that system and comes into conflict with it (Braverman 1974).[7] The defining anecdote is the tragicomic tale, recounted by Marx, of a Mr. Peel, who took with him from England to the Swan River district of western Australia £50,000 in cash and 3,000 working-class men, women, and children. Mr. Peel overlooked one thing: the need to keep his workers separated from the means of production.

> Finding land freely available in this empty region, they abandoned their employer, leaving him without even a servant to make his bed or fetch him water from the river. "Unhappy Mr Peel," Marx writes, "who provided for everything except the export of English relations of production to the Swan River." (Wheen 2006, 69)

We can think about this interplay between technology and the social relations of production in a slightly more practical way. Productivity improvements depend crucially on the cooperation of workers and upon their tacit knowledge, ideas, and suggestions, which will be withheld if workers feel their jobs are at risk as a consequence.[8] Hence, in regulated, cooperative industrial relations systems, workers presumably are less suspicious of and resistant to productivity-enhancing automation, and perhaps are even involved in planning and implementing it, because their employment security reduces their fear of technology-spurred layoffs. This is an important paradox: the more rigid the industrial relations system, the more flexible and open to technological progress the social organization of production. The argument is that worker cooperation, commitment, and participation depend to a large extent on the trustworthiness of the employers in honoring their commitments to long-term employment and a fair productivity gain sharing. The most solid foundation for this kind of trust, as Edward Lorenz (1992) has eloquently argued, is the ability of labor to enforce those commitments. This, in turn, requires a national institutional and regulatory environment that offers legal protections to workers' rights and opportunities for effective (and safe) worker participation in firm decision making. Hence, labor economists Stephen Nickell and Richard Layard (1999, 3065) write, "There is no reason to be surprised that employment protection shows up with a positive coefficient in . . . productivity regressions." Similarly, David Levine (1993, 174) concludes that theory and evidence strongly suggest that "employment security policies have desirable macroeconomic consequences and therefore warrant support of national policymakers." The upshot of this is that, expressed in terms of the productivity regime equation (4.1), we expect coefficient β_3 to be positive.

Table 4.2 summarizes what in our view are the major statistical studies on the macroeconomic impact of labor market policies on productivity growth. At first sight, the empirical evidence appears rather inconclusive—eight of the

Table 4.2. OECD productivity growth and labor market regulation: selected studies

Independent variables:	Dependent variable: Labor productivity growth	Source and period of analysis
Employment protection legislation	+0.09***	Nickell and Layard (1999); 1976–1992
Replacement ratio	insignificant	
Total tax rate	−0.031*	
Benefit duration	insignificant	
Worker rights and labor-management cooperation index	+0.45**	Buchele and Christiansen (1999); 1979–1994
Employment protection legislation:		Scarpetta and Tressel (2004); 1984–1998;
• for all OECD countries	insignificant	
• for OECD countries featuring sectoral wage bargaining without national coordination	−1.151***	TFP growth
Average job tenure	+0.16***	Auer, Berg, and Coulibaly (2005); 1992–2002
Dismissal costs	Positive	Autor, Kerr, and Kugler (2007); 1976–1999; U.S. data
Employment protection legislation	−0.02***	OECD (2007); 1982–2003
Minimum wage	+0.17*** / +0.20***	
Unemployment benefits	+0.15***	
Employment protection legislation	+0.23***	
Replacement rate	1.37***	Dew-Becker and Gordon (2008)

Notes: ** and *** denote statistical significance at 5% and 1%, respectively.

eleven impacts found to be statistically significantly different from zero are positive, three indicators are found to have no impact, and another three indicators are negatively associated with productivity growth. Two of the three negative impacts are quantitatively small, and only one—the impact of employment protection, in Scarpetta and Tressel 2004—is substantive. But this finding is not a general one, as it applies to a subset of OECD countries that feature sectoral wage bargaining without national coordination; for all OECD countries, these authors find no impact of employment protection on productivity growth.

However, three of the more substantive studies attest to the positive association between labor market regulation and productivity growth ($\beta_3 > 0$). The first one is by U.S. labor economists Robert Buchele and Jens Christiansen (1999), who study differences in labor productivity growth rates in fifteen major OECD countries during the period from 1979 to 1994. They examine the effect on productivity growth of their own composite measures of the countries' systems of labor market regulation, which they derive from a careful factor analysis of a number of different dimensions of those systems. Their composite measure of regulation (integrating information on employment protection, unemployment insurance, collective wage bargaining coverage, job tenure, and wage compression) makes more sense than using individual indicators separately, as is done in most other studies, because the individual indicators are strongly interrelated (or collinear). In their statistical analysis, Buchele and Christiansen control for the effect of capital deepening, which of course has a positive influence on productivity growth rates. After pointing out all the quantitative bells and whistles, they feel comfortable concluding that if other things are equal, protective labor market regulation (that is, cooperative labor relations) has a positive and statistically significant impact on OECD productivity growth: "Strong worker rights and cooperative labor relations promote productivity growth" (ibid., 107).

A second suggestive piece of evidence comes from ILO economists Peter Auer, Janine Berg, and Ibrahim Coulibaly (2005), who present evidence that tenure (the amount of time that a worker has spent working for the same employer, including when that person's job within the firm changes) is necessary for both workers' security and firms' productivity. They treat shorter average tenure as a proxy for greater labor market flexibility. They find, using sectoral data for thirteen European countries for the period from 1992 to 2002, a significant positive impact of tenure on labor productivity; also, longer tenure is associated with stricter employment protection legislation. Auer et al. explain their findings by arguing that strict employment protection stimulates firm-specific training investments that raise productivity growth, as in the firm-specific human capital model. At the aggregate level,

> a strong incidence of stable employment relationships can help an econ-
> omy by ensuring constancy of aggregate demand. The financial stability
> created by long-term employment relationships creates economic stabil-
> ity, as a steady and growing purchasing power over the life cycle be-
> comes a positive source of consumption and, thus, sustained aggregate
> demand growth. (Auer, Berg, and Coulibaly 2005, 335)

This brings us back to square one: the Kaldor-Verdoorn effect. Sustained
growth and low unemployment reinforce the positive relationship between
regulation and productivity growth.

Finally, we mention U.S. economists Ian Dew-Becker and Robert Gordon
(2008), who studied the role of labor market regulation in the slowdown of
productivity growth in fifteen European countries between 1980 and 2003.
The strength of their analysis is that they try to capture the impact of regulation on productivity growth both directly and indirectly, the latter through its
negative impact on employment growth and output growth. They find that
"two of the policy variables (the replacement rate of unemployment benefits
and an index of employment protection legislation) have significant direct
positive effects on productivity growth in addition to their indirect [negative]
effects through employment." These effects are highly significant. Hence,
their analysis suggests that "some of the policy reforms that are at the top of
the European 'reform' agenda [such as labor market deregulation] may raise
employment but reduce productivity, leaving as in our simulations perhaps
negligible effects on output per capita" (ibid., 4, 29).

Our Empirical Strategy

We study differences in the growth rates of labor productivity per hour worked
among twenty OECD economies over two periods: 1984–1994 (with 1989 as
the central year) and 1994–2004 (with 1999 as the pivotal year). This means
that our number of observations is forty. We are pooling period-average data
pertaining to the end of the 1980s and data pertaining to the end of the
1990s—both of which are time frames for which reliable data on labor market
regulation and macroeconomic performance are available—to investigate the
impact of structural variables (i.e., regulatory labor market institutions) on
longer-term labor productivity growth. Our choice to use period averages
rather than pooled time-series data avoids rather artificially inflating the R^2
through across-time correlation of independent variables within countries; it
must also be noted that the time-series data on labor market variables are often rather unreliable, because many of these have been mechanically obtained
by means of interpolation or are not strictly comparable over time (Baker et al.
2005b). We emphasize that we use *national* data and not industry-level data

because most labor market regulations (and especially employment protection legislation) vary across countries but are identical across industries. The impact of labor market regulation should therefore be visible in aggregate (hourly) labor productivity growth. We have checked for country-specific effects by including country dummies, but in general we found (unless stated otherwise in the text and the tables) that these country dummies were not statistically significant, which suggests that we have included the relevant control variables.[9] Table 4.9 (in the Appendix to this chapter) presents our database for the sample of twenty OECD countries for the two periods; summary statistics are given in Table 4.3. Data sources are listed in the book's Appendix.

Important qualitative aspects of industrial relations are hard to quantify; however, we believe that these unquantifiable aspects are correlated with one or more of the following quantitative indicators:

1. An index of employment protection legislation (EPL) (OECD 1999; Nicoletti, Scarpetta, and Boyland 2000), designed as a multidimensional indicator of the strictness of legal protection against dismissals for permanent as well as temporary workers. The higher this index, the more restricted a country's employment protection legislation.[10]
2. The percentage of the nonagricultural labor force working in administrative and managerial occupations. This management ratio is used as an indicator of the intensity of supervision and monitoring by management (Gordon 1994, 1996); it can be interpreted as a (negative) indicator of the extent to which management trusts employees, and of the degree of autonomy workers have in organizing and coordinating their work activities.
3. Union density, that is, union members as a percentage of employees.
4. Collective bargaining coverage, that is, the percentage of the employed labor force whose pay is determined by collective agreement.
5. The unemployment benefit duration index.
6. An index of the extent of coordination in wage bargaining (range 1–3); "coordination" refers to mechanisms whereby the aggregate employment implications of wage determination are taken into account when wage bargains are struck. An industrial relations systems can be said to be coordinated when (1) the wage-bargain occurs in a centralized way or coordination among employers and/or trade unions sets a uniform band of wages; (2) employers and labor unions cooperate in regard to decision making inside the firm; and (3) employers' associations have an active role in solving free rider problems across firms.
7. The unemployment benefit replacement ratio, defined as unemployment benefit entitlement before tax as a percentage of previous earnings before tax.

Table 4.3. Summary statistics

	No. of observations	Mean	Standard deviation	Coefficient of variation	Minimum	Maximum
Labor relations indicators						
Employment protection legislation	40	2.18	1.17	53.58	0.2	3.9
Labor market regulation	36	0.00	0.96	—	-2.18	1.09
Management ratio	40	6.00	4.08	68.00	2.0	16.4
Union density	38	41.87	21.13	50.47	10.0	87.0
Bargaining coverage	37	67.80	25.88	38.17	14.0	99.0
Benefit duration	38	0.47	0.32	67.79	0.1	1.0
Wage bargaining coordination	38	2.03	0.57	28.10	1.0	3.0
Replacement ratio	38	0.48	0.18	37.50	0.2	0.8
Total labor tax	38	0.50	0.12	24.46	0.3	0.8
Earnings inequality	38	3.03	0.73	24.06	2.0	4.6
Median job tenure	40	9.88	1.77	17.88	5.9	13.5
Macroeconomic variables						
Labor productivity growth	40	2.13	0.84	39.18	0.18	4.70
Real wage growth	40	1.66	0.89	53.74	-1.22	3.18
Capital intensity growth	40	2.12	1.17	55.42	-0.37	4.57
Real GDP growth	40	2.77	1.10	39.56	1.15	7.67
Investment growth	40	3.37	2.32	68.99	-2.27	10.65
Unemployment (%)	40	7.50	3.18	42.37	2.50	16.10

Sources: See the Appendix in the backmatter and Table 4.9.

8. The total labor tax rate (including the payroll tax rate, the income tax rate, and the consumption tax rate).
9. Earnings inequality, defined as the ratio of the top 10 percent of earnings to the bottom 10 percent of earnings, which is taken as a (negative) indicator of how fairly compensated employees are likely to feel. The lower this ratio, the fairer workers will perceive their share of earnings to be.
10. Median job tenure, that is, the length of time that workers remain in their present jobs or self-employed; job tenure is an indicator of the prevalence of long-term employment relations or job stability in each country.

Following Buchele and Christiansen (1999), our starting point is that many features of a country's industrial relations systems tend to vary together—as can be seen from Table 4.4, in which appear the pairwise correlation coefficients for the various dimensions of labor market regulation in the twenty OECD countries. We find a particularly strong (statistically significant at 5 percent or less) and positive correlation between employment protection (measured by the EPL index), on one hand, and the management ratio, bargaining coverage, and bargaining coordination, on the other. The strong association (at 1 percent significance) between stricter employment protection and greater long-term job stability, reflected by longer average job tenure, is confirmed both by Buchele and Christiansen (1999) and Auer, Berg, and Coulibaly (2005). Earnings dispersion is very significantly negatively correlated with union density (which is confirmed by Faggio and Nickell 2007, even when controlling for the dispersion of skills), bargaining coverage, and wage bargaining coordination. Figure 4.1 presents a graphical illustration of four major regulatory complementarities, which in our view are a defining feature of OECD labor markets.[11] These complementarities allow us to draw out generalizations—for example, if an industrial relations system features weak employment protection, it is likely to display relatively high supervision intensity but relatively little wage bargaining coordination, a low level of collective bargaining coverage, and less job stability (short job tenure). Statistically, the high collinearity between labor market variables poses problems for estimating their separate impacts on labor productivity growth. First, the higher the degree of collinearity between the explanatory variables, the larger the standard errors of the ordinary least squares (OLS) estimators; as a result, the estimated coefficients become sensitive to even small changes in the data and/or model specification. Second, because of this, it may be impossible to isolate the individual effects of the explanatory variables. Unlike many earlier studies (see Table 4.2), we take advantage of these regulatory

Table 4.4. OECD labor relations (1984–2004): pairwise correlation matrix (Pearson's rho)

	EPL	MR	UD	BC	DUR	COORD	RR	Tax	Earnings inequality
EPL	1.00 (40)								
MR	-0.72*** (40)	1.00 (40)							
UD	0.04 (38)	-0.13 (38)	1.00 (38)						
BC	0.47*** (37)	-0.45** (38)	0.40** (38)	1.00 (37)					
DUR	-0.29 (38)	0.28* (38)	0.17 (36)	0.34** (36)	1.00 (38)				
COORD	0.49*** (38)	-0.70*** (38)	0.22 (38)	0.51*** (36)	0.08 (38)	1.00 (38)			
RR	0.27 (38)	-0.45*** (38)	0.11 (38)	0.27 (38)	-0.16 (38)	0.27 (38)	1.00 (18)		
Tax	0.28 (38)	-0.03 (38)	0.47*** (38)	0.53*** (38)	0.01 (38)	0.11 (38)	0.31* (18)	1.00 (18)	
Earnings inequality	-0.24 (38)	0.33** (38)	-0.59*** (38)	-0.43*** (36)	-0.13 (38)	-0.45*** (38)	-0.19 (38)	-0.51** (38)	1.00 (18)
Tenure	0.77*** (40)	-0.71** (40)	0.08 (38)	0.29 (37)	-0.36** (38)	0.42*** (38)	0.23 (38)	0.22 (38)	-0.19 (38)

Notes:

a. EPL = index of strictness of employment protection legislation; MR = management ratio (the proportion of managers in the nonagricultural labor force); UD = union density (in %); BC = collective bargaining coverage; DUR = unemployment benefits duration index; COORD = index of the extent of coordination in wage bargaining (range 1–3); RR = replacement ratio, defined as unemployment benefit entitlement before tax as a percentage of previous earnings before tax; Tax = total labor tax rate (including the payroll tax rate, the income tax rate, and the consumption tax rate); Earnings inequality = ratio of the 90th to 10th percentile earnings; and Tenure = median job tenure.

b. *, **, and *** denote statistical significance, in a two-tailed test, at 10%, 5%, and 1%, respectively. Figures within parentheses give the number of observations (*n*).

complementarities and use multivariate measures of the extent of labor market regulation in our productivity growth regressions.

To minimize the multicollinearity problem, we adopt a two-pronged approach. First, we use the EPL index as our measure of the nature of a country's labor relations: the higher the EPL, the more cooperative labor-management relations are and the more coordinated wage bargaining is (see Figure 4.1). Second, we used factor analysis to create a factor score of the nature of the labor relations systems. The factor score—called labor market regulation

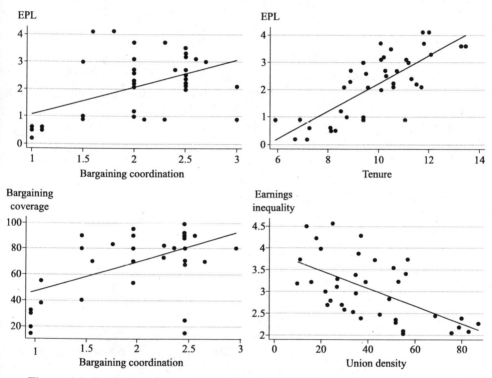

Figure 4.1. Regulatory complementarities in OECD labor markets.

Notes: The curves are based on the following OLS regressions (we report robust *t*-values):

Upper left panel: $EPL = 0.08$ $+ 1.00$ bargaining coordination
$\qquad\qquad\qquad$ (0.14) $\qquad$ $(3.45)^{***}$ $\qquad$ $\overline{R}^2 = 0.22$

Upper right panel: $EPL = -2.87$ $\quad + 0.51$ tenure
$\qquad\qquad\qquad$ $(5.16)^{***}$ $\quad (9.09)^{***}$ $\qquad$ $\overline{R}^2 = 0.59$

Lower left panel: bargaining coverage $= 22.79 + 23.06$ bargaining coordination
$\qquad\qquad\qquad\qquad\qquad\qquad (1.69)^{*} \ (3.43)^{***} \quad \overline{R}^2 = 0.24$

Lower right panel: earnings inequality $= 3.88 \ \ - 0.02$ union density
$\qquad\qquad\qquad\qquad\qquad\qquad (19.21)^{***} (5.78)^{***} \ \ \overline{R}^2 = 0.33$

$* =$ statistically significant at 10%; $*** =$ statistically significant at 1%.

(LMR)—is created for eighteen OECD countries, has a mean value of zero for the two periods combined, and loads highly on employment protection, the management ratio, earnings inequality, bargaining coordination, and collective bargaining coverage (for details, see the Appendix to this chapter). (Note that Ireland and Greece are excluded because of lack of comparable data on earnings inequality, bargaining coverage, the replacement ratio, and bargaining coordination.) The higher the labor market regulation, the more intensively regulated a country's labor market. Figure 4.2 ranks the estimates of labor market regulation by country in descending order for the periods from 1984 to 1994 and from 1994 to 2004. The ranking generally confirms most observers' views that countries in southern Europe have the most highly regulated labor markets, followed by France, Germany, and the Scandinavian countries, while the United States, Canada, the United Kingdom, and Australia are at the opposite end of the spectrum. As can be seen by comparing the upper and lower panels of Figure 4.2, there has been little change in the ranking of countries between 1984–1994 and 1994–2004; the rank correlation according to Spearman's rho $= 0.89$ (p $> |t| = 0.0000$). This is perhaps surprising, because many OECD countries have embarked on reforms to deregulate the labor market, but in practice most of the reforms have been marginal (affecting workers on temporary contracts, not regular workers) and in about 30 percent of cases reforms have tightened rather than loosened labor market regulations (Boeri 2005).

The biggest change occurred in Denmark, which ranked ninth in the first period, when its score was above average, and thirteenth in the second, when its score was below average. This change is due to the reform of the Danish industrial relations system toward a system of "flexicurity," alternatively called "protected mobility" (Auer 2007), which combines reduced employment protection and increased social protection (especially higher unemployment benefits and active labor market policies). The extent of regulation also declined (but less significantly so) in Germany, Norway, Spain, and Sweden, but it increased in Finland and remained more or less unchanged in the other Continental European countries and Japan. Finally, there has been hardly any change in the labor market regulation scores and ranking of the Anglo-Saxon countries.

Determinants of OECD Productivity Growth

Table 4.5 presents our labor productivity growth regressions. Direct estimation of the productivity regime equation (4.1) did not yield robust statistical results—mainly because of problems of simultaneity, which violate OLS assumptions. The simultaneity concerns both real wage growth (which affects

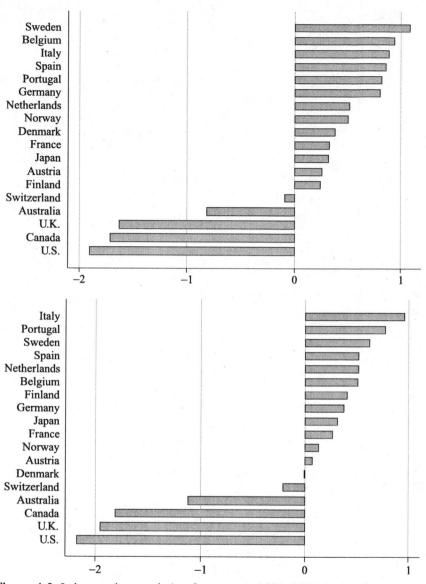

Figure 4.2. Labor market regulation factor score, 1984–1994 *(top)* and 1994–2004 *(bottom)*.
Source: Authors' estimation.

Table 4.5. OECD productivity growth: estimation results (1984–2004)

	(1) EPL			(2) LMR		
	GDP growth	Capital intensity growth	Labor productivity growth	GDP growth	Capital intensity growth	Labor productivity growth
Constant	0.36 (1.56)	0.43 (1.59)	−0.17 (1.13)	0.36 (1.56)***	1.06 (4.58)***	−0.03 (0.12)
Export growth	0.29 (7.64)***			0.18 (3.96)***		
Investment growth	0.25 (7.62)***			0.24 (7.12)***		
Government deficit (% GDP)	0.06 (2.76)***			0.05 (2.51)**		
Real wage growth		0.58 (5.31)***			0.70 (5.41)***	
EPL index		0.32 (4.02)***				
LMR factor score					0.37 (3.41)***	
GDP growth			0.46 (12.63)***			0.39 (5.59)***
Capital intensity growth			0.45 (10.12)***			0.46 (10.21)***
Country dummies						
Canada, 1989			−0.82 (3.61)***			−0.78 (3.49)***
Denmark, 1989		1.36 (2.31)**			1.12 (1.85)*	
Finland, 1989		2.21 (3.68)***	0.79 (3.07)***		1.95 (3.14)***	0.71 (2.78)***
France, 1989		1.65 (2.80)***			1.58 (2.61)***	

	EPL (1)	EPL (1)	EPL (1)	LMR (2)	LMR (2)	LMR (2)
Ireland, 1989			1.17 (5.07)***			
Japan, 1989		2.93 (4.88)***			2.93 (4.74)***	
Norway, 1989			0.71 (3.14)***			0.74 (3.30)***
Austria, 1999			0.72 (3.09)***			0.70 (3.04)***
Belgium, 1999		-1.52 (2.59)***			-1.85 (3.03)***	
Finland, 1999		-2.91 (4.87)***	1.15 (4.53)***		-3.19 (5.12)***	1.26 (4.92)***
Germany, 1999			0.63 (2.73)***			0.56 (2.37)**
Netherlands, 1999		-1.41 (2.40)**			-1.68 (2.77)***	
Portugal, 1999			-0.64 (2.70)***			-0.62 (2.68)***
Spain, 1999			-1.59 (6.76)***			-1.48 (6.30)***
Sweden, 1999		-1.62 (2.71)***	0.78 (3.33)***		-1.94 (3.09)***	0.82 (3.55)***
R^2	0.84	0.72	0.92	0.70	0.74	0.89
χ^2 (prob>χ^2)	212.2 (0.000)	127.5 (0.000)	454.4 (0.000)	83.4 (0.000)	113.5 (0.000)	279.6 (0.000)
No. of observ.	40	40	40	36	36	36
Standard error	0.433	0.607	0.228	0.382	0.617	0.225

Notes: Table 4.5 presents the 3SLS estimation results for a three-equation system. The equations reported in column 1, using EPL as explanatory variable, are estimated for 20 OECD countries. The equations in column 2, which includes LMR as one of the determinants, are estimated for 18 countries; Greece and Ireland are excluded because of lack of LMR factor scores. z-statistics appear in parentheses. *, **, and *** denote statistical significance at 10%, 5%, and 1%, respectively. Figures in parentheses in the χ^2-row are p-values. Finally, we included all statistically significant (at 10% or less) country dummies in the regression of the capital intensity growth and productivity growth equations. The maximum number of country dummies is 20, as we have 20 countries and the dummies are meant to capture structural (period-invariant) country-specific effects.

productivity growth but is also itself influenced by productivity growth) and real GDP growth (which similarly is related to and determined by productivity growth). To get around these simultaneity problems, we follow an indirect, somewhat more complicated route and reformulate equation (4.1) in terms of the following three equations, which were estimated by three-stage least squares (3SLS) regression:

$$(4.2) \qquad \hat{x} = \varphi_0 + \varphi_e \hat{e} + \varphi \hat{i} + \varphi_g deficit$$

$$(4.3) \qquad \hat{k} = \xi_0 + \xi_1 z + \xi_2 \hat{w} \qquad \xi_1, \xi_2 > 0$$

$$(4.4) \qquad \hat{\lambda} = \gamma_0 + \gamma_1 \hat{k} + \beta_1 \hat{x} \qquad \gamma_1 > 0; \, 0 < \beta_1 < 1$$

Equation (4.2) specifies demand-determined real GDP growth as a function of export growth $\hat{e}$, investment growth $\hat{i}$, and the government budget deficit *(deficit)*.[12] In equation (4.3), capital intensity growth $\hat{k}$ is a positive function of real wage growth (reflecting capital-labor substitution) and the extent of labor market regulation. Equation (4.4), which can be derived from a CES production function, states that labor productivity growth depends positively on capital intensity growth and real GDP growth, with β_1 being the Kaldor-Verdoorn coefficient. From this three-equation system, we can derive the productivity regime equation (4.1) as follows:

$$(4.1) \qquad \hat{\lambda} = [\gamma_0 + \gamma_1 \xi_0] + \beta_1 \hat{x} + \gamma_1 \xi_2 \hat{w} + \gamma_1 \xi_1 z = \beta_0 + \beta_1 \hat{x} + \beta_2 \hat{w} + \beta_3 z$$

where $\beta_0 = \gamma_0 + \gamma_1 \xi_0$, $\beta_2 = \gamma_1 \xi_2 > 0$, and $\beta_3 = \gamma_1 \xi_1 > 0$. This shows that the three coefficients of the productivity regime can be derived from the estimated equations (4.2)–(4.4).

Turning to the estimation results in Table 4.5, column 1 presents the results when we use the EPL index as our measure of labor market regulation. In column 2 appear the results using the LMR factor score; note that the number of observations is thirty-six in this case. Let us first consider the estimation results for equation (4.2): real GDP growth. The explanatory power of the estimated equation is high—the adjusted R^2 is 0.84 and 0.70 in column 1 and column 2, respectively. All coefficients (for exports, investment, and the government deficit) are statistically significant and positive—we therefore have obtained a plausibly instrumented estimate of real GDP growth. Second, the estimated equations for capital-intensity growth (4.3) are quite satisfactory: the explanatory power is relatively high (0.72 when using EPL, 0.74 when using LMR) and the coefficients have the expected signs. We find that ξ_2 takes values (statistically significant at 1 percent) of 0.58 and 0.70, respectively; ξ_2 can be interpreted as the elasticity of capital-labor substitution, and our results correspond to available estimates of the economywide elasticity of capital-labor substitution (Rowthorn 1999). Also, ξ_2 is statistically significantly different from (smaller than) unity. We further find that ξ_1, the impact of labor market regulation on capital intensity growth, is about 0.32–0.37 and statistically significantly different from zero at 1 percent. (We have checked that the statistical significance of the estimated coefficients does not depend on one particular country.) Finally, we consider the estimated labor productivity growth equation (4.4). The coefficient for capital intensity growth takes a value of 0.45 in column 1 (0.46 in column 2) and is statistically very significant at 1 percent. We also find a positive and statistically significant (at 1 percent) Kaldor-Verdoorn coefficient β_1; its values of 0.46 and 0.39, respectively, are comparable to available estimates (as we have seen in Table 4.1).

Based on these results, we calculated the coefficients of the productivity regime equation (4.1). Our reduced-form estimate of the coefficient of real-wage-growth-induced technological progress is $\beta_2 = 0.29$, that is, a 1 percentage point rise in real wage growth will lead to a rise in labor productivity growth of 0.29 percentage points. This result is in line with the findings of Rowthorn (1999) and Hein and Tarassow (2009), as is clear from Table 4.1. Our reduced-form estimate of $\beta_3 = 0.16$ means that an increase in the EPL index by 1 point (on a 0–4 scale) raises labor productivity growth by 0.16 percentage points—which resembles findings by Buchele and Christiansen (1999), Nickell and Layard (1999), Auer, Berg, and Coulibaly (2005), and Dew-Becker and Gordon (2008). We note that the impact of labor market regulation on productivity growth as measured by LMR is of similar sign and magnitude as the impact of EPL. This similarity in results based on alternative measures of labor market regulation reinforces our conclusion that higher employment protection and more extensive labor market regulation are associated with higher labor productivity growth.

From the regression analysis, we learn that the main factor explaining the positive association between labor market regulation and hourly labor productivity growth is capital deepening. Capital deepening is higher in countries featuring stricter employment protection legislation and higher levels of labor market regulation. This is illustrated in Figure 4.3 for the EPL index. It attests to the crucial role played by wage-cost-induced technological progress in capitalist economies.

Productivity Growth in Liberal and Coordinated Economies

So far we have assumed that differences in labor market regulation are continuous, but the vast literature on cross-national differences in institutional systems governing production relations (Gordon 1996; Hall and Soskice

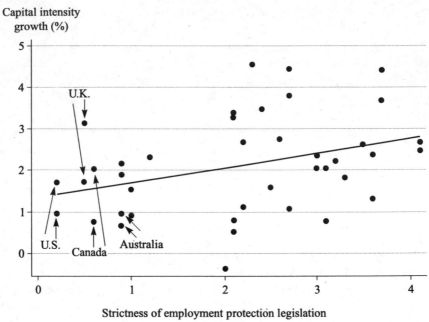

Figure 4.3. Capital intensity growth is higher when the labor market is more regulated.

Note: The Anglo-Saxon economies feature weak employment protection and low capital-intensity growth.

2001; Faggio and Nickell 2007) as well as the observed complementarities between structural dimensions of labor market regulation point to categorical differences across OECD economies between "coordinated/rigid" and "liberal/flexible" industrial relations systems. What can we learn from comparisons across country groupings featuring different kinds of industrial relations systems? Here, at least at first blush, the evidence seems to confirm our conclusion that economies most clearly featuring cooperative social relations of production have strong comparative advantage on the productivity front. We take the simplest possible categorical approach to OECD productivity growth, grouping our twenty countries into three groups (not four groups, as we did in Chapter 2): the four Scandinavian (Nordic) countries, the European Continental (EC) countries, and the Anglo-Saxon (AS) countries. We have reviewed the main differences in labor market policies between these groups in Chapter 2. Briefly, the Nordic countries and the EC countries all are coordinated market economies; the main difference between the rather diverse EC group of countries and the Nordics is that unemployment benefit systems in Scandinavia are arguably more "activating"—the Danish "flexicurity" system is a case in point (Auer 2007). In contrast, the AS countries have comparatively unregulated labor markets, low employment protection, relatively low labor taxes, weak unions, little coordination of wage bargaining, benefit systems that are worker unfriendly, and relatively high earnings inequalities.[13]

To see if our classification into three groups makes sense, Table 4.6 decomposes the total sum of squared deviations (from the overall OECD mean) into a within-group and a between-groups mean variation for each of our indicators of labor market regulation. It can be seen that the classification is valid. Differences across country groups capture more than 60 percent of the variation in OECD industrial relations systems during 1984–2004: the between-groups variation accounts for more than 62 percent in the case of the EPL index and as much as 86 to 88 percent in the case of the LMR factor score. The between-groups variation is high (> 50 percent) in the case of wage bargaining coordination, union density, job tenure, and the replacement rate during the years from 1994 to 2004. The categorical variation in regulation thus is significant—but is it significant enough to show up in differential productivity performance?

We use regression analysis to see whether OECD labor productivity growth can be explained by our categorical country grouping based on distinctive industrial relations regimes. To do so, we created separate dummy variables for the Nordic and AS countries. We regressed hourly labor productivity growth on these group dummies while controlling for capital intensity growth (and including an additional dummy for Ireland).[14] We thus postulated that the productivity growth functions of the three country groups in relation to capital intensity growth would have the same slope but different intercepts.

The results appear in column 1 of Table 4.7. They suggest that the categorical grouping contains about as much information as the continuous country scoring on our indicators for EPL or LMR (reported in Table 4.5). The $\bar{R}^2$ values, 0.72 and 0.74, are high. In column 1 of Table 4.7, the coefficient on the Nordic group dummy is statistically significant (at the 10 percent level) and carries a positive sign. This means that Nordic labor productivity growth is 0.44 percentage points higher than productivity growth in EC and AS countries for a similar rate of capital intensity growth. The impact of the Nordic system of industrial relations is therefore very strong.

If we run the same regression including a dummy variable for Denmark, which is the only Nordic country to have experienced fundamental labor market reform (e.g., significant decline in employment protection) as well as

Table 4.6. Decomposition of the differences in labor market regulation: eighteen OECD countries (1984–1994 and 1994–2004)

	Period: 1984–1994				Period: 1994–2004			
	Between-groups variation (%)	Within-group variation (%)			Between-groups variation (%)	Within-group variation (%)		
		Nordic countries	European Continental countries	Anglo-Saxon countries		Nordic countries	European Continental countries	Anglo-Saxon countries
Unemployment benefit duration	3.9	13.6	52.2	30.3	4.1	31.9	34.4	29.6
Replacement ratio	18.3	10.2	59.6	11.9	57.1	4.3	27.2	11.5
Expenditure on active labor market policies	29.3	33.0	33.7	4.0	56.1	13.2	29.4	1.3
Collective bargaining coverage	43.4	6.6	20.9	29.2	39.3	2.4	37.0	21.3
Total labor taxes	44.4	10.2	41.9	3.5	36.8	8.5	50.4	4.4
Earnings inequality (D9/D1)	48.9	1.1	33.3	16.8	43.3	0.8	44.1	11.8
Wage bargaining coordination	51.6	5.4	19.9	23.1	57.0	3.6	35.9	3.6
Union density	52.8	6.8	30.8	9.6	74.7	6.7	14.7	4.0
Average job tenure	61.7	3.4	30.7	4.2	63.4	8.5	24.6	3.6
Employment protection legislation (EPL)	65.4	4.5	29.2	0.9	62.1	5.1	31.6	1.2
Labor market regulation (LMR)	86.4	2.6	6.6	4.4	88.4	1.5	6.2	4.0

Source: Authors' calculations.

Table 4.7. Determinants of OECD labor productivity growth: a categorical analysis

Dependent variable	Average annual labor productivity growth	
	(1)	(2)
Constant	0.35	0.35
	(1.53)	(1.49)
Capital intensity growth	0.38***	0.39***
	(5.48)	(5.94)
Real GDP growth	0.31***	0.30***
	(3.45)	(3.21)
Dummy Nordic	0.44*	0.59**
	(1.88)	(2.26)
Dummy Anglo-Saxon	−0.16	−0.15
	(0.76)	(0.68)
Dummy Ireland	1.47***	1.49***
	(5.07)	(5.12)
Dummy Denmark		−0.64*
		(1.74)
$\bar{R}^2$	0.72	0.74
F (prob > 0)	69.53	66.86
	(0.000)	(0.000)
Standard error	0.476	0.466
No. of observations	40	40

Notes: The equations are estimated using OLS for 20 OECD countries (1984–2004). Robust t-statistics appear in parentheses. *, **, and *** denote statistical significance at 10%, 5%, and 1%, respectively. Figures in parentheses in the F-row are p-values.

a considerable decline in its productivity growth, we get an even more significant result, as can be seen from column 2 in Table 4.7. Nordic labor productivity growth excluding Denmark is 0.59 percentage points higher than productivity growth in EC and AS countries for a similar rate of capital intensity growth. Europe's Nordic economies, all featuring regulated and highly coordinated industrial relations systems, structurally outperform the other OECD countries in terms of labor productivity growth. The coefficient on the AS dummy is negative in both regressions but not significant; hence, there is no structural difference between productivity growth in the AS countries and the supposedly sluggish EC countries. Overall, the results reported in Table 4.7 suggest that a categorical distinction among countries is at least as useful an approach to controlling for the impact of labor market regulation on labor productivity growth as a continuous approach (Gordon 1994). They reinforce the conclusion that a relatively regulated and coordinated (rigid) industrial relations system promotes long-run labor productivity growth.

The Productivity Regime: Stylized and Fact

Our empirical analysis for twenty OECD countries in the period from 1984 to 2004 has confirmed that the productivity regime equation (4.1) makes sense as a stylized description of the supply side of the advanced OECD economies. We have found a positive impact of real GDP growth on labor productivity growth (the Kaldor-Verdoorn effect) as well as a significant impact of real wage growth on productivity advance (the Marx-Hicks effect). Last but not least, we find a significant positive association between protective labor market interventions and aggregate labor productivity growth, which confirms, at the aggregate level, the mountain of microeconomic evidence that productivity is higher, if all other things are equal, in enterprises that feature relatively more substantive worker involvement in production, decision making, and profit-sharing. Paraphrasing Robert Solow, we conclude that there is no doubt that our findings are stylized, but it is not unreasonable to treat them as facts.

In view of this association, it is wrong to assume, as is done in the NAIRU model, that labor productivity growth is *not* affected by labor market reform: it is, because it affects workers' motivation, work effort, and work intensity. This point was highlighted in Figure 1.3, which shows that more protective labor market regulation does raise wage claims (the wage-setting curve WS) as well as labor productivity levels (reflected by an upward shift of the price-setting curve PS). The ultimate impact on the inflation-safe unemployment rate is not clear beforehand: it may rise or fall depending on whether wage claims or productivity is affected most. We explore the impact on structural unemployment of labor market deregulation in Chapter 6 in much more empirical detail.

Our findings in this chapter, finally, contradict the claim that excessive labor market regulation or rigid labor markets are a major cause of slow labor productivity growth (à la OECD 2007) and should caution against overly optimistic assessments of the possible productivity impacts of labor market deregulation and real wage restraint. Further deregulation and increasing flexibility of OECD labor markets will lead to deteriorated productivity performance because they depress capital accumulation and growth, retard the pace of technological progress, and fail to effectuate the contribution that workers can make to the process of organizational and technological innovation, which raises productivity. The lesson is that, contrary to common opinion, unregulated labor markets, weak employment protection, low taxes, high earnings inequalities, and weak unions are not at all necessary to sustain high rates of labor productivity growth; in actual fact, they are detrimental to technological dynamism, "imposing costs on all of us whether or not we think we've evaded the blows of the Stick," as David Gordon wrote (1996, 97).

Further Reading

Kaldor's (1966) inaugural address at Cambridge University and Kaldor (1972) remain excellent expositions of the Kaldor-Verdoorn effect (also known as Kaldor's second law of growth). Allyn Young's (1928) older piece on the importance of increasing returns to scale is also still pertinent. David Gordon's (1996) *Fat and Mean* is a penetrating, broad-canvas exposition of how the social relations of production affect productivity growth, macro performance, and societal welfare at large. Robert Buchele and Jens Christiansen (1999) present a careful statistical evaluation of the impact of labor relations on OECD productivity growth. Edward Lorenz (1992) presents an eloquent, historically embedded argument that as organizational flexibility increases, labor-management relations become more cooperative; his comparative analysis of how computer-numerical-control machine tools were introduced in high-trust Germany (with the cooperation of workers) and low-trust Britain (with much worker opposition) should be textbook material. Peter Auer (2007) and Giulia Faggio and Stephen Nickell (2007) provide useful, nuanced overviews of contemporary cross-national differences in the social relations of production.

Appendix

We use factor analysis to reduce seven measures of labor market regulation to one factor, measuring the extent of labor market regulation. The eigenvalue of this first factor is 3.47 (>1) and this (unrotated) factor solution represents 88.7 percent of the variance in the data. We report only one factor, because the eigenvalues of the second and third factors were well below 1 (0.586 and 0.192, respectively) and they lacked substantive interpretation. The factor loadings and factor scoring coefficients are shown in Table 4.8; the latter were used to calculate each country's factor score. Because of missing data, Greece and Ireland are not included. Table 4.9 presents the database used in the statistical analysis in this chapter.

Table 4.8. Factor loadings

Variables	Factor loadings	Factor scoring coefficients
Employment protection legislation	0.8558	0.3023
Collective bargaining coverage	0.6311	0.1012
Management ratio	−0.8929	−0.3495
Wage bargaining coordination	0.7636	0.1630
Replacement ratio	0.4090	0.0390
Earnings inequality	−0.4547	−0.1023
Average job tenure	0.7650	0.1254

Table 4.9. Labor productivity growth, capital intensity growth, GDP growth, and labor relations (1984–1994 and 1994–2004)

Period: 1984–1994

	P	KL	W	GDP	GFCF	UNEMP	UD	COORD	CBC	Ltax	RR	DUR	EAP	Earnings	EPL	MR	Tenure	LMR
Australia	1.57	0.67	1.05	3.33	3.78	8.00	49	2.3	82.5	39	0.23	1.02	0.42	2.83	0.9	10.0	5.9	-0.82
Austria	2.13	2.68	1.61	2.44	3.65	4.58	51	2.5	99	58	0.34	0.75	0.27	3.54	2.2	6.1	10.6	0.26
Belgium	2.21	2.04	2.14	2.29	4.18	4.68	52	2.6	90	46	0.5	0.79	1.31	2.34	3.1	3.5	11.1	0.94
Canada	1.19	2.02	1.28	2.82	3.14	7.05	37	1.1	38	42	0.57	0.25	0.64	4.28	0.6	13.1	7.3	-1.71
Denmark	2.59	3.30	1.37	2.19	3.95	4.76	79	2.5	70.5	59	0.67	0.62	1.14	2.18	2.1	4.3	8.7	0.38
Finland	3.35	4.57	2.18	1.43	-2.27	4.70	69	2.0	95	58	0.38	0.61	0.9	2.44	2.3	4.9	8.9	0.25
France	2.20	3.79	1.23	2.11	2.16	4.92	16	2.0	90	65	0.61	0.37	0.66	3.22	2.7	5.6	10.3	0.33
Germany	2.26	2.23	2.63	2.81	3.30	5.14	34	2.5	92	50	0.38	0.61	0.8	2.52	3.2	3.8	10.2	0.81
Greece	1.42	1.32	0.42	1.37	-0.51	4.62									3.6	2.4	13.5	
Ireland	3.79	1.89	2.91	4.08	1.30	10.21	56	2.1		37	0.5	0.4	1.52	3.40	0.9	3.5	11.1	
Italy	2.35	2.67	1.43	2.30	1.58	5.51	45	1.8	84	56	0.02	0	0.62	2.47	4.1	3.7	12.0	0.88
Japan	3.18	4.45	0.67	3.44	4.34	4.08	27	2.5	25	33	0.29	0	0.17	3.11	2.7	4.1	10.7	0.32
Netherlands	1.78	1.07	0.72	2.83	3.55	5.86	30	2.4	81	55	0.67	0.66	1.16	2.58	2.7	4.2	8.9	0.52
Norway	3.00	2.06	3.02	3.12	-0.61	6.05	55	2.7	70	65	0.56	0.49	0.61	2.07	3.0	6.9	9.4	0.50
Portugal	2.62	2.48	2.03	3.06	3.55	6.88	57	1.6	71	33	0.44	0.11	0.33	3.73	4.1	2.0	11.8	0.81
Spain	2.96	4.42	2.17	2.86	4.28	6.22	11	2.3	73	40	0.75	0.21	0.33	3.73	3.7	2.0	10.1	0.85
Sweden	1.51	2.61	1.77	1.70	1.29	4.21	83	2.5	89	77	0.7	0.05	2.1	2.08	3.5	3.1	10.5	1.09
Switzerland	0.69	0.92	0.10	1.93	2.58	3.57	29	2.0	53	36	0.48	0	0.19	2.69	1.0	2.6	8.7	-0.09
U.K.	2.32	3.12	2.82	2.53	3.52	4.68	53	1.1	55	51	0.26	0.71	0.75	3.22	0.5	14.4	8.1	-1.63
U.S.	1.40	0.96	1.28	3.41	4.19	8.33	20	1.0	19	44	0.3	0.17	0.25	3.97	0.2	10.0	7.2	-1.90

Period: 1994–2004

	P	KL	W	GDP	GFCF	UNEMP	UD	COORD	CBC	Ltax	RR	DUR	EAP	Earnings	EPL	MR	Tenure	LMR
Australia	1.94	0.96	1.51	3.80	6.60	7.26	35	1.5	80	39	0.25	1	0.42	2.97	0.9	11.4	6.9	-1.12
Austria	3.02	3.37	1.87	2.23	1.77	4.14	39	2.0	95	66	0.42	0.68	0.44	3.22	2.1	6.9	10.6	0.07
Belgium	1.55	0.52	1.86	2.31	2.71	8.52	52	2.0	90	51	0.46	0.78	1.42	2.28	2.1	4.0	11.7	0.51
Canada	1.47	0.76	0.73	3.47	5.40	8.27	36	1.0	32	53	0.49	0.42	0.5	3.86	0.6	14.9	8.1	-1.81
Denmark	1.62	2.31	1.78	2.41	5.12	5.49	76	2.0	80	61	0.66	1	1.66	2.04	1.2	4.9	8.5	-0.01
Finland	2.53	-0.37	2.30	3.74	5.38	11.53	80	2.5	90	62	0.54	0.63	1.4	2.38	2.0	5.2	10.1	0.41
France	2.08	2.34	1.69	2.26	3.07	10.25	10	1.5	90	68	0.59	0.47	1.3	3.18	3.0	6.4	11.2	0.27
Germany	1.88	1.58	1.59	1.54	0.49	8.38	27	2.5	68	50	0.37	0.75	1.26	3.29	2.5	4.3	10.3	0.38
Greece	2.41	2.38	3.18	3.57	6.71	10.23		3.0	30						3.6	2.7	13.3	
Ireland	4.70	2.16	2.82	7.68	10.65	7.59	43	3.0		33	0.35	0.77	1.54	3.72	0.9	4.0	9.4	0.96
Italy	1.03	1.81	0.11	1.63	2.86	10.07	37	2.5	80	64	0.6	0	1.12	2.39	3.3	4.2	12.1	0.32
Japan	1.89	3.48	1.16	1.15	-0.73	4.25	22	2.5	15	37	0.37	0	0.09	2.99	2.4	3.6	11.3	0.52
Netherlands	1.66	0.80	1.90	2.78	3.11	4.32	24	3.0	80	43	0.7	0.64	1.74	2.78	2.1	4.8	9.6	0.14
Norway	2.65	2.74	1.85	3.28	4.37	4.23	55	2.0	70	60	0.62	0.6	0.9	2.03	2.6	7.9	9.5	0.77
Portugal	2.04	3.69	2.50	2.64	3.80	5.81	25	2.0	80	39	0.65	0.58	0.78	4.56	3.7	2.2	11.8	0.52
Spain	0.18	0.78	-1.22	3.48	5.88	14.02	18	2.0	80	45	0.63	0.29	0.7	4.22	3.1	2.3	10.1	0.63
Sweden	2.45	1.11	2.37	2.99	4.20	7.27	87	2.0	90	77	0.74	0.02	1.97	2.26	2.2	3.5	11.5	
Switzerland	1.36	1.52	1.50	1.37	2.13	3.56	23	1.5	40	36	0.74	0.31	0.77	2.68	1.0	3.0	9.4	-0.21
U.K.	2.21	1.73	2.00	3.05	4.83	6.33	35	1.0	30	44	0.17	0.96	0.34	3.38	0.5	16.4	8.3	-1.95
U.S.	2.09	1.68	2.04	3.28	5.33	5.15	14	1.0	14	45	0.29	0.22	0.17	4.50	0.2	14.4	6.7	-2.18

Sources: See the Appendix in the backmatter.

Notes: P=labor productivity growth (per hour worked); KL=capital intensity growth; W=real wage growth; GDP=real GDP growth; GFCF=investment growth; UNEMP=unemployment rate; UD=union density; COORD=wage bargaining coordination; CBC=collective bargaining coverage; Ltax=labor tax; RR=replacement ratio; DUR=unemployment benefit duration; EAP=expenditure on active labor market programs; Earnings=earnings inequality (D9/D1); EPL=index of the strictness of employment protection legislation; MR=the management ratio; Tenure=average job tenure; LMR=labor market regulation (factor score).

5

OECD Demand Regimes

Two souls, alas! are housed within my breast,
and each will wrestle for the mastery there,
the one has passion's craving crude for love,
and hugs a world where sweet the senses rage;
the other longs for pastures fair above,
leaving the murk for lofty heritage.

JOHANN WOLFGANG VON GOETHE, *THE TRAGEDY OF FAUST*

Goethe's Doctor Faust, a physician, lawyer, and theologian, in a famous piti-ful soliloquy, despairs of the futility of his scholarly pursuits of the spiritual world and yearns to fully experience the joys and sorrows of earthly life. He invokes the Spirit of the Earth, who shows him clearly his divided nature, the dualistic dilemma between spiritual longing and earthly desires, aspira-tion and indulgence. Lance Taylor (2010), who knows his Goethe, uses the analogy of Goethe's "two-souls problem" to describe the distributive strife within capitalism between the soul of labor and the soul of capital. As Faust, aggregate demand hosts within its breast two souls that struggle there for undivided reign. The outcome of this wrestling ultimately reveals itself in either the wage-led or profit-led nature of a country's aggregate demand—as we have analyzed in far less poetic terms in Chapter 3.

Quite unlike our approach, conventional (NAIRU-based) wisdom in mac-roeconomics holds that aggregate demand in the OECD economies has only one soul, a profit-led one—which, only slightly paraphrasing Goethe, has pas-sion's craving crude for a low wage share and a high profit share. In this view, profits, investment, and exports play a dominant role in expanding aggre-gate demand insofar as any reduction in consumption due to lower real wage growth is more than compensated for by the positive response by private in-vestment and exports to that lower real wage. To illustrate, it is commonplace in discussions of the demise of the "golden age" of capitalism—the period from 1950 to 1973—to accord a central role to the decline in profitability (the high-employment profit squeeze), which in turn was brought about by high real wage growth as well as energy price increases (Marglin and Schor 1990; Cornwall and Cornwall 2001; Bowles, Edwards, and Roosevelt 2005; Glyn 2006). Not surprisingly, therefore, a near consensus has emerged that a recovery of profitability, to be achieved by means of real wage restraint in conjunction with a more general deregulation of labor markets, is a necessary condition to improve the long-run macroeconomic performance of the OECD countries. However, despite the fact that in almost all OECD countries real wage growth was significantly restrained after 1980, allowing profitability to recover to its golden-age level, post-1980 macroeconomic performance is in general characterized by lower output growth, lower rates of investment, and higher rates of unemployment than witnessed during the period from 1960 to 1980 (see Table 5.1 later in the chapter). The disappointing performance raises the question of why the redistribution of income from wages to profits in a supposedly profit-led demand regime has so far failed to bring about more adequate long-run economic performance. Is it true that an economywide decline in real wage growth will lead to higher investment and GDP growth and will cause unemployment to decline? This is the question that is addressed in this chapter for twelve major OECD countries in the period from 1960 to 2000: Belgium, Denmark, Finland, France, Germany, Italy, Japan, the Netherlands, Spain, Sweden, the United Kingdom, and the United States.

Wrestling for Mastery

Capitalism, in conventional economic and sociological accounts (Tsakalotos 2006), is seen as a zero-sum game of conflicting claims on the income it generates. The prominent social conflict is that between the soul of labor (workers) and the soul of capital (firms and capital owners), and inflation and/or stagflation are often believed to be the result if this conflict is not resolved or successfully mediated.

Keynesian economists view this conflictual zero-sum capitalism as being inherently unstable, prone to cycles of overheating (inflation) and recession (high unemployment) (Galbraith 2008; Taylor 2010). For Keynesians, unregulated market forces could, at best, offer suboptimal equilibria and unemployment, and at worst, crises of the magnitude of the crisis of the 1930s and of 2008–2011. However, Keynesians claim that the conflict can be resolved (and the system stabilized) by translating and guiding private self-interest into optimal social outcomes. Necessary to do so are special collective bargaining institutions, under a strong agency from the state, so as to secure both growth and full employment—this further develops Michał Kalecki's (1943) brilliant insight that capitalism is incompatible with full employment unless there are major institutional arrangements to incorporate workers into the macro decision-making system (Rehn 1999; Bowles,

Edwards, and Roosevelt 2005; Tsakalotos 2006; Moene 2008; Palma 2009). In 1943, at the height of enthusiasm for Keynesian full employment policies, Kalecki (1943, 326) wrote:

> Indeed, under a regime of permanent full employment, the "sack" would cease to play its role as a disciplinary measure. The social position of the boss would be undermined, and the self-assurance and class-consciousness of the working class would grow. Strikes for wage increases and improvements in conditions of work would create political tension. . . . "[D]iscipline in the factories" and "political stability" are more appreciated than profits by business leaders. Their class instinct tells them that lasting full employment is unsound from their point of view, and that unemployment is an integral part of a "normal" capitalist system.

Full employment is therefore achievable only if it is backed up by a grand social bargain, or compromise, between workers, firms, and the state. The Keynesian case in point is the golden age (1950–1973), in which the OECD economies experienced almost full employment, rapid growth, and impressive productivity performance. This high-growth episode was structurally underpinned by a "Keynesian compromise" over the distribution of income and a commitment to full employment, which entailed high growth rates of real wages as well as of productivity and aggregate demand. The Keynesian compromise made possible a long investment boom and high real GDP growth, which in turn made the distributional struggle more manageable—because firms' total profits could grow even though the profit share in income declined (and the wage share increased). To see this in more detail, let us return to equation (1.7) of Chapter 1, which shows that the profit rate has three main determinants: the real wage w, labor productivity λ, and capacity utilization Θ (if we ignore p/p_k).

$$(1.7) \qquad \rho = (1 - w\lambda^{-1}) * \frac{p}{p_k} * \Theta$$

Even if real wages grow more rapidly than labor productivity, making the wage share $w\lambda^{-1}$ grow, the profit *rate* can rise if strong demand growth raises capacity utilization Θ strongly enough. As Amit Bhaduri and Stephen Marglin (1990, 382) put it: "Given the accountants' book value of capital in the short period, a higher total profit would also mean a higher profit rate despite the lower profit . . . share." This, in their view, is a critical condition for the cooperative positive-sum solution to the wage-profit wrestle. It reflects Keynesian optimism that the economic system can be stabilized and its performance be improved by appropriate collective action and government guidance.

The Keynesian compromise underlying the golden age collapsed by the early 1970s, partly in response to external factors (rising energy prices) and partly because of its failure to resolve mounting internal contradictions. Domestically, the profit share began to decline significantly as a result of a slowdown in productivity growth (in turn due to the exhaustion of the prevailing Fordist techno-economic paradigm), rising real input costs, tighter labor market conditions (which had led to a long-lasting improvement of workers' bargaining position), and intensified foreign competition. Tensions between trade unions and employers' associations mounted everywhere.[1] Internationally, the collapse of the Bretton Woods system, the consequent deregulation of international financial markets, and the oil price shock of 1973 had serious implications for economic activity, employment, and macroeconomic policy. The energy price hike added to the rising inflationary pressures. The share of profits in GDP dropped sharply. This profit squeeze has been extensively analyzed.[2] The profit squeeze, and the dramatic rise in macroeconomic uncertainty, led to a significant decline in investment growth, which in turn has been argued to have been the major cause of the slowdown of output growth and rising OECD unemployment. Rowthorn (1995), for example, finds for ten OECD countries from 1960 to 1992 that each 1 percent of extra growth in capital stock is associated with between 0.48 and 0.61 percent faster employment growth. Cornwall and Cornwall (2001) find that restrictive monetary policy and sluggish international demand conditions accounted for the bulk of the increase in unemployment over time. This, in essence, is the Keynesian story.

There exists another, polar opposite take on the problem of social conflict and the demise of the golden age: the NAIRU approach. Reflecting the optimism of Friedmanian monetarism, it identifies capitalism as a system based on institutional inequalities that create continuous struggles between economic interests (e.g., labor versus capital) and featuring mechanisms that secure its stability. Acquitting markets of the ills of which they are often accused, monetarists view competitive struggle not only as constituting a "natural" harmonic order but also as furthering the social good (Foley 2006; Palma 2009). The key stabilizing mechanism, of course, is changes in equilibrium unemployment, which discipline workers and force their real wage demands back in line with preordained productivity growth and firms' profit share. Bowles, Edwards, and Roosevelt (2005) call this the invisible hand (or *laissez faire et laissez passer et le monde va de lui-même*) solution, which has to be contrasted with the Keynesian "visible handshake," outlined above. The end of the golden age, in this view, must be attributed to a profit squeeze caused by excessive real wage growth, which in turn was due to workers having too much bargaining power, and too much government

interference in the system in general; stagflation was the inescapable outcome of overregulation at the cost of market forces. (In the Keynesian explanation, the stagflation is due not to overregulation or regulation per se but
to regulatory failure: incorrect macro policy responses based on weakening social compromises.) Accordingly, in the monetarist view, the revival of
growth and of employment depends upon a recovery of private-sector investment growth, which in turn requires a restoration of profitability or (in a
zero-sum world) a decline in the wage share. This is possible only by means
of real wage restraint and a more general deregulation of labor markets—a
bitter but supposedly necessary medicine, as we explained in Chapter 2.

This discussion of conflicting wage-profit claims may appear rather arcane, especially because mainstream macroeconomics does not care much
about distribution, and also because it is held that the wage share is more or
less stable in the long run; hence the wage share (or profit share) does not
feature prominently in most macro policy debates. But because of this focus
on the very long run, one glosses over major changes in distribution actually
occurring in the medium-to-long run. Figure 5.1 illustrates for the twelve
OECD economies during the years 1960–2000 that there is actually a lot of
distributional dynamics going on. The year 1980 represents a breaking point
in the data: up until then, the twelve high-income countries experienced a
general rise in the wage share (except Germany), and Scott Carter (2007)
shows that this wage share increase (and profit share decline) was accompanied by a general fall in the rate of profit. After 1980, the trend reverses
(except for Japan and Spain) as the share of wages falls and the profit share
rises, and Carter's data show that the profit rate increases as well. The decline in the wage share after 1980 is a signal of a much more general deterioration in the position of workers, brought about by, as Andrew Glyn (2006)
makes clear, a counterrevolution in macroeconomic policy and labor market
deregulation. The change in macro policy saw tight monetary policy (drastically higher real interest rates) and fiscal austerity imposed in the name of
defeating inflation—a process of which the deregulation of labor markets
was also a major aspect. The idea was, as discussed in Chapter 2, that capitalist growth required that capital (profits) regain the upper hand via an economic environment that was permanently unstable and highly insecure for
workers as well as the state (Palma 2009). Goodbye to welfare capitalism,
welcome to Greenspan's traumatized workers! Making up the balance sheet
of macro policy changes in the OECD, Glyn concludes:

> The period since 1979 provides an extraordinary contrast with the
> gains made by labour over the previous 30 years which covered jobs,
> pay, working conditions and worker representation. In the Golden Age

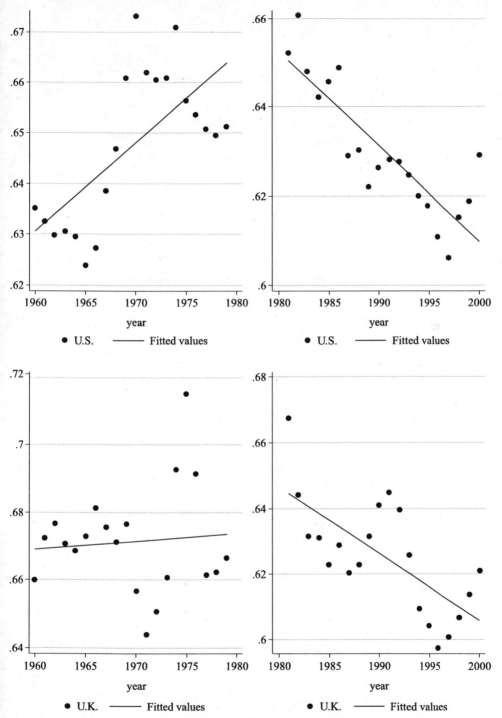

Figure 5.1. The evolution of the wage share, 1960–1980 and 1980–2000: the United States and the United Kingdom.

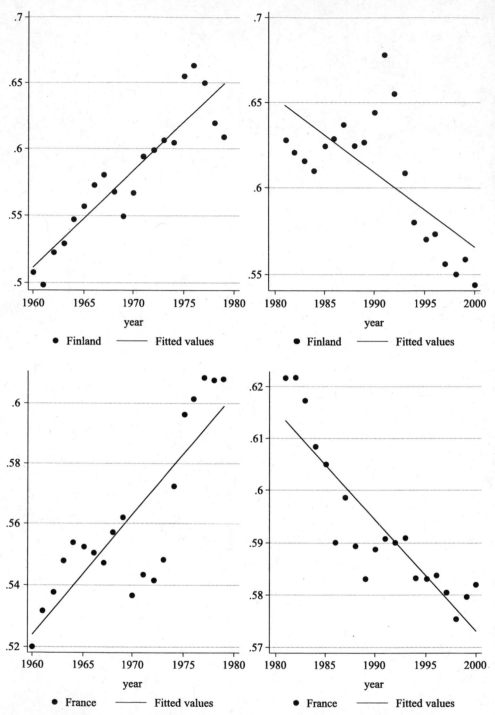

Figure 5.1. *(continued)* The evolution of the wage share, 1960–1980 and 1980–2000: Finland and France.

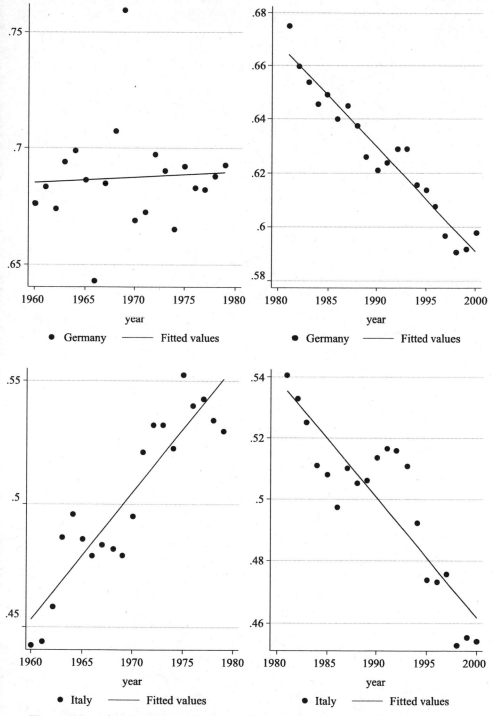

Figure 5.1. *(continued)* The evolution of the wage share, 1960–1980 and 1980–2000: Germany and Italy.

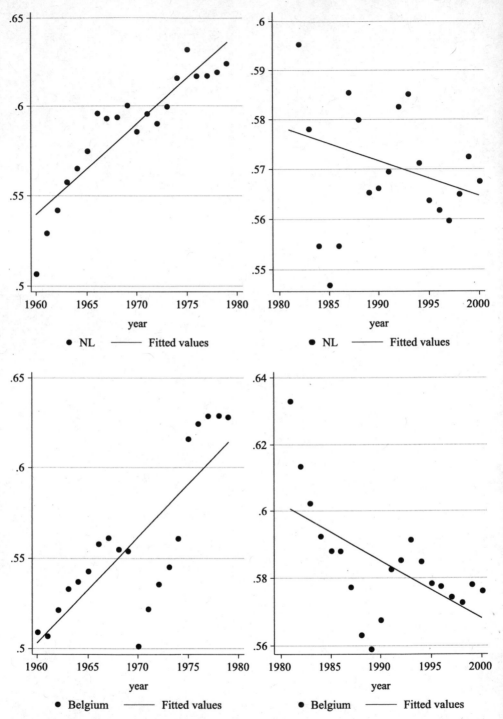

Figure 5.1. *(continued)* The evolution of the wage share, 1960–1980 and 1980–2000: The Netherlands and Belgium.

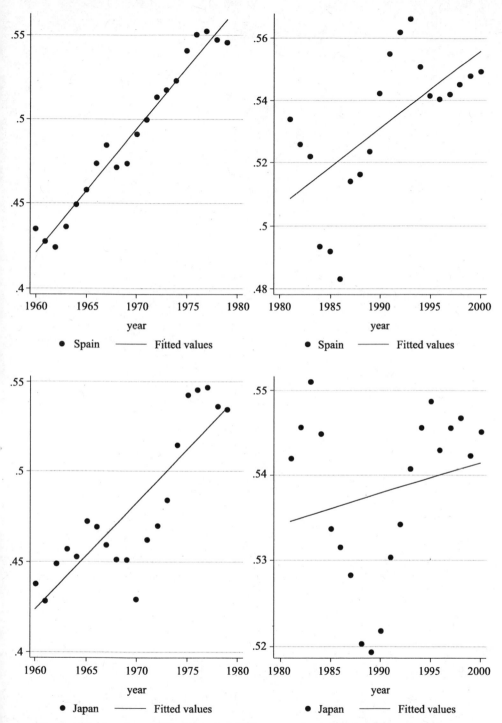

Figure 5.1. *(continued)* The evolution of the wage share, 1960–1980 and 1980–2000: Spain and Japan.

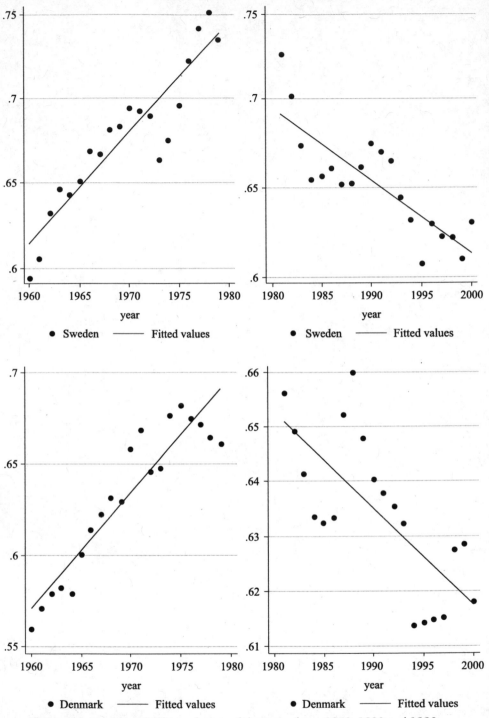

Figure 5.1. *(continued)* The evolution of the wage share, 1960–1980 and 1980–2000: Sweden and Denmark.

unemployment fell to very low levels and workers moved out of agriculture into better paid jobs in industry and services. Pay levels rose steadily, differentials were narrowed, hours of work fell and legal protection for workers was extended. Unions became stronger and exerted this strength in industrial action. Since 1979 labour markets have slackened and the unskilled men who lost jobs in industry have shifted into poorly paid service jobs, unemployment or even out of the labour force. For women job opportunities have improved but many of these jobs are still low paid. Average pay levels rose in real terms slowly if at all. Those at the top of the pay distribution tended to gain substantially relative to the middle. Work intensity typically increased. Employment protection legislation, particularly affecting temporary workers, was scaled back. Outside Scandinavia the proportion of employees in unions fell substantially. . . . It seems impossible to depict all of this as signalling anything other than a major retreat for labour. (Glyn 2006, 126–127)

Thus, the victory by the soul of capital, which took place in the name of bringing down inflation, required high and rising unemployment, which was "a price worth paying. Inflation is a *terrible cancerous disease* that takes radical action," as the president of Chase Manhattan noted.[3] According to our data, every percentage point increase in the unemployment rate is associated with a 0.7 percent rise in the profit share; this is exactly the same impact found by Glyn (1997) for fifteen OECD countries.

The sharp rise in unemployment after 1980 (see Table 5.1) put the labor unions in a tight corner and made them agree to real wage growth restraint. In all our countries, post-1980 real wage growth has been moderated and kept close to the rate of labor productivity growth. The average annual growth rate of real wages in the twelve OECD economies declined by as much as 3.6 percentage points between 1960–1980 and 1980–2000. Such drastic real wage growth restraint was accomplished in various ways. In the Anglo-Saxon economies, it was achieved less by bargaining and legislation than by deflationary domestic macroeconomic policies[4] and by spectacular government victories in marathon disputes with public sector unions (see Dore, Lazonick, and O'Sullivan 1999 for a discussion).[5] Paul Volcker at the U.S. Federal Reserve underlined the links between tight monetary policy and the broader issue of the weakening of labor. Volcker believed that "the most important single action of the administration in helping the anti-inflation fight was defeating the air traffic controllers' strike." Furthermore, the Fed chief thought that "this action had rather a profound, and from his standpoint, constructive effect on the climate of labor-management relations" (Glyn 2006, 27). The consistency in Fed thinking—from Volcker's "constructive intervention" in

Table 5.1. Lower wage shares do not necessarily mean higher investment ratios, more growth, and lower unemployment rates

	Percentage point change in the wage share		Percentage point change in the investment-to-GDP ratio		Real GDP growth (average annual growth rate %)		Average unemployment (standardized rate %)	
	Between 1960–1965 and 1975–1980	Between 1975–1980 and 1995–2000	Between 1960–1965 and 1975–1980	Between 1975–1980 and 1995–2000	1960–1980	1980–2000	1960–1980	1980–2000
	(1)	(2)	(3)	(4)	(5)	(6)	(7)	(8)
Belgium	10.2	−5.1	−1.0	−0.5	4.2	2.2	3.9	9.4
Denmark	9.1	−5.0	0.4	−0.1	3.2	1.8	2.9	6.9
Finland	10.9	−7.7	−3.2	−9.5	4.2	2.7	2.9	8.5
France	6.6	−2.6	0.7	−0.7	4.6	2.1	3.1	10.0
Germany	0.0	−8.7	−5.5	−1.8	3.6	2.1	1.8	6.1
Italy	6.9	−7.4	−5.7	−2.8	4.7	2.0	4.3	7.9
Japan	9.1	0.5	6.2	−0.3	7.5	2.8	1.5	3.0
Netherlands	7.6	−5.7	−3.2	−1.2	4.0	2.5	2.9	7.3
Spain	10.7	−0.1	2.7	1.9	5.5	2.8	4.1	17.6
Sweden	10.1	−10.9	−2.1	−1.4	3.3	2.1	1.5	4.8
U.K.	0.9	−7.2	0.7	1.5	2.4	2.3	3.9	8.7
U.S.	2.3	−3.7	0.1	3.6	3.6	3.1	5.4	6.3
Unweighted average	7.0	−5.3	−0.8	−1.0	4.4	2.5	3.2	8.1

Source: Authors' calculations.

labor-management relations in 1979 to Greenspan's traumatized workers twenty years later—cannot escape the eye.

In contrast, in the European Continental (EC) countries and Japan, employers and unions cooperated to varying degrees to deliver wage restraint. Such cooperation was possible in these countries because both parties to the bargaining were willing to think in terms of a common national interest in stable prices and reduced unemployment. The Dutch example provides a good illustration: in a 1982 central agreement between labor unions, employers' organizations, and government, voluntary real wage restraint by workers was exchanged for a promise by firms to increase investment and hence employment, and for a promise by government to maintain entitlements under the Dutch welfare state at prevailing levels. Since then, average annual real wage growth in the Netherlands has been 0.4 percent (compared to an average annual growth rate of about 5 percent during 1960–1980). As a result, the profit share in GDP of Dutch firms increased by 5.7 percent between 1975–1979 and 1995–2000, almost restoring profitability to the levels realized in the early 1960s.[6] The evidence provided by Figure 5.1 suggests that real wage restraint in the 1980s and 1990s has brought about a decisive profit recovery in almost all OECD economies. International institutions, including the OECD and IMF, and many economists expected that the improved profitability would lead to increased investment and higher GDP growth, in effect reducing unemployment. Table 5.1 shows that these expectations proved to be false.

A Pyrrhic Victory for Capital?

Table 5.1 puts numbers on the change in the average wage shares of the twelve OECD countries between 1960–1965 and 1975–1980 and between 1975–1980 and 1995–2000. On average, the wage share increased by 7 percentage points in the 1960s and 1970s, and it increased in all countries (except Germany, where it remained stable). Belgium, Finland, Spain, and Sweden experienced a wage share increase of more than 10 percentage points; in Denmark, France, Italy, Japan, and the Netherlands, the wage share increase was also very pronounced. The U.S. wage share increased by 2.3 percentage points, while in Britain and Germany the increases were smaller. The 1960s and 1970s thus were a period of generally declining profit shares. However, this general decline in profit shares is not statistically significantly associated with a general decline in the investment-to-GDP ratio (even though, on average, the investment-to-GDP ratio declined by 0.8 percentage points). Using the data in columns 1 and 3 of Table 5.1, a simple bivariate regression gives the following nonsignificant result for the first period 1960–1980 (t-values are given in parentheses):

Change in investment-to-GDP ratio = −2.27 + 0.21 change in the wage share
$$(-1.18) \ (0.84) \qquad \overline{R}^2 = 0.0; \ n = 12$$

In other words, the increase in the wage share up to 1980 did not affect the investment-to-GDP ratio either positively or negatively.

The second period (1980–2000), in contrast, is a period of profit share recovery: on average, the OECD wage share (profit share) declines (increases) by 5.3 percentage points. We see that the wage share declines strongly (by more than 7 percentage points) in Finland, Germany, Italy, Sweden, and the United Kingdom. The smaller European countries, Belgium, Denmark, and the Netherlands, experienced a wage share decline of more than 5 percentage points, while the U.S. wage share declined by 3.7 percentage points. However, strong profit share recovery did not lead to a corresponding investment growth recovery: on the contrary, after 1980, investment as a share of GDP declined, on average, by 1 percentage point. Drops in the investment ratio were large in Finland, Italy, Germany, Sweden, and the Netherlands. Using the data in columns 2 and 4 of Table 5.1, we find that the wage share is positively and significantly (at 10 percent) associated with the investment-to-GDP ratio:

Change in investment-to-GDP ratio = 1.23 + 0.41 change in the wage share
$$(1.23) \ (1.88)^* \qquad \overline{R}^2 = 0.11; \ n = 12$$

(where * means statistically significant at 10 percent). This means that after 1980 in the OECD countries, a lower wage share (a higher profit share) is associated with a lower investment-to-GDP ratio—not something one can easily square with the logic of the NAIRU approach.

Table 5.1 provides further data on average real GDP growth and average unemployment in the two periods. In the 1960s and 1970s, GDP growth was high (4.4 percent per annum on average) and in many countries there was nearly full employment, especially during the years 1960–1973 (the average rate of unemployment in our sample of countries was 3.2 percent during the years 1960–1980). Unemployment rates were below 2 percent in Germany, Japan, and Sweden, and unemployment was highest (at 5.4 percent of the labor force) in the United States. Analyses of the golden age have shown that this superior performance depended upon there being no constraint on aggregate demand, which grew without serious interruption over the period. Export growth and investment growth were strong components of the growth in aggregate demand. Investment rose at a historically high pace, helped by the stability of aggregate demand growth; through the multiplier process the rapid investment growth generated high GDP growth, justifying past investment and encouraging its continuation in a positive feedback loop.

Real GDP growth declined after 1980 in all countries, notwithstanding the recovery of profitability. Even for the United States, average annual real GDP growth declined by 0.5 percentage points even though the profit share increased by 3.6 percentage points and was higher during 1995–2000 than it was in the early 1960s. Statistically, our data show that countries that experienced a larger increase in their profit share (or a decline in their wage share) during 1980–2000 recorded lower real GDP growth than countries experiencing a smaller revival of profitability:

Annual real GDP growth (1980–2000) =
2.69   + 0.06 change in the wage share from 1975–1980 to 1995–2000
(16.54)*** (3.12)** $\bar{R}^2 = 0.18; n = 12$

(where *** and ** mean statistically significant at 1 percent and 5 percent, respectively). A higher wage share, in other words, is not detrimental to economic growth. Also, it is not associated with higher unemployment.

In fact, despite the significant real wage restraint, there was a considerable deterioration in the unemployment picture that continues today: the unweighted average unemployment rate for the OECD countries in our study increased from 3.2 percent during 1960–1980 to more than 8.1 percent during 1980–2000; in our twelve countries alone, about twenty-one million workers were unemployed in 2000. Unemployment increased in all countries—notwithstanding the often large declines in the wage share. For example, the United Kingdom wage share declined by 7.2 percentage points after 1980, but average unemployment rose by 4.8 percentage points. In Germany, the wage share declined by 8.7 percentage points (the profit share increased by the same magnitude), but the unemployment rate grew by 4.3 percentage points. Sweden cut down its wage share after 1980 by almost 11 percentage points, only to see its unemployment rate rise by 3.3 percentage points. If cutting down the wage share to restore profitability is so important for raising growth and reducing unemployment, the effect does not show up in the data. Not at all, in fact. Even in the United States, where the wage share fell by 3.2 percentage points after 1980, the average rate of unemployment rose by almost 1 percentage point. It is therefore not surprising that every percentage point increase in unemployment after 1980 is associated with a rise in the profit share of 0.7 percentage points. This disappointing performance raises the question of why the redistribution of income from wages to profits in a supposedly profit-led demand regime has so far failed to bring about adequate long-run macroeconomic performance. To answer this question, we need to do some soul-searching and find out whether OECD aggregate demand is profit-led (as conventional macro theory holds) or wage-led.

The Two Souls Defined

We defined the demand regime in Chapter 3 as follows:

(5.1)
$$\hat{x} = \frac{\psi_i \varphi_0 \hat{b} + \psi_g \hat{g}^* + \psi_e \hat{e} - \psi_i \varphi_3 r_k}{1 - \psi_i \varphi_2}$$
$$+ \frac{[\xi(\sigma_\pi - \sigma_w) - \psi_i \varphi_1 \theta - \psi_e \varepsilon_1]}{1 - \psi_i \varphi_2}[\hat{w} - \hat{\lambda}]$$

Equation (5.1) is the same as equation (3.15). Demand-led output growth thus depends on five factors:

(i) the growth of autonomous investment $\hat{b}$
(ii) the growth of net public current expenditure $\hat{g}^*$
(iii) the growth of autonomous exports $\hat{e}_0$
(iv) the real interest rate r_k
(v) the growth rate of real unit labor cost $\hat{v} = \hat{w} - \hat{\lambda}$

Let

$$\Theta = \frac{\psi_i \varphi_0 \hat{b} + \psi_g \hat{g}^* + \psi_e \hat{e} - \psi_i \varphi_3 r_k}{1 - \psi_i \varphi_2}$$

and

$$C = \frac{[\xi(\sigma_\pi - \sigma_w) - \psi_i \varphi_1 \theta - \psi_e \varepsilon_1]}{1 - \psi_i \varphi_2}.$$

Then (5.1) becomes

(5.2) $$\hat{x} = \Theta + C[\hat{w} - \hat{\lambda}]$$

where C captures the two souls of aggregate demand. To see this, let us determine the impact of a change in unit labor cost growth $\hat{v} = \hat{w} - \hat{\lambda}$ on demand growth, or:

(5.3) $$\frac{d\hat{x}}{d\hat{v}} = C = \frac{[\xi(\sigma_\pi - \sigma_w) - \psi_i \varphi_1 \theta - \psi_e \varepsilon_1]}{1 - \psi_i \varphi_2}$$

The sign of equation (5.3), that is, the sign of coefficient C, is not clear a priori, because any excess of real wage growth over labor productivity growth (i.e., $\hat{v} > 0$ or $\hat{w} > \hat{\lambda}$) has two opposing effects on output growth. On one hand, it increases the size of the multiplier, because it entails a redistribution of income from profits toward wage income and a consequent decline in the aggregate savings propensity (because $\sigma_w < \sigma_\pi$). But on the other hand, any such excess reduces investment growth (via the profit share elasticity ϕ_1) and export growth (via the export cost elasticity ε_1), and consequently it will lower output growth. Accordingly, the total effect on demand growth of a rise in unit labor cost growth given by equation (5.2) can be additively decomposed into three components:

(5.4) $\qquad +\dfrac{\xi(\sigma_\pi - \sigma_w)}{1 - \psi_i \varphi_2}$: a *positive* impact on consumption growth

(5.5) $\qquad -\dfrac{\psi_i \varphi_1 \theta}{1 - \psi_i \varphi_2}$: a *negative* effect on investment growth (via the profit share)

(5.6) $\qquad -\dfrac{\psi_e \varepsilon_1}{1 - \psi_i \varphi_2}$: a *negative* effect on export growth (via unit labor costs)

If impact (5.4) is larger in absolute terms than the sum of impacts (5.5) and (5.6), then $(d\hat{x}/d\hat{v})$ is positive ($C > 0$) and aggregate demand is wage-led. On the other hand, if consumption growth impact (5.3) is smaller in absolute terms than the sum of effects (5.4) and (5.5), $(d\hat{x}/d\hat{v})$ is negative ($C < 0$) and demand growth is profit-led. In the latter case, higher labor cost growth reduces demand and output growth—because the consequent fall in profits and investments as well as exports is larger than the stimulus imparted to consumption.

Distribution and Consumption Growth

The first step in our empirical investigation of the demand regime is to determine if the distribution of income between wages and profits affects the level of savings and hence consumption. We start by noting that the classical assumption that the savings rate out of wages is smaller than the savings rate out of profit income, or $\sigma_w < \sigma_\pi$, is generally in line with available empirical evidence. Amit Bhaduri and Stephen Marglin (1990), for instance, find an average value for $(\sigma_\pi - \sigma_w)$ of 0.37 for a sample of sixteen OECD countries (1960–1985), and the average estimate of $(\sigma_\pi - \sigma_w)$ for France, Germany, Japan, the United Kingdom, and the United States by Samuel Bowles and Robert Boyer (1995) is 0.46. Eckhard Hein and Lena Vogel (2008) report a statistically significant average saving differential for France, Germany, the Netherlands, the United Kingdom, and the United States during 1960–2005 of 0.43. Bowles and Boyer (1995, 152) conclude: "Among all but economists, the proposition that the rich save a larger fraction of their income has come to be taken as a sociological fact of life requiring little explanation."

Following Bowles and Boyer, our estimates of the effect of income distribution on savings are based on a transformation of the following identity for real private savings s:

$$(5.7) \qquad s = [\sigma_w v + \sigma_\pi \pi] x$$

Recall that $v = 1 - \pi$, so we can write the aggregate savings propensity ($\sigma = s/x$) as

$$(5.8) \qquad \sigma = s/x = \sigma_w + (\sigma_\pi - \sigma_w) \pi$$

As argued by Bowles and Boyer, (5.8) is not a behavioral equation but rather it is a way of summarizing the empirical relationship between aggregate savings and the distribution of income under given institutional conditions. Our estimates of (5.8) appear in Table 5.2 for our twelve OECD countries. We have limited our investigation to estimating the effects of only variables identified in our model and have deliberately refrained from determining the influence of other variables.

The estimated parameters are consistent with the two-propensity hypothesis that $\sigma_W < \sigma_\pi$ (i.e., the propensity to save out of wage income is less than the propensity to save out of profit income), and the overall fit of the equations is high. Estimates of $(\sigma_\pi - \sigma_W)$ vary between 0.6 (Denmark) and 0.22 (the United States); the average value of our estimates of $(\sigma_\pi - \sigma_W)$ is 0.41, which is in line with earlier estimates mentioned above. It is useful to compare our country-specific findings with the country findings by Hein and Vogel (2008), whose period of analysis (1960–2005) is much the same as ours. Hein and Vogel's estimates for Germany (0.41), the Netherlands (0.56), and the United Kingdom (0.45) are similar to our results: 0.39, 0.57, and 0.43, respectively. Our estimates for France (0.30) and the United States (0.22) are somewhat lower than their savings differentials of 0.44 and 0.30, respectively, but still comparable. With these several results, we can generally confirm the plausibility of our findings, which suggest quite a substantial influence of the functional distribution of income on the savings rate. A redistribution from profits to wages therefore leads to a significant increase in consumption demand in the OECD countries. The mechanism underlying the wage-led aggregate demand regime is thus strongly supported.

Investment Growth and the Profit Share

The second channel through which real wage growth affects aggregate demand is through profitability and investment, as indicated by equation (5.5).

Table 5.2. Estimated savings propensities: twelve OECD economies (1960–2000)

Country	σ_w	$(\sigma_\pi - \sigma_w)$	Trend	$\bar{R}^2$	F	DW	Period
OLS estimates							
Finland	0.03 (1.72)**	0.58 (8.74)***	−0.12 (4.68)***	0.71	49.1 (0.000)	1.73	1960–2000
France	0.10 (1.74)**	0.30 (2.06)**		0.82	140.1 (0.000)	1.96	1970–2000
Germany	0.09 (1.54)*	0.39 (2.68)***		0.76	63.2 (0.000)	2.05	1960–2000
Italy	0.17 (1.74)**	0.35 (1.92)**		0.74	59.2 (0.000)	2.10	1960–2000
Japan	0.12 (2.55)***	0.38 (3.91)***		0.80	161.4 (0.000)	1.85	1960–2000
Netherlands	0.15 (3.75)***	0.57 (4.75)***	−0.22 (5.16)***	0.83	79.4 (0.000)	1.90	1969–2000
Spain	0.12 (1.57)*	0.26 (4.65)***		0.96	401.7 (0.000)	1.62	1964–2000
Sweden							
U.S.	0.12 (1.62)*	0.22 (2.70)***		0.77	68.8 (0.000)	2.15	1960–2000

(continued)

Table 5.2. *(continued)*

Log likelihood	σ_w	$(\sigma_\pi - \sigma_w)$	AR(1)	AR(2)	Wald χ^2	Log likelihood	Period
Belgium	0.16	0.34	0.64		15.0	−40.7	1970–2000
	(1.76)*	(1.56)	(3.82)***		(0.001)		
Denmark	0.02	0.60	1.29	−0.48	151.1	−48.5	1970–2000
	(0.31)	(3.06)**	(6.41)***	(2.02)**	(0.000)		
Sweden	0.05	0.44	1.29	−0.47	216.4	−76.3	1960–2000
	(0.77)	(2.17)**	(9.07)***	(3.30)***	(0.000)		
U.K.	0.04	0.43	1.21	−0.46	75.3	−62.6	1960–2000
	(0.71)	(2.89)***	(7.37)***	(2.89)***	(0.000)		
Mean		0.41					
Standard deviation		0.13					

Notes:

a. The dependent variable is gross domestic savings divided by gross domestic product (at factor cost).

b. The columns headed σ_w and $(\sigma_\pi - \sigma_w)$ are the estimated constant and coefficient of the profit share π in equation (18).

c. Figures in parentheses are t-statistics. *, **, and *** denote statistical significance at 10%, 5%, and 1%, respectively.

d. Equations for most countries are estimated using the Cochrane-Orcutt AR (1) method. The equations for Belgium, Denmark, Sweden, and the United Kingdom are estimated using ARIMA correcting for first- and second-order autocorrelation.

e. The equation for Germany was estimated including a dummy variable for the year 1990 (the German unification); the estimated coefficient takes a value of −1.75 ($t = 2.32$).

f. AR(1) and AR(2) are first-order and second-order autoregressive processes to correct for autocorrelation in the error term.

The profit-driven model of investment has generated much debate and little consensus among economists. The profit-driven investment argument holds that

> firms' investment decisions are influenced by future profits and by the firms' liquidity, both of which co-vary with current profits. Additionally, profitability may favorably influence firms' willingness to build new capacity in the face of uncertain product demand conditions. Other influences on investment typically included in profit-driven models are the level of expected future demand as measured by current capacity utilization or an accelerator term and the cost of borrowing. (Bowles and Boyer 1995, 155)

Typically, measures of expected future demand dominate other independent variables in econometric studies of aggregate investment, but, as has been pointed out in a major review of the literature by Glyn (1997), the available evidence consistently shows that profitability plays an important role, particularly in the slowing down of investment growth after 1973 (see also Bhaskar and Glyn 1995). Gordon (1995), based on quarterly data for U.S. nonresidential investment during the period from the fourth quarter of 1955 to the second quarter to 1989, obtained a value of about 0.73 for our coefficient φ_1, meaning that a 1 percentage point rise in profitability is associated with an increase in investment of 0.73 percentage points. That "profits have been an important influence on investment is buttressed by a number of time-series studies of OECD investment trends. . . . When investment is regressed on profitability alone (or with only a lagged dependent variable added), profitability is almost always significant," concluded Glyn (1997, 597). The profit sensitivity of investment has been confirmed by studies more recent than Glyn's. For example, using data pooled for eighteen OECD countries over thirty-six years (1960–1996), Alberto Alesina et al. (2002) find a significant and high profit sensitivity of investment: an increase in profitability by 1 percentage point would, according to their estimates, lead to a rise in investment of about 0.9 percentage points. Likewise, using quarterly aggregate U.K. manufacturing data over a twenty-eight-year period (1972–1999) while controlling for capacity utilization and demand uncertainty, Ciaran Driver, Paul Temple, and Giovanni Urga (2005) find a profit-investment elasticity of 0.65–0.78; their result is in line with findings by Alan Carruth, Andy Dickerson, and Andrew Henley (2000) that the short-run profit-investment elasticity for U.K. aggregate investment is about 0.17, while the corresponding long-run elasticity is about 0.85 (their period of analysis is from the third quarter of 1964 to the fourth quarter of 1995).

We estimated the investment equation with variables expressed in logarithms, thus avoiding spurious correlations between variables with common trends. We have checked that the transformation of the original level variables in growth rates stabilizes their means and variances through time (i.e., the variables are stationary), so OLS estimation indeed can be used. To avoid simultaneity, the profit share π and aggregate demand x are introduced with a one-year lag. Specifically, we estimated the following investment demand function in logarithmic form:

(5.9) $\log (i/x) = \Xi + \varphi_1 \log \pi + (\varphi_2 - 1) \log x$

where (i/x) is the ratio of gross fixed investment to GDP. Using this ratio means that we assume that investment and GDP normally grow in tandem (i.e., a 1 percentage point increase in GDP growth is associated with a 1 percentage point increase in investment growth, keeping the ratio unchanged); any deviation from this norm would be captured by the coefficient $(\varphi_2 - 1)$ being statistically significantly different from zero. If $(\varphi_2 - 1) > 0$, demand growth has strong accelerator effects on investment growth; if $(\varphi_2 - 1) < 0$, the accelerator effect is rather weak. We finally note that differentiation of equation (5.9) with respect to time yields the investment growth equation (3.12) of Chapter 3.

The regression results appear in Table 5.3. Only the equation for the Netherlands is quite unsatisfactory, indicating little explanatory power. But the coefficient of the profit share is found to be statistically significant (at 5 percent) and positive, taking a value of 0.47, which is consistent with earlier, more satisfactory results by Naastepad (2006), who—using data from a different source but for the same period, 1960–2000—obtains a coefficient of 0.39. For the other countries, the coefficients of π have the expected sign and are statistically significant at the 5 percent level, except for Spain; the profit-investment coefficient for Spain is significant at the 10 percent level. The mean of the country-specific profit elasticities is 0.43, which is higher than the average estimate of 0.28 for France, Germany, Japan, the United Kingdom, and the United States for 1953–1987 by Bowles and Boyer (1995). It is about half of the estimate of 0.9 for eighteen OECD countries by Alesina et al. (2002), which appears to be on the high side compared to other cross-country studies. Our average profit sensitivity of investment is, for example, similar to Glyn's (1997) estimate of 0.44 for twelve OECD countries during the years 1973–1992.

Turning to the country-specific findings, our estimate of the profit sensitivity of investment for the Netherlands (0.47) is close to the estimated value of 0.34 by Hein and Vogel (2008) for the period from 1970 to 2005. We find a coefficient value for the United Kingdom of 0.54, which is close to

Table 5.3. Estimated investment growth equations: twelve OECD economies (1960–2000)

Country	Constant	$\log^{\pi_{-1}}$	$\log^{x_{-1}}$	Trend	$\bar{R}^2$	F	DW
OLS estimates							
Belgium	0.23	0.62	0.02			3,863.7	1.97
	(0.27)	(1.77)*	(0.22)		0.95	(0.000)	
Germany	−1.12	0.56	0.27	−0.006		13.7	1.43
	(−0.73)	(3.07)***	(1.13)	(−2.35)**	0.50	(0.000)	
Japan	−0.04	0.60	0.06			6.2	1.60
	(−0.05)	(3.52)***	(0.75)		0.22	(0.005)	
Netherlands	−0.62	0.47	0.24	−0.007		2.2	1.62
	(−0.32)	(1.79)**	(0.67)	(−1.60)*	0.08	(0.110)	
Sweden	−2.74	0.23	0.60	−0.002		956.6	1.45
	(2.09)**	(2.50)***	(2.90)***	(−3.07)***	0.98	(0.000)	
U.K.	−1.36	0.54	0.30			11.2	1.61
	(−2.27)**	(2.11)**	(2.47)***		0.47	(0.001)	

(continued)

Table 5.3. (*continued*)

Log likelihood	Constant	$\log^{\pi_{-1}}$	$\log^{x_{-1}}$	Dummy	AR(1)	AR(2)	Wald χ^2	Log likelihood
Denmark	-0.15 (-0.15)	0.64 (2.20)**	0.08 (0.53)	0.04 (4.44)***	1.33 (7.62)***	-0.49 (-2.69)***	254.2	96.0
Finland	2.36 (2.19)**	0.34 (1.36)	-0.31 (1.88)*		1.49 (12.48)***	-0.65 (-4.69)***	429.7	97.9
France	1.49 (3.52)***	0.29 (2.21)**	-0.11 (2.24)**		1.32 (7.77)***	-0.65 (-4.79)***	115.8	111.3
Italy	0.68 (0.50)	0.50 (1.69)**	-0.03 (-0.16)		1.23 (8.15)***	-0.60 (-4.22)***	216.5	119.6
Spain		0.26 (1.57)*	0.16 (3.20)***		1.45 (9.85)***	-0.61 (-4.37)***	7,104.0	110.7
U.S.	-0.32 (-0.62)	0.48 (1.93)**	0.12 (1.72)**		1.25 (7.30)***	-0.51 (-2.31)**	169.9	116.8
Mean		0.43						
Standard deviation		0.20						

Notes:

a. The period of estimation is 1960–2000, except for France (1967–2000) and the United Kingdom (1976–2000). The dependent variable is the logarithm of the ratio of gross domestic fixed investment to GDP. Equations for Belgium, Germany, Japan, the Netherlands, Sweden, and the United Kingdom are estimated using Cochrane-Orcutt AR (1). The equations for Denmark, Finland, France, Italy, Spain, and the United States are estimated using ARIMA (correcting for first- and second-order autocorrelation). For Denmark we included a time dummy for the years 1964 and 1976 in the regression.

b. Figures in parentheses are *t*-statistics (or, in the case of ARIMA estimations, *z*-statistics). *, **, and *** denote statistical significance at 10%, 5%, and 1%, respectively.

c. *F* is the *F*-statistic and the figure in parentheses is the associated probability of observing an *F*-statistic that large or larger. DW is the transformed Durbin-Watson statistic.

d. $\log^{\pi_{-1}}$ = the one-period lagged logarithm of the profit share; $\log^{x_{-1}}$ = one-period lagged log of real GDP at market prices.

e. AR(1) and AR(2) are first-order and second-order autoregressive processes to correct for autocorrelation in the error term.

Driver, Temple, and Urga's (2005) value of 0.65–0.78 and falls within the range of values (0.17–0.85) reported by Carruth, Dickerson, and Henley (2000) and the range of values (0.38–0.79) reported by Bond and coauthors (2003). Our coefficient estimate for France is 0.29—again very close to the value of 0.22 found by Hein and Vogel (2005) and of 0.25 found by Bowles and Boyer (1995), but considerably higher than the 0.09 obtained by Bond, Elston, and coauthors (2003), who use firm-level data for the years from 1978 to 1989. Our estimate of 0.56 for Germany is higher than the estimate (of 0.33) by Bowles and Boyer (1995), but far lower than the estimate of 1 by Pugh (1998). And our coefficient for Japan (0.60) is similar to the influence (0.53) found by Bowles and Boyer (1995). Finally, our estimated coefficient value for the United States, 0.48, is lower than the coefficient (0.73) found by Gordon (1995); the difference is likely caused by the difference in the data periods.[7]

Turning to the impact on investment of demand, we find that demand growth has a significant effect on investment growth, taking a value that is not statistically significantly different from unity for Belgium, Denmark, Germany, Japan, the Netherlands, and Italy. This can be concluded from the fact that the coefficient $(1 - \varphi_2)$ is not statistically significantly different from zero in these regressions. Its impact is found to be larger than unity in Spain, Sweden, the United Kingdom, and the United States and less than proportional for Finland and France. If $(\varphi_2 - 1) > 0$, as for instance is true for Sweden, where we find $(\varphi_2 - 1) = 0.6$, then the elasticity of investment with respect to demand growth (φ_2) takes a value of 1.6. This means that a change in demand growth become cumulative, because it leads to higher investment growth, and therefore a second round of demand growth. This accelerator effect is captured in equations (5.4) to (5.6) by the multiplier term $1/(1 - \psi_i \varphi_2)$; a higher φ_2 implies that a change in demand has a larger multiplier effect on demand and output growth. On the other hand, if $(\varphi_2 - 1) < 0$, as for France, where $(\varphi_2 - 1) = -0.11$, the elasticity of investment with respect to demand growth φ_2 has a value of 0.89. Here the accelerator effect, expressed by $1/(1 - \psi_i \varphi_2)$, is less strong.

Export Growth and Unit Labor Costs

The third channel through which the real wage affects aggregate demand is through relative unit labor costs, as in equation (5.6). We must emphasize that this export effect can materialize only at the level of individual national economies; in the aggregate, because the world economy is closed, this effect must disappear. What we have at hand here is a good example of what Keynes called a fallacy of composition: it would be wrong to infer that something is true of the whole (i.e., the global economy) from the fact that it is true of some part of the whole (a specific country). This implies that if we were to consider the OECD as a whole, the export effect surely would be diminished (given that many OECD countries moderated wage growth simultaneously) and, in consequence, our analysis is likely to overstate the importance of the export effect. Keeping this important caveat in mind, we now investigate the export effect at the national level of our twelve OECD countries.

We start by noting that there is a strong consensus in the literature that cost competitiveness matters for the export performance of OECD countries, but only in a very modest way. William Milberg and Ellen Houston (2005, 140), analyzing aggregate export growth for seventeen OECD countries during the years from 1975 to 1995, conclude that "among OECD countries relative unit labor costs are often not statistically significant in explaining variations in international competitiveness over time." Hein and Vogel (2008) find zero effects of a change in unit labor costs on net exports in France, Germany, the United Kingdom, and the United States (during 1960–2005). A recent analysis by the European Commission (2010) finds that Germany's massive export boom over the period from 1999 to 2010 is almost completely due to the growth of its export markets, whereas the contribution of more competitive pricing to German export growth is barely noticeable. Germany specializes in products and services that the more dynamic emerging economies such as Brazil, China, and India are most eager to buy (e.g., machinery, telecom equipment, transport infrastructures, luxury automobiles, etc.). This type of specialization pattern has the effect of making the demand for Germany's exports price-inelastic; it is embodied technical know-how and quality that count (Janssen 2011).

Not surprisingly, therefore, a sophisticated econometric analysis of the impact of cost competitiveness using industry-level data for fourteen OECD countries during 1970–1992 finds a long-run elasticity of exports with respect to cost of only −0.26 (Carlin, Glyn, and van Reenen 2001). This means that an increase in unit labor cost growth of 1 percentage point would reduce export volume growth by 0.26 percentage points. But if instead data for *total* manufacturing are used, the long-run elasticity between exports and relative unit labor costs is found to be only −0.03, insignificantly different from zero.

There is no clear relationship for *the manufacturing sector as a whole* between change in export market share and in cost competitiveness. No country is observed with the combination of declining relative costs and increasing export market share. Indeed . . . there appears to be a tendency for countries with rising relative costs to have increased their market shares for manufacturing as a whole. (Carlin, Glyn, and van Reenen 2001, 135–136; emphasis added)

The finding that export market shares (export growth rates) are higher for countries experiencing increasing relative unit labor costs may appear remarkable, because traditionally we are used to thinking of costs and prices as being the most important factors in international competition. But appearances are deceptive. Nicholas Kaldor (1978) was the first to point out that countries with the fastest improvement in export performance were those with the fastest increases in costs—and so the "Kaldor paradox" was born.[8] The reason for the paradox is that other factors, including differences across countries in technological capabilities, investment, innovative effort, the nature of labor relations, and the extent of social protection, are often more important than costs.[9] Kaldor, as usual, puts it best himself:

The customary statistical measures of "competitiveness" . . . are arbitrary and not an adequate indicator of a country's true competitive position . . . a rise in export unit values may therefore signify no more than that a country is trading "up-market," i.e. selling machinery of higher quality, while the countries with falling export values are trading "down-market" selling machinery of the more primitive kind. (1978, 106)

To estimate the long-run elasticity of exports and unit labor cost growth $\hat{v}$, or coefficient ε_1 in equation (5.6), we used the following export growth equation:

$$(5.10) \qquad \hat{e} = \hat{e}_0 wtgrowth - \varepsilon_1 \hat{v}$$

We do not expect to find high values (in absolute terms) for the long-run export–unit labor cost elasticity ε_1. Table 5.4 presents the regression results for the twelve countries for the period from 1960 to 2000. Overall, the results are consistent with prior expectations. The general fit of the equation is high (the adjusted R^2 is about 0.8). For Belgium, Finland, France, Germany, the Netherlands, and the United States, the coefficient of world trade growth *wtgrowth* takes a (statistically significant at 1 percent) value that is not significantly different from unity; hence, exports of these countries tend to grow in line with world trade. The elasticity of exports with respect to world trade is (statistically significantly) larger than unity for Italy, Spain, and especially Japan, and it is below unity for Denmark, Sweden, and the United

Table 5.4. Estimated export growth equations: twelve OECD economies (1960–2000)

Country	wtgrowth	$\hat{\nu}$	Trend	$\bar{R}^2$	F	DW	Estimates by Carlin, Glyn, and van Reenen (2001)
Belgium	1.09 (13.45)***	−0.04 (−1.03)		0.88	99.1 (0.000)	1.63	+0.041 (0.46)
Denmark	0.75 (12.53)***	−0.06 (−1.59)*		0.80	80.9 (0.000)	1.89	+0.224 (2.07)**
Finland	0.94 (8.71)***	−0.26 (−3.78)***		0.71	51.3 (0.000)	1.64	−0.356 (−1.61)*
France	1.05 (21.32)***	−0.06 (−1.74)**		0.92	236.1 (0.000)	1.93	+0.172 (1.76)**
Germany	0.99 (14.81)***	−0.12 (−2.63)***		0.84	110.3 (0.000)	1.75	−0.124 (−0.77)
Italy	1.17 (8.87)***	−0.12 (−2.01)**	−0.06 (−1.49)*	0.78	47.3 (0.000)	1.91	−0.033 (−0.14)
Japan	1.88 (9.96)***	−0.23 (−2.23)**	−0.15 (−2.73)***	0.76	44.3 (0.000)	1.72	−0.400 (−1.96)**
Netherlands	0.95 (15.62)***	−0.003 (−0.08)		0.86	123.0 (0.000)	1.90	+0.164 (1.31)*

Spain	1.26 (11.43)***	-0.16 (-2.45)***	0.78	73.3 (0.000)	2.24	-0.670 (-14.25)***
Sweden	0.89 (11.97)***	-0.16 (-3.19)***	0.79	78.1 (0.000)	1.54	-0.246 (-2.44)***
U.K.	0.72 (12.98)***	-0.12 (-2.78)***	0.83	96.7 (0.000)	1.86	-0.287 (-2.16)**
U.S.	1.09 (9.35)***	0.16 (0.35)	0.69	44.8 (0.000)	1.95	
Mean	1.07	-0.10				-0.14
Standard deviation	0.30	0.11				0.28

Notes:

a. The period of estimation is 1960–2000. The dependent variable is the annual growth rate of real exports. Equations for all countries were estimated using Cochrane-Orcutt AR (1). The equations for Japan and the United Kingdom were estimated using the one-period lagged growth rate of unit labor cost.

b. Figures in parentheses are t-statistics. *, **, and *** denote statistical significance at 10%, 5%, and 1%, respectively.

c. F is the F-statistic and the figure in parentheses is the associated probability of observing an F-statistic that large or larger. DW is the transformed Durbin-Watson statistic.

d. *wtgrowth* = the growth rate of the volume of world trade; $\dot{p}$ = the growth rate of relative unit labor cost.

e. The estimates by Carlin, Glyn, and van Reenen (2001) are based on countrywise regressions using data pooled across 12 major manufacturing industries during 1970–1992.

Kingdom—in the latter case indicating a long-run loss of world export market share.[10]

A majority of the estimated coefficients of relative unit labor cost (eight out of twelve coefficients) is negative and significant at the 5 percent (or 1 percent) level. The mean of the country-specific elasticities is -0.10, which is close to the mean elasticity of -0.14 across eleven of the twelve country-specific elasticities obtained by Carlin, Glyn, and van Reenen (2001). Our results for Belgium and Germany are consistent with those of Carlin et al., and in the case of Finland, Japan, Sweden, and the United Kingdom we find a somewhat smaller (in absolute terms) cost sensitivity. Our results of low wage-cost sensitivity of exports for France, Germany, the United Kingdom, and the United States are comparable with findings by Hein and Vogel (2008).[11] But for Denmark and France we obtain a negative cost elasticity (rather than a positive one, as by Carlin et al.), and the Netherlands and the United States have a statistically insignificant cost elasticity, suggesting negligible price sensitivity of their exports.[12]

Demand Regimes in Twelve OECD Countries

Depending on the relative size (in absolute terms) of these three effects, the total effect of a 1 percentage point rise in real wage growth—given by equation (5.3)—may be positive or negative. Estimates of these three effects as well as the total effect appear in Table 5.5 for each of the twelve economies in question.

We find that the redistribution from profits to wages, implied by a rise in real wage growth of 1 percentage point, raises consumption growth, thereby augmenting demand growth by on average 1.2 percentage points. But country-specific effects vary considerably (the standard deviation is 0.6 percentage points). In Belgium and the Netherlands, for example, a rise in real wage growth of 1 percentage point is associated with a rise in demand growth of only 0.30–0.53 percentage points. This below-average effect is due to the fact that of the twelve countries in our sample, the Belgian and Dutch economies are the ones that are the most open to international trade; as a consequence, a large proportion of the demand stimulus, implied by the income redistribution, leaks abroad. Italy is another country where the impact of increased real wage growth is limited. This is not so much due to the openness of the Italian economy as to the fact that of the twelve countries, Italy has the lowest wage share v; as a result, the demand-augmenting impact of a redistribution of income is smaller in Italy than elsewhere (other variables remaining constant).[13] The impact on demand through consumption is comparatively large in Japan (more than two standard deviations above the average), Sweden, and the United States: a 1 percentage point increase in

Table 5.5. The effect of an increase in real wage growth (by 1 percentage point) on aggregate demand growth

	Impact through (in percentage growth rates):				Nature of demand regime
	Consumption growth 1	Investment growth 2	Export growth 3	Total effect 4	5
Belgium	0.30	−0.29	negligible	±0.0	undefined
Denmark	1.19	−0.75	−0.07	0.37	wage-led
Finland	0.92	negligible	−0.20	0.72	strongly wage-led
France	0.83	−0.45	−0.06	0.32	wage-led
Germany	0.98	−0.80	−0.13	0.06	wage-led
Italy	0.55	−0.36	−0.08	0.12	wage-led
Japan	2.62	−2.84	−0.33	−0.55	profit-led
Netherlands	0.53	−0.25	negligible	0.28	wage-led
Spain	0.94	−0.46	−0.19	0.28	wage-led
Sweden	2.03	−0.67	−0.32	1.04	strongly wage-led
U.K.	1.43	−0.97	−0.15	0.31	wage-led
U.S.	1.75	−1.98	negligible	−0.23	profit-led
Mean	1.16	−0.84	−0.15	0.23	
Standard deviation	0.63	0.79	0.10	0.37	

Sources: Authors' estimates; the period of estimation is 1960–2000.

Notes: How do our results compare to those of other studies? Stockhammer, Onaran, and Ederer (2009) find the euro area countries (1960–2004), when taken together, to be wage-led, and Hein and Vogel's (2007) results indicate that France and Germany are wage-led economies (1960–2005). Bowles and Boyer (1995) also find that Japan is profit-led and the United Kingdom is wage-led. According to Naastepad (2006) and Tavani, Flaschel, and Taylor (2011), the Dutch economy is wage-led. Equally in line with our results for the United States, Gordon (1995), using data for the period 1955–1988, Barbosa-Filho and Taylor (2006), based on data for 1948–2002, and Tavani, Flaschel, and Taylor (2011) for the period 1956–2004, all find the United States to be profit-led. But in deviation from our results, Hein and Vogel (1995) find the United States to be wage-led and the Netherlands to be profit-led. Their results for the United States hinge on their findings that changes in the profit share do not affect investment, which appears unrealistic in view of the considerable effects reported in the literature. Hein and Vogel's results for the Netherlands follow mostly from their findings that Dutch export growth will rise significantly when there is a decline in real wage growth (a rise in profit share growth); this finding is at odds with findings by Carlin, Glyn, and van Reenen (2001), see Table 5.4 in this volume.

real wage growth raises aggregate demand and GDP growth by 2.6, 2, and 1.8 percentage points, respectively. For Japan and the United States, these significant impacts occur mainly because the import leakages in these countries are small (their average import-to-GDP ratios being less than 10 percent). Real wage growth has a much larger impact on consumption and GDP growth in Sweden, mainly because of bigger income-demand accelerator effects on investment in Sweden; in terms of equation (5.3), this is reflected in a relatively large accelerator coefficient ϕ_2 (see Table 5.3). The same holds true for the United Kingdom: the rise in consumption and aggregate demand, triggered by the income redistribution, raises investment demand, thus further augmenting aggregate demand growth.

The second column of Table 5.5 shows that in all countries except Finland, higher real wage growth reduces demand and GDP growth. On average, a rise in real wage growth (by 1 percentage point) reduces OECD demand growth by 0.8 percentage points because it reduces profitability and hence investment. But this average conceals a wide variability in the strength of this profitability-investment-growth nexus, as is shown by the value of the standard deviation (0.79). In fact, the profitability-investment-growth nexus is found to be particularly strong in Japan, Britain, and the United States, whereas it is relatively weak in the EC countries. The average impact of a 1 percentage point rise in real wage growth on demand growth through reduced profits and investment is −0.48 percentage points for the nine EC countries (with a standard deviation of 0.21), whereas its average impact on growth in Japan, the United Kingdom, and the United States is −1.93 percentage points (standard deviation 0.94). The difference between these two groups of countries in the strength of the profitability-investment-growth nexus is a reflection of systemic differences. Profitability is less important in the bank-based financial systems of the EC countries, and in Germany in particular, because firms in these countries fund their activities mostly from retained earnings or by long-term bank loans (Hall and Soskice 2001; Vitols 2001); this explains their willingness to make long-term investments and to accept lower returns on capital (Dore, Lazonick, and O'Sullivan 1999). In contrast, profitability is more important in the stock-market-based financial systems of the United Kingdom and the United States. Firms in these countries tend to rely more heavily on bond and equity markets for external finance, and the terms on which they can secure finance are heavily dependent on their valuation in equity markets, which in turn depends significantly on current profitability (Hall and Soskice 2001). We will say more about this systemic difference below, when dealing with the "third soul" of OECD capitalism.

A word must be said about Japan, which is quite different from the other OECD countries in our sample when it comes to the profit sensitivity of investment. Japan's very strong profit-investment nexus must be attributed to East Asia's corporate financing system. This system—with heavy reliance on long-term bank loans from state development banks (not private banks), a relatively insignificant role for the stock market, and controlling shares in the hands of other firms within the group *(keiretsu)* or close business relations—has allowed firms to retain an unusually high proportion of their profits instead of paying dividends (Singh 1998; Storm and Naastepad 2005a). As a result, and given the overall growth orientation of the Japanese economy, Japan's investment-to-GDP ratio is by far the highest of all countries in our sample, which through the multiplier-adjusted investment share ψ_i augments through investment growth the impact of a real wage change on output growth.

In column 3 of Table 5.5 appears the impact of real wage growth on demand growth through its effect on cost competitiveness. In line with our findings (in Table 5.4) that the cost sensitivity of exports is rather small, the effects on demand of a 1 percentage point rise in real wage growth (through export demand) turn out to be small as well: on average, aggregate demand growth is found to decline by only 0.15 percentage points. Japan and Sweden show the highest sensitivity to cost competition, with demand growth declining by about 0.3 percentage points; in contrast, changes in cost competitiveness have hardly any impact on demand growth in France and Italy and no impact whatsoever in Belgium, the Netherlands, and the United States.

Looking at the consumption, investment, and export growth effects combined gives us an indication of the nature of the demand regime of the country concerned. It can be seen that the combined effects of a real wage growth increase on demand is positive in France, Germany, Italy, the Netherlands, Spain, and the United Kingdom; these countries therefore exhibit a wage-led aggregate demand regime. The total effect is negative in Japan and the United States, indicating that their demand regimes are profit-led. It is striking that all EU economies (including the United Kingdom's) are wage-led, whereas the two non-European OECD economies turn out to be profit-led. The main cause of this difference is systemic and, as we have seen, lies in the much stronger profitability-investment-growth nexus in Japan and the United States.

Finally, we must remark that for some countries, notably Belgium, Germany, and Italy, the magnitude of C is close to zero. This being the case, the nature of the demand regime may change—shifting from wage-led to profit-led—in response to small changes in the estimated model parameters. Therefore, in these cases, the conclusion that the demand regime is wage-led remains a cautious one—we are back to Figure 3.6, in which the demand regime is a horizontal curve. A decline in wage growth does not affect output growth, but it raises employment growth by depressing labor productivity growth (indicated by the leftward shift of the productivity regime). Wage restraint thus reduces unemployment in Belgium, Germany, and Italy, but it does so by raising the labor intensity of growth (and retarding technological progress), not by raising the rate of growth.

For the other countries, the magnitude of C is more significantly different from zero. It is clear from Table 5.5 that increased profitability, to be achieved by means of real wage restraint in conjunction with a more general deregulation of labor markets, is not a necessary condition to improve the long-run macroeconomic performance of the OECD countries. Seven out of the twelve OECD economies under investigation are found to be significantly wage-led, which implies that aggregate demand growth will *decline*, not rise, in response to the orthodox policy recommendation of real wage growth restraint. The relevant illustrations here are Figures 3.4 and 3.5, portraying strong and weak wage-led demand regimes. The higher the value of C, the larger the shift in the demand regime curve when there is a change in real wage growth. Real wage growth restraint reduces productivity growth, which (keeping other factors constant) will raise employment, but it reduces demand growth, which reduces employment growth.

Remarkably, in the case of Sweden, where $C > 1$, a reduction in real wage growth by 1 percentage point initially forces down output growth by more than 1 percentage point; however, labor productivity is also forced down, which has additional impacts on output growth. Using reduced-form equation (3.28), and if we assume that the Kaldor-Verdoorn coefficient $\beta_1 = 0.45$ and the coefficient of wage-cost-induced technological progress $\beta_2 = 0.29$, we estimate that Swedish equilibrium output growth will decline by 0.5 percentage points.[14] Swedish productivity growth also declines due to reduced wage growth, also by 0.5 percentage points, as we can calculate from equation (3.29). This means that Swedish unemployment is not affected by real wage restraint—the non-NAIRUvian outcome depicted by Figure 3.4. Roughly the same conclusion holds for Finland, where $C = 0.72$; in Finland, a 1 percentage point reduction in real wage growth depresses output growth by 0.39 percentage points and productivity growth by 0.46 percentage points; hence, employment growth marginally increases by 0.07 percentage points, which is not a very significant impact.

But for Denmark, France, the Netherlands, Spain, and the United Kingdom, productivity growth declines more than output growth (due to a decline in real wages), and hence employment growth is stimulated and unemployment is likely to fall. This is the weakly wage-led economy, illustrated in Figure 3.5. It cannot be emphasized often enough that even though this unemployment outcome in weakly wage-led systems appears to resemble the NAIRUvian prediction, the underlying macroeconomic changes are not the same. Here, lower wage growth reduces both demand and productivity growth, which is a low-level equilibrium, and because productivity growth declines more strongly than output growth, employment increases. But the jobs so created are not only of low productivity but also low-paid. This is capitalism where, like in Lewis Carroll's *Through the Looking-Glass*, one has to run harder all the time just to stay in the same place.[15] Not an attractive proposition, we would argue.

Demand Regimes and the Degree of Openness

It has been argued that OECD countries are becoming more profit-led due to the increased openness in trade. Bowles and Boyer (1995, 161), for instance, conclude that export and import shares of 10 percent of GDP or less support wage-led aggregate demand regimes, within which "the negative impact on profits and investment of egalitarian and solidaristic social policies are . . . attenuated by the induced increases in output." But when trade openness increases, the nature of the demand regime is likely to change from wage-led to profit-led.[16] This shift has significant implications for policy, as Amit Bhaduri and Stephen Marglin (1990, 388) explain:

> A dominant trade effect tends to make the stagnationist [wage-led] logic increasingly irrelevant in a world characterised by high trade interdependence. The left social democratic emphasis on wage-led expansion derived from the stagnationist logic may be given up in the pursuit of export surplus by following restrictive macroeconomic policies to keep down real wages (and inflation) for greater international price competitiveness.

In such an open and (as the argument goes) therefore profit-led economy, a rise in employment can be sustained in the long run only by a fall in real wages, even if such a fall is not required to make production profitable.[17] This is exactly the same fundamental conclusion as the one drawn by Wendy Carlin and David Soskice (2006, 401) from their NAIRU model: "The fall in real wages is necessary to raise competitiveness and secure a satisfactory external account." The only (nontrivial) problem with this beggar-thy-neighbor strategy, Bhaduri and Marglin (1990, 388) add, is that it is impossible for all countries to achieve a trade surplus simultaneously—this is Keynes's fallacy of composition, mentioned earlier. "And yet, the lure of this impossibility has contributed substantially to the disintegration of the traditional social democratic ideology without any coherent alternative taking its place" (ibid.).

Whether or not the trade (or openness) effect on the wage-led or profit-led nature of the demand regime is dominant depends on the magnitude of exports' and imports' shares of GDP. Consider first the effects of a higher export share, given by an increase in coefficient ψ_e in equation (5.8). From this equation, one can see that when ψ_e is larger, the export-growth-depressing impact of an increase in real wage growth is also larger. It is therefore true, in theory, that if ψ_e is sufficiently large, the effect given by equation (5.8) may dominate the consumption effect, so the sign of the total impact of higher wage growth on demand growth in equation (5.3) is negative and the economy is profit-led. But in reality, this is not likely to happen, one reason being that the wage-cost elasticity of exports ε_1 is small or even zero; this being the case, even large increases in ψ_e do not substantially magnify the negative impact of higher wage growth on demand growth (captured by coefficient C). To illustrate this point, Figure 5.2 plots coefficient C for varying export GDP shares for Spain, Sweden, and the United Kingdom (the three wage-led countries in our sample where increased openness has had the largest impact on the demand regime). Sweden had an export-to-GDP ratio of 30.1 percent during 1960–2000; the corresponding value of C (from Table 5.5) is 1.04. We see that C does decline when the export share rises, but it would take an export share far higher than 100 percent of GDP to turn Swedish wage-led demand into profit-led demand. For more realistic increases in the export-to-GDP ratio (from 30.1 percent to, say, 45 percent), the decline in the value of C is limited (from 1.04 to about 0.89). The situa-

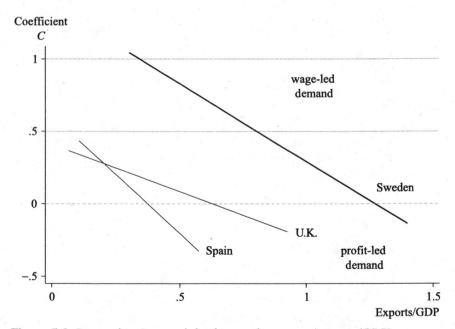

Figure 5.2. Demand regimes and the degree of openness (exports/GDP).

tion is different for Spain, however. Spain is already much less strongly wage-led than Sweden, and the value of C for Spain is only 0.28 given an average export-to-GDP ratio of 16.3 percent during 1960–2000. Figure 5.2 shows that for Spain, C declines more rapidly in response to increases in the export-to-GDP ratio and becomes zero when the export share is about 40 percent; this is still far beyond Spain's actual export-to-GDP ratio during 2000–2004, which was 27.3 percent. Higher export shares would mean that Spanish aggregate demand becomes less wage-led. Likewise, British demand becomes more weakly wage-led when the export share rises, but it is only for unrealistically high export shares (beyond 80 percent) that British demand would become profit-led.

While the Spanish, Swedish, and British demand regimes are sensitive to higher export shares, this is clearly not true for Belgium, the Netherlands, and the United States, because the exports of these three countries are not sensitive to labor costs (Table 5.4). Likewise, wage-led demand in Denmark, Finland, France, Germany, and Italy is also not very sensitive to higher export-to-GDP ratios. Japan, finally, would turn more profit-led with further increases in its export share. We note that Japan's export-to-GDP ratio is only about 10 percent, and despite its relatively limited integration in world markets, it is a strongly profit-led economy—quite unlike the generalization made by Bowles and Boyer.

Of course, we should not only look at what happens when the export share increases but also investigate the impact of higher import-to-GDP ratios. In our model, imports depend on GDP and are not affected by changes in the real wage rate (or the wage share). This reflects the fact that a large proportion of OECD imports is complementary to output and not very cost sensitive. A rise in the import share, consequently, cannot alter the nature of the demand regime (from wage-led to profit-led), but it does weaken the multiplier process—higher import-to-GDP ratios mean higher leakages from the circular flow, and hence the impact on demand growth of an increase in real wage growth becomes smaller and eventually vanishes when the import share becomes very high. This holds true for both wage-led and profit-led systems. In combination with a higher export share, a higher import share could, in principle, have a significant impact on the nature of the demand regime. This is illustrated in Table 5.6. In column 1 appear the countrywise average export and import shares during 1960–2000. Column 2 presents the corresponding value of coefficient C (which is the same as in Table 5.5). In column 3 appear the export and import shares per country for the period from 2000 to 2004. It can be seen that both export and import ratios have increased significantly for all economies except Japan. For instance, for

Table 5.6. Demand regimes and the degree of openness: twelve OECD countries

	Less globalized		More globalized	
	Export/GDP *Import/GDP* 1960–2000 1	Coefficient C 2	Export/GDP *Import/GDP* 2000–2004 3	Coefficient C 4
Belgium	0.602 *0.591*	0.00	0.823 *0.778*	−0.03
Denmark	0.324 *0.316*	0.37	0.443 *0.385*	0.28
Finland	0.276 *0.264*	0.72	0.396 *0.314*	0.56
France	0.192 *0.192*	0.32	0.275 *0.258*	0.23
Germany	0.244 *0.223*	0.06	0.356 *0.327*	0.00
Italy	0.201 *0.195*	0.12	0.274 *0.263*	0.07
Japan	0.112 *0.100*	−0.55	0.114 *0.099*	−0.57
Netherlands	0.506 *0.488*	0.28	0.631 *0.577*	0.25
Spain	0.163 *0.178*	0.28	0.290 *0.307*	0.07
Sweden	0.301 *0.282*	1.04	0.442 *0.381*	0.61
U.K.	0.245 *0.251*	0.31	0.265 *0.284*	0.28
U.S.	0.080 *0.089*	−0.23	0.103 *0.146*	−0.13

Source: Authors' calculations.
Note: Figures in italics are import/GDP ratios.

Belgium the export (import) share in 2000–2004 was 82.3 percent (77.8 percent), which is higher than the average export (import) share of 60.2 percent (59.1 percent) during the period from 1960 to 2000.

If we use these recent trade shares to calculate coefficient C, what happens? Not much for most countries, as column 4 makes clear. For Belgium, Denmark, Finland, France, Italy, Japan, the Netherlands, the United Kingdom, and the United States, there is a small quantitative change but no qualitative one. Germany's weakly wage-led coefficient C becomes zero because of the higher trade integration. The biggest changes occur for Spain and Sweden. The wage-led coefficient C of 0.28 for Spain drops to close to zero, which means that Spanish demand is only weakly wage-led if at all. For Sweden, the decline is from a value of 1.04 to a value of 0.61, which is still high relative to the other OECD countries but considerably below unity. We analyze the implications for the Keynesian visible handshake of this weakening of wage-led demand for Sweden in Chapter 7, where we deal with Europe's Nordic economies in greater detail. A fair bottom line of the above discussion is that greater openness to trade does indeed reduce the strength of a wage-led demand regime, but for the actual increases in trade integration (between the 1960s and 2000–2004) the changes in coefficient C are quite small. By implication, the effects on demand growth of more rapid real wage growth reported in Table 5.5 do stand.

The Soul of Finance

Johann Wolfgang von Goethe's "two-souls problem" has resonated with later writers. One prominent example is Charles Dickens, who was once interviewed by his Russian colleague Fyodor Dostoevsky. To him, Dickens confessed that "There were two people in him," one good, one bad. The Russian shot back, "Only two people?" (Slater 2009, 502).[18] Dostoevsky's insistence on the possibility of having more than two souls provides a pointer for the present analysis: capitalist distributive strife involves not just the two souls of labor and capital but also a third soul—that of finance. We argue that the soul of finance has a crucial influence on the two-soul struggle. Specifically, differences in financial systems between countries show up in differences in aggregate investment behavior, especially in the profit sensitivity of firms' investment demand.

Other authors—including Bhaduri and Marglin (1990), Bowles and Boyer (1995), and Hein and Vogel (2008)—have claimed that the wage sensitivity of net export growth is the crucial factor determining the nature of aggregate demand (accepting that higher real wage growth raises demand growth through higher consumption). We don't think the evidence in support of this claim is convincing: our estimates in Tables 5.5 and 5.6 suggest that increased trade openness and globalization have a fairly small impact on the demand regime. What we find instead is that the wage-led consumption growth effect, in column 1 of Table 5.5, is overruled by a very strong negative profit-led impact of higher wage growth on investment in the profit-led economies (Japan and the United States), but not in the wage-led economies. Hence, what in our view emerges from Table 5.5 is that the profit sensitivity of aggregate demand growth is key to determining whether the demand regime is wage-led or profit-led. In turn, the differences in the profit sensitivity of aggregate demand growth are related to differences in financial systems across our sample of OECD countries. This is where the soul of finance plays its role.

If we zoom in on the profit-led United States versus wage-led Europe (and neglect Japan), what comes to mind immediately is that the U.S. financial system (as well as that of the United Kingdom) is stock-market-based, while the European financial system (and especially the German system) is bank-based.[19] In the stock-market-based system of the United States and United Kingdom, share ownership is dispersed, and the monitoring of the firm takes place in public by outsiders and shareholders. Stock markets are relatively "thick" and active, and therefore an unhappy shareholder can "exit" by selling shares. U.S. and U.K. firms are strongly obliged to satisfy their many small shareholders in the short run, such as the next quarter, which is not conducive to long-term strategic investment. It also explains why dividend payouts (as a percentage of sales) and stock repurchases are higher in economies having stock-based financial systems in which shareholders enjoy strong legal protections (Lazonick 2009).

In contrast, in the bank-based German system, share ownership and share management are concentrated in a small number of large shareholders, often banks. As Stephen Bond, Dietmar Harhoff, and John van Reenen (1999, 2) explain:

> Share ownership in Germany tends to be more concentrated than in Britain, which may mitigate asymmetric information and conflicts of interest between shareholders and managers. Bank representation on supervisory boards and long-term repeated relationships between banks and firms in Germany may mitigate asymmetric information between lenders and borrowers. Large German firms are more likely to remain unquoted, hostile takeovers are extremely rare, and dividend payout ratios tend to be both lower and less rigid in German firms than in British firms.

Stock markets place relatively little pressure on the firm, because firms fund their activities mostly from retained profit earnings or through long-term bank loans; this explains their willingness to make long-term investments and to accept lower returns on capital. Unhappy shareholders in this system will not leave but will use their "voice"—that is, try to improve firm performance by negotiating for change. The classic exposition of the strengths of the bank-based financial system is that of economic historian Alexander Gerschenkron (2000, 137):

> The German investment banks—a powerful invention, comparable in its economic effects to that of the steam engine—were in their capital-

supplying functions a substitute for the insufficiency of the previously created wealth willingly placed at the disposal of entrepreneurs. . . . From their central vantage point of control, the banks participated actively in shaping the major . . . decisions of individual enterprises. It was they who very often mapped out a firm's path of growth, conceived farsighted plans, decided on major technological and locational innovations, and arranged for mergers and capital increases.

What is relevant for our argument here is that short-run profitability plays a much more important role in determining investment by firms in a stock-market-based system than in the bank-based system. The reason is that external investment finance is more costly than internal finance in a stock-market-based system, because outside investors (mostly banks), kept at arm's length by firms' managers, demand a higher cost premium, as they are less well informed than managers about the risks involved in a firm's investment projects and/or the true value of the firm's assets.[20] In effect, the availability of internal finance—that is, profits—is a more important constraint on firm investment in a stock-market-based financial system than in a bank-based one. In addition, firms in stock-market-based systems tend to rely more heavily on bond markets for external finance (rather than on loans) and the terms on which they can secure finance are heavily dependent on their valuation in equity markets, which in turn depends significantly on current profitability. In contrast, firms in Germany, France, and other countries featuring bank-based financial systems rely more on nonpublic sources of often long-term finance provided by banks, other firms, or networks involving the government.

Econometric evidence at the firm level supports the claim that profitability matters more for investment by firms in a stock-market-based system than for firms in a bank-based system. For instance, findings based on data for three large panels of firms in the United States, France, and Japan by Hall et al. (1998) show that U.S. investment is much more sensitive to cash flow (current profits) than is investment in the other two economies. Investigating the role of financial factors in investment in Belgium, France, Germany, and the United Kingdom, Stephen Bond et al. (2003, 161) conclude, "For each of the investment models we have considered, the cash-flow and profits variables appear to play a much more important role in the sample of U.K. firms than in the remaining countries."

But perhaps surprisingly, there has been little investigation of whether these differences between financial systems may be related to differences in the profit sensitivity of investment at the macroeconomic level. Our evidence on the profit sensitivity of investment in twelve OECD countries can be used to check if differences in financial systems show up at the macroeconomic level. To do this, Figure 5.3 plots the stock market capitalization rate (SMCR, defined as the ratio of average stock market capitalization in a country to its GDP) during the period from 1989 to 2005 against the impact of a higher profit share on aggregate demand growth through investment growth. This impact is the absolute value of the impact of higher real wage growth on demand growth, given in column 2 of Table 5.5. Figure 5.3 shows that, as expected, stock market capitalization is highest in the Anglo-Saxon economies (the United States and the United Kingdom), followed by the Netherlands (where stock market capitalization is high because of the presence of a few prominent Anglo-Dutch multinationals), Sweden, and Finland. SMCR is much lower in Belgium, Denmark, France, Germany, Italy, and Spain. As Figure 5.3 shows, there exists a statistically significant (at 5 percent) positive association between the SMCR and the profit sensitivity of investment and demand growth. The sensitivity of investment to profit-

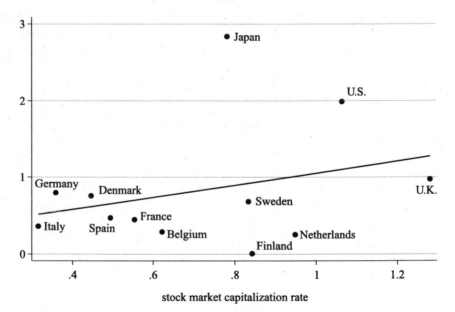

Figure 5.3. The profit sensitivity of investment increases with stock market capitalization.

Notes:

a. The fitted curve is based on the following OLS regression:

profit sensitivity of investment = +1.10 stock market capitalization rate
(in absolute terms) (3.40)***
No. of observations = 12; $\overline{R}^2 = 0.52$

b. *** = statistically significant at 1%.

ability thus is higher in countries in which the stock market plays a more prominent role. It follows from this that countries featuring profit-led aggregate demand are likely to have a stock-market-based financial system; wage-led demand, in contrast, is associated more with bank-based finance. We therefore conclude that profit-led aggregate demand is the macroeconomic corollary of a stock-market-based financial system; likewise, a wage-led demand regime is the macroeconomic complement of a bank-based financial system.

Systemic Complementarities

The complementarity we observed between type of financial system and nature of demand regime has to do with systemic consistency—an economy with a particular structural feature likely develops complementary features in other dimensions as well. Two systemic features can be said to be complementary if the presence or efficiency of one reinforces the presence, functioning, or efficiency of the other.[21] Hence, systemic features are not distributed randomly across nations but are clustered—for instance, along the dimensions that divide regulated (coordinated or "rigid") economies from unregulated (liberal or "flexible") ones. The most widely recognized example of a systemic or institutional complementarity concerns the domains of industrial relations and the financial system. The often-told story is that for reasons of systemic consistency, stock-market-oriented financial sectors and shareholder-oriented corporate governance systems go together with flexible, deregulated labor markets, whereas bank-based financial sectors and "insider" corporate governance systems are associated with regulated labor markets.[22]

What explains this particular complementarity? Several theoretical arguments have been made to explain it (see Höpner 2005 for a review), which all essentially boil down to the following commonplace observations. On one hand, the buildup of a firm-specific skilled workforce (which is highly productive) requires not only patient capital (i.e., investors having a long time horizon) but also coordinated wage setting and regulated labor markets in order to minimize the risk of poaching (Hall and Soskice 2001). This is the gain from complementarity in a bank-based system having regulated industrial relations. On the other hand, the complementarity advantage of market-based systems featuring deregulated labor markets stems from its high degree of flexibility, facilitated by short-term finance and a "hire-and-fire" system of employment protection.[23] In addition, it can be argued that industrial relations systems that produce low degrees of income inequality support bank-based savings regimes and bank-based corporate governance systems (Vitols

2001); the reason is that middle-income households have a greater preference for less risky assets such as bank deposits, whereas high-income groups
prefer high-risk securitized assets. It is in this sense that the high income
inequality in the United States is tightly associated with high-risk assets and
high-risk financial innovation (Palma 2009; Lysandrou 2011).

Figure 5.4 presents evidence on this important complementarity between
financial and labor markets. The horizontal axis again measures SMCR. On
the vertical axis, we measure the extent of labor market regulation in terms
of our index of labor market regulation (LMR): LMR is low (negative) for
countries with flexible labor markets and high when a country has a rigid,
heavily regulated labor market (see Chapter 4). There exists a strong (statistically significant at 1 percent) negative association between SMCR and LMR,
which can be interpreted as a regulatory complementarity. Further clustering of systemic features appears in Figures 5.5 and 5.6, which show that
countries featuring market-based financial systems have relatively deregulated product markets and relatively small welfare states. However, statistical
association by itself is only an indication of compatibility, not proof of complementarity. Hall and Gingerich (2004) go beyond statistical association
and test whether OECD countries featuring consistent configurations of labor and financial markets produce better outcomes than inconsistent ones,
on the assumption that complementarity leads to reciprocal reinforcement

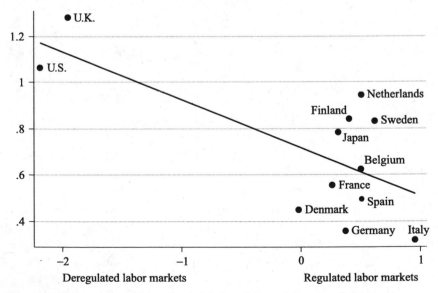

Figure 5.4. Countries with stock-market-based financial sectors feature
deregulated labor markets.

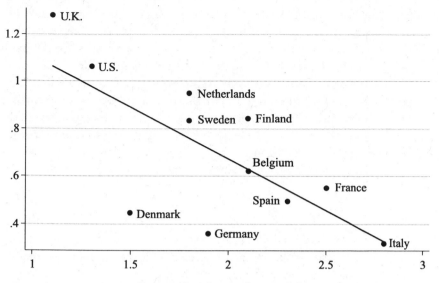

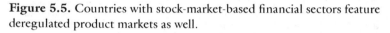

Figure 5.5. Countries with stock-market-based financial sectors feature deregulated product markets as well.

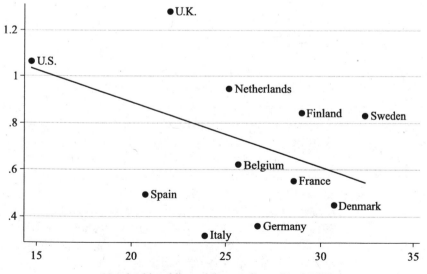

Figure 5.6. Countries with stock-market-based financial sectors feature smaller welfare states.

(as explained above) and hence better national economic performance. Combining different industrial relations measures and corporate governance indicators, they find that countries featuring inconsistent configurations experienced lower growth rates between 1971 and 1997. This could be taken as evidence of the importance of systemic complementarities. It is an important conclusion, implying that because of the mutually reinforcing complementarities, a wage-led demand regime featuring regulated labor markets and bank-based finance (also known as "stakeholder capitalism") can perform as well as a profit-led system having deregulated labor markets, a stock-market-based financial system, and shareholder-oriented corporate governance.

And Then There Was One?

If increased shareholder orientation and stock-market-based capitalism tend to be associated with profit-led demand, we must ask how the increased shareholder orientation of European firms from the late 1990s onward and the resulting reorientation of companies from growth to short-run profitability have been affecting the wage-led demand regime. This increased shareholder orientation resulted from the rise of institutional investors as shareholders of European companies, which in turn was a result of the international diversification of the assets of Anglo-American funds and of internal restructuring within European firms as European managers grasped the opportunity to raise their salaries by adopting Anglo-American management standards including stock-based compensation (Höpner 2005). The perturbation in the financial sphere, which undermines the conditions for "patient capital," has the effect of undermining institutional arrangements in other spheres, notably the corporate governance system and the labor market. The resulting increase in capital market orientation has indeed been accompanied by some—although not yet very significant—deregulation of labor markets (Boeri 2002; Glyn 2006). However, as Martin Höpner (2005) reports, there has been a silent hollowing-out of crucial labor market institutions, such as the German system of co-determination (with works councils avoiding confrontations over pay inequality and employee participation in shareholder-oriented firms), and the apparent stability of European industrial relations systems may be misleading, as this may hide functional convergence to Anglo-Saxon-style industrial relations. Anke Hassel (1999) provides substantial evidence of the erosion of the German system of industrial relations. Under pressure of cross-border capital mobility, this combination of stock market orientation and functional labor market deregulation may eventually lead to Europe's demand regime becoming profit-led. There is economic pressure to converge to a profit-led system among capitalist economies; in an important way, the title of Chris Howell's (2003) review of the varieties-of-capitalism literature, "And Then There Was One?," sums it all up.

However, convergence is not an inescapable historical tendency. First, systemic change of wage-led European economies is unlikely to be a radical, quick jump to a different model, simply because the system's interlocking, interdependent features render it resistant to change. What further complicates matters is that there is no single superior system—as we explain in Chapter 7, the Scandinavian wage-led model performs at least as well as, and in many ways better than, the Anglo-Saxon profit-led model in terms of growth, technological dynamism, competitiveness, and unemployment. As Peter Swenson (2002, 10) writes:

> Some of the most astonishing evidence shows that the Swedish Employers' Confederation was remarkably eager to create a more level structure of wages across firms and industries, well before the unions unified behind a "solidaristic wage policy" in the 1930s onward. The power of well-organized unions helped employers achieve results that their organization could not achieve on its own in the face of market forces.

The point here is that the political power of labor can be crucial if it is conceived not as "power against capital" but as "power for capital," as Swenson argues. Labor, in fact, can bring capital into a social bargain in which concerted wage negotiation and welfare state provision serves the purpose of reducing market uncertainties and raising productivity growth. As William Lazonick (2009, 60) writes:

> In [today's] era of open standards, rapid technological change, convergence of technologies, and intense global competition, business enterprises do need to be flexible in the deployment of capital and labor. One way of attaining this flexibility is by giving the organized labor force a major role in enterprise governance, as for example the Japanese, Germans and Swedes have done, each in their own particular ways. In such a system, there is the possibility of an interaction between business and government to provide widespread economic security in employment and retirement while permitting business enterprises to remain innovative and competitive on a global scale.

The other way of attaining this flexibility is the profit-led American way, which involves stock-market-based finance aiming for maximum shareholder value, plus deregulated labor markets featuring employable workers traumatized by economic insecurity and high inequality. However, American "capitalism without compulsions" has run amok, U.S. unemployment has increased beyond one in ten workers, and excessive stock market orientation, or maximizing shareholder value, has been the dominant ideology behind its current crisis. In Lazonick's view, this ideology has contributed to the sharp rise of economic insecurity and inequality by legitimizing a "downsize-and-distribute" allocation regime at the firm level in which companies downsized their labor forces and increased the distribution of profits to shareholders (via dividends as well as stock repurchases)—reversing the earlier "retain-and-reinvest" regime that characterized these companies in the post–World War II decades, when labor forces were expanded on long-term contracts and profits were reinvested in organization and technology. In their quest for shareholder value, companies have been using profits to pay out dividends and to do massive buybacks to boost their stock prices (including the prices of stock options for their management).[24] The main casualty of this disgorging of the free cash flow of firms, to use Michael Jensen's (1986) evocative term, has been firms' innovative investments, as Lazonick shows. Six major information, communication, and technology (ICT) companies—Microsoft, Cisco Systems, Intel, Oracle, Texas Instruments, and Applied Materials—spent more on stock repurchases than on R&D and became much less research-intensive over time, relying instead on a compliant government's investments in the high-tech knowledge base. This is the main weakness of stock-market-based capitalism: "Shareholders want financial liquidity; investments in innovation require financial commitment," as Lazonick (2009, 56) writes. Longer-term financial commitment, needed for innovation, is not compatible with short-run, impatient capital. .

The other problem with the United States' capitalism without compulsions is that it is not sustainable, the current crisis being its anticlimax. U.S. growth, led by consumption and not by investment, has become dependent on excessive debt accumulation by households and ever-increasing asset prices, as Thomas Palley (2009, 14) argues:

> Maintaining growth of spending on consumption requires continued excessive borrowing and continued reduction in savings rates. Continued excessive borrowing requires ever increasing asset prices and debt/income ratios: hence, the systemic need for bubbles (which eventually burst). Meanwhile, when the savings rate hits zero, little further reduction is possible. Consequently, both drivers of demand eventually exhaust themselves.

Eventually the housing bubble exploded and America's growth model imploded, writes Palley, who believes that without drastic reform, the U.S. economy will not manage to escape the pull of economic stagnation. Financial capitalism without the required level of compulsions for oligopolistic capital is "probably no more efficient than Communism without workers' control over the bureaucracy," concludes Palma (2009, 864). The deep crisis of 2008–2011, in other words, has revealed the inadequacy of a deregulated profit-led and stock-market-based growth model, and the roles of the state and of regulation are now being reconsidered.

Our emphasis on systemic complementarities has important implications for labor market policy in both profit-led and wage-led economies. We can now understand why in a profit-led economy such as the United States, the introduction of a more regulated industrial relations system based on employee co-determination, strong employment, and wage bargaining coordination will not improve macroeconomic performance if the nature of the financial and corporate governance systems is not changed at the same time. In other words, in a profit-led system such as the United States, there exists a conflict between workers' interest and the interests of firms and the financial sector. The complementarity between the industrial relations system and the financial system makes life difficult for labor unions: progressive and growth-promoting policies must be based on simultaneous attempts to reform the labor market in the interest of wage earners and employees and of the financial sector (reducing its obsession with short-run shareholder value orientation).[25] For workers and unions in Europe's wage-led economies, the implication of our analysis is that efforts should be directed not only at maintaining labor market arrangements but also at curbing further growth in the shareholder orientation of firms and firm management. Perhaps the latter task, basically persuading capitalists that it is in their interest to support regulation of financial and labor markets, is the more important one.

Further Reading

Amit Bhaduri and Stephen Marglin (1990) is the landmark publication on wage-led or profit-led growth. Gerald Epstein and Herbert Gintis (1995) is a useful collection of follow-up studies in the Bhaduri-Marglin approach. John and Wendy Cornwall (2001) present a well-structured Keynesian-Schumpeterian framework that explains the rise and fall of the golden age of OECD capitalism. Andrew Glyn (2006) narrates what happened after the golden age. Excellent sources on the varieties of capitalism are Hall and Soskice (2001), Amable (2003), and Höpner (2005). William Lazonick (2009) provides a readable review of the New Economy business model that led to the financial-economic crisis of 2008–2011. Robert Wade (2009) offers a hard-hitting stocktaking of the rise and fall of the "New Wall Street System." Palley (2009), Palma (2009), and Taylor (2010) are insightful political-economy analyses of the causes of the current crisis.

Appendix: Accounting for the OECD Growth Decline

The estimated model coefficients are used to understand why OECD economic growth performance during the period from 1980 to 2001 failed to recover sufficiently to significantly reduce unemployment, despite the fact that in all twelve OECD countries post-1980 real wage growth was restrained to historically low levels. To do so, we express the reduced-form equation (5.1) in first differences:

$$(5.11) \qquad \Delta \hat{x} = \frac{\psi_i \varphi_0}{1 - \psi_i \varphi_2} \Delta \hat{b} + \frac{\psi_e \varepsilon_0}{1 - \psi_i \varphi_2} \Delta \hat{z} + C \Delta \hat{w} - C \Delta \hat{\lambda}$$

where $C = (d\hat{x}/d\hat{w})$, that is, the partial derivative of demand growth with respect to real wage growth. Demand (or GDP) growth will thus decline if:

- There is a decline in the growth rate of $\hat{b}$, that is, the "animal spirits" of investors are becoming depressed.
- World trade growth declines, that is, $\Delta \hat{z} < 0$; note that $\psi_e \varepsilon_0 / (1 - \psi_i \phi_2)$ is the foreign-trade multiplier (in growth rates)—analogous to Thirlwall's (2002) dynamic trade multiplier.
- Real wage growth declines ($\Delta \hat{w} < 0$), assuming that $C > 0$, that is, the demand regime is wage-led.
- Labor productivity growth rises, that is, $\Delta \hat{\lambda} > 0$, again assuming that $C > 0$.

Using equation (5.11), we estimated the change in real GDP growth in our twelve countries between 1960–1980 and 1980–2000; the results of this growth accounting exercise appear in Table 5.7. These results are compared to the actual decline in real GDP growth, listed in row 9 of Table 5.7. The second and third rows present the countrywise changes (actually declines) in real wage growth and labor productivity growth; in the first row appears the decline in world trade growth (by 1.4 percentage points) between the two periods. Rows 4, 5, and 6 present the estimated country-specific contributions to real GDP growth decline by the decline in world trade growth, real wage growth, and productivity growth, respectively. Row 7 is the sum of rows 5 and 6, thus showing the contribution of the change in real unit labor cost growth. In row 8, finally, appear the estimated country-specific total effects on OECD real GDP growth.

To illustrate how the findings in Table 5.7 are to be interpreted, we consider the case of Germany in some detail. The first cause of the slowdown in German GDP growth between 1960–1980 and 1980–2000 is the decline in world trade growth (by 1.4 percentage points), which—according to our estimates—had an almost one-to-one effect on German growth (i.e., a decline of 1.4 percentage points). Second, the decline in real wage growth (by as

Table 5.7. Percentage of the change in average real GDP growth between 1960–1980 and 1980–2000 explained by the growth model variables

	Belgium	Denmark	Finland	France	Germany	Italy	Japan	Netherlands	Spain	Sweden	U.K.	U.S.
Actual changes between 1960–1980 and 1980–2000												
1 Change in world trade growth: $\Delta\hat{z}$	-1.4	-1.4	-1.4	-1.4	-1.4	-1.4	-1.4	-1.4	-1.4	-1.4	-0.8	-1.4
2 Change in real wage growth: $\Delta\hat{w}$	-4.2	-2.9	-2.9	-3.7	-3.9	-5.4	-5.3	-4.7	-5.1	-2.1	-1.8	-0.7
3 Change in labor productivity growth: $\Delta\hat{\lambda}$	-2.8	-1.9	-1.4	-2.8	-3.7	-3.7	-4.3	-3.3	-4.0	-1.9	-1.4	-0.3
Change in real GDP growth caused by:												
4 $\Delta\hat{z}$	-1.3	-1.4	-1.1	-1.3	-1.4	-1.1	-3.8	-1.1	-2.0	-2.9	-0.7	-1.4
	(103.1)	(79.0)	(82.3)	(82.8)	(99.4)	(84.6)	(117.6)	(74.2)	(86.5)	(77.8)	(84.5)	(106.2)
5 $\Delta\hat{w}$	0.1	-1.1	-2.1	-1.2	-0.2	-0.6	2.9	-1.3	-1.4	-2.0	-0.6	0.2
	(-9.1)	(58.4)	(97.8)	(74.6)	(15.5)	(50.5)	(-90.5)	(87.2)	(74.6)	(77.8)	(67.5)	(-11.8)
6 $\Delta\hat{\lambda}$	-0.1	0.7	1.0	0.9	0.2	0.4	-2.3	0.9	1.1	2.1	0.4	-0.1
	(6.0)	(-37.3)	(-47.9)	(-57.4)	(-14.8)	(-35.1)	(72.8)	(-61.5)	(-57.4)	(-55.6)	(-52.0)	(5.6)
7 Change in unit labour cost growth: $\Delta\hat{w} - \Delta\hat{\lambda}$	0.0	-0.4	-1.1	-0.3	-0.0	-0.9	0.6	-0.4	-0.3	-0.8	-0.1	-0.1
	(-3.1)	(21.0)	(49.9)	(17.3)	(0.6)	(15.4)	(-17.6)	(25.8)	(17.3)	(22.2)	(15.5)	(-6.2)
8 Total predicted change in real GDP growth	-1.3	-1.8	-2.1	-1.6	-1.4	-1.3	-3.3	-1.5	-2.4	-3.7	-0.8	-1.3
	(69.1)	(131.8)	(140.3)	(63.7)	(88.4)	(46.7)	(66.9)	(97.8)	(85.1)	(248.8)	(84.5)	(207.6)
9 Actual change in real GDP growth between 1960–1980 and 1980–2000	-1.8	-1.4	-1.5	-2.5	-1.6	-2.7	-4.9	-1.5	-2.8	-1.5	-0.6	-0.6

Notes:

a. The estimated in changes in real GDP growth were calculated using equation (5.11).

b. The predicted change in real GDP growth for the United Kingdom is based on actual changes in world trade growth, real wage growth, and productivity growth between the periods 1960–1970 and 1980–2000; the actual change in average GDP growth between 1960–1980 and 1980–2000 being very small (only –0.1 percentage point), our model overestimates the decline in GDP growth due to the variables included in the analysis by a factor of 11 (the estimated change being –1.4 percentage points). Clearly, other factors have been important in containing the decline in British GDP; however, the model performs in a more satisfactory manner when we compare GDP growth in the periods 1960–1970 and 1980–2000.

c. Figures in parentheses in rows 4, 5, 6, and 7 are percentages of the total predicted change in real GDP growth (row 8). Figures in parentheses given in row 8 are percentages of the actual change in real GDP growth (in row 9).

much as 3.9 percentage points) also led to a decline in German GDP growth (by 0.2 percentage points), the German demand regime being wage-led. Third, the slowdown of labor productivity growth (by as much as 3.7 percentage points), on the other hand, had a positive impact (by 0.2 percentage points) on German GDP growth, because it implied a redistribution of income from higher-savings profits to lower-savings wages. The net effect of these three changes is an estimated decline of 1.4 percentage points in German GDP growth between 1960–1980 and 1980–2000; this means that the model explains about 88 percent of the actual decline in average annual real GDP growth of Germany (1.6 percentage points). The overriding cause of Germany's growth slowdown is therefore the decline in world trade growth: about 99 percent of the decline in Germany's GDP growth rate between the two periods must be attributed to slower world trade growth. Real wage growth restraint and the consequent improvement in profitability did not result in higher GDP growth, since Germany's aggregate demand regime is wage-led. Hence, the decline in real wage growth reduced GDP growth, but our estimates show—perhaps surprisingly—that (1) the significant decline in real wage growth contributed only 15.5 percent to the decline in GDP growth, and (2) this negative impact on growth of real wage restraint was almost fully offset by the positive growth effects of the equally significant decline in labor productivity growth.

In many respects, the German case is exemplary for the other wage-led economies. Specifically, sluggish world trade growth in the 1980s and 1990s explains on average 86 percent of the decline in real GDP growth in the other wage-led economies. This brings up the question of what caused the slowdown in world trade growth. Beyond doubt, the growth of international trade has been affected negatively by the breakdown of the stable regime of international trade and finance under the Bretton Woods agreement after 1971–1973 (Marglin and Schor 1990; Cornwall and Cornwall 2001). One reason is increased exchange rate volatility and uncertainty, caused by large and persistent payments imbalances. Another reason is that the increased prominence and mobility of financial capital post-1980 has encouraged the use of deflationary macroeconomic policies, designed to appease the inflation-averse international financial community (Setterfield and Cornwall 2002). In addition, following the deregulation of international financial markets, national governments now perceive increased risk in pursuing expansionary macro policies and increased pressures to adopt deflationary policies, to defend credibility in global financial markets (Glyn 2006). Our findings indicate that only a trend toward increase in the rate of growth of world economic activity can offer the prospect of substantial long-run improvement in OECD growth and employment. This points to one important lesson: the need to revise the rules of the global trading and financial system so as to provide the OECD countries with a more stable and coordinated international economic environment, which allows them enough macroeconomic policy space to pursue domestic goals.

But real wage growth restraint led to larger declines in GDP growth in the other wage-led economies compared to Germany: in the other eight wage-led countries, on average as much as 74 percent of the decline in GDP growth between 1960–1980 and 1980–2000 is caused by real wage restraint. But as in Germany, to a large extent, this negative effect is largely offset by the slowdown of labor productivity growth; on average, the decline in productivity growth raised real GDP growth by 51 percent. Accordingly, the combined macroeconomic effect of the decline in wage growth and the decline in productivity turns out to be quite small: on average, the decline in average annual unit labor cost growth accounts for 23 percent of the decrease in post-1980 GDP growth.

While it is clear that real wage restraint did not generate the desired improvements in macroeconomic performance in the wage-led economies, Table 5.7 shows that it also did not work in the two profit-led economies, Japan and the United States. In the United States, the decline in real wage growth did indeed raise GDP growth, but only by 0.2 percentage points, which was by far insufficient to offset the 1.4 percentage points decline in GDP growth caused by stagnating world trade growth. In the United States, GDP growth declined by an additional 0.1 percentage points, because of the long-term slowdown of its labor productivity growth. In profit-led Japan, considerable real wage growth restraint raised GDP growth by as much as 2.9 percentage points, but this was still insufficient to compensate for the 3.8 percentage point decline in GDP growth, caused by falling world trade growth; in fact, stagnating trade more than completely explains the decline in Japanese growth. In addition, Japan's GDP growth suffered from the sharp decline in its productivity growth; the resulting decline in GDP growth by 2.3 percentage points accounts for about 73 percent of the deterioration in Japan's economic growth.

It can be seen that the model performs reasonably well for Belgium, France, Germany, Japan, the Netherlands, Spain, and the United Kingdom, in each case explaining more than 60–65 percent of the slowdown in growth. The model clearly underestimates the decline in Italian real GDP growth (by as much as 54 percent) and Japan. The fact that the model consistently underestimates the decline in the post-1980 real GDP growth rate in the five EC countries may point to a common factor: all five became members of the Economic and Monetary Union (EMU), which according to the conditions of the Maastricht Treaty required them to reduce their government budget deficit to below 3 percent of GDP and cut their public debt to below 60 percent of GDP. The deflationary fiscal policies adopted during much of the 1990s, in conjunction with the restrictive monetary policy pursued by the newly established European Central Bank, have depressed the growth of aggregate demand in France, Germany, Italy, the Netherlands, and Spain further than our estimates indicate (Galbraith and Garcilazo 2004). The fact that actual GDP growth in Japan declined more than is predicted by our model must be attributed to factors not included in the model, the most important of which are the stock market collapse, the consequent fall in land and real estate prices of the early 1990s, and the resulting banking crisis. The decline in the wealth of consumers led them to cut spending and raise their savings rates, which—by depressing aggregate demand—had a negative impact on investor confidence. As a result, and despite historically very low real interest rates and a large budget deficit, Japan suffered from deficient aggregate demand and GDP growth has actually gone down beyond the level predicted by the model. But "the devastating loss of national self-confidence, particularly after a premature burst of fiscal prudence halted the 1995–96 recovery from the post-bubble recession" (Dore, Lazonick, and O'Sullivan 1999, 116), has been perhaps the most important factor behind Japan's fall into a liquidity trap. We *over*estimate the wage-moderation-induced decline in growth in Denmark, Finland, and especially Sweden. Clearly, there have been other, compensating influences that have kept up real GDP growth after 1980; we may note relatively expansionary fiscal policy during the 1980s and low (real) interest rates after 1995 as two major macro factors keeping up Nordic growth. Chapter 7 goes into the Nordic model in more policy detail.

Finally, our demand regime model seriously overestimates the decline in the GDP growth rate of the United States. How can this be explained? We think the basic cause of the better-than-predicted U.S. growth performance lies in the debt-financed consumption boom, which was the primary engine of U.S. growth in the second half of the 1990s. Estimates by Robert Pollin (2003, 65) indicate that the rise in the stock market and real estate prices between 1995 and 1999 injected "roughly 2–4 percent more spending into the [U.S.] economy, which in turn stimulated further growth through its impact on investment and jobs"; it must be noted that this rise in spending was driven almost entirely by a considerable increase in consumption by the richest 10 percent of households, whose rapidly growing wealth enabled them to do this (Palma 2009). The consumption boom, in turn, raised U.S. investors' animal spirits, thus augmenting aggregate demand growth. Because this "wealth effect" and the improvement in animal spirits are not included in the model, Table 5.7 overestimates the decline in post-1980 U.S. growth.

6

The Generalization of the NAIRU Theory

Long-run equilibrium is a slippery eel.

JOAN ROBINSON, *ECONOMIC PHILOSOPHY*

The growth model analysis of Chapter 3 has shown that NAIRU-based policies of real wage restraint and labor market deregulation may actually depress accumulation and growth, petrify technological progress, and thus stifle productivity growth without significantly reducing unemployment. These effects were found to occur in strongly wage-led economies, but we have seen that NAIRU-based policy is likely to reduce labor productivity growth in profit-led systems as well. While the growth model analysis has yielded important insights into the differential macro adjustments to labor market reform in wage-led and profit-led economies, it could be claimed that the steady-state growth paths analyzed in Chapter 3 represent not long-run but merely provisional or conditional equilibrium (Setterfield 2002). The reason is that we are not assuming (as is done in the NAIRU approach) that both the rate of unemployment and the rate of inflation are constant, or, alternatively, that the wage-profit distribution is constant. Hence, the wage-led and profit-led steady states analyzed so far imply ever-changing (accelerating or decelerating) inflation and a constantly shifting (growing or declining) wage or profit share. This may be realistic in the medium run, in fact: data for the OECD countries show, for instance, that the profit share has more or less continuously increased during 1984–2004 (Carter 2007). But longer-run data show otherwise: Marquetti (2004), as mentioned, finds a roughly constant wage or profit share for the U.S. economy over the 130-year period from 1869 to 1999. Long-run equilibrium is therefore generally defined by imposing the condition that inflation is constant or that income distribution between wages and profits is constant (which amounts to the same thing). As a corollary, the unemployment rate will also be constant, and this, in fact, explains the NAIRU: it is the particular unemployment rate at which inflation is constant, because inflation is fully anticipated (we are in a world where somehow the future has already happened) and the various claims on income by workers and firms are mutually consistent. This chapter imposes this long-run equilibrium condition on the growth model of Chapter 3 to identify the determinants of equilibrium unemployment. We claim that our model is more general than the conventional NAIRU model, because we allow aggregate demand, investment, and demand-induced endogenous technological progress to play a major role in determining inflation-safe unemployment. Using our more general model, we show that (1) aggregate demand has long-run effects on unemployment and (2) labor market *de*regulation does not necessarily lead to reduced unemployment. We test our more general NAIRU model using cross-country data for twenty OECD countries in the period from 1984 to 2004.

The Slippery Eel

The concept of equilibrium is an indispensable tool of economic analysis, of course. But as Joan Robinson (1962, 78) argued:

> To use the equilibrium concept, one has to keep it in its place, and its place is strictly in the preliminary stages of an analytical argument, not in the framing of hypotheses to be tested against the facts, for we know perfectly well that we shall not find facts in a state of equilibrium.

Yet NAIRU theory seems to conceive the long run as a date somewhere in the future that we shall get to someday. The NAIRU itself is seen as an attractor, as in dynamic systems theory—a stable equilibrium point to which the dynamic economic system evolves after a long enough time. Specifically, the actual unemployment rate always adjusts to the level of the NAIRU, not vice versa. Consider the case of a positive demand shock, which results in actual unemployment falling below the NAIRU. Lower actual unemployment strengthens the bargaining position of workers and leads to wage claims exceeding productivity growth. The wage increases provoke firms to increase their prices, because they want to maintain their profits, and the inevitable result is a wage-price inflationary spiral. The accelerating inflation can be halted only if real wage claims are brought back in line again with exogenous productivity. This requires additional unemployment, which is created by the system either by means of a Pigouvian real balance effect or by higher interest rates. Inflation becomes constant again once the actual unemployment rate has been pushed up to the NAIRU.

While long-run equilibrium can be a useful metaphor, the concept cannot be easily applied to actual economic life because it is incompatible with historical time. As Robinson wrote, it is "a metaphor based on movements in space applied to processes taking place in time. In space, it is possible to go to and fro and remedy misdirections, but in time, every day, the past is irrevocable and the future unknown." It was precisely from this timeless con cept of long-run equilibrium that Keynes was struggling to escape: "As he was concerned to account for an actual phenomenon—unemployment—in an actual economy—contemporary capitalism—he had to discuss it in terms of processes taking place in actual history" (Robinson 1979, xiv). The NAIRU is evidently such a timeless concept. We can therefore legitimately ask how long it would take to get actual unemployment, once perturbed from the long-run position, back to the constant NAIRU level.

In our derivation of equilibrium unemployment, we follow both Keynes and Robinson in one important respect: our generalization of the NAIRU model is an attempt to treat the analysis of accumulation and technological progress in historical time. Specifically, going back to our earlier example of a positive demand shock that causes actual unemployment to fall below the NAIRU, we take into account that the additional demand has a positive Kaldor-Verdoorn impact on productivity. And we allow for the possibility that the higher real wage growth induces higher labor productivity growth (along the lines of Marx and Hicks). The result is that equilibrium unemployment itself will change once the system is perturbed out of equilibrium, and it is now no longer clear what the new equilibrium will be. In our model, change is therefore *path-dependent*, in the jargon of evolutionary economists (Dosi 1997), meaning that there is no unique and predetermined equilibrium (such as the conventional NAIRU attractor); rather, the new equilibrium depends significantly on the nature of the perturbation and the process of getting there. Because of this, demand and demand policy do have long-run, permanent effects.

Long-Run Equilibrium

The growth model of Chapter 3 can be reduced to three equations: the productivity regime (3.1), the demand regime (3.20), and the real wage growth equation (3.24):[1]

(3.1) $\qquad \hat{\lambda} = \beta_0 + \beta_1 \hat{x} + \beta_2 \hat{w} + \beta_3 z \qquad \beta_0, \beta_2, \beta_3 > 0; \ 0 < \beta_1 < 1$

(3.20) $\qquad \hat{x} = \Theta + C[\hat{w} - \hat{\lambda}]$

where

$$\Theta = \frac{\psi_i \varphi_0 \hat{b} + \psi_g \hat{g}^* + \psi_e \hat{e} - \psi_i \varphi_3 r_k}{1 - \psi_i \varphi_2},$$

as in equation (3.19).

(3.24) $\qquad \hat{w} = \alpha_0 - \alpha_1 u + \alpha_2 \hat{\lambda} + \alpha_3 z \qquad \alpha_0, \alpha_2, \alpha_3 > 0$

This is a systems of three equations in four unknowns: labor productivity growth $\hat{\lambda}$, real GDP growth $\hat{x}$, real wage growth $\hat{w}$, and the unemployment rate u. This means that one additional restriction needs to be imposed to close the system. We assume that in the long run real wages must grow at the same rate as labor productivity, so that

(6.1) $\hat{w} = \hat{\lambda}$

Condition (6.1) is the fundamental condition for long-period equilibrium, which implies that both inflation and the distribution of income across wages and profits are constant.[2] Using equation (6.1) and equation (3.19) from Chapter 3, we immediately obtain the reduced-form expression for long-run equilibrium income growth $\hat{x}^*$ from equation (3.20):

(6.2) $\hat{x}^* = \Theta = \dfrac{\psi_i \varphi_0 \hat{b} + \psi_g \hat{g}^* + \psi_e \hat{e} - \psi_i \varphi_3 r_k}{1 - \psi_i \varphi_2}$

Interestingly, the wage-led or profit-led nature of the demand regime, while being of crucial importance in the medium run (analyzed in Chapter 3), turns out to be immaterial for long-run income growth; this is not surprising, however, since we are keeping the distribution of income between wages and profits unchanged by imposing restriction (6.1). Long-run growth thus depends on autonomous investment growth $\hat{b}$ and export growth $\hat{e}$, the growth of net public expenditure $\hat{g}^*$ (the fiscal policy stance), and the real interest rate r_k (the monetary policy stance).

Substitution of equations (6.1) and (6.2) into the productivity regime (3.1) gives us the reduced-form expression for equilibrium labor productivity growth $\hat{\lambda}^*$:

(6.3) $\hat{\lambda}^* = \dfrac{\beta_0}{1 - \beta_2} + \dfrac{\beta_1}{1 - \beta_2} * \dfrac{\psi_i \varphi_0 \hat{b} + \psi_g \hat{g}^* + \psi_e \hat{e} - \psi_i \varphi_3 r_k}{1 - \psi_i \varphi_2} + \dfrac{\beta_3}{1 - \beta_2} z$

Provided $\beta_1 > 0$, that is, the Kaldor-Verdoorn coefficient is positive, long-run productivity depends positively on the growth of autonomous demand and negatively on the real interest rate (assuming that $1 - \beta_2 > 0$). In addition, if $\beta_3 > 0$, any rise in the extent of labor market regulation (captured by a rise in z) will raise productivity growth through a process of labor-saving technological progress.

Turning to the labor market, we note that by combining equations (6.1) and (3.24) we can derive the equilibrium unemployment rate u^* as follows:

(6.4) $u^* = \dfrac{\alpha_0 - (1 - \alpha_2)\hat{\lambda} + \alpha_3 z}{\alpha_1}$

(Note that this is also equation (1.3) in Chapter 1.) Substitution of (6.3) into (6.4) finally gives the following reduced-form expression for u^*:

(6.5)
$$u^* = \frac{\alpha_0(1-\beta_2)-\beta_0(1-\alpha_2)}{\alpha_1(1-\beta_2)} + \left[\frac{\alpha_3(1-\beta_2)-(1-\alpha_2)\beta_3}{\alpha_1(1-\beta_2)}\right]z$$
$$-\left[\frac{(1-\alpha_2)\beta_1}{\alpha_1(1-\beta_2)}\right]*\left[\frac{\psi_i\varphi_0\hat{b}+\psi_g\hat{g}^*+\psi_e\hat{e}-\psi_i\varphi_3 r_k}{1-\psi_i\varphi_2}\right]$$

Two insights follow directly from equation (6.5). First, unlike in the conventional NAIRU model, demand factors $\hat{b}$, $\hat{g}^*$, $\hat{e}$, and Δr_k can have permanent effects on equilibrium unemployment. If $\alpha_1>0$; $0<\alpha_2<1$; $0<\beta_1<1$; and $0\le\beta_2<1$, it follows that an increase in the growth rate of autonomous investment, net public expenditure, and exports will reduce equilibrium unemployment, whereas a rise in the real rate of interest will reduce u^* by depressing investment demand:

(6.6)
$$\frac{\partial u^*}{\partial\hat{g}^*} = -\left[\frac{(1-\alpha_2)\beta_1}{\alpha_1(1-\beta_2)}\right]\left[\frac{\psi_g}{1-\psi_i\varphi_2}\right]<0$$

(6.7)
$$\frac{\partial u^*}{\partial\hat{e}} = -\left[\frac{(1-\alpha_2)\beta_1}{\alpha_1(1-\beta_2)}\right]\left[\frac{\psi_e}{1-\psi_i\varphi_2}\right]<0$$

(6.8)
$$\frac{\partial u^*}{\partial r_k} = \left[\frac{(1-\alpha_2)\beta_1}{\alpha_1(1-\beta_2)}\right]\left[\frac{\psi_i\varphi_3}{1-\psi_i\varphi_2}\right]>0$$

According to (6.6)–(6.8), demand manipulation by means of fiscal and/or monetary policy causes the NAIRU itself to change over time. Note that the mechanism through which this happens is different from the one suggested by Hargreaves Heap (1980) and Ball (1999), who argue that demand expansions can reduce u^* because the long-term unemployed do not put downward pressure on wages and hence do not affect inflation. Their reason is that unemployed workers supposedly lose skills (or their skills become obsolete) and employers hold negative views of the capacities of job seekers who have been unemployed for a long time. In our case, the inflationary impact of demand expansions is at least partly mitigated because they lead to faster productivity growth (via the Kaldor-Verdoorn coefficient β_1); hence output growth, wage growth, and employment growth can be increased permanently in a noninflationary manner.

Second, from equation (6.5), it follows that the sign of the impact on equilibrium unemployment of an increase in z is ambiguous. Increased regulation leads to higher equilibrium unemployment (as conventional wisdom holds) only if

(6.9) $\dfrac{\partial u^*}{\partial z} = \dfrac{\alpha_3(1-\beta_2)-(1-\alpha_2)\beta_3}{\alpha_1(1-\beta_2)} > 0$

Assuming that $\alpha_1 > 0$ and $(1-\beta_2) > 0$, condition (6.9) can be restated as:

(6.10) $\dfrac{\partial u^*}{\partial z} > 0$ if $\dfrac{\alpha_3}{(1-\alpha_2)} > \dfrac{\beta_3}{(1-\beta_2)}$

This inequality has a straightforward interpretation. Its right-hand side is the impact of an increase in z on labor productivity growth from equation (6.3):

$$\frac{\partial \hat{\lambda}^*}{\partial z} = \frac{\beta_3}{1-\beta_2} > 0.$$

Because of the increase in productivity growth, equilibrium real wage growth can also increase while keeping the rate of inflation constant. Accordingly, we can define

$$\Delta \hat{w}_W = \frac{\partial \hat{\lambda}^*}{\partial z} = \frac{\beta_3}{1-\beta_2}$$

as the increase in real wage growth warranted by increased productivity growth. The left-hand side of equation (6.10) reflects the extra real wage growth demanded by workers in response to an increase in z. To see this, we rewrite equation (3.24) in terms of real wage growth, using equation (6.1):

(6.11) $\hat{w} = \dfrac{\alpha_0}{1-\alpha_2} - \dfrac{\alpha_1}{1-\alpha_2} u + \dfrac{\alpha_3}{1-\alpha_2} z$

From (6.11), it follows that

$$\frac{\partial \hat{w}}{\partial z} = \frac{\alpha_3}{1-\alpha_2} > 0.$$

Let us denote the additional wage growth demanded by $\Delta \hat{w}_D$. According to condition (6.10), $\Delta \hat{w}_D > \Delta \hat{w}_W$, that is, the extra wage growth claimed exceeds the wage growth increase warranted by the increased productivity growth. This can only be reconciled by a rise in equilibrium unemployment, which—as shown by equation (6.11)—forces workers to reduce their wage growth demands until, in equilibrium, $\Delta \hat{w}_D = \Delta \hat{w}_W = \Delta \hat{w}^*$. But condition (6.10) need not be satisfied, and hence it is equally possible that

(6.12) $\dfrac{\partial u^*}{\partial z} < 0$ if $\dfrac{\alpha_3}{(1-\alpha_2)} < \dfrac{\beta_3}{(1-\beta_2)}$

Now, $\Delta \hat{w}_D < \Delta \hat{w}_W$, that is, the extra wage growth claimed by workers is less than the wage growth increase warranted by the increased productivity growth. This means that in this case—and in contrast to what the standard NAIRU model predicts—increased labor market regulation will lead to a permanent decline in u^*.

Finally, it may be useful to compare our generalized NAIRU model with a more standard model. The first thing to note is that more conventional models generally assume that equilibrium productivity growth is exogenous, that is, $\hat{\lambda}^* = \hat{\lambda}$, and consequently these models must treat possible influences of productivity growth on unemployment as being due to exogenous productivity growth shocks. In terms of our productivity regime equation (3.1), this requires that the Kaldor-Verdoorn coefficient β_1 is zero (demand growth does not affect labor productivity growth) and that the coefficient of wage-led technological progress β_2 is equal to unity (in terms of a neoclassical production function, the elasticity of capital-labor substitution is equal to unity). By assuming that β_2 is equal to unity, capital-intensity growth and real wage growth will vary in a one-to-one manner in the very short run. As a result, if there is investment and consequently actual unemployment declines and the real wage rate increases, firms will substitute labor for capital until the loss of jobs on the installed capital stock is equal to the additional jobs created on the new equipment; u^* thus remains unchanged.[3]

From restriction (6.1), it follows that $\hat{w}^*$ must adjust to the exogenously given growth rate of labor productivity. Given these assumptions ($\beta_1 = 0$, $\beta_2 = 1$), equilibrium productivity and real wage growth and equilibrium unemployment u^* are determined. This leaves equilibrium demand growth $\hat{x}^*$ to be determined. It is clear that $\hat{x}^*$ must be consistent with u^* and stable inflation. To achieve this, more-standard NAIRU models introduce the real balance effect (Stockhammer 2004; Taylor 2004, 2010). Alternatively, it is sometimes argued that "most OECD countries now set monetary policy on the basis of an inflation target which *naturally* moves real demand and unemployment towards the equilibrium" consistent with stable inflation (Nickell, Nunziata, and Ochel 2005, 3; emphasis added). In terms of our model, this second option can be taken to imply that the real rate of interest becomes endogenous and as such takes care of the alignment between $\hat{x}^*$ and u^*, with $\hat{x}^*$ thus becoming a negative function of u^* and r_k:

(6.13) $\hat{x}^* = f(u^*, r_k)$

Table 6.1 lists the full set of equations of a conventional NAIRU model and compares these to the reduced-form equations of our extended model.

Table 6.1. Key equations

Dependent variable	The extended NAIRU model $\alpha_1 > 0$; $0 < \alpha_2 \leq 1$; $0 \leq \beta_1 \leq 1$; and $0 \leq \beta_2 \leq 1$.	A basic NAIRU model $\alpha_1 > 0$; $\alpha_2 = 1$; $\beta_1 = 0$; and $\beta_2 = 1$.
Income growth	$\hat{x}^* = \dfrac{\psi_i \varphi_0 \hat{b} + \psi_g \hat{g}^{*} + \psi_c \hat{c} - \psi_i \varphi_3 r_k}{1 - \psi_i \varphi_2}$	$\hat{x}^* = f(u^*, r_k)$
Labor productivity growth	$\hat{\lambda}^* = \dfrac{\beta_0}{1-\beta_2} + \dfrac{\beta_1}{1-\beta_2} * \dfrac{\psi_i \varphi_0 \hat{b} + \psi_g \hat{g}^{*} + \psi_c \hat{c} - \psi_i \varphi_3 r_k}{1-\psi_i \varphi_2} + \dfrac{\beta_3}{1-\beta_2} z$	$\hat{\lambda}^* = \hat{\lambda}$
Equilibrium unemployment	$u^* = \dfrac{\alpha_0(1-\beta_2) - \beta_0(1-\alpha_2)}{\alpha_1(1-\beta_2)} + \left[\dfrac{\alpha_3(1-\beta_2)-(1-\alpha_2)\beta_3}{\alpha_1(1-\beta_2)}\right]z$ $- \left[\dfrac{(1-\alpha_2)\beta_1}{\alpha_1(1-\beta_2)}\right] * \left[\dfrac{\psi_i \varphi_0 \hat{b} + \psi_g \hat{g}^{*} + \psi_c \hat{c} - \psi_i \varphi_3 r_k}{1-\psi_i \varphi_2}\right]$	$u^* = \dfrac{\alpha_0 - (1-\alpha_2)\hat{\lambda}^* + \alpha_3 z}{\alpha_1}$
Real wage growth	$\hat{w} = \hat{\lambda}^*$	$\hat{w} = \hat{\lambda}^*$

Explaining Unemployment in the OECD, 1984–2004

Our theoretical results suggest that (1) monetary policy and other determinants of aggregate demand have long-run effects on unemployment, and (2) the impact of increases in labor market regulation, which lead to increased wage bargaining power of workers, on steady-inflation unemployment is inherently ambiguous. Here we present an empirical investigation of the determinants of equilibrium unemployment in twenty OECD countries during the period from 1984 to 2004. As in Chapter 4, we are interested in finding the impact of structural variables (that is, regulatory labor market institutions, monetary and fiscal policies, and export growth) on longer-term unemployment and labor productivity growth in the OECD countries.[4] To do so, as explained in Chapter 4, we pool structural data pertaining to the periods from 1984 to 1994 and from 1994 to 2004. We have checked for country-specific effects by including country dummies, but in general we found country dummies to be statistically insignificant unless stated otherwise in the text and the tables. Our indicators of labor market regulation (i.e., our catchall variable z) are the same as in Chapter 4: the employment protection legislation (EPL) index, developed by the OECD (1999), and the labor market regulation (LMR) factor score, created for eighteen OECD countries.

To explain OECD unemployment, we estimated three equations: the productivity regime equation (3.1), the long-run equilibrium growth equation (6.2), and the real wage growth equation (3.24). The estimation results for the productivity regime have already been discussed in Chapter 4; these appear in Table 4.5. Based on these results, we obtained the following coefficient values: the Kaldor-Verdoorn coefficient $\beta_1 = 0.42$; the coefficient of real-wage-growth-induced technological progress $\beta_2 = 0.29$; and our estimate of $\beta_3 = 0.16$, which means that an increase in the EPL index by 1 point (on a scale of 0–4) raises labor productivity growth by 0.16 percentage points. In terms of equation (3.1), this gives us

$$(6.14) \qquad \hat{\lambda} = \beta_0 + 0.42\hat{x} + 0.29\hat{w} + 0.16z$$

Table 6.2 presents the results for the real wage growth equation—that is, equation (3.24) of our model. The real wage growth equation is estimated by two-stage least squares (2SLS) using labor productivity growth as the instrumented variable to avoid simultaneity bias. Column 1 presents the results when we use the EPL index as our measure of labor market regulation; in column 2 are the results when we use the LMR factor score. The estimation results are similar across columns 1 and 2, and the explanatory power of both specifications is relatively high ($\overline{R}^2$ is about 0.6). The coefficient of unemployment is statistically significant (at 5 percent and 10 percent, respectively) and

Table 6.2. OECD real wage growth equations: estimation results (1984–2004)

	Dependent variable: real wage growth	
	(1)	(2)
Constant	1.45	1.08
	(3.57)***	(1.17)
Unemployment	−0.11	−0.10
	(2.06)**	(1.83)*
EPL index	−0.06	
	(0.65)	
LMR factor score		−0.06
		(0.55)
Labour productivity growth	0.54	0.64
	(4.31)***	(1.84)*
Country dummies:		
Finland, 1999	0.92	0.83
	(3.09)***	(2.10)**
Greece, 1999	1.81	
	(7.51)***	
Ireland, 1989	1.23	
	(2.14)**	
Japan, 1989	−2.05	−2.18
	(6.89)***	(5.80)***
Spain, 1989	1.17	0.92
	(2.24)**	(1.29)
Switzerland, 1989	−1.30	−1.10
	(5.34)***	(1.93)*
$\bar{R}^2$	0.60	0.57
F (prob > F)	5.76	5.08
	(0.000)	(0.001)
No. of observations	40	36
Standard error	0.56	0.55

Notes: Equation (1) in column 1, using EPL as explanatory variable, is estimated for 20 OECD countries. Equation (2), which includes LMR as one of the determinants, is estimated for 18 countries; Greece and Ireland are excluded because of lack of LMR factor score. Regressions in columns 1 and 2 are estimated by instrumented (2SLS) regression with robust standard errors; labor productivity growth is instrumented using capital intensity growth; in addition, significant country dummies are included for Finland (1999), Greece (1999), Ireland (1989 and 1999), Japan (1989), Spain (1989), and Switzerland (1989). The first-stage regressions are not reported in the table. Robust *t*-statistics appear in parentheses. *, **, and *** denote statistical significance at 10%, 5%, and 1%, respectively. Figures in parentheses in the F-row are *p*-values.

negative (-0.1), as is to be expected. The coefficient of productivity growth is statistically significantly different from zero (at 1 percent in column 1 and at 10 percent in column 2) and positive. It is notable that its values (0.54 and 0.64, respectively) conform to similar coefficient estimates for twenty OECD countries (1960–1994) by Nunziata (2005) and for Britain (1871–1999) by Hatton (2007). The estimated coefficients are also statistically significantly different from unity; the null hypothesis $H_0: \alpha_2 = 1$ must therefore be rejected (at 1 percent), which is in line with earlier results by Carter (2007) for fifteen OECD countries (1963–1996). Finally, perhaps surprisingly, we find that real wage growth is not statistically significantly affected by either the EPL index or the LMR factor score. More will be said on this finding below.

In Table 6.3 appear the results for aggregate demand growth, which in Keynesian fashion is estimated as a function of export growth, investment growth, and the government deficit as a percentage of GDP. Investment growth, in turn, is estimated a function of the long-term real interest rate and statistically significant country dummies for Japan (1999) and the group of Anglo-Saxon countries (1989 and 1999). The two equations are estimated separately by OLS (reported in column 1 of Table 6.3) and jointly by three-stage least squares (3SLS) (reported in column 2). The results are comparable; the explanatory power of the demand growth equations is high ($\bar{R}^2$ is about 0.82).

First, export growth emerges as a major determinant of real GDP growth: the statistically significant (at 1 percent) elasticity of GDP with respect to exports is 0.3. Second, a 1 percentage point increase in the government deficit is associated with a rise in real GDP growth of 0.06 percentage points. Third, the coefficient of real fixed investment growth is statistically significant (at 1 percent) and positive. We further find a statistically significant and negative effect of real interest rates on investment growth (in columns 1# and 2#). According to the estimated coefficients of Table 6.3, a 1 percentage point increase in the real interest rate is associated with a decline in real GDP growth of about 0.1 percentage points.

Long-Run Effects of Labor Market Regulation

Using the estimation results of Tables 6.2, 6.3, and 4.5, we calculated the reduced-form coefficients of the equilibrium unemployment equation (6.5). The implied impacts of specified changes in each of the independent variables—demand growth, real interest rate changes, and indicators of labor market regulation—appear in Table 6.4. First we look at the impact on unemployment of labor market regulation. We calculated the implied impact of a one-unit increase in the EPL index as well as the LMR factor score (i.e., more extensive

Table 6.3. OECD demand equations: estimation results (1984–2004)

	OLS estimates Dependent variable:		3SLS estimates Dependent variable:	
	GDP growth (1)	Fixed investment growth (1#)	GDP growth (2)	Fixed investment growth (2#)
Constant	0.30	6.28	0.54	6.83
	(0.99)	(5.24)***	(2.19)**	(7.02)***
Real interest rate		−0.42		−0.48
		(2.67)**		(3.97)***
Fixed investment growth	0.25		0.18	
	(5.14)***		(2.65)***	
Export growth	0.30		0.31	
	(5.32)***		(6.44)***	
Government deficit (% of GDP)	0.06		0.07	
	(2.20)**		(3.03)***	
Country dummies:				
Japan, 1999		−6.11		−5.84
		(6.93)***		(3.01)***
Anglo-Saxon countries, 1989 and 1999		1.84		1.42
		(2.32)**		(2.11)**
$\bar{R}^2$	0.84	0.35	0.82	0.34
F (prob > F)	35.76	6.48		
	(0.000)	(0.001)		
χ^2 (prob > χ^2)			139.03	21.22
			(0.000)	(0.000)
No. of observations	40	40	40	40
Standard error	0.46	1.95	0.46	1.87

Notes: Equations (1) and (1#) are estimated using OLS. Equations (2) and (2#) are estimated using 3SLS. In the investment growth equations, we have included a country dummy for Japan for 1999, which experienced extremely low real interest rates during 1994–2004, and a group dummy for the five Anglo-Saxon countries (Australia, Canada, Ireland, the United Kingdom, and the United States) in our sample. Robust *t*-statistics appear in parentheses for the OLS estimations; *z*-statistics appear in parentheses for the 3SLS estimations. *, **, and *** denote statistical significance at 10%, 5%, and 1%, respectively. Figures in parentheses in the *F*-row are *p*-values.

Table 6.4. The effects on equilibrium unemployment of labor market deregulation, export growth, and an increase in the real interest rate

	Indicators of labor market regulation		Demand variables		
	$\partial u^*/\partial$ EPL	$\partial u^*/\partial$ LMR	$\partial u^*/\partial \hat{e}$	$\partial u^*/\partial r_k$	$\partial u^*/\partial$ deficit
1 Our estimate	−0.92	−0.92	−0.77	+0.25	−0.15
Earlier findings					
2 Elmeskov, Martin, and Scarpetta (1998)	+1.43				
3 Blanchard and Wolfers (2000)	+0.24				
4 Belot and van Ours (2001)	+0.87				
5 Nicoletti and Scarpetta (2003)	+0.91				
6 IMF (2003)	+0.52				
7 Nickell, Nunziata, and Ochel (2005)	+1.21				
8 Baccaro and Rei (2005)	−0.95			+0.20 / 0.30	

Notes: The impact on equilibrium unemployment of the EPL index and LMR factor score is based on a 1-unit increase in this index.

Sources: Row 1 is based on authors' calculations; based on our estimations, we assume that $\alpha_1 = 0.10$; $\alpha_2 = 0.59$; $\alpha_3 = 0$; $\beta_1 = 0.42$; $\beta_2 = 0.29$; *and* $\beta_3 = 0.16$. Rows 2 to 4 are from Baker et al. (2005a), table 3.5. Rows 5 and 6 are based on Baker et al. (2005b), tables 2 and 3; the IMF estimate is based on variant three of the IMF's (2003) four regression equations. Row (7) is based on Nickell, Nunziata, and Ochel (2005), table 5, column 2; the impact of the EPL index is evaluated at its mean value and includes the impact of EPL on raising unemployment persistence. Row 8 is from Baccaro and Rei (2005); the EPL estimate (rescaled) is from table 11; the interest rate effect represents the authors' conclusion (p. 41).

labor market regulation) using equation (6.9) and find that these changes lead to a decline in the NAIRU of 0.9 percentage points. The reason for this outcome lies in the fact that more regulation leads to a larger increase in labor productivity growth (through more rapid technological progress) than in real wage growth; as a result, there is downward pressure on the price level, and equilibrium unemployment has to fall (to generate more real wage growth) so as to keep income distribution and inflation constant. Formally, this result follows from condition (6.15), which states that the extra wage growth demanded by workers (due to higher z) is less than the real wage growth warranted by the increased productivity growth:

$$(6.15) \qquad \frac{\partial u^*}{\partial z} < 0 \text{ if } \frac{\alpha_3}{(1-\alpha_2)} = \frac{0}{1-0.59} = 0 < \frac{\beta_3}{(1-\beta_2)} = \frac{0.16}{1-0.29} = 0.23$$

In terms of the standard NAIRU model formulation, an increase in regulation—represented by a rise in our wage-push factor z—shifts up the price-setting curve from PS to PS' as in Figure 6.1, because the ensuing higher productivity growth now warrants a higher real wage growth (keeping the profit share constant). The wage-setting curve WS does not shift, because $\alpha_3 = 0$, that is, more labor market regulation does not lead to higher wage growth claims. The result is a decline in the inflation-safe unemployment rate from u_1^* to u_2^*.

This empirical result may be overly strong, however, as it is partly based on our finding that $\alpha_3 = 0$. It follows, ceteris paribus, that for higher values of α_3, $\partial u^*/\partial z \to 0$, that is, the more sensitive real wage growth claims are to z, the smaller the unemployment-reducing impact of labor market regulation. It can be calculated from equation (6.15) that if $\alpha_3 = 0.093$, $\partial u^*/\partial z = 0$. The available evidence on the impact of regulation on real wage growth is weak, nonrobust, and mixed, and therefore does not warrant strong conclusions. Nunziata (2005), for instance, finds that $\alpha_3 > 0$, but Holden and Nymoen (2002) and Nymoen and Rødseth (2003) find

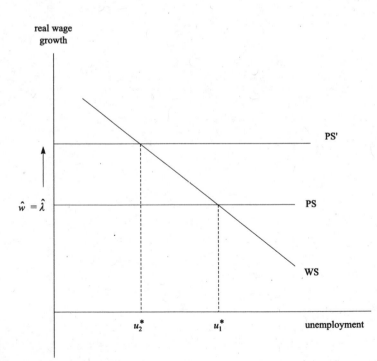

Figure 6.1. More labor market regulation (and higher real wage growth) reduces the NAIRU.

no statistically significant impact. We cannot exclude the empirical possibility that $\alpha_3 > 0$, but the coefficient is not likely to be very large. Therefore, we interpret our finding as pointing to a small but negative association between long-run unemployment and labor market regulation. Empirical support for this interpretation can be found in the work of Lucio Baccaro and Diego Rei (2005), who find, using their preferred model, that the estimated coefficient of EPL on unemployment is generally negative and statistically significant; in their preferred specification, the estimated coefficient is -0.95, which is close to our reduced-form estimate of $\partial u^*/\partial z$.[5] It needs no comment that our conclusion stands in sharp contrast to the unemployment-creating effects of regulation predicted by the standard NAIRU model, as is clear from Table 6.4, which lists the findings from six well-known NAIRU studies. But none of these studies has included the productivity-enhancing effects of protective labor market interventions. It is in this sense that these findings are empirically and intellectually unsatisfactory.

Demand Policy Does Have Permanent Effects

The pinnacle of conventional NAIRU theory is that macro policy efforts to reduce actual unemployment below its equilibrium rate would be unsuccessful in the long run, because they would soon generate accelerating inflation, the intolerability of which would force a retreat to the NAIRU. This argument is essentially due to Milton Friedman (1968) and Edmund Phelps (1968). Friedman formulated a thought experiment within which unemployment could vary in response to macroeconomic policy in the short run because of unfulfilled inflation expectations but would be constant—by construction—in the long run because in a rational world expectations must be satisfied. While the core of his argument was macroeconomic, Friedman was rather hazy about how precisely the economy would revert back to the NAIRU after being perturbed by demand policy and how long this process would take. One could infer from his paper that equilibrium unemployment would be restored by means of Pigouvian real balance effects, whereby changes in inflation affect wealth, consumption, and aggregate demand. On the length of the adjustment process, he ventured a personal judgment, based on his examination of the historical evidence for the United States, stating that "a full adjustment to the new rate of inflation takes . . . a couple of decades" (Friedman 1968, 11). The rhetorical power of Friedman's argument was so great that it swept the field—notwithstanding its haziness (Eisner 1997; Galbraith 1997). But is the argument right?

Our theoretical argument and empirical analysis suggest that the answer is no. As is shown in Table 6.4, we find that demand factors do have a permanent impact on equilibrium unemployment. Specifically, we find the following:

1. A decline of 1 percentage point in autonomous OECD export growth leads (via the foreign trade multiplier) to an increase in equilibrium unemployment of 0.77 percentage points. Actual OECD export growth (estimated from OECD data) declined from 7.6 percent per annum during 1960–1980 to 4.3 percent per year during 1980–2000. This 3.3 percentage point decline in export growth must have led to a rise in equilibrium unemployment between 1960–1980 and 1980–2000 by about 2.5 percentage points—which in itself explains about 50 percent of the actual increase in OECD unemployment over these periods.[6]

2. Fiscal policy influences steady-inflation unemployment—a 1 percentage point increase in the government deficit is found to lead to a decline in the unemployment rate by 0.15 percentage points. Our finding is probably an overestimate, because over longer periods of time than that covered by our analysis, the impact of fiscal policy on unemployment will be smaller because of fiscal solvency requirements. Still, when we apply it to the increase in the average structural budget deficit of OECD governments, from 1 percent during 1960–1980 to 3.1 percent during 1980–2000 (Baker et al. 2005a), our impact estimates translates into a reduction of OECD unemployment by about 0.3 percentage points. More recently, many European governments reduced their budget deficits in response to the 1992 Maastricht Treaty, which—according to our findings—must have led to rising EU unemployment. Gordon (1999) and Galbraith and Garcilazo (2004) confirm our inference and pin the responsibility for rising European unemployment after 1992 on this fiscal tightening.

3. A rise in the real interest rate by 1 percentage point results—by depressing investment demand—in an increase in unemployment of about 0.25 percentage points. Our quantitative estimate is broadly similar to earlier findings by Ball (1999, table 5) and Baccaro and Rei (2005) that an increase of 1 percentage point in the real interest rate leads to an increase in the unemployment rate of about 0.2—0.5 percentage points. According to estimates by Baker et al. (2005a), the actual average real interest rate in the OECD area increased by 3.7 percentage points between 1960–1980 and 1980–2000, which—according to our estimates—must have raised OECD equilibrium unemployment by another 0.9 percentage points (explaining another 17.9 percent of the actual rise in OECD unemployment).

We therefore find that as much as 68 percent, or two-thirds, of the actual long-term increase in OECD unemployment between 1960–1980 and 1980–2000 can be attributed to the lower growth rate of world exports and the higher level of real interest rates after 1980. Clearly, demand factors are the dominant determinants of equilibrium unemployment in the OECD area. This finding highlights the seriousness of omitting demand from the analysis of unemployment.

To illustrate the claim that demand policy matters for structural unemployment, we constructed Figure 6.2, which plots period-average real interest rates against structural unemployment rates in our group of twenty OECD countries for the ten-year periods from 1984 to 1994 and from 1994 to 2004. The

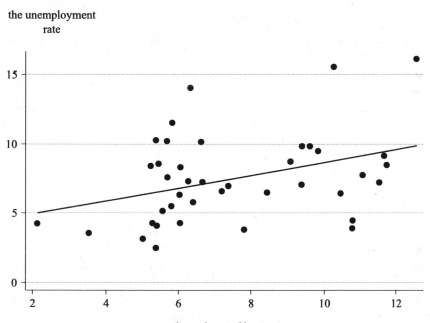

Figure 6.2. Structural unemployment is higher when the real interest is higher.

Notes:

a. Data points are for twenty OECD countries in two periods: 1984–1994 and 1994–2004. The curve is based on the following OLS regression (robust t-value in parentheses):

$$\text{Unemployment rate} = 3.22 + 0.56\ r_k$$
$$(2.27)^{**}\ (2.83)^{***}\ \ \overline{R}^2 = 0.21$$

b. ** = statistically significant at 5%; *** = statistically significant at 1%.

statistical association is strong (significant at less than 1 percent) and positive, indicating that countries featuring above-OECD-average real interest rates over prolonged periods of time (ten years) experience above-average unemployment. Our explanation of this association is as follows: due to the higher real interest rates, investment and overall demand are lower; this leads to slower labor productivity growth, which in turn increases a country's proneness to inflationary pressures; hence, the lower productivity growth translates into higher equilibrium unemployment so as to maintain inflation constant and conflicting income claims mutually consistent.

Egalitarianism, Beyond Ideology

We have tried to generalize the conventional NAIRU model by endogenizing technological change and labor productivity growth in terms of the major variables of the model. In our extended NAIRU model, labor productivity growth is included in the wage bargaining process but is not fully reflected in real wage growth, and labor productivity growth itself depends positively on demand growth (the Kaldor-Verdoorn relation) and labor market regulation (through wage-cost-induced technological progress), as we have explained in Chapter 4. The logical consequence of this broadening of the theoretical canvass has been that the NAIRU becomes endogenous itself and ceases to be an attractor—Friedman's natural, stable, and timeless equilibrium point from which the system cannot permanently deviate. In our model, a deviation from the initial equilibrium affects not only wages and prices (keeping the rest of the system unchanged) but also demand, technology, workers' motivation, and work intensity; as a result, productivity growth and ultimate equilibrium unemployment will change. There is, in other words, nothing natural or inescapable about equilibrium unemployment, as is Friedman's presumption, following Wicksell; rather, the NAIRU is a social construct, fluctuating in response to fiscal and monetary policies and labor market interventions. Its ephemeral (rather than structural) nature may explain why the best economists working on the NAIRU have persistently failed to agree on how high the NAIRU actually is and how to estimate it.

It is important to further think through our model. If we do so, we discover how NAIRU-based macro policies may in actual fact have perverse outcomes. The implication of our finding that demand matters for unemployment is that deflationary macro policies (e.g., high interest rates and balanced budgets) not only reduce GDP growth but simultaneously raise the economy's inflationary threshold because of their negative (Kaldor-Verdoorn) impact on productivity growth, thus raising equilibrium unemployment. With lower productivity growth, the NAIRU has to be higher to lower wage claims, bringing them back in line with productivity. This being the case, a vicious circle may develop: trying to keep inflation low and stable, the monetary and fiscal policy authorities follow a high interest rate policy and a restrictive budget policy; the result is a decline in demand growth; the consequent fall in productivity growth reduces the scope for real wage growth claims and raises the steady-inflation unemployment rate; once the scope for wage claims becomes more circumscribed, the likelihood increases that wage growth demand exceeds productivity growth; if this happens, it will be countered by a new round of deflationary policies (because those making macroeconomic policy stick to conventional NAIRU wisdom). The economic and social costs of such NAIRUvianism are high and avoidable: unnecessarily high rates of unemployment, low real wage growth, and unnecessarily low labor productivity growth—as has been characteristic of European Monetary Union countries, which have been more Catholic than the Pope in their fervor to follow the NAIRU policy prescriptions (Galbraith and Garcilazo 2004; Arestis, Baddeley, and Sawyer 2007).

How do our findings compare with those of the recent literature? First, our finding that demand and demand policies have long-run effects on unemployment reinforces the conclusions of Arestis and Biefang-Frisancho Mariscal (1998), Ball (1999), Galbraith and Garcilazo (2004), and Arestis, Baddeley, and Sawyer (2007). But theoretically, we offer a new explanation: demand affects unemployment through its effect on productivity growth. Empirically, we present additional evidence of a statistically significant association between demand factors (export growth and the real interest rate) and long-term unemployment, which contradicts the conventional view that demand does not influence the NAIRU. Second, regarding the unemployment effects of labor market regulation, we interpret our findings as indicating that the effects on long-run unemployment of labor market institutions should not be overemphasized, as these are likely to be rather small. A similar point has been made by Ball (1999); by Blanchard and Wolfers (2000), who deemphasize the direct impact of labor market regulation; by Baccaro and Rei (2005, 44), who conclude that "unemployment is mostly increased by policies and institutions that lead to restrictive macroeconomics policies. The claim that systematic deregulation of labour markets would solve the unemployment problem . . . appears unwarranted based on our results"; and by Baker et al. (2005a) and Howell et al. (2007). Thus, the recent literature seems to accept that the impact of excessive labor market regulation on long-run unemployment is small (compared to the impact of depressed demand) but negative. Instead, we have argued that more extensive labor market regulation could, in principle, lead to reduced unemployment, mainly because it will stimulate productivity growth and technological progress. For macroeconomic policy, our findings have obvious implications. First, the rise in structural unemployment in major OECD countries over the last three decades cannot be attributed to increased labor market regulation, but (and this is the second implication) must be attributed to a slowdown of autonomous demand growth and a structural rise in real interest rates. All this points to the most important lesson to be drawn from the analysis: the need to revive aggregate demand, both domestically and globally, so as to enable the OECD countries to reduce their high levels of structural unemployment.

Further Reading

Joan Robinson's (1962) *Economic Philosophy* continues to be a relevant treatment of fundamental issues in economics that nowadays are (incorrectly) taken for granted, including morals, ideology, values, and historical and logical time. Robert Eisner (1997) and James Galbraith (1997) provide honest evaluations of NAIRU-based macroeconomics, which are still relevant more than ten years later. Laurence Ball (1999), Marika Karanassou and Dennis Snower (2004), and Philip Arestis, Michelle Baddeley, and Malcolm Sawyer (2007) are among the few researchers rejecting Friedman's claim that demand does not matter in the long run.

7

Europe's Nordic Model

> The animal species, in which individual struggle has been reduced to
> its narrowest limits, and the practice of mutual aid has attained the
> greatest development, are invariably the most numerous, the most
> prosperous, and the most open to further progress. The mutual
> protection which is obtained in this case, the possibility of attaining
> old age and of accumulating experience, the higher intellectual
> development, and the further growth of sociable habits, secure the
> maintenance of the species, its extension, and its further progressive
> evolution. The unsociable species, on the contrary, are doomed
> to decay.
>
> PYOTR ALEXEYEVICH KROPOTKIN, *MUTUAL AID*

Partly in response to social Darwinism, which is so characteristic of mainstream economics, Russian prince (and anarchist) Pyotr Kropotkin argued
that cooperation and mutual aid are as important in the evolution of the species as competition, antagonism, and mutual strife, if not more so. Kropotkin's ideas, though unorthodox, have become scientifically respectable and
have found their way into modern sociobiology.[1] Kropotkin did not deny
the competitive form of struggle, but he argued, as evolutionary biologist
Stephen Jay Gould explained, that

> the co-operative style had been underemphasized and must balance or
> even predominate over competition in considering nature as a whole. . . .
> I would hold that Kropotkin's basic argument is correct. Struggle does
> occur in many modes, and some lead to co-operation among members
> of a species as the best pathway to advantage for individuals. If Kropot-
> kin overemphasized mutual aid, most Darwinians . . . had exaggerated
> competition just as strongly. If Kropotkin drew inappropriate hope for
> social reform from his concept of nature, other Darwinians had erred
> just as firmly . . . in justifying imperial conquest, racism, and oppression
> of industrial workers as the harsh outcome of natural selection in the
> competitive mode. (Gould 1997, 21)

Likewise, and translated to our context, the NAIRU mode of thought has
overemphasized the importance of dog-eat-dog competition and worker-
business conflict while underemphasizing or even ignoring the potential

187

advantages of cooperation and coordination. The NAIRU approach sees capitalism as a zero-sum game: if workers win (obtain a higher wage share), firms must lose (profits). Such an unbalance cannot persist indefinitely, because it would wipe out profits, investment, and growth and lead to dismal stagnation. Hence, to maintain growth, the wage share has to be reduced again (so as to restore profitability), which is possible only by disciplining workers by means of additional unemployment. Similarly, Darwin thought of ecology as a world stuffed full of competing species—so balanced and crowded that a new life-form could gain entry only by pushing a former inhabitant out.[2]

In the group of OECD economies, the advantages of cooperation and mutual aid, emphasized by Kropotkin, are undoubtedly exemplified best by Europe's Scandinavian countries: Denmark, Finland, Norway, and Sweden. These Nordic countries on average outperform the other countries of the OECD on most measures of economic performance, notwithstanding the fact that they have the highest level of social expenditures, the highest taxes, and extensive labor market regulation, which ensures one of the most compressed wage structures in the world and generous universal unemployment benefits. What most economists see as a recipe for serious economic trouble has, in the Nordic countries, led to high growth, low unemployment, low inequality, and a fairly efficient allocation of resources. How do the open, dependent, and globalized Nordic countries manage to escape the supposedly ubiquitous NAIRU trade-off between growth and low unemployment, on one hand, and egalitarian outcomes, on the other? This is the issue addressed in this chapter.

A Provisional Utopia

"Kropotkin was no crackpot," writes Gould. Neither were Swedish economists Gösta Rehn and Rudolf Meidner, the two architects of the unique economic policy model (Meidner and Rehn 1953) that shaped Swedish economic policies during the past five decades and has also influenced policies in the other Nordic economies. Building on Keynes, the two men understood that social welfare, corporate governance, and macroeconomic management needed to be brought together if full employment and fair wages were to be maintained with low inflation and rapid growth. The Rehn-Meidner model can be seen as a form of modified Keynesianism that, by combining private ownership and free markets with strong regulation and coordination, comes close to being a "provisional utopia":

The values of the highest priority are full employment and equality. Both come into conflict with other goals, notably price stability and efficiency. The conflict between full employment and price stability can be solved by a policy which combines restrictive general demand management and [active] labour market policy. Equality pursued by a system of general welfare, by a large public sector and by a wage policy of solidarity has to be compatible with the goals of efficiency and economic growth. (Meidner 1993, 217–218)

We can distinguish five major components of the Swedish model. First, total demand should be kept high by fiscal and monetary policy, but not so high as to lead to excessive demand and rising inflation. Second, the fulfillment of social needs should not depend upon individual purchasing power in the market; hence, the state should guarantee universal pensions, unemployment insurance, and health care—unlike Anglo-Saxon-style corporate welfare, which offered private corporations tax incentives to take on (in a decentralized manner) the task of supplying social insurance to their own workers. Third, wage growth should be restrained and wages should be set according to a solidaristic wage policy (equal work should be equally paid, regardless of the profitability of the firm, its size, and the location of the workplace). Fourth, active labor market policy was a central original component of the Rehn-Meidner model, crucial to achieving full employment in a noninflationary manner. And fifth, to solve the dilemma (inherent in the wage policy of solidarity) that wage restraint in profitable firms leaves the latter more profit than they would earn in an unregulated market, excess profits should be transferred into so-called tax-exempt wage earners' funds, which were collectively owned by the employees; the idea was to strengthen employees' influence at the workplace through co-ownership.[3] But unlike the other components of the model, the idea of setting up wage earners' funds was never pursued in practice (beyond a symbolic gesture).

Two features of the Rehn-Meidner model are of special importance in the context of our larger argument.[4] First, its two architects well understood the fact that regulation (and coordination) need not be counterproductive in terms of technological progress and productivity growth, but can in fact be productivity-enhancing. Many in the economics profession are of the view that too much equality, too much worker security, and too much regulation stifle the dynamics of entrepreneurial creativity—the essence of capitalism. But as Rudolf Meidner writes:

High public expenditures may look like a heavy burden for the taxpayers, but what is frequently overlooked is the fact that a considerable part of public expenditures are investments in human capital and consequently highly productive. . . . Firms unable to pay the "normal" wage (set in the central negotiations) have to rationalize their production or, if they have exhausted that potential, will be squeezed out from the market. (Meidner 1993, 215–217)

Rapid labor productivity growth is therefore perfectly compatible with wage equality, as equal remuneration for identical jobs puts cost pressure on low-productivity firms, requiring them to increase productivity or die; the closure of inefficient firms frees resources for the expansion of more dynamic firms (Moene and Wallerstein 1995, 1997; Agell 1999; Erixon 2008). A study of productivity growth in Sweden by Hibbs and Locking (2000) finds evidence that the gain in efficiency was substantial and the cumulative impact on the distribution of wages and salaries was large. Furthermore, a wage policy of solidarity strengthens the incentives for productivity-raising structural change by inducing larger profit differentials between industries and firms (for evidence, see Edin and Topel 1997). Second, Rehn and Meidner rejected the idea that unions should be disciplined by unemployment, as is the case in the NAIRU model. Their preference was a combination of self-discipline by the unions, keeping real wage growth in line with productivity growth, and a discipline imposed on firms and capital owners, forcing them to accept and adjust to the compressed wage structure and to transfer excess profits to wage earners' funds. These two features make the Rehn-Meidner model the counterpart to the NAIRU approach.

The Nordic Visible Handshake

Samuel Bowles, Richard Edwards, and Frank Roosevelt (2005, 473) have called the Nordic policy model the "visible handshake" approach. According to them, it is "the only viable way to achieve full employment."[5] The handshake "refers to deals struck between business and labor to share the increased output associated with higher employment in ways that (a) are fair and (b) also allow for a high enough rate of profit to stimulate investment." In the visible handshake approach, the wage-profit claims conflict is solved by negotiating and coordinating wages and working conditions between unions and firms in a way that is based on notions of reciprocity, trust, and fairness. Unions are willing to forgo using the bargaining power that high employment gives them and accept that workers need to be flexible and mobile (supported by active labor market programs) to facilitate firms' adjustment. At the same time, firms give up the bargaining power that high unemployment gives them:

What labor agrees to do in the handshake must have its counterpart in a corresponding commitment on the part of business—otherwise it will be no deal. Employers must commit themselves to providing employment security both at the level of the firm . . . and as a macroeconomic strategy (supporting the government to achieve high employment). (Bowles, Edwards, and Roosevelt 2005, 474)

"One should not underestimate the importance of strong employer associations to the system," writes Norwegian political economist Karl Ove Moene (2008, 370). "The role of employers is often forgotten by critics of the system. If the employers so desired, they could easily dissolve the system by withdrawing from central wage negotiations."

The second element in the handshake approach would be the expansion of built-in stabilizers, such as unemployment insurance and other welfare provisions. This would not only strengthen income-support programs but also help maintain a stable level of aggregate demand, which would be beneficial to both business and labor.

While the visible handshake approach is a good, essentialist characterization of the Nordic model, we are aware that there is no single Nordic model, and still less an unchanging Nordic model. But as Jeffrey Sachs (2006a, 2) writes, "What has been consistently true for decades is a high level of public social outlays as a share of national income, and a sustained commitment to social insurance and redistributive social support for the poor, disabled, and otherwise vulnerable parts of the population." This comes out clearly in our comparison of four OECD country groupings in Chapter 2. As Table 2.3 shows, even if the Nordics are very similar to the other European Continental (EC) countries in terms of policies, three major differences stand out. First, the Nordic countries combine high social spending and fiscal surpluses, which means that their levels of taxation are high enough to match their social ambitions, unlike the EC and European Mediterranean (EM) countries, which feature fiscal deficits. Scandinavian fiscal policy is thus very restrictive compared to these other countries, not only to control inflation but also to redistribute income to labor and increase public savings (at the expense of firm savings) for purposes of industrial and technology policy; this prudential fiscal policy stance goes back directly to the Rehn-Meidner model. Second, the Nordics spend more on activating labor market policies than the EM countries do (but not significantly more than the EC countries). And finally, the Nordic countries invest more heavily in knowledge and research and development (R&D) and have prospering information, communication, and technology (ICT) manufacturing sectors; a big part of these investments are financed from public savings. The huge differences in policies between the

Nordic and the Anglo-Saxon (AS) countries, highlighted in Chapter 2, need no further elaboration. Figure 7.1 brings out—in various ways— Rudolf Meidner's key insight that egalitarianism is compatible with technological dynamism. In the upper left panel, for example, we see that the more egalitarian OECD countries feature higher R&D expenditures (as a percentage of their GDP), and the upper right panel shows that R&D expenditure is significantly higher in economies having more strongly regulated labor markets (captured by more strict employment protection). The lower left panel shows that R&D expenditures as a percentage of GDP are higher when labor taxation is higher—as in the Rehn-Meidner model where tax revenues were to be used for industrial policy. The lower right panel indicates that there is no association between earnings inequality and the share of ICT value added in total business sector value added.

Opinions about the Nordic model vary across authors and also over time, depending on whether the Scandinavian countries were facing periodic financial difficulties and episodes of high unemployment (Erixon 2008; Holmlund 2009). But recent overall assessments are positive and in line with the substantive evidence reviewed in Chapter 2: the Nordic model on average does not perform worse than the other countries of the OECD and in fact outperforms them on most measures of economic performance, including productivity growth and unemployment. As Jeffrey Sachs (2006b) writes, comparing the Nordic and AS economies: "Poverty rates are much lower there [than in the Anglo-Saxon countries], and national income per working-age population is on average higher. Unemployment rates are roughly the same in both groups. . . . The budget situation is stronger in the Nordic group, with larger surpluses as a share of GDP." Our Table 2.4 (in Chapter 2) shows that Nordic earnings and income inequalities, poverty, and long-term unemployment and youth unemployment have been the lowest within the OECD.[6] Hence Belgian economist André Sapir (2005, 9) concludes that the "Nordics enjoy an envious position, with a social model that delivers both efficiency and equity."

Nordic Exceptionalism Explained?

Nordic macroeconomic performance conflicts with the cornerstone of mainstream macro theory: the idea of a ubiquitous trade-off between growth and low unemployment, on the one hand, and equity and strong social protection, on the other. This contradiction is a powerful cause of cognitive dissonance, as we argued in Chapter 2. As in other such cases of dissonance, responses vary from the outright denial of the disconfirming evidence to rationalization, basically arguing that superior Nordic macro performance is

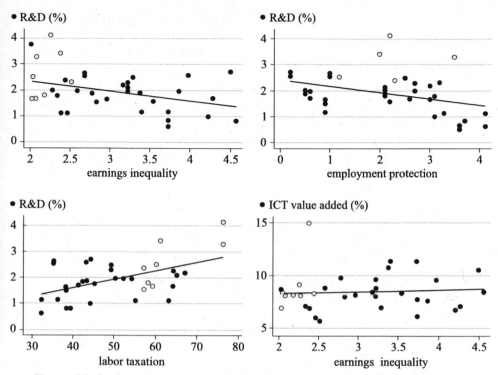

Figure 7.1. Egalitarianism is compatible with technological dynamism.

Notes:

a. Scatter points of the Nordic countries are indicated in lighter-shaded circles. The curves are based on the following OLS regressions (we report robust *t*-values):

Upper left panel:

R&D expenditure (% GDP) = 3.11   −0.38 earnings inequality

                    $(5.30)^{***}$ $(2.05)^{**}$ $\bar{R}^2 = 0.12$

Upper right panel:

R&D expenditure (% GDP) = 2.40   −0.24 employment protection (*EPL*)

                   $(11.45)^{***}$ $(2.57)^{**}$ $\bar{R}^2 = 0.11$

Lower left panel:

R&D expenditure (% GDP) = 0.27   +0.27 labor taxation

                   (0.48) $(2.93)^{***}$ $\bar{R}^2 = 0.25$

Lower right panel:

ICT value added (% business
    sector value added)   = 8.05   +0.14 earnings inequality

                   $(6.35)^{***}$ (0.37) $\bar{R}^2 = 0.00$

b. ** = statistically significant at 5%; *** = statistically significant at 1%.

due to idiosyncratic causes. Perhaps the best example of outright denial is provided by monetarist economists Lars Ljungqvist and Thomas J. Sargent (1995), who blame the higher Swedish unemployment rate during the years 1990–1995 on labor market regulations introduced in the 1960s and 1970s; the lags involved strain credibility and remind one of Milton Friedman's conclusion that unemployment adjustments to inflation may take decades (see Chapter 6). In contrast to Ljungqvist and Sargent, the available evidence suggests that changes in Nordic labor market regulation do not at all explain actual changes in structural unemployment. As Ragnar Nymoen and Asbjørn Rødseth (2003, 26) conclude, based on an analysis of Nordic wage curves between 1965 and 1994: "The shifts in the wage curve [due to increased regulation] are small relative to the large actual increases in unemployment." And Bertil Holmlund (2009, 124) notes that it is "difficult to identify sharp changes in the usual suspects—benefits, labour-market institutions, taxes, etc.—that could explain the [change] in unemployment."

The most frequently mentioned idiosyncratic cause of superior Nordic employment performance is these countries' higher levels of expenditure on activating labor market policies and systems of "flexicurity" (Ploughmann and Madsen 2005; Auer 2007). However, unlike foreign economists, Nordic economists in general have been skeptical about this favorable interpretation of Nordic labor market policies, because the weight of the empirical evidence indicates that these programs do *not* raise reemployment probabilities but, instead, raise real wage growth, as unemployed workers are presented with an attractive alternative to unemployment (Calmfors and Forslund 1991; Nymoen and Rødseth 2003; Erixon 2008; Forslund, Gottfries, and Westermark 2008). Swedish studies have shown that the positive effects on regular employment of active labor market programs were either small or nonexistent and that their mobility-stimulating and inflation-dampening effects should not be overstated (Forslund and Krueger 1997; Calmfors et al. 2001; Nymoen and Rødseth 2003). Hence, activating labor market policies add to the puzzle, because they not only reduce both directly and indirectly the much-needed real wage flexibility of firms to respond to intensifying global competition but also raise labor costs. Hence, unsurprisingly, most studies of Nordic unemployment conclude that "the perspective should be broadened, particularly by looking for explanations of . . . unemployment that do not focus solely on a malfunctioning labour market" (Holden and Nymoen 2002, 102).

Macroeconomic shocks are the second idiosyncratic cause that is frequently invoked to explain the evolution of Nordic unemployment. The steep rise in Nordic unemployment during 1990–1995, for example, is generally attributed to a series of adverse macroeconomic shocks, especially high real interest rates due to contractionary monetary policy to protect the exchange rate. Holmlund (2009, 115) concludes that "around half of the Swedish unemployment [during 1994] was due to contractionary monetary policy." And Nymoen and Rødseth (2003, 27) argue that "most of the action must have been on the demand side. . . . [L]arge demand shocks may cause disequilibria that remain significant for several years." Without denying the importance of demand factors, we think this invocation of demand shocks is not convincing: demand policy should be treated as an integral part of the explanatory framework, along the lines set out in Chapter 6.

A third idiosyncratic cause of superior Nordic performance concerns these countries' lavish expenditure on R&D and higher education, which explains their rapid productivity growth and innovativeness. "All of them, but especially Sweden and Finland, have taken to the sweeping revolution in information and communications technology and leveraged it to gain global competitiveness," writes Sachs (2006b). "On average, the Nordic nations spend 3 percent of GDP on R&D, compared with around 2 percent in the English-speaking nations." While their commitment to R&D and innovation must have produced considerable gains in productivity and competitiveness, we believe that the focus on R&D and education investments per se is too narrow and fails to recognize the larger macroeconomic and industrial-relations context (à la the Rehn-Meidner model) within which these investments have, in fact, generated significant economywide returns. This larger context, we argue, is that of a wage-led macroeconomic growth regime, within which the Nordic economies manage to exploit the cumulative growth potential of the Kaldor-Verdoorn relationship. Due to coordinated real wage growth and supporting fiscal and monetary policies, they keep up aggregate demand growth as well as productivity growth, and this in turn helps to maintain firms' profitability and investment, stimulating growth and keeping a check on structural unemployment. Hence, redistributive and regulatory interventions in the labor market have not led to higher steady-inflation unemployment, because labor productivity has been raised at the same time.

The Model (Again)

Let us briefly recapitulate the main features of our growth model, which has been outlined in Chapter 3 and applied to all OECD countries in Chapter 6. The model can be condensed to three equations: the productivity regime (7.1), the demand regime (7.2), and the real wage growth equation (7.3).

(7.1) $\hat{\lambda} = \beta_0 + \beta_1\,\hat{x} + \beta_2\,\hat{w} + \beta_3\,z$ $\beta_0, \beta_2, \beta_3 > 0;\quad 0 < \beta_1 < 1$

(7.2) $\hat{x} = \Theta + C\,[\hat{w} - \hat{\lambda}]$

where $\Theta = \dfrac{\psi_i\varphi_0\hat{b} + \psi_g\hat{g}^* + \psi_e\hat{e} - \psi_i\varphi_3 r_k}{1 - \psi_i\varphi_2}$, as in equation (3.19).

(7.3) $\hat{w} = \alpha_0 - \alpha_1\,u + \alpha_2\,\hat{\lambda} + \alpha_3\,z$ $\alpha_0, \alpha_2, \alpha_3 > 0$

This is a system of three equations in four unknowns: labor productivity growth $\hat{\lambda}$, real GDP growth $\hat{x}$, real wage growth $\hat{w}$, and the unemployment rate u. Variable z is our catchall indicator of the nature of labor market regulation. Long-run autonomous investment growth is denoted by $\hat{b}$, export growth by $\hat{e}$, the growth of net public expenditure by $\hat{g}^*$ (which is the fiscal policy stance), and the real interest rate by r_k (the monetary policy stance). Equations (7.1) to (7.3) were estimated for the four Nordic countries using data for the period from 1984 to 2004.

Long-run equilibrium requires real wages to grow at the same rate as labor productivity, so that

(7.4) $\hat{w} = \hat{\lambda}$

Using equations (7.2) and (7.4), we get long-run equilibrium income growth $\hat{x}^*$:

(7.5) $\hat{x}^* = \Theta = \dfrac{\psi_i\varphi_0\hat{b} + \psi_g\hat{g}^* + \psi_e\hat{e} - \psi_i\varphi_3 r_k}{1 - \psi_i\varphi_2}$

Substitution of equations (7.4) and (7.5) into the productivity regime (7.1) gives us the reduced-form expression for equilibrium labor productivity growth $\hat{\lambda}^*$:

(7.6) $\hat{\lambda}^* = \dfrac{\beta_0}{1-\beta_2} + \dfrac{\beta_1}{1-\beta_2} * \dfrac{\psi_i\varphi_0\hat{b} + \psi_g\hat{g}^* + \psi_e\hat{e} - \psi_i\varphi_3 r_k}{1 - \psi_i\varphi_2} + \dfrac{\beta_3}{1-\beta_2}z$

just as in Chapter 6. Finally, we derive the equilibrium unemployment rate u^* by combining equations (7.3), (7.4), and (7.6):

(7.7) $u^* = \dfrac{\alpha_0(1-\beta_2) - \beta_0(1-\alpha_2)}{\alpha_1(1-\beta_2)} + \left[\dfrac{\alpha_3(1-\beta_2) - (1-\alpha_2)\beta_3}{\alpha_1(1-\beta_2)}\right]z$

$$-\left[\dfrac{(1-\alpha_2)\beta_1}{\alpha_1(1-\beta_2)}\right]*\left[\dfrac{\psi_i\varphi_0\hat{b} + \psi_g\hat{g}^* + \psi_e\hat{e} - \psi_i\varphi_3 r_k}{1 - \psi_i\varphi_2}\right]$$

Equation (7.7) has already been analyzed and interpreted in detail in Chapter 6.

The Empirics of Nordic Growth

There is not much econometric evidence on the wage-led or profit-led nature of Nordic macroeconomic growth in the existing empirical literature. Our cross-country analysis of Nordic growth is a first attempt to fill this gap. To estimate the Nordic productivity and demand regimes, we use countrywise average annual growth rates for Denmark, Finland, Norway, and Sweden in the regression analysis for four periods of five years each: 1984–1989, 1990–1994, 1995–1999, and 2000–2004. This means that the maximum number of observations is sixteen. To take care of problems of endogeneity and simultaneity, we estimate the productivity and demand regime equations in combination with the equation for endogenous real wage growth using 3SLS. The estimation results appear in Table 7.1. Data sources are listed in the book's Appendix. We include and report statistically influential country dummies. However, before proceeding, we emphasize that the primary purpose of our econometric analysis is exploratory—it is an attempt to examine the quantitative importance of the various causal relations and "a means of suggesting possibilities and probabilities rather than anything else," which need to be "taken with enough grains of salt and applied with superlative common sense" (John Maynard Keynes, 1939 letter E. J. Broster, in Garrone and Marchionatti 2004, 11n11). However, when comparing our findings to the results from other econometric studies for the Nordic economies, we do find (in Table 7.2 below) that our estimations fall well within the range of "stylized facts" on Nordic wage setting, unemployment, and growth.

Consider first the estimation results for the demand regime (column 1). Our main interest here is to obtain the impact on demand growth of real unit labor cost growth, or coefficient C in equation (7.2); note that $[\hat{w}-\hat{\lambda}]$ is the growth rate of real unit labor costs. We use the government deficit (as a percentage of GDP) as our empirical indicator of a country's fiscal policy stance, and the real interest rate as the monetary policy instrument. The estimated equation has a good fit ($\bar{R}^2 = 0.69$) and the estimated coefficients have the expected signs. Important is that our estimate of C (statistically significant at 1 percent) equals 0.83, which means that a 1 percentage point increase in unit labor cost growth raises Nordic demand and output growth by 0.83 percentage points. How does this estimate compare to our earlier estimates for Denmark, Finland, and Sweden in Chapter 5? From Table 5.5, we can see that the present estimate for the group of four Nordic countries is consistent with countrywise estimations: C takes a value of 0.37 for Denmark, 0.72 for Finland, and 1.04 for Sweden, respectively.[7] Nordic demand growth thus is wage-led, and relatively strongly so in comparison to other wage-led European economies. As reported in Table 5.6, coefficient C for

France, Germany, and the Netherlands takes values of, respectively, 0.32, 0.06, and 0.12. This implies that similar real wage growth has much stronger output effects in the Nordic economies than in the EC countries.

In addition, we find that Nordic growth is stimulated by deficit spending and is reduced by higher real interest rates. The coefficient for deficit spending is statistically significant at 10 percent, but the coefficient for the real interest rate is significant at only 13 percent. We accept (and retain in our empirical analysis) the negative interest rate effect, because it is a well-established, uncontroversial stylized fact of Nordic macroeconomic performance. Holmlund's (2009) comprehensive review of Swedish macroeconomic experience after 1980, for instance, shows that high real interest rates accounted for as much as 50 percent of Swedish unemployment in the early 1990s. Nymoen and Rødseth (2003), Forslund, Gottfries, and Westermark (2008), and Karanassou, Sala, and Salvador (2009) find similar substantial effects for the other Nordic economies as well.

The estimation results for the productivity regime appear in column 2 of Table 7.1. As in Chapters 4 and 6, we operationalized variable z using the employment protection legislation (EPL) index. The choice of a single indicator for labor market regulation may appear surprising at first sight, as it seems not rich enough to reflect the manifold dimensions of labor market regulation. But we have two reasons to justify our choice of the EPL index. First, as shown in Chapter 4 for twenty OECD countries, the EPL index covaries in a statistically very significant manner with other major features of labor market regulation. For the Nordics, our labor market regulation factor score, based on seven dimensions of regulation, is strongly correlated with the EPL index ($\bar{R}^2 = 0.76$, with $p < 3$ percent), which indicates that the EPL index is by itself a useful proxy for the larger regulatory structure. Second, while the system of labor market regulation is not perfectly identical in the four Nordic economies, national idiosyncrasies are relatively small (Nymoen and Rødseth 2003). There is one important exception: the Nordics differ rather substantially in terms of the strictness of employment protection legislation. Denmark, in particular, features weak employment protection, almost Anglo-Saxon style, as part of its "flexicurity" approach to the labor market (Auer 2007), deviating significantly from the other Nordics. It is this limited variation in labor market regulation that we want to capture in our estimations.

Turning to the results in column 2 of Table 7.1, we find that Nordic labor productivity growth has been positively associated with real GDP growth: the estimated Kaldor-Verdoorn coefficient takes a value of 0.31 (significant at 1 percent), which is in line with the OECD literature (see Table 4.1). The impact of endogenous real wage growth on Nordic productivity growth is 0.51 (significant at 5 percent), which corresponds to findings by Nordic

Table 7.1. 3SLS estimation results (1984–2004)

	Dependent variable		
	(Demand regime) GDP growth (1)	(Productivity regime) Labor productivity growth (2)	Real wage growth (3)
Constant	3.49 (3.72)***	−1.04 (1.67)*	2.24 (4.72)***
Real unit labor cost growth	0.83 (3.29)***		
Government deficit	0.14 (1.74)*		
Real interest rate	−0.28 (1.53)		
Real wage growth		0.51 (2.42)**	
Unemployment			−0.13 (4.04)***
Real GDP growth		0.31 (3.04)***	
Labor productivity growth			0.57 (5.00)***
EPL index		0.54 (2.67)***	−0.22 (1.45)
Country dummies:			
Sweden, 1984–1989		−1.32 (2.82)***	
Denmark, 1990–1994	2.49** (2.44)	1.96 (3.84)***	−1.67 (4.91)***
Finland, 1990–1994		2.35 (4.11)***	
Norway, 1990–1994	2.40 (2.59)*		
Finland, 1995–1999	2.81 (3.19)***		
Denmark, 2000–2004	−1.98** (2.22)		
Finland, 2000–2004			0.82 (2.68)***
Norway, 2000–2004		1.56 (2.80)***	−2.24 (6.71)***
Pseudo $\bar{R}^2$	0.69	0.70	0.84
χ^2 (prob > χ^2)	38.9 (0.000)	47.4 (0.000)	95.3 (0.000)
No. of observations	16	16	16

Notes: Equations are estimated using 3SLS. z-statistics appear in parentheses. *, **, and *** denote statistical significance at 10%, 5%, and 1%, respectively. Figures in parentheses in the χ^2-row are p-values.

authors including Nymoen and Rødseth (2003, 26) (see again Table 4.1 for evidence for most OECD countries). Finally, we obtain a highly significant (at 1 percent), robust, positive association between labor market regulation and productivity growth in the Nordic countries—which vindicates earlier findings, at the macroeconomic level, of a positive association between productivity growth and forms of regulation (see Buchele and Christiansen 1999; Auer, Berg, and Coulibaly 2005; Dew-Becker and Gordon 2008; and Chapter 4 in this book).

Column 3 of Table 7.1 presents evidence on Nordic real wage growth, expressed in terms of equation (7.3). We stress that our specification of the determinants of real wage growth is the canonical model, used by most Nordic authors with only slight variations. For example, Forslund, Gottfries, and Westermark (2008) derive equation (7.3) from a strategic Nash bargaining model with unions and firms bargaining over the scope for wage increases, that is, the sum of productivity growth and price increases (see also Eriksson 2005; Carlin and Soskice 2006). Wage setters are assumed to build the underlying labor productivity growth into their real wage claims, with their share in productivity growth being dependent on the (perceived) state of the labor market and on the nature and extent of labor market regulation. Real wage growth can then be shown to depend on $\hat{\lambda}$, u, and z (see also Nymoen and Rødseth 2003). Coefficient α_1 reflects the (negative) impact on the real wage of a rise in unemployment: because higher unemployment weakens workers' bargaining power, they are forced to accept a lower real wage.

Coefficient α_2 represents the extent to which labor productivity growth is reflected in the real wage bargain (Hatton 2007; Forslund, Gottfries, and Westermark 2008). A higher z reflects workers' strengthened bargaining position, which increases real wage growth demanded by workers at a given unemployment rate, hence $\alpha_3 > 0$. Earlier research (Holden and Nymoen 2002; Nymoen and Rødseth 2003; Forslund, Gottfries, and Westermark 2008) has shown no evidence of important structural differences in the wage equations between Denmark, Finland, Norway, and Sweden, which means that information from all four countries can be usefully pooled. Column 3 of Table 7.1 shows that the estimated real wage growth equation has a good fit, is relatively robust regarding changes in specification, and comes close to resembling the canonical Nordic wage-setting equation.

Coefficient α_1 takes a value of -0.13 (significant at 1 percent). The negative α_1 indicates that Nordic real wages are negatively sensitive to variations in unemployment. Our numerical estimate implies that a ceteris paribus increase in Nordic unemployment from 3 to 4 percentage points reduces real wages by around 6–7 percentage points, which corresponds closely to findings by Calmfors and Forslund (1991), Nymoen and Rødseth (2003), and Forslund,

Gottfries, and Westermark (2008). Our estimate of α_2 is 0.57 (significant at 1 percent) and is statistically significantly different from unity, which means that a rise (or fall) in productivity growth will not be matched by a corresponding rise (or fall) in real wage growth. Our estimate of α_2 is very close to that of Calmfors and Forslund (1991), who find elasticities lying in the 0.30–0.70 interval with an average of 0.47; their coefficients were always significantly different from unity. Our estimate is also comparable to estimates by Holden and Nymoen (2002) and Nymoen and Rødseth (2003), as reported in Table 7.2.

Finally, we do not find a statistically significant impact on unemployment of labor market regulation: our estimate of α_3, which unexpectedly takes on a negative sign, is not significant at 10 percent. This lack of significant association is, however, also a stylized fact of Nordic real wage formation: the available evidence on the impact of regulation on Nordic real wage growth is weak, nonrobust, and mixed. For example, Calmfors and Forslund (1991) find statistically significant positive effects on wage growth of labor market programs and labor taxes, whereas Holden and Nymoen (2002) and Nymoen and Rødseth (2003) find no such effects. And while Calmfors and Forslund (1991) conclude that there is no significant association between unemployment benefits and wage growth, Forslund, Gottfries, and Westermark (2008) report significant positive impacts. Hence, Nymoen and Rødseth (2003) and Holmlund (2009) conclude that the evidence on $\alpha_3 > 0$ is weak and conflicting and does not warrant strong conclusions. We cautiously interpret the available evidence on α_3 as reflecting a rather weak positive association between labor market policies and real wage growth.

Provisional Equilibrium

Let us assume for the moment that real wage growth is exogenously determined and does not match labor productivity growth. This brings us back to the conditional equilibrium growth model of Chapter 3. If we insert estimated parameter values from our demand and productivity regime equations in Table 7.1 in equations (7.1) and (7.2), we can compute the total impact of an increase in Nordic real wage growth on Nordic output growth, productivity growth and employment growth. Doing so, we find that an increase in real wage growth by 1 percentage point raises real GDP growth by 0.3 percentage points (using equation (3.28)) and labor productivity growth by 0.6 percentage points (using equation (3.29)). As a result, employment growth is *reduced* by 0.3 percentage points.[8]

This finding is sobering. Whereas Scandinavia's strongly wage-led economies face no conflict between egalitarianism and economic growth or

Table 7.2. Estimated (long-run) elasticities

	Elasticity of the real wage with respect to			Elasticity of unemployment with respect to
	Unemployment	Labor productivity	Labor market regulation	Real interest rate
Calmfors and Forslund (1991)[a]	−0.15	0.3–0.7	±0.16	
Holden and Nymoen (2002)[b]	insignificant	0.41	insignificant	
Nymoen and Rødseth (2003)[c]	−0.13	0.36	insignificant	1.20
Sveriges Riksbank (2007)[d]				0.80
Forslund, Gottfries, and Westermark (2008)[e]	−0.12		±0.30	
Karanassou, Sala, and Salvador (2009)[f]	−0.59/−0.67	0.22–0.31	0.17–0.27	0.20–0.47
Holmlund (2009)[g]			insignificant	0.43
Average	−0.25	0.39	±0.23	0.69
Our estimates	−0.13	0.57	insignificant	0.59

Notes:

a. Calmfors and Forslund (1991) present an econometric analysis of real wage determination and labor market policies for Sweden (1960–1990). This study is included to highlight the stability of Nordic wage-setting processes. The authors find no impact on wages of unemployment benefits, but positive significant effects of activating labor market programs and payroll and income taxation.

b. Based on annual data for 1964–1994, Holden and Nymoen (2002, 92) find that deviations from the NAIRU have "no predictive power for the change in wage growth" and hence the NAIRU "explains nothing of the actual variation in [Nordic] wage acceleration." They find "no changes in wage-setting behavior for any of the four Nordic countries, nor do we detect changes in the explanatory variables in wage setting that can explain the [change] in unemployment" (2002, 100). Specifically, they find no consistent effects on wages of income tax rates, payroll and income tax wedges, centralization of bargaining, and replacement rates.

c. Nymoen and Rødseth (2003) analyze Nordic wage setting and structural unemployment during 1968–1994; they find no statistically significant impacts on Nordic wage setting of changes in benefit replacement rates, the degree of centralization of wage bargaining, and activating labor market programs. They conclude that shifts in the wage curve due to changes in regulation are small relative to the large actual changes in unemployment, and hence it appears that the demand side of the labor market must have played an important part in all Nordic countries.

d. Estimates of Sveriges Riksbank (2007) are based on model-based simulations of monetary policy for Sweden.

e. Forslund, Gottfries, and Westermark (2008) use data for the period from 1968 to 1994/1997. Their results suggest that higher replacement rates and higher unemployment benefits do raise wages and hence unemployment, but the effects are relatively small. They find no clear evidence that activating labor market programs contribute to wage restraint. Their overall conclusion is that, in the medium term, demand-side factors are important determinants of Nordic unemployment.

f. Karanassou, Sala, and Salvador (2009) analyze wage setting in Denmark (1973–2005), Finland (1976–2005), and Sweden (1966–2005). The labor market variables used are the tax wedge for Finland and direct taxation for Sweden. The elasticity of unemployment with respect to the real interest rate has been calculated assuming an interest rate elasticity of investment of unity.

g. Holmlund's (2009) estimates are based on a structural vector autoregression model to examine how monetary policy affected Swedish unemployment in the early 1990s.

technological dynamism, they cannot escape the nasty trade-off between egalitarian outcomes and employment growth. The theoretical analysis of Chapter 3 highlighted—in Figure 3.4—the possibility of a strongly wage-led economy in which higher real wage growth would increase output growth about as strongly as productivity growth, keeping employment growth (and unemployment) more or less unaffected. We can now conclude that our assessment of the strongly wage-led case has perhaps been too optimistic: employment growth in the most strongly wage-led OECD nations, the Nordics, declines as real wage growth rises. The Nordic case is illustrated in Figure 7.2.

Superficially, the outcome of the present analysis for the Nordic economies looks rather like that of the conventional NAIRU model in which higher real wage growth leads to higher unemployment. But this is as far as the similarity goes. In the NAIRU model, higher real wage growth is associated with slower investment and output growth, because of the higher real

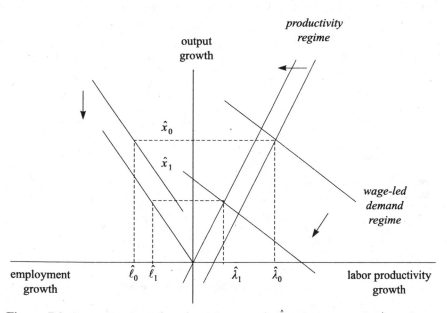

Figure 7.2. Determination of productivity growth ($\hat{\lambda}$), output growth ($\hat{x}$), and employment growth ($\hat{\ell}$): the Nordic economies.

Note: The arrows indicate shifts in the demand, productivity, and employment regime curves caused by a decline in real wage growth, which is in turn due to a weakening of the bargaining power of workers caused by labor market deregulation (a decline in z). In this wage-led economy, labor market deregulation has a stronger impact on demand growth than on productivity growth—hence employment growth falls and unemployment rises.

interest rate needed to create the additional unemployment to bring wage growth back in line with the given unchanging rate of productivity growth.

In contrast, in our model, the higher real wage growth is associated with both higher output growth and higher (endogenously induced) labor productivity growth. The difference is crucial, both theoretically and in terms of its practical implications, as can be seen from the Nordic resolution of the trade-off between egalitarian outcomes and unemployment—a resolution both simple and bold: more regulation and coordination. Specifically, by sharing available employment hours, the Nordic economies have ensured that lack of, or even negative, employment growth does not lead to increased unemployment (Bowles and Park 2005). This employment sharing, based on (often centralized) bargaining and coordination, is reflected in the lower annual hours worked per employee in the Nordic economies compared to the AS and EM countries (Faggio and Nickell 2007); at the same time, Nordic employment rates are the highest in the OECD and Nordic unemployment is relatively low. We believe that this solution (coordinated employment sharing) is predicated on the fact that the economic system responds to higher wage growth by expanding output and raising labor productivity; it would not be feasible when the economy contracts in reaction to higher real wage growth.[9]

Why is this coordinated egalitarian model acceptable to organized Nordic private sector firms? The answer is that because firms and workers are operating under a fairness constraint (Akerlof 1982, 2007), firms obtain more worker commitment, higher labor productivity, more demand, and greater worker willingness to cooperate in engendering labor-saving technological progress in exchange for a higher wage and a more egalitarian outcome.[10] Crucially, the more rapid demand growth and even higher labor productivity growth enables firms to maintain their profitability in real terms. To see this, let us define profit income Π in real terms as the product of the profit share π and output (that is, $\Pi = \pi x$). It follows that profit income growth is equal to

$$(7.8) \qquad \hat{\Pi} = \hat{\pi} + \hat{x} = -[\hat{w} - \hat{\lambda}] + \hat{x}$$

The impact of an increase in real wage growth on profit income growth then is

$$(7.9) \qquad \frac{\partial \hat{\Pi}}{\partial \hat{w}} = -1 + \frac{\partial \hat{\lambda}}{\partial \hat{w}} + \frac{\partial \hat{x}}{\partial \hat{w}}$$

Based on the estimated Nordic parameter values, we find that the impact of a 1 percentage point increase in real wage growth on Nordic profit income growth is very small:

$$(7.10) \qquad \frac{\partial \hat{\Pi}}{\partial \hat{w}} = -1 + 0.62 + 0.32 = -0.07$$

The relative insensitivity of profitability to higher real wages, which is in large measure due to the relatively strong responsiveness of productivity growth to wage growth, provides the foundation for the Nordic version of cooperative capitalism (Bhaduri and Marglin 1990; Hall and Soskice 2001). This is the Nordic macro bargain between workers, firms, and government—the visible handshake. Swedish employers agreed to concerted wage negotiations, regulated industrial relations, and universal social benefits because they saw that this type of system could serve their interests. In short, as political scientist Peter A. Swenson beautifully expressed it, Swedish capitalists were willing to act "against markets" because they were reciprocated in terms of higher productivity, stable demand, and supportive public policies.[11] Swenson writes: "History shows that Swedish employers were anything but foot draggers when it came to [social reform] . . . and were, in some cases, even more generous reformers than the Social Democrats themselves" (2002, 10–11).

Swedish employers favored social legislation over no legislation, favored the more expensive universalistic pension scheme over a cheaper means-tested version, and actively endorsed active labor market policies.

> Organized employers were not merely resigned to hegemonic Social Democrats and hoping to appease them for special consideration on particular details, for nicer treatment in other domains, or to avoid public disfavour. They knew what they wanted. Sometimes they liked best what they got and got what they liked best. (Swenson 2002, 11)

Politically, support for the Nordic model increased in a self-reinforcing process: the small wage differentials that centralized wage setting created provided support for universal welfare state arrangements, and the generous welfare state, in turn, supported weak groups in the labor market, thus compressing the wage distribution even further (Moene 2008).

The Nordic model should be contrasted to the European Continental model. We specifically consider the Dutch case, examined by Naastepad (2006), which arguably is representative of other EC countries. In the Dutch case, an increase in real wage growth of 1 percentage point results in a decline in employment growth by 0.3 percentage points, which is similar to the employment growth impact we find for the Nordic economies. But unlike the Nordic case, the decline in Dutch employment growth due to higher real wage growth is the net effect of a very small increase of demand growth (0.04 percentage points) and a larger increase in labor productivity growth (0.34 percentage points). Dutch demand growth, in other words, is weakly wage-led, and because of this, Dutch profit income growth turns out to be quite sensitive to real wage growth. In fact, using Naastepad's estimates, we calculate the impact of a 1 percentage point increase in real wage growth on Dutch profit income growth as follows:

$$(7.11) \qquad \frac{\partial \hat{\Pi}}{\partial \hat{w}} = -1 + 0.34 + 0.04 = -0.62$$

Clearly, granting workers higher real wages is not an option for Dutch firms, as their profitability will suffer. This sharp trade-off between real wage growth and profit growth helps to explain why Dutch unions did not push for higher pay but instead decided to bargain for more jobs by means of a social compromise, entailing a long-term voluntary commitment to real wage growth restraint. Predictably, this real wage restraint did lead to the recovery of firm profitability as well as to the "Dutch employment miracle" (Auer 2000), which has been—as we can now see—the by-product of a wage-moderation-induced productivity growth slowdown and technological regression. The contrast with the technologically more dynamic Nordic model being obvious, we may call the Nordic model "social productivist," while labeling the Dutch model "social stagnationist." The label "social stagnationist" applies to most other EC economies, including France and Germany as well as Italy and Spain. This is apparent from Figure 7.3, which shows that, all other coefficients being the same, a higher coefficient C (meaning that the economy in question is more strongly wage-led) is associated with lower sensitivity of profit income growth to increases in real wage growth. For Germany, $\partial \hat{\Pi} / \partial \hat{w}$ would be the same (-0.62) as for the Netherlands, for Italy the sensitivity of profit growth to real wage growth is -0.56, and for France and Spain it would take a value of about -0.4. These European Continental countries feature a weakly wage-led aggregate demand similar to the Dutch one and have also opted for high employment growth and low wage growth rather than high productivity growth, high wage growth, and employment sharing. Figure 7.3 also features the profit-led U.S. economy (having $C < 0$): with profit-led demand, a 1 percentage-point increase in real wage growth translates into a decline of 1 percentage point in profit income growth. Nowhere in the OECD is the conflict between wage growth and profit growth more pronounced than in the United States.

Demand, Regulation, and Long-Run Unemployment

Our model analysis so far has been predicated on the assumption that $\hat{w} \neq \hat{\lambda}$, which is not sustainable in a long-run context, because it implies a constantly increasing or decreasing profit share (Setterfield 2002). We now use the model for long-run analysis and concentrate on the determinants of equilibrium unemployment, u^*, or the nonaccelerating inflation rate of un-

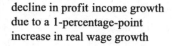

decline in profit income growth
due to a 1-percentage-point
increase in real wage growth

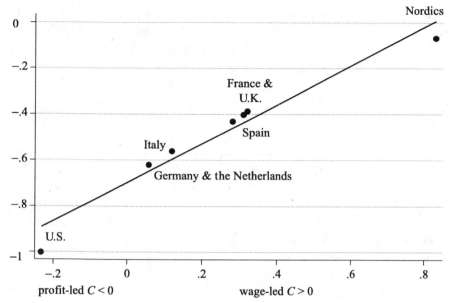

Figure 7.3. The more strongly wage-led the economy, the less sensitive is profit income growth to real wage growth.

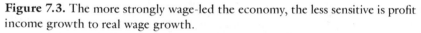

Note: The scatter points indicate the sensitivity of profit income growth to a change in real wage growth by 1 percentage point (as defined in equation (7.9)). The observed variation across countries in this sensitivity is only due to country-wise variations in the (wage-led/profit-led) coefficient C—all other coefficient values are identical to the Nordic coefficients $\beta_1 = 0.31$, $\beta_2 = 0.51$, and $\beta_3 = 0.54$. C coefficients are given in Table 5.5.

employment. Equilibrium unemployment is given by equation (7.7). Using the parameter estimates appearing in Table 7.1, we find for the Nordic countries that

(7.12) $$\frac{\partial u^*}{\partial \hat{g}^*} = -0.29$$

and

(7.13) $$\frac{\partial u^*}{\partial r_k} = +0.59$$

Demand policy therefore matters directly for Nordic steady-inflation unemployment. A 1 percentage point increase in the government deficit (in equation (7.12)) leads to a decline in the unemployment rate by 0.29 percentage points, which is higher than our estimate of 0.15 percentage points for twenty OECD countries in the same period (see Chapter 6). Fiscal stimulus has a permanent impact, because it raises productivity growth and thus reduces the system's inflationary threshold. From equation (7.7), it follows that autonomous (non-interest-rate sensitive) investment demand would have an impact similar to that of fiscal stimulus. Estimates by Karanassou, Sala, and Salvador (2009) show that a 1 percentage point decline in capital accumulation reduces the equilibrium unemployment rate in Denmark by 0.47 percent, in Sweden by 0.36 percent, and in Finland by 0.20 percent. Karanassou, Sala, and Salvador (2009, 994) conclude that "feeding through the labour market system, the investment downturns give rise to the unemployment rate upturns and drive their intensity and longevity." Our estimate of the unemployment impact of a fiscal stimulus falls in the same ballpark as their estimates of the unemployment impact of an investment change. We must qualify our finding in equation (7.12) in one respect: over a period of time longer than that covered by our analysis, the impact of fiscal policy on unemployment may be smaller because of requirements of fiscal solvency. In fact, the Nordic countries stand out in the OECD area for their fiscal conservatism: they have by far the lowest government deficits and public debts, even if Norway (with its huge oil revenues) is excluded. Nordic governments (again excluding Norway) reduced their deficits by 3.9 percentage points between the 1990s and 2000–2006, which according to our estimate in equation (7.12) must have raised their equilibrium unemployment rate by 1.1 percentage points.

Crucially, the considerable decline in public deficits motivated Nordic central banks to drastically reduce interest rates—real interest rates declined by 3.7 percentage points between 1990–1999 and 2000–2006.[12] We find according to equation (7.13) that a 1 percentage point decline in the real interest rate reduces the Nordic equilibrium unemployment rate by 0.59 percent— which, we note, is roughly the average of the impacts found by Holmlund (2009) and the Sveriges Riksbank (2007; see also Table 7.2). An interest rate decline of 3.7 percentage points between 1990–1999 and 2000–2006 must have reduced Nordic unemployment by 2.2 percentage points (or by about 25 percent). The combined impact of restrictive fiscal policy and relatively low interest rates accounted for a 1.1 percentage point decline in the inflation-safe unemployment rate. The Nordic combination of very prudent fiscal policy and relatively accommodating monetary policy has paid off very handsomely in terms of reduced structural unemployment and higher labor productivity growth. This has been the government's contribution to the Nordic visible handshake.

Finally, we can investigate the impact of labor market regulation on steady-inflation unemployment. From equation (7.7), we know that the sign of the impact on equilibrium unemployment of an increase in z is ambiguous. Increased regulation leads to higher equilibrium unemployment (as conventional wisdom holds) only if

(7.14) $$\frac{\partial u^*}{\partial z} > 0 \text{ if } \frac{\alpha_3}{(1-\alpha_2)} > \frac{\beta_3}{(1-\beta_2)}$$

assuming that $\alpha_1 > 0$ and $(1-\beta_2) > 0$. The right-hand side of equation (7.14) is the impact of an increase in z on productivity growth. The left-hand side reflects the extra real wage growth demanded by workers in response to an increase in z. Using our parameter estimates (from Table 7.1), we find for the four Nordic economies that *more* labor market regulation is associated with *lower* unemployment:

(7.15) $$\frac{\partial u^*}{\partial z} < 0 \text{ because } \frac{\alpha_3}{(1-\alpha_2)} = \frac{0}{1-0.57}$$
$$= 0 < \frac{\beta_3}{(1-\beta_2)} = \frac{0.54}{1-0.51} = 1.10$$

This empirical result is overly strong, however, because it is partly based on our finding that $\alpha_3 = 0$ (more regulation does not lead to higher wage growth claims). But it can be checked that condition (7.14) continues to hold if we use much higher values for α_3, for instance, $\alpha_3 = 0.3$, as is suggested by Forslund, Gottfries, and Westermark (2008). Only if $\alpha_3 > 0.47$ do we find that $\partial u^*/\partial z > 0$, but such values for α_3 we deem unrealistic in light of the comparative evidence appearing in Table 7.2 (see also Nymoen and Rødseth 2003). We therefore feel confident concluding that Scandinavian labor market regulation has been paying off well in two respects: it has contributed to higher productivity growth as well as to lower steady-inflation unemployment.

This conclusion is vital to macroeconomic policy making, the main challenge of which is to find ways to reconcile growth and low unemployment with equality and social protection. Our Nordic case study has shown that the dominant claim against egalitarianism is off the mark, as it is falsified by the superior long-run performance of Europe's Nordic economies. The wage-led model of Nordic growth presented here and the supporting empirical evidence underscore Jeffrey Sachs's (2006b) conclusion that "Von Hayek was wrong . . . a generous social welfare system is not a road to serfdom but rather to fairness, economic equality and international competitiveness." All-important is the larger macroeconomic context within which

Nordic policy interventions generate significant economywide returns. This larger context, as we have argued, is that of a strongly wage-led macroeconomic growth regime. Our analysis brings out the main reason supposedly costly egalitarian redistribution in these open economies has succeeded: it did lead to growth of wage-led aggregate demand as well as to growth of labor productivity, which has been sufficient to keep intact firms' profits as well as government tax revenues. This, in essence, constitutes the foundation of the Nordic macroeconomic bargain between workers, firms, and government. It needs no elaboration that the mechanics of Nordic growth and the underlying political economy bargain are fundamentally different from the workings of conventional NAIRU models, which resemble profit-led economies (see Chapter 3).

Is the Nordic Model Transferable and Sustainable?

Our evidence would at least seem to suggest that other OECD countries, such as France, Germany, and the Netherlands, that are now stuck in social stagnationist modes (creating more rather low-wage jobs at the expense of productivity growth) have a true choice: either to go further down the inegalitarian path of deregulation, liberalization, welfare state downsizing, tax reductions, and expenditure cutting, emulating the profit-led Anglo-Saxon model, or to opt for the egalitarian, social productivist course favored by the wage-led Nordics, in which the inherent conflicts of interest between employers and workers are resolved by negotiation, regulation, and coordination— that is, by the so-called visible handshake. In strongly wage-led systems, there exists one inescapable conflict that must be resolved: namely, balancing egalitarianism and employment growth. The Nordic model, concludes Lennart Erixon (2008, 385), "retains a message for today" as a third way between the liberal Anglo-Saxon model and the European Continental model. Karl Ove Moene (2008, 369), a longtime close observer of Nordic social democracy, has become only "more certain that the Nordic lessons were highly relevant for social reformers in other parts of the world." Of course, the transferability to other OECD countries of the Nordic model, which has been fundamentally shaped by and embedded in the larger sociological, political, and cultural structures and norms of the four Scandinavian countries (Moene 2008), is open to question. Still, unless the Nordic case is entirely idiosyncratic (which we do not think to be the case), our analysis suggests that the commonplace opposition between growth and open-economy egalitarianism is considerably overdrawn at the least, and perhaps plain wrong.

Globalization could be a threat to the sustainability of the Nordic model, as it could undermine the ability to levy high enough tax rates to underpin government's contribution to the visible handshake. But as Rudolf Meidner (1993, 227) wrote: "The concept of a society which is built on moral values is, in my view, too promising to be extinguished by inhuman market forces." The Nordic countries have so far managed to keep unemployment low, find generally accepted norms for the wage policy of solidarity, and support wage policy by some kind of collective capital formation and technological progress. They succeeded in combining internationally open capital markets, a relatively low rate of taxation on capital, and relatively high rates of indirect taxation and labor taxation. Nordic governance has shown strong transformative capacity in overcoming macroeconomic difficulties, ranging from a big financial crisis (in the early 1990s in Sweden) and oil-based foreign exchange booms (in Norway) to the collapse of major export markets (in Finland after 1990). The Nordic model has worked for more than forty years and has not led to long-term political or economic deterioration.[13] The Nordic economies have also managed to weather the negative impacts of the recent global recession. The mutual protection by workers, firms, and government has paid off very well, and there is no reason to doubt that the Nordic model is, in Kropotkin's language, "open to further progress."[14]

Further Reading

Gøsta Esping-Andersen (1990) presents a classic (though increasingly criticized) comparative typology of OECD policy models, which separates the Nordic social democratic model from the German and French conservative model and the U.S. and U.K. liberal one. Lennart Erixon (2008) provides a useful assessment of the ups and many downs of the Swedish Rehn-Meidner model; Rudolph Meidner (1993) testifies to the deep insights on which the model is based. Karl Ove Moene and Michael Wallerstein (1995, 1997) and Moene (2008) explain how Scandinavian policies and complementary institutions fit together and strengthen one another to create a viable model of egalitarian growth, especially in Norway and Sweden. The political economic history of the making of Swedish industrial relations and its welfare state is given in Peter Swenson's (2002) book *Capitalists against Markets*. Marika Karanassou, Hector Sala, and Pablo Salvador (2009) explain why capital accumulation matters for unemployment and provide a Nordic case study. Guy Standing (1988) and Bertil Holmlund (2009) offer thoughtful assessments of the Swedish unemployment experience, concluding that institutional factors play no important role in determining unemployment changes in Sweden.

Macroeconomics Beyond
the NAIRU

The great enemy of clear language is insincerity. When there is a gap
between one's real and one's declared aims, one turns as it where
instinctively to long words and exhausted idioms, like a cuttlefish
spurting out ink.

GEORGE ORWELL, *POLITICS AND THE ENGLISH LANGUAGE*

James Galbraith, in an early critique of NAIRU economics (1997), asks
whether economics can live without the NAIRU. Galbraith thinks this is not
only possible but desirable, because momentous public policy decisions cannot be based on a theoretical and empirical construct this weak.[1] We agree.
The NAIRU, as a constant attractor, cannot provide appropriate guidance to
public policy making—because it does not exist. The fundamental assumption of NAIRU economics that demand adjusts to supply, while supply is independent of demand, is wrong. We presented, in Chapters 3, 4, and 5, the
contrary theoretical argument that supply is influenced by demand factors,
via endogenous technological change and labor productivity growth, and we
argued that demand-supply interaction depends critically on the wage-led or
profit-led nature of aggregate demand. We provided clear-cut empirical evidence that demand growth does influence capital accumulation and labor
productivity growth. Fiscal and monetary policies do therefore have permanent effects on unemployment and growth. Friedman's policy ineffectiveness theorem does not hold water.

Likewise, the unconditional NAIRU argument that labor market deregulation reduces equilibrium unemployment is flawed. Chapter 2 made clear
that NAIRU theory does not match with the empirical evidence, and we
discussed the major anomalies. The mismatch between theory and evidence
calls for serious macroeconomic rethinking—which is what we tried to do in
Chapter 6, making the case that labor market regulation has not just one but
two opposing effects on unemployment: it leads to higher wage demands
and higher unemployment, but at the same time it raises labor productivity
growth, which reduces the NAIRU. In theory, the impact of labor market
deregulation on steady-inflation unemployment is ambiguous, but Chapter 6
has shown, based on empirical analysis, that empirically the net effect of

deregulation is a rise in OECD unemployment. Chapter 7 discussed the anomaly of Europe's Nordic economies, which manage to combine egalitarian growth, rapid technological progress, and low unemployment through appropriate macroeconomic and labor market regulation. Regulation of labor markets pays off in terms of higher productivity growth and lower equilibrium unemployment.

In this final chapter, we want to go beyond the boundaries of the formal model and the narrow confines of the statistical discussions of the empirical evidence to address the deeper foundations of NAIRU economics. We believe that its views of the social order and of human nature are of crucial importance if one wants to understand both the appeal of NAIRU economics and the true damage done by it. However, before proceeding, we must first address the social cost of NAIRU-based economics: an avoidable, self-induced decline in the trend rate of productivity growth and a consequent increase in the estimated natural and actual rate of unemployment. James Galbraith rightly calls it "a self-inflicted wound, a socio-psychological disability, of colossal proportions" (Galbraith 1997, 99).

The Self-Inflicted Wound

One fundamental implication of NAIRU economics is that central bank interest rate policy supposedly has no long-run effect on equilibrium unemployment. NAIRU theory thereby allows the Federal Reserve and the European Central Bank to take full employment off the table while conveniently absolving them of charges that their policies may actually contribute to higher unemployment. As we have argued in this book, the central bank *does* influence the NAIRU, and substantially so. The higher the real interest rate, the lower the investment growth and labor productivity growth, and the higher the equilibrium unemployment rate needed to keep wage claims in line with productivity growth. James Galbraith (1997, 99) has been one of the first to recognize this possibility, arguing that "if growth policies had been more sustained, disciplined and aggressive, then the perceived decline in the trend productivity growth rate would have been smaller than it was, and the estimated natural rate [of unemployment] would also have been lower than it has appeared to be." Likewise, Robert Eisner (1995, 61) stated that "we ought to be trying to reduce [unemployment], not only by supply-side measures, but by ensuring that the economy is not starved for adequate aggregate demand or productivity-increasing public investment."

We can use our estimates for all OECD economies in Tables 6.3 and 6.4 to illustrate how big these avoidable costs of NAIRU-based policy errors actually are. Let us suppose that initially the rates of actual and equilibrium unemployment are equal. Assume now that world export growth increases permanently by 1 percentage point because of factors external to the OECD economies. The initial impact of this world demand shock is higher output growth; according to Table 6.3, output growth will rise by 0.3 percentage points. In effect, labor demand increases and actual unemployment falls—the latter leading to higher real wage claims and rising inflation. The OECD economy is now outside long-run equilibrium. To stop the inflation, the central bank, following NAIRU logic, raises the interest rate. To bring the OECD economy back to steady-inflation equilibrium, the real interest rate must rise by 3 percentage points, in the process curtailing investment growth and raising actual unemployment. Erring policymakers believe they can do this without changing the NAIRU; what they claim is that the inflation is stopped from accelerating at no cost in terms of additional long-run unemployment. This is wrong. Our estimates (reported in Table 6.4) show that a real interest rate increase of 3 percentage points leads to a permanent increase in the NAIRU by 0.75 percentage points, or three million additional jobless workers in the OECD area as a whole.

But this is by no means the full cost of NAIRU policy. As we have argued in Chapter 6, the world demand shock, if not neutralized by an interest rate hike, actually would have reduced steady-inflation unemployment by 0.77 percentage points, or three million OECD workers. The reason, as explained, is that the ensuing higher demand growth would have increased labor productivity growth (by the Kaldor-Verdoorn effect), thus creating the opportunity for a lower inflation-safe unemployment rate. The true cost of erring macroeconomic policymakers, enthralled by the illusion of a constant natural rate of unemployment, is not only constant-inflation OECD growth that is permanently lower than would have been necessary, but also a staggering six million additional unemployed workers. This is what Galbraith means when he talks of a self-inflicted wound of colossal proportions. Of course, our example is specific, but it illustrates the general point that policymakers who base their decisions on the NAIRU approach will tend to prematurely and systematically kill off economic expansions above trend. What it means is that the business cycle peak is endogenous to policy. The consequent avoidable cost of high unemployment must rest on the conscience of the economics profession.

Our example highlights one more relevant point. If we follow our model, actual unemployment will increase by 0.75 percentage points above the NAIRU estimate after inflation has been stabilized, and will show no tendency to decline. Such persistent discrepancies occur frequently in practice, and the usual response has been to explain them away in ad hoc fashion; all of a sudden, analysts discover that "the demographic characteristics of workers are deteriorating, or that the job-wage and wage-price dynamics has become unstable" (Galbraith 1997, 101), with the result that the NAIRU must have been higher than before. This practice has led to the most recent incarnation of the theory in which the NAIRU is basically the trend rate of actual unemployment (Staiger, Stock, and Watson 2001). "Whatever trend is observed is natural—case closed," writes Thomas Palley (2006, 5). The policy implication of this is crucial. When higher actual unemployment is accompanied by a higher NAIRU, there is no case for expansionary macro policy, since a higher proportion of actual unemployment is seen as necessary to keep inflation stable. As a result, NAIRU economics must always lean against policies to support full employment.

The second implication of NAIRU economics is that structural unemployment can be reduced only by labor market deregulation. Deregulation of labor markets is not a trivial affair; Chapter 2 highlighted the considerable social costs of uncontrolled labor markets, using the United States as a case. Deregulation is a momentous decision of public policy, and therefore the theoretical case that it does reduce unemployment must be impeccable and the supporting evidence strong. This isn't what has happened. Our own analysis suggests that labor market deregulation is likely to raise unemployment, because it reduces productivity growth more than real wage growth. To illustrate, based on Table 6.4, if European labor markets are deregulated U.S. style, not only would European employees be worse off in terms of employment protection, social welfare, and job security, but more than 2 million European workers would likely lose their jobs (and that is a cautious assessment). We agree with Baker et al. (2005a, 109) that "the empirical case has not been made that could justify the sweeping and unconditional prescriptions for labor market deregulation that pervade much of the policy discussion." What is more, the productivity growth slowdown caused by the deregulation locks the European economies into a vicious circle in which they become more (not less) inflation-prone at higher rates of unemployment. If the litmus test of macroeconomic policy is its effectiveness in reconciling reasonable price stability with acceptable growth at the highest achievable levels of employment and in managing shocks with the least disruption, NAIRU economics fails the test.

The Monetarist Moment

If NAIRU economics is so colossally damaging, why are most economists persuaded by it? To explain this, we need to understand why NAIRU doctrine triumphed in academia and policy circles, and this requires us to go back to the mid- and late 1970s, when most OECD countries where experiencing stagflation—the simultaneous existence of high unemployment, low growth, and high inflation (Bruno and Sachs 1985). To most macroeconomists, stagflation came as a big surprise, because most believed that stagnating growth could only mean low, not high and accelerating, inflation. Most economists at that time accepted the so-called Phillips curve mechanism, according to which there exists a trade-off between higher output (lower unemployment) and higher inflation, even in the long run. This defining moment of crisis and general confusion provided monetarists with an opening, and they were prepared to make use of it. As Milton Friedman (1962, ix) famously observed:

> Only a crisis—actual or perceived—produces real change. When that crisis occurs, the actions that are taken depend on the ideas that are lying around. That, I believe, is our basic function: to develop alternatives to existing policies, to keep them alive and available until the politically impossible becomes politically inevitable.[2]

Monetarists made two claims. Their first claim was that stagflation proved Keynesianism fatally wrong: the combination of accelerating inflation and high unemployment, in their view, "proved" that there was no long-run Phillips curve (as most Keynesians argued). That is, there is no trade-off between inflation and unemployment in the long run, because unemployment cannot permanently deviate from its natural rate; as a corollary, demand factors cannot affect natural supply in the long run. "That the predictions [of Keynesian economics] were wildly incorrect, and that the doctrine on which they were based was fundamentally flawed, are now *simple matters of fact*, involving no subtleties in economic theory," stated Robert Lucas and Thomas Sargent victoriously (1978, 49; emphasis added).

Their second claim was that stagflation could be explained by monetarist theory, the NAIRU model in particular. Assuming rational expectations, the monetarists argued—following Friedman (1968) and Edmund S. Phelps (1968)—that anticipated macro policy attempts to reduce unemployment below the natural rate of unemployment à la Keynes were bound to fail and would have lasting effects on inflation. Lucas (1981, 560) summarizes this second claim well:

> Now, Friedman and Phelps had no way of foreseeing the inflation of the 1970s, any more than did the rest of us, but the central forecast to which their reasoning led was a conditional one, to the effect that a high inflation decade should not have less unemployment on average than a low-inflation decade. We got the high inflation decade, and with it as clear-cut an experimental discrimination as macroeconomics is ever likely to see, and Friedman and Phelps were right.

In the monetarist account, stagflation was a self-propelling market process, dominated by positive feedback from higher wage claims to higher prices, and it could be halted only by interest-rate shock therapy imposed by a credible independent outside technocracy (the central bank). Furthermore, a repeat of stagflation could be avoided only by structurally weakening the position of organized labor while strengthening deregulated market forces.

This hard-line position was backed by the rising academic prestige of monetarism. Too, in its simplicity it was also politically attractive, perhaps even irresistible, because it had the effect of off-loading responsibility for inflation control from the government. Thus, monetarism came to guide macroeconomic policy as newly independent central banks (especially the Federal Reserve) launched their anti-inflation offensive. Short-term interest rates were raised sharply, demand collapsed, and inflation came down. But the disinflation had huge costs: unemployment shot up dramatically. Two institutional changes ensured that monetarist reforms were made permanent and low inflation could be sustained for most of the years after 1982, as Galbraith (2008, 44) explains:

> The collapse of labor union power and pattern bargaining in industrial wages, and globalization: the increased reliance of American consumers on manufactured imports produced in low-wage countries. Together these facts transformed the structural environment of American price setting. Together they created a low-inflation, postindustrial, deunionized economy, much more unequal than before but nevertheless with reasonable high living standards ensured by cheap imports.[3]

This, in Thomas Palley's (2009) words, became America's growth paradigm, based on low (or no) real wage growth, flexible (even disposable) workers, low inflation, cheap low-wage imports, and rising inequality, and relying on household and firm debt and asset price inflation to drive demand. Neither the Federal Reserve nor the government tried to promote full employment, as any attempt to deviate from the natural rate could only fail. Over time, central bankers persuaded themselves, and many economists, that "being known for being tough on inflation" would discourage workers from demanding wage increases that they might otherwise seek, for fear of retribution in the form of higher interest rates and higher unemployment.

The monetarist interpretation of the stagflation of the 1970s, which has become a cliché of mainstream economic history, rests on the evidence of a long-run vertical Phillips curve. The fundamental policy implication following from this view is that of tight limits on the rate of economic growth, lest inflation accelerate beyond control. However, the empirical evidence for longer periods of time (longer than the 1970s) is in almost uniform agreement that inflation reacts only very slowly to higher growth and lower actual un-employment, and that whatever limits may exist are at worst highly elastic (Galbraith 1997). This is, for instance, clearly illustrated by the Clinton-era boom (1994–2000), when unemployment fell to well below the natural rate, inflation did not rise, and the Federal Reserve did nothing. Instead, produc-tivity growth increased—quite understandably, because when businesses have difficulty finding labor, they look for ways to get the same output with less of it. "Economists reacted to the declining unemployment rate first with dire warnings that sapped the credibility of the profession," writes Galbraith (2008, 47–48).

> Then came a wave of articles that the natural rate must be lower than anyone had realized. Ultimately the articles more or less stopped com-ing, and silence settled over the grave of the natural rate [of unemploy-ment]. For years, conservative economists had argued that low unem-ployment rates were dangerous, and most of Washington had believed them. Greenspan, by the simple act of doing nothing, blew all of that away. We had full employment; it did not cause inflation. Monetarism, the natural rate doctrine, and the idea that the Federal Reserve must be eternally vigilant against inflation—all of that was wrong! Who knew?

To paraphrase Lucas and Sargent, it is now a simple matter of fact, involving no subtleties in economic theory, that the natural rate doctrine itself is fun-damentally flawed. In Chapter 3, we provided an alternative theoretical framework within which the nonconstancy of the natural rate of unemploy-ment can be explained. We found that the NAIRU is a constant attractor (as in monetarism) only when one unrealistically assumes that (1) all labor productivity growth is absorbed in higher real wages and (2) productivity growth does not change in response to demand growth, wage growth, and changes in the social relations of production. In general, these two condi-tions are not satisfied, and our empirical analysis, in Chapters 4, 6, and 7, shows that they don't actually apply to OECD reality. Nevertheless, the NAIRU doctrine is not dead, as Galbraith appears to believe; it is still the dominant macroeconomic narrative found in textbooks and policy-making circles. Empirical evidence and theoretical reasoning by themselves are not enough to convince the mainstream to change its view, certainly not in macroeco-nomics, because as Joan Robinson (1962, 76) wrote, "In a subject where there is no agreed procedure for knocking out errors, doctrines have a long life."

There are other factors explaining the triumph of the NAIRU doctrine as well. It is to these broader and deeper factors that we now turn.

An Illegible Regime of Power

Milton Friedman devoted his life to fighting a battle of ideas against the Keynesians, who believed that governments could and should intervene in the market to bring macroeconomic stability and soften the market's sharp edges. Friedman believed that history "got off on the wrong track" when economists and politicians began listening to John Maynard Keynes, who proposed a mixed, regulated economy—a system of social compromises, progressive checks and balances, and democratic management of aggregate demand—to reconcile the interests of capitalists and workers so as to avoid the vagaries of the business cycle and crisis. But the price of progressive Keynesianism was big government, establishing countervailing power against the authority of private corporate business (Galbraith 2008). It is against big government and in favor of personal freedom that Friedman (1962) acted with such missionary zeal: his advocacy of a minimalist state is, without doubt, the hallmark of his contributions to political economy. "The major error, in my opinion," Friedman wrote in a letter to Chile's dictator Augusto Pinochet in 1975, is "to believe that it is possible to do good with other people's money" (Klein 2007, 21). In Friedman's view, free, uncontrolled markets and a rather minimalist state minimize the external restrictions on individual action, thus promoting freedom from coercion and external constraints by an exterior social body (the state), as in Erich Fromm's (2001) and Isaiah Berlin's (1969) negative notions of liberty. In the free market, Friedman wrote, "each man can vote, as it were, for the color of tie he wants" (1962, 15).

Friedman's mission rested on his conviction that decentralized markets provide a "spontaneous" social order, built around the natural rate of unemployment. The use of the adjective "natural" is deliberate; the aim is to legitimize laissez-faire capitalism, in which free market solutions are preferred over regulation, as the spontaneous social order. It captures the essence of Friedman's social thinking that the economic forces of supply, demand, inflation, and unemployment are like the forces of nature, fixed and unchanging. Just as ecosystems self-regulate and maintain balance, so does the market system, left to its own devices. As Harvard sociologist Daniel Bell argues, this love of an idealized system is the defining characteristic of radical free-market economics; capitalism is envisaged as a "celestial clockwork . . . a work of art, so compelling that one thinks of the celebrated pictures of Apelles who painted a cluster of grapes so realistic that the birds would come and pick at them" (1981, 57–58). We must add that to justify the epithet "natural," Friedman could invoke the authority of no less an economist than Adam Smith, who in *The Wealth of Nations* used the same analogy to argue that the division of labor stems from the natural psychological propensities to barter and exchange.

Assuming individual freedom in market transactions and equality of bargaining partners when exchanging "equivalent values," Smith's invisible hand ensures that these individual propensities lead to an optimal division of labor (Foley 2006); hence, the spontaneous and harmonious order of the market is analogous to the spontaneous and harmonious order of nature. This has become today's dominant philosophical frame, in which laissez-faire capitalism is equated with individual freedom.

To explain the appeal of NAIRU-based economics is no great challenge: it combined "simplicity together with apparent logical completeness" and "idealism with radicalism," as Don Patinkin (1981, 4) explained. More specifically, the radical ideal of "economic freedom," ensured by this harmonious market order and dependent upon humanity's natural dispositions, struck a responsive chord among the populations of the OECD countries, which were in the throes of a rapid, historically unprecedented process of emancipation and apparent individualization.[4] This process of emancipation has led to growing opposition to public controls as representing illegitimate constraints on personal freedom and choice. "The market is [seen as] the necessary counterpart to economic freedom," writes James Galbraith (2008, 19); "it is the broker, the means of detached and dispassionate interaction between parties with opposed interests. The market ensures that one person's freedom interferes with no other." As Milton and Rose Friedman defined it in the title of their 1980 best-seller, economic freedom for them means being "free to choose."[5] Who would be opposed to freedom and hence to free markets? Who would not prefer "flexible" markets over "rigid" ones, "choice" over "limits"? The important point is that words and labels are often used in a consciously euphemistic and even dishonest way, as George Orwell (1946) observed. That is, words such as "natural" and "flexible" have their own private definitions to the user, but allow hearers to think something quite different is meant. "Such phraseology is needed if one wants to name things without calling up mental pictures of them," wrote Orwell. The epithet "natural" is used to cover up some difficult questions concerning freedom and power.

Here's the snake in the grass. We have seen that in order to remain in balance, the "natural" capitalist order needs a reserve army of the unemployed (euphemistically called equilibrium unemployment), amounting to one in ten or one in twenty workers.[6] It further needs increased job insecurity, deregulated labor markets, and traumatized workers to keep wage claims in line with labor productivity growth and to maintain profits. And it needs an activist, permanently vigilant central bank to counter even a small decline in the reserve army, to avoid the risk of runaway inflation and social destabilization. "The new [capitalist] order substitutes new controls rather than simply abolishing the rules of the past—but these new controls are also hard to understand. The new capitalism is an often illegible regime of power," writes sociologist Richard Sennett (1998, 10). In this illegible regime of power, responsibility for inflation control has been off-loaded to central banks, independent from democratic control, since it could not be left to democratic governments or parliaments, vulnerable to Keynesian impulses. Paradoxically, therefore, it turns out that the invisible hand needs quite a bit of visible help—the disciplining hands of independent central bankers. The "natural" order imagined by Friedman is that of a capitalist economy existing on a knife edge, "teetering forever on the brink of an inflationary abyss" and in which "the eternal vigilance of the central bankers could never be dispensed with, and every year that passed with no inflation would be just another testament to their wisdom and public spirit" (Galbraith 2008, 46). This is Friedman's dishonesty: unlike nature, which is capable of self-regulation, the economic system is not—not even in the monetarist model. The NAIRU order is constructed by human design so as to maintain stability in an otherwise unstable market system—by unilaterally imposing discipline on one group (workers) while protecting the other groups (business and finance).[7] Monetarists are not upset by this dishonesty, however. Even if theirs is not a natural order, they claim in relentlessly Panglossian fashion, it is the best one possible, as only the NAIRU order strikes a satisfactory balance between individual freedom and a stable macro order (in the process legitimizing sharply increased inequalities).[8] Are they right?

A Dog-Eat-Dog World

To answer this question, we must recognize that NAIRU theory assumes that workers and firms are motivated only by their self-interest (rational self-love), narrowly conceived, and that these private interests clash. This is (perhaps remarkably) also the view of most Marxists and others on the Left, who stress the importance of conflicting claims and reject talk of a public interest as obscuring underlying class, race, or gender conflict and as mainly serving the interests of the ruling capitalist class. The NAIRU world is a world of zero-sum conflict, of Darwinian dog-eat-dog competition, which can be formalized in terms of the so-called prisoner's dilemma (Mansbridge 1990a).[9] The prisoner's dilemma is the classic illustration of how uncoordinated self-seeking by each party produces an inferior social outcome (for instance, stagflation) that is worse for both than the result of both parties choosing the unselfish strategy (Rapoport and Chammah 1965). This inferior outcome persists even if the game is repeated many times. The superior outcome, however, can be achieved only by coordination between the different parties. How to achieve this? The standard answers to this question all involve self-interest. One class of utilitarian solutions, for instance, involves introducing additional incentives (rewards or punishments) to induce less self-interested behavior in coordinated fashion (Olson 1965; see Mansbridge 1990c, 134–135, for examples). Anatol Rapoport's "tit-for-tat" strategy of reciprocal altruism also belongs to this class of solutions (Axelrod 1984; Dawes and Thaler 1988).

Another option introduces a "sovereign" who imposes the external punishment necessary to change the balance of self-interested incentives from defection to cooperation. This is Thomas Hobbes's (1651) solution of authoritarian third-party control; "covenants, without the sword, are but words and of no strength to secure a man at all," as Hobbes famously wrote. Jane Mansbridge (1990b, 5) explains how it is supposed to work: "Self-interest can lead one voluntarily to submit to a sovereign, authorizing the sovereign's action as if they were one's own; self-interest can thus provide the basis for political legitimacy." Replace Hobbes's "authoritarian sovereign" by Friedman's "central banker" and what we have is the NAIRU solution to the problem of individual freedom and macro order.[10] As N. Gregory Mankiw and Mark P. Taylor write:

> Most economists—at least the majority of us who believe in a long-run vertical Phillips curve—would rather hand control of monetary policy to the central banker, particularly if the central banker in question had a reputation for being tough on inflation. . . . It is a testimony to the power of macroeconomic theory that this [NAIRU] argument has persuaded many governments around the world to grant independence to their central bank in the conduct of monetary policy. The European Central Bank, for example, has been independent since its inception in 1998, and the Bank of England was granted independence in 1997. . . . The US Federal Reserve is also independent in both the design and implementation of monetary policy. . . . A long-run vertical Phillips curve is a compelling case for taking control over monetary policy out of the hands of politicians and handing it over to a "conservative" central banker. (Mankiw and Taylor 2010, 765, 767)

In this view, independent central bank control, imposing constant inflation on the economy, is a crude but effective solution to the macroeconomic prisoner's dilemma. It represents an unobjectionable form of paternalism, self-imposed, just like the case of Odysseus, who ordered his men to tie him to the mast no matter how much he would beg, so as not to fall prey to the Sirens' song. Of course, the NAIRU solution also "implies a pretty cynical view of politics," as Mankiw and Taylor write, "assuming that governments do not have the long-term well-being of the economy at heart but only want to be re-elected at any cost." Because unemployment is never a vote winner, governments will be tempted to reduce interest rates to reduce unemployment, in the process creating only a higher rate of inflation, not lower unemployment. Public-spirited behavior just does not exist, or, if it exists, it cannot be relied upon to persist in the face of the political class's private interests.[11]

The NAIRU order is the present-day version of Hobbes's Leviathan, with the central bank in the role of sovereign—equally authoritarian and antidemocratic in that after having given the sovereign the right to act for them, people cannot change the form of government, no matter what the sovereign does. NAIRU paternalism should not be taken lightly, however. We can do no better than quote philosopher Jon Elster on this:

> For one thing, the opportunity to choose—including the right to make the wrong choices—is a valuable, in fact, indispensable means to self-improvement. For another, there is a presumption that people are the best judges of their own interest. . . . Paternalism is appropriate only when freedom to choose is likely to be severely self-destructive, especially when it will also harm other people. . . . [Paternalism] can also . . . be a technique of domination and manipulation. (1990, 47–48)

Paternalism is "the greatest despotism imaginable," writes Isaiah Berlin (1969, 11), because it tampers with human beings, conditions them, and treats them as objects without wills of their own, thereby denying their human essence. Paternalistic central banks are a clear violation of "positive liberty of collective self-direction": the liberty given to people in choosing their governments, to participate in the macroeconomic governance of society, and to learn from their mistakes. But likewise the "freedom from" or negative liberty is compromised, because in the NAIRU order, the "freedom" of workers to sell one's services to the highest bidder in the market is eclipsed by the need to do so—under the combined pressures of increased job insecurity, deregulated labor markets, stagnating real wages, crumbling social protection, a lack of decent work opportunities, and a reserve army of millions of unemployed workers, kept intact by an interest rate policy aiming to maintain inflation constant. Workers, in other words, are not free—they are forced to be "flexible" (Sennett 1998). While workers may enjoy some negative liberty ("freedom from external state control over at least some segment of their life space"), their positive liberty ("freedom to emancipate and codetermine the constraints that affect other segments of their life space") is seriously compromised (Lowe 1988, 5).

If not for workers, who is market freedom for? It is a freedom for business alone, concludes Galbraith (2008, 23), "for stable large corporations with substantial political power, for only such business can muster the power to exercise that freedom in the fullest." This is capitalism without compulsions for big business and finance, in Gabriel Palma's (2009) definition. Indeed, the monetarist concept of economic freedom opposes any measures such as universal health care, free public education, and social security, particularly if they are to be financed by redistributive and progressive taxation. Meanwhile, the free market regime of Augusto Pinochet, in this conception, brought economic freedom to the people of Chile, even though they did not have any voice in politics at all.[12] Hence, when you come down to it, the monetarist concept of freedom is very narrow: it is, in James Galbraith's words, only the "freedom to shop," to express one's free will through one's consumer choices (glossing over the fact that oligopolistic corporations actually manipulate consumers' wants). Economic freedom, in this sense, has nothing to do with positive freedom as the power of self-determination over the range of issues open to human decision making. We must see through the harmonist, naturalist pretense of the idea that markets promote economic freedom and are instrumental to further emancipation. They do not and they are not.

Self-Interest Misperceived

NAIRU economists have been socialized by their university training to believe that the Hobbesian solution to the problem of freedom and macro order is the only rational one, and also the realist one—because they have come to accept that capitalism is founded on the full-blooded pursuit of self-interest. That NAIRU economics can explain much social injustice and apparent cruelty as an inevitable incident in the scheme of "natural" progress, and attempts to change such things as likely to do more harm than good, even appears to commend it to authority. The earlier statements by Mankiw and Taylor do indeed reflect what most mainstream economists actually believe: that there is a static zero-sum power game between the worker and capitalist classes. This "gloomy vision" (Hirschman 1970) is grounded in a set of pessimistic assumption about behavior and sees the primary purpose of social theory as solving the "negative problem" of restricting the social costs arising from human imperfections (Ghoshal 2005).[13] In this uncooperative zero-sum world, the balance of class power may shift from capital to labor (or vice versa), depending on their political strength, but without the sovereign central banker the system will underperform macroeconomically. However, what NAIRU economists fail to notice in their enthusiasm for the rule by authoritarian, conservative central bankers is that their interpretation of the behavior by and interests of firms and employees is excessively parsimonious, to use Albert Hirschman's (1982) words, as well as static.

To illustrate this point, we return to the prisoner's dilemma and note that we don't need Leviathan to get to the socially superior outcome, even if firms and workers are motivated by self-interest alone. One already mentioned alternative mechanism whereby worker-firm coordination of decision making can be realized is reciprocal altruism (Axelrod 1984). As in the "high commitment" efficiency wage model (Akerlof 1982), workers and firms understand that reciprocity sustains exchange. Cooperative behavior is likely to elicit cooperation from others, because one cannot successfully fake being cooperative for an extended period of time (Frank 1988). Hence, it is highly probable that a cooperative act will be reciprocated with cooperation, to the ultimate benefit of the initial cooperator. Both firms and workers will tend to cooperate until they learn from experience that the other party is taking advantage of them. Cooperation is still motivated by self-interest (firms and workers know that most probably they will gain by cooperating), but the world no longer is a fixed, unchanging place of "war of all against all." NAIRU economics denies the possibility of cooperation based on reciprocal altruism and social learning, even though the underlying behavior is not in conflict with self-interest.

Fascinating comparative evidence of real-life capital-labor cooperation based on reciprocal altruism has been presented by political scientist Peter Swenson (2002, 2004). Based on a mass of historical detail, Swenson argues that welfare state development in both the United States and Sweden has been based on an alignment of the (supposedly conflicting) interests of labor and capitalists. The reason: "social policies often regulate competition among capitalists in ways that protect the profits of a politically significant portion of them" (Swenson 2004, 3). Social regulation "was a benefit in and of itself" (ibid., 4), and it made possible cross-class alliances. One consequence of minimum wages, for instance, is that wages are taken out of competition and there is less disruptive price competition between firms; the monopoly rents thus created are shared between employers and employees. The idea that whatever is a benefit to labor must be at the expense of capital is wrong.[14] What Peter Swenson finds is that labor market regulation can serve labor *and* capital, not labor at the expense of capital. In his masterly book *The Great Transformation* (2001, 156), social historian Karl Polanyi put it as follows:

Ultimately . . . it is the relation of a class to society as a whole which maps out its part in the drama; and its success is determined by the breadth and variety of the interests, other than its own, which it is able to serve. Indeed, no policy of a narrow class interest can safeguard even that interest well.

Major U.S. corporations (and their associations), for example, understood Polanyi's insight and aligned behind Roosevelt's New Deal, as it would reduce competition in their own interest. In 1935, M. C. Rorty, president of the American Management Association, praised employers who consistently paid above-market wages and preached against the "evils of excessive wage reductions." Wage cuts, he thought, would do more harm than wage rigidity (Swenson 2004, 6). By encouraging firms to invest less in labor-saving technology and slow down the scrapping of older capital stock, wage cuts would lead to price slashing, massive layoffs, and substandard competition at considerable cost to workplace harmony, efficiency, and labor productivity, as we explained in Chapter 4.

The situation in Sweden was much the same: its welfare state was developed in the 1940s and 1950s on the basis of a strong cross-class alliance. In a firsthand account of efforts to promote costly active labor market policies (ALMP), Swedish economist Gösta Rehn never mentions employer resistance—but that is because there was no such resistance. Employers liked these policies and even defended them against the Social Democratic government, which wanted to reduce the ALMP budget (Swenson 2004, 18). Likewise, employers favored a pension scheme that was more expensive and universalistic than the one preferred by the fiscally conservative Social Democratic government. What Swenson's analysis persuasively shows is that interactions among self-interested workers and firms are strategically more complex than NAIRU theory presumes and that conflictual power relations are not static but can be transformed in progressive cross-class win-win alliances, founded on reciprocity. Our findings in Chapters 4 and 7 that higher wages and regulated labor markets are associated with more rapid labor productivity growth can be taken as evidence of such worker-firm reciprocity. It is precisely what is neglected by the NAIRU approach.

Homo Homini Lupus Est: Or Not?

Like the NAIRU order, a solution based on reciprocal altruism still assumes that economic agents are motivated only by self-interest. A deeper, foundational critique of the NAIRU order rejects its inherently pessimistic view of human nature as well as its deep skepticism of any possibility of learning and human improvement. This is brought out in Hobbes's motto "Homo homini lupus est," or "A man is a wolf to his fellow man." This particular view of human nature has been a persistent one in economics—witness the assertion by Francis Ysidro Edgeworth (1881, 104), in his *Mathematical Psychics* that "the first principle of economics is that every agent is actuated only by self-interest." It is certainly the first principle of the NAIRU approach. But it is not a particularly realistic starting point. This purely economic human must be seen, according to Amartya Sen, as a social moron—a "rational fool"—and Sen gives the following tongue-in-cheek illustration of what a society of rational fools would look like:

> "Where is the railway station?" he asks me. "There," I say, pointing at the post office, "and would you please post this letter for me on the way?" "Yes," he says, determined to open the envelope and check whether it contains something valuable. (1990, 35)

Choices based on purely egoistic motives consistently lead to suboptimal outcomes for all involved.[15] As Sen's illustration makes clear, individual behavior and social organization cannot be reduced to universal egoism. Rather, social order depends on pro-social motivations, genuine concern for others ("we-feeling"), commitment to moral and spiritual principles (often a socially instilled conscience), and readiness to cooperate even when cooperation does not serve self-interest (Mansbridge 1990a).[16] People often see cooperation as a "good thing in itself," irrespective of its results for personal welfare, and are motivated to "do the right thing"—this is what Sen means by commitment: acting out of a sense of obligation that goes beyond the consequence for one's own welfare. Commitment may lead us to forgo actions that harm collective welfare, regardless of individual consequences.

Sociologists are not surprised. From Talcott Parsons's *The Structure of Social Action* (1937) to Amitai Etzioni's *The Moral Dimension* (1988) and Robert Putnam's *Bowling Alone* (2000), social stability has been argued to be grounded in cooperation and consensus, not merely in exchange or conflict. "From the most primitive to the most advanced societies, a higher degree of cooperation takes place than can be explained as merely pragmatic strategy of egoistic man," as Jack Hirshleifer (1985, 55) summarizes the historical evidence. Hundreds if not thousands of controlled experiments in laboratory conditions with prisoner's dilemma and other games that actually reward self-interested behavior at the expense of the group indicate a stubborn refusal on the part of 30–35 percent of the participants to take self-interested action, even when acting in isolation under conditions of complete anonymity with no possibility of group punishment. These people act as social beings, concerned about the fairness of the deal they are being offered and about other matters quite irrelevant to narrow utility maximization. And experimenters can raise the level of cooperative behavior to 85 percent by allowing discussion and other procedures that increase feelings of group identity (Dawes and Thaler 1988; Dawes, van de Kragt, and Orbell 1990). These are remarkably subversive findings. The selfish economist may try to blame the players, arguing that they are "not strategically sophisticated enough" to figure out the only rationally defensible strategy and that it is "this intellectual shortcoming [which] saves them from losing."[17] But this will not wash. A more fruitful approach lies in permitting the possibility that people are in fact more sophisticated than the theory allows—as Albert Hirschman (1982) and Amartya Sen (1990) conclude. "Perhaps," write Robyn Dawes and Richard Thaler (1988, 196), "we need to give more attention to 'sensible cooperators'" than to rational fools. Yale economist John E. Roemer's paper "Kantian Equilibrium" (2010) is a recent theoretical attempt to do just this. Here people are assumed to be motivated by Immanuel Kant's categorical imperative, which says that one should take those actions and only those actions that one would advocate all others take as well. Roemer argues that if people can agree to live by Kantian norms, the inefficiency of the prisoner's dilemma can in general be resolved by means of cooperation (provided that the utility from cheating is not excessively high). If people are made to realize the consequences of their noncooperative behavior, they sensibly go for the superior cooperative solution. It is a solution based on voluntary self-restraint—quite unlike the restraint imposed by an external authority that impinges on freedom.

Once we start seeing people as sensible cooperators, we can recognize the narrowness of both the monetarist explanation of the stagflationary episode of the 1970s and its solution, the imposition of NAIRU order. Authoritarian third-party control over macroeconomic policy is a solution only if we assume that firms, unions, and government are incapable of learning from mistakes and of realizing the impacts of noncooperative behavior and are unable to alter their practices in the face of changing social necessities. But if we assume sensible cooperators, capable of self-restraint and committed behavior, alternative joint actions could have been possible to restore stability and slow down inflation without drastically reducing output and creating much additional unemployment—for example, a system of coordinated wage-price guideposts and income policies in a context of regulated labor markets and relatively low real rates of interest, a system that worked successfully in the 1960s and which continues to work well in a somewhat toned-down version in the Nordic economies. The key issues to be explained are why the earlier cross-class alliance of labor and capital (as documented by Swenson and others) became precarious and eventually broke down in the 1970s, and how a similar alliance could be revived.[18] One of the most damaging consequences of economists' preoccupation with the NAIRU has been the almost total neglect of these issues, in favor of a "there is no alternative" attitude that monopolizes thinking while abrogating egalitarianism.

The comparison of a Kantian solution to the Hobbesian NAIRU solution is relevant in one more respect: Kant believed firmly in the possibility of human improvement, whereas Hobbes was skeptical thereof (Williams 2003). For Kant, the essence of humans is that they are autonomous beings— "authors of values, of ends in themselves, the ultimate authority of which consists precisely in the fact they are willed freely" (Berlin 1969, 11). Kant consequently focused on learning and the evolution of human nature. Hobbes saw human nature as fixed and unchanging, and humans as natural objects whose choices can be manipulated by rulers, whether by threats of force or offers of rewards. Hobbes's authoritarian solution appears to be "outside history," just as the NAIRUvian authoritarian solution of central bank independence appears to be ahistorical. When moving from theory to practice, we side with Kant, and follow Lowe (1988, 3) in seeing human history as an evolutionary process of progressive emancipation, driven by one and the same underlying impulse: "to cast off the fetters forged by a harsh nature, by even harsher human masters, and by the harshest despot of all: ignorance." However, this process of emancipation is creating new challenges for social order and stability: "The weakening of the former barriers to economic freedom is removing an essential stabilizer of the past: the uniform behavior patterns that had ensured the self-correcting movements of the system," writes Lowe (1988, 37). Personal "freedom from" at the micro level needs a stable macro order if it is to persist—and long-term macro stability, in turn, requires restrictions on the behavior of its micro units so as to help the system self-correct. "But need such constraints [on micro behavior] be imposed by external forces . . . ? Can they not be engendered by self-restraint on the part of the micro units—an attitude we explicitly excluded from the list of freedom-limiting factors?" Can people learn to live by Kantian norms?

The Afflictions of the NAIRU Order

Now we come to our main point. The NAIRU order denies the constructive potential of emancipation—it is the antithesis of the free, democratic society. It is a society of "cheerful robots," as depicted by American sociologist Charles Wright Mills (1959, 166ff), conforming to external, rational rules and regulations, which are alien to and in contradiction with "all that has been historically understood as individuality."

> The advent of this [cheerful robot] points to freedom as trouble, as issue, and—let us hope—as a problem for social scientists. Put as trouble

of the individual . . . it is the trouble called "alienation." As an issue for publics . . . it is no less than the issue of democratic society, as fact and as aspiration. (Mills 1959, 170–172)

The NAIRU order compromises "positive liberty" while overemphasizing "negative liberty" (for some). It violates egalitarian freedom, the transformative power of self-determination (which also includes the right to make wrong choices), in a way that has become self-reinforcing and self-perpetuating. First, the NAIRU order systematically raises—to use prisoner's dilemma terms—the payoff from noncooperative behavior, relative to that of cooperative behavior, and people respond by acting more self-interestedly, just as experimental studies have shown (Mansbridge 1990b). Second, by atomizing workers, weakening group and social identities, and reintroducing individual risk and uncertainty (in the form of insecure jobs, insecure pensions, and lower entitlements to social security), the deregulated labor markets of the NAIRU order systematically undermine group solidarity and mutual commitment, thereby weakening a major basis of cooperative behavior; this manifests itself, for example, in the growing tendency of more highly skilled workers to opt out of collective bargaining and rely instead on individual bargaining, weakening the traditional constituency and bargaining power of unions.

The combined result of both changes has been what sociologist Richard Sennett (1998, 10) has called "the corrosion of character," where "character is expressed by loyalty and mutual commitment, or through the pursuit of long-term goals, or by the practice of delayed gratification for the sake of a future end." The basic message of today's flexible and insecure capitalism is "No long term," writes Sennett, and this motto is altering the very meaning of work: long-term jobs are being replaced by short-term "projects," corroding trust, work identity, loyalty, standards of authority, and mutual commitment. "No long term" is a deeply self-destructive message, as workers' engagement with work becomes superficial and both collective responsibility and commitment break down. "No long term" means that workers become reluctant to invest in "firm-specific human capital," as they have little prospect of reaping returns on these investments over the course of their careers. The damage is not only to them but to the economy as a whole (Lazonick 2009). Under shareholder capitalism, supposedly anonymous financial market pressures are used as an excuse for firms to be in a constant state of restructuring and reorganization, absolving them and their managers of responsibility—it is the "anonymous market" that makes constant change imperative. As a result, authority vanishes, for no one can be held responsible, and no one feels responsible any longer. Workers, under constant pressure to adjust, feel powerless and often are led to behave more selfishly themselves if they think their firms are acting selfishly (Mansbridge 1990b). Or they feel alienated and become disengaged. The NAIRU order, in other words, inhibits the development of "full human personality" and fashions a predictable one-dimensional human personality (Hirschman 1977). It is increasingly turning us into rational fools rather than sensible cooperators.

At the macro level, similar mechanisms are at work. First and foremost, the NAIRU order, in Gabriel Palma's words, is "a deliberate attempt to shift the economy (and much else) from a 'stable' to a somehow 'unstable' equilibrium." It is

> a movement away from Keynesian attempts to manage risk and reduce uncertainty via national and international policy coordination, closed capital accounts, stable exchange rates, low and stable interest rates, low levels of unemployment and unemployment benefits for those out of work, public health services and the other aspects of the welfare state, and a state autonomous enough to be capable at least of some "disciplining" of the capitalist elite, toward an intended movement in reverse. (Palma 2009, 845)

The NAIRU order is a return to a Hobbesian state of emergency, based on precarious jobs, unemployment, weak social safety nets, and insufficient and insecure pensions. With workers thus "traumatized" (see Chapter 2), the door has been opened wide to the rule of "experts," a depoliticized technocracy with authoritarian power over monetary as well as fiscal policy, in the process creating a low-intensity democracy within which increasingly unequal market outcomes could be legitimized. NAIRU economics breeds inequality; Figure 2.1 illustrates this clearly for our twenty OECD countries. Inequality, in turn, "promotes [survival] strategies that are more self-interested, less affiliative, often highly anti-social, more stressful and likely to give rise to higher levels of violence, poorer community relations, and worse health," writes social epidemiologist Richard Wilkinson (1996, 24).

Wilkinson and Kate Pickett (2009), using evidence from twenty-three rich countries and from each of the states in the United States, show that the most unequal countries or states do worse according to almost every quality-of-life indicator. Whether the test is life expectancy, infant mortality, obesity, homicides, learning, teenage pregnancy, illegal drug use, depression, or mental illness, the more equal a society, the better the performance is. The best predictor of how countries or states rank is not the differences in wealth between them but the differences in wealth within the country or state itself. People in more equal societies (for instance, Sweden, Norway, and Finland) are less oriented toward dominance and more towards inclusiveness and empathy. Wilkinson and Pickett argue that when disparities grow, the distance between social groups widens, contacts between them diminish, misconceptions about the others grow, stereotyping increases, tolerance decreases, and distrust becomes more prevalent. It is not the level of income or well-being that creates trust within a society but the degree of equality that prevails within it. Greater inequality implies a steeper social gradient, deeper social divisions, and stronger status competition. It forces people to establish coping mechanisms that may vary from self-centered individualism to mistrust. Just as bad money drives out good money, competition crowds out solidarity and cooperation; hence, labor market deregulation leads to workers who are less cooperative, less committed, and more disengaged.[19] This, we think, explains the large presence of external controllers (supervisors as a percentage of the labor force) in deregulated markets, as we highlighted in Figure 2.2. The flexible work ethos, we believe, also underlies our finding in Chapter 4 that labor productivity growth is lower in countries featuring more competitive, uncoordinated, and unequal labor markets.

Rising income inequality has also been closely associated with increased financial deepening and rising stock market capitalization in a process of simultaneous causation (Boyer 2000; Dore 2008; Palma 2009). Much of the rising inequality must be ascribed to the shift in income distribution from wages to financial-sector profits—as shown in our Figure 5.1—but the income concentration has reinforced inequality, as it has led to higher values of financial assets owned, further capital gains, and excessive consumerism by the rich. Those who are not rich, on the other hand, had to put in more hours of low-wage work to earn the income needed to meet their aspirations or to finance spending from debt (Irvin 2011; Lysandrou 2011). As Palma (2009, 842) writes, the American dream has been "hijacked by a rather tiny minority—for the rest, it has only been available on credit!"

Crucially, the increased inequality is closely associated with rising shareholder power: long-term employment is not feasible where the financial system provides capital on terms that are very sensitive to current profitability. This is a matter of institutional complementarity, as we argued in Chapter 5. A highly developed stock market thus indicates greater reliance on market modes of coordination in the sphere of industrial relations (see Figure 5.4). This is explained by Sanford Jacoby as follows:

> As investors press for larger returns, employees are forced to bear the increased risk. Wages and employment volatility have risen since 1980; pension plans have shifted from defined benefit to defined contribution; and employer-provided health insurance is disappearing. However, what is telling is that the volatility effects occur only in public firms; private

firms exhibit a *decline* in employment volatility, suggesting an association with financial markets. There is also an association between shareholder power and reduced levels of employee tenure. (Jacoby 2007, cited in Dore 2008, 1108; emphasis added)

Higher stock market capitalization rates are associated with profit-led aggregate demand, as we observed in Chapter 5. That is, shareholder-oriented economies are likely to grow and have lower unemployment when the wage share is reduced, income and wealth inequality rises, and unions are highly constrained. Macroeconomically, such profit-led systems provide no basis whatsoever for a more sensibly cooperative, egalitarian capitalism. They are locked into a conflictual social order in which the rewards of the moment are overrated and both firms and workers blind themselves to the requirements of a viable future in order to pursue short-term partisan gain and factional interests at the expense of larger public needs (Lowe 1988). The general effect of the NAIRU order has been a depersonalization of firm-worker relationships. Once these relationships depended on trust, mutual responsibility, and fairness, and carried some sense of personal or corporate obligation. Now they are only contractual (very flexible) relationships that can be enforced only in courts. This erosion of trust spills over into large costs in the broader society, undermining notions of longer-term collective responsibility and "helping erode whatever sense of community and cooperation we may once have shared," wrote David Gordon (1996, 98). "Anger and frustration boil over in the political arena as well, contributing to cynicism, declining citizen participation, volatile rejection of political leadership and even of the efficacy of government itself."[20] We all pay the price and we all suffer the consequences (Marglin 2008). NAIRU economics makes us believe that the NAIRU order and its rules and institutions are inexorable, unchanging, and objective powers, as inescapable as the laws of nature. We maintain that this is an illusion, the spell of which can only be broken by being analyzed and understood; indeed, only understanding is the basis for appropriate action.

Cooperation for the Benefit of Us (Not Me)[21]

How is egalitarian freedom (as power of self-determination over the range open to human decision making) compatible with a stable social order? The answer depends on our views of human nature. If people are rational fools, incapable of self-restraint and unable to transcend the "natural selfish passions of men," then order can be maintained only by a visible external authority, such as the central bank. This order comes at the cost of positive liberty: it limits our freedom of self-determination, constrains emancipation, and alienates us from the human condition by reducing us to cheerful robots. But if people are sensible cooperators, capable of voluntary self-restraint, socially conscious, and able to learn and improve their practices in light of social necessities and experience, then there is less or even no need for external control. Indeed, in that case, we ourselves become responsible for realizing the constructive potential of emancipation. The key question therefore is, what makes people sensible cooperators?

The question cannot be answered with certainty. What we can say is that at the deepest level, it requires a new consciousness—what Erich Fromm (1977, 8) called "a radical change of the human heart," a change away from "the pathogenic nature of present social character" (ibid., 137) and toward a "human solidarity" based on reciprocity, responsibility, and empathy. Education and knowledge are critical in this process of consciousness change. What we mean is *"education* in the widest sense of the term," the way Adolph Lowe (1988, 128) intended it.[22] This involves not merely the intellectual-cognitive training necessary for understanding the social implications of individual behavior, but also education meant to integrate the "rational with the moral," to shape and encourage a critical and creative social consciousness, and to further emancipative participation in the democratic governance of society.[23] Education should orient people in their lives and help them to alter their practices and create new ones in the face of changing social necessities—including overcoming paralyzing class conflict by cross-class bridge building, which involves fulfilling tasks set by interests wider than their own. This is what Kant meant by realizing the potential of human improvement—and it is exactly what Hobbes and NAIRU economics deny.

The implication for economics is that it should give up false scientific ("naturalist") pretenses and stop claiming that economics is a nonpolitical subject, eliding issues of power and inequality and reducing humans to rational fools. Failure to do so destroys its relation to the real world, turning economic debates into chummy conservations between Tweedledum and Tweedledee. "The victims of that," wrote John Kenneth Galbraith,

> are those we instruct in error. The beneficiaries are the institutions whose power we so disguise. Let there be no question: Economics, so long as it is thus taught, becomes, however unconsciously, a part of an arrangement by which the citizen or student is kept from seeing how he is, or will be, governed. (1973, 6)

NAIRU-based economics itself is an obstruction to cooperative behavior and has to change if economics is to revive its original sense of purpose and worthiness, which the discipline has lost over the last three decades.

In a world of sensible cooperators, "reform based on cross-class compromise and agreement could reconcile efficiency and society, allowing classes to work together for socially . . . healthy growth, political stability, and a widely shared, non-utopian kind of freedom," as Peter Swenson (2002, 321) writes. But we must recognize that large inequalities, persistent unemployment, corporate power, job insecurity, and the existence of power without responsibility in the workplace and in macroeconomic policy are fundamental obstacles to social cohesion and cross-class bridge building. Large inequalities in income, wealth, political power, and status also compromise positive liberty, because these reduce access to the means on which depends the attainment of a person's chief ends. Anatole France's (2010) famous taunt—"the law, in its majestic equality, forbids the rich as well as the poor to sleep under bridges, to beg in the streets and to steal bread"—captures the constraints on freedom imposed by inequality. Such blocks to freedom and constraints on cooperative behavior are not laws of nature; they are in principle removable, and thus legitimate targets of public control, as Adolph Lowe (1988, 6) argues.[24]

James Galbraith (2008, xiii–xiv) writes:

> The setting of wages and the control of the distribution of pay and incomes is a social, and not a market, decision. It is not the case that technology dictates what people are worth and should be paid. Rather, society decides what the distribution of pay should be, and technology adjusts to that configuration. . . . And more egalitarian standards [for pay]— those that lead to a more just society—also promote the most rapid and effective forms of technological change, so that there is no trade-off, in a properly designed economic policy, between efficiency and fairness.

This, in a nutshell, is what we argued in this book.

Egalitarianism, however, is macroeconomically compatible only with wage-led aggregate demand. In profit-led economies, such as that of the United States, it will lower growth, slow down technological progress and productivity growth, and increase unemployment (see Figure 3.3). Profit-led systems have to be transformed into wage-led ones to make egalitarian growth feasible. The single most important relationship that has to be transformed to achieve this is the relationship between financial and productive capital. What John Maynard Keynes (1931a) wrote concerning the recovery of the 1930s crisis is as true for us today:

> A wide gulf . . . is set between the ideas of lenders and the ideas of borrowers for the purpose of genuine capital investment. . . . [T]here

cannot be a real recovery, in my judgment, until the ideas of lenders and the ideas of productive borrowers are brought together again. . . . Seldom in modern history has the gap between the two been so wide and so difficult to bridge. (1931a, 145–146)

What it means is a drastic tightening of regulation of financial capital, not just to control its speculative and manipulative excesses but also to direct it toward financing productive investment (Palma 2009; Wade 2009). Undoubtedly, the political imperative to come out of the current crisis, which we hope serves the purpose of opening up the consciousness of the public to its true interests, may help facilitate the transition to more regulated, less volatile financial markets. But this is not enough. To sustain this countervailing power, its rationale has to be fully understood and accepted as a socially legitimate form of "self-restraint"—in Lowe's profound sense of term—which enhances public freedom or self-governance in other segments of our life space. Otherwise, tight governance of financial markets will not last, because "he who's convinced against his will / is of the same opinion still" (Robinson 1962, 26).

A detailed discussion of which restrictions are needed is beyond the scope of this concluding chapter; David Gordon (1996, chapter 9), Sanford Jacoby (2007), Ronald Dore (2008), Robert Wade (2009), Lance Taylor (2010), and others provide important clues. The general point is that the excessive shareholder value orientation of firms' management must be curbed. In our view, this requires two fundamental reforms. First, for the sake of generating stable and equitable growth, the role played by the stock market in the corporate allocation of resources needs to be reformed. The general objective of reform should be to control the forces of stock price speculation and manipulation (by means of corporate stock repurchases, executive stock options, and other devices), so that the stock market can function to support (and stock price movements reflect) truly innovative firm performance.[25] The necessary first step is a rejection of the deification of shareholder returns as an indicator of superior economic performance. What must be recognized is that shareholder value ideology does not comport with an innovative economy. William Lazonick explains why:

> Investment in innovation is a direct investment that involves, first and foremost, a strategic confrontation with technological, market, and competitive uncertainty. Those who have the abilities and incentives to allocate resources to innovation must decide, in the face of uncertainty, what types of investments have . . . potential. . . . Then they must mobilize committed finance to sustain the innovation process until it generates the higher-quality, lower-cost products that permit financial returns.

What role do public shareholders play in this innovation process? Do they confront uncertainty by strategically allocating resources to innovative investments? No. As portfolio investors, they diversify their financial holdings across the outstanding shares of existing firms to minimize risk. They do so, moreover, with limited liability, which means that they are under no legal obligation to make further investments of "good" money to support previous investments that have gone bad. Indeed, even for these previous investments, the existence of a highly liquid stock market enables public shareholders to cut their losses instantaneously by selling their shares—what has long been called the "Wall Street walk."

Without this ability to exit an investment easily, public shareholders would not be willing to hold shares of companies over the assets of which they exercise no direct allocative control. It is the liquidity of a public shareholder's portfolio investment that differentiates it from a direct investment, and indeed distinguishes the public shareholder from a private shareholder who, for lack of liquidity of his or her shares, must remain committed to his or her direct investment until it generates financial returns. (Lazonick 2009, 55–56)

Lazonick sums it up by stating that "public shareholders want financial liquidity; investments in innovation require financial commitment." To turn public shareholders into more committed investors, the payoff for speculative behavior should be drastically reduced by enacting legislation that restricts or even forbids the practice of corporate stock repurchases, reins in top executive pay, and raises taxes on stock-based income (whether in the form of dividends or capital gains). These measures will help bring together again the views of lenders and productive borrowers.

Second, we must recognize that the wealth produced by corporations is the joint product of all resource providers, including shareholders, employees, and government. Each stakeholder has a right to expect returns for its investment in the firm as well as accountability from its management. Government subsidy, funded by current taxation, is a major source of innovation investment finance (as documented by Lazonick), with the state bearing the risks that the nation's firms would further develop and utilize these productive capabilities in ways that would ultimately benefit the nation—but without any contractually stated guarantee. Similar to government, workers also make investments in their own firm-specific productive capabilities, which they supply to their firm without a guaranteed contractual return; just like shareholders, workers are dependent on their employer for generating returns on their firm-specific investments (Blair 1995), but unlike liquid shareholders who can sell their stocks easily, most workers are often not in a position to find another job. Hence, "in every substantive sense, employees carry more risks than do the shareholders. Also, their contributions of knowledge, skills, and entrepreneurship are typically more important than the contributions of capital by shareholders," wrote Sumantra Ghoshal (2005, 80). This stakeholder reinterpretation of the nature of the corporation has profound implications for governance as well as for corporate wealth distribution.

One such implication is giving the organized labor force a major role in enterprise governance and strategic decision making, as, for example, the Germans and the Swedes have done, each in their own particular ways. Economic democratization in the form of worker co-determination is helpful to the firm in various ways. It helps firms attain internal flexibility in the allocation of capital and labor, much needed in this era of rapid technological change and intense global competition (Lorenz 1992; Lazonick 2009). It helps firms mobilize workers' tacit knowledge, which is important for innovation. And it helps make capital more committed, because workers have a longer-term orientation—they are interested in keeping the firm in business to maintain their jobs. One particular form of worker co-determination, relevant to our argument, is the idea advanced by Rudolf Meidner (1978) to establish wage earners' funds. These would be financed by a nonpunitive levy on annual profits and operated by worker representatives and local authorities. The effect would be to dilute traditional shareholder power without weakening the corporation as a productive concern.[26] Wage earners' funds absorb the windfall profits (or rents) for firms with above-average productivity created by labor market regulation, and guarantee that these rents are used for productive investment. As the wage earners' funds grow, these will be able to play an increasing part in strategic decision making in the firms that they partially own. Meidner's plan found an echo in Martin Weitzman's (1984) plea for a "share economy," which, it is argued, not only boosts employee morale and labor productivity—as has been duly noted by industrial relations experts for years—but also creates the much-needed wage flexibility at full employment. Finally, we emphasize that worker co-determination, if it is to be meaningful, should also apply to corporate research agendas and the development of new technologies, because technology is a major factor helping to shape work contexts and the social relations of production, as we argued in Chapter 4.[27]

The final major obstacle to egalitarian growth in a wage-led economy is an inherent one: the specter of technological unemployment. We found in Chapter 7 that even in the most strongly wage-led countries in the OECD, the Nordic ones, egalitarian growth has not created jobs, as is illustrated in Figure 7.2. The reason is that egalitarian growth is strongly associated with rapid labor-saving technological progress and high rates of labor productivity growth; the resulting lack of employment growth poses a major obstacle to egalitarianism. One remedy intended to create extra jobs is an overall reduction of individual working hours, as in Scandinavia; ignoring some organizational complications, no valid objections can be raised so long as wages are reduced in proportion to the reduction in working hours and the growth of labor productivity. (We must note that if a reduction in working hours raises unit labor costs for firms, it will likely induce further labor-saving innovations, and the real effect of the measure would then be a further rise in technological unemployment—the contrary of what workers expect.) A second remedy is what Adolph Lowe (1988) called "planned domestic colonization": the creation of public sector jobs to strengthen public infrastructure and provide essential services in health, education, and general welfare.[28] Lowe's proposal, which ties in with the basic income scheme proposed by Andrew Glyn (2006), Richard Sennett (2005), and many others, advocates "a type of investment that will enlist millions of job-seeking workers, whom the private domain cannot employ, in productive activity" (Lowe 1988, 110). However, while the problem of egalitarian growth can thus be resolved, it stands to reason that the lack of employment growth in dynamic, strongly wage-led economies may not be much of a problem in the decades to come, because of significant demographic change in the OECD countries. The populations and labor forces in these countries are aging, with the expected result that labor force growth in most economies has already turned negative or will turn negative shortly.[29] In these demographic circumstances, a steady reduction of labor input per unit of output—a true saving of labor—will no longer stand in the way of achieving full employment. To the contrary, realizing a steady high rate of labor productivity growth is the only viable way to maintain economic welfare in the graying OECD economies. That the requisite productivity growth, based on labor-saving technological progress, is perfectly compatible with rapid (wage-led) egalitarian growth needs no further elaboration.

Is It Practical?

Our book constitutes a manifesto for feasible egalitarian growth. It rejects NAIRU economics, which is based on a narrow, static view of human nature and social organization and fundamentally denies not only positive liberty but also humanity's ability to learn and to self-improve. The book offers an agenda for discussion on how macroeconomics has to be reconstructed if we wish to allow for more cooperative behavior and acknowledge that coordination and regulation pay off in terms of more rapid labor productivity growth. It has argued for a more complex and dynamic view of human nature and social order—a view that acknowledges the importance of pro-social motivations and commitment, cross-class cooperation (which may go beyond self-interest), learning and constructive emancipation, and mutual responsibility. This is what is involved in creating egalitarian growth. Clearly, we offer just a beginning; more work is needed, and the challenges in creating an alternative macroeconomics are daunting.

Our critique of the NAIRU order, of its demeaning effects on human existence and on our social relations, will be derided for being unrealistic, maverick, and naive. The alternative order we propose, of which the Nordic egalitarian growth analyzed in Chapter 7 may be an example, will be regarded as idiosyncratic or even dangerously utopian, a threat to negative liberty. But the current crisis of NAIRU-based capitalism is too big and too visible to pass over without any major change. "We cannot go on living like this," writes Tony Judt.

> The little crash of 2008 was a reminder that unregulated capitalism is its own worst enemy: sooner or later it must fall prey to its own excesses and turn again to the state for rescue. But if we do no more than pick up the pieces and carry on as before, we can look forward to greater upheavals in years to come.
>
> And yet we seem unable to conceive of alternatives. (2010b, 2)

This collective inability to imagine alternatives is reflected in macroeconomics' current state of disarray and controversy, to a degree that we have not witnessed for a long time. The frustration and disappointment with NAIRU-based economics likely will create demands for radical changes in economic theory as well as policy. We hope our book will provide a foundation for such demands and open up the agenda for alternatives.

We are not denying the problems involved in creating a feasible egalitarian alternative, nor are we assuming that such problems can easily be solved. But we are not paralyzed by them, because it is the attempt to improve the world itself that matters and provides meaning. Perhaps this is the most valuable message provided by our book: a better, more human economic order is possible once we realize that we ourselves can give shape and meaning to life and are co-creators of the social-economic order. There is much to be done, and it will not be easy. But as the angels said as they carried Faust to heaven: "Whoever strives with all his power, we are allowed to save."

Further Reading

Adolph Lowe's (1988) masterly treatise on balancing freedom and order, *Has Freedom a Future?*, has been a main inspiration in writing this chapter. Forstater (2000) is a useful introduction to Lowe's work. Martin Weitzman's *The Share Economy* (1984) is a plausible attempt to make capitalism more stable by changing the relationship between workers and their firms. Richard Sennett (1998) wrote a provocative essay on the personal consequences of flexibility and downsizing. Friedman (1962) is the essential text on Friedman's views on liberty and order. Counterviews are given by James Galbraith's *The Predator State* (2008) and Naomi Klein's *The Shock Doctrine* (2007), a rich history of the machinations required to impose monetarist free market policies in the real world. Mansbridge (1990a) is an excellent collection of papers on human motivation and social and political order, including Amartya Sen's paper on rational fools. Finally, William Lazonick (2009) analyzes the transformation of U.S. capitalism into a flexible, shareholder-value-driven model and highlights its perverse and unsustainable outcomes.

Appendix: Data Sources

The countries in the sample are:

Australia	Finland	Italy	Spain
Austria	France	Japan	Sweden
Belgium	Germany	The Netherlands	Switzerland
Canada	Greece	Norway	United Kingdom
Denmark	Ireland	Portugal	United States

Employment Protection Legislation index for 1989 and 1999 is provided by Nicoletti, Scarpetta, and Boyland (2000). The management ratio was calculated based on data on employment by occupation from ILO, *Yearbook of Labour Statistics*, various issues. Data on the benefit duration index (for 1980–1987 and 1999), collective bargaining coverage (in 1980 and 1994), and the co-ordination index (1980–1987 and 1995–1999) are all from Nickel, Nunziata, and Ochel (2005). Duration of unemployment benefits is based on a measure of how the longer-term generosity of benefits compares to the one-year replacement rate. Collective bargaining coverage refers to the percentage of the employed labor force whose pay is determined by collective agreement. Data on union density (during 1980–1987 and 1996–1998), the replacement ratio (for 1980–1987 and 1999), expenditure on active labor market policies (1985 and 1998), and total labor taxes (for 1980–1987 and 1996–2000) are from Nickell, Nunziata, and Ochel (2005). Data on average tenure (1985–2004) are from OECD (1997). The source of the data on earnings inequality (1984–2001) is *OECD Employment Outlook* (various years).

Real GDP growth is from the OECD Economic Outlook Database. Labor productivity growth is defined as the average annual growth rate of real GDP (at factor cost) per hour worked. Data on hours worked are from the GGDC Total Economy Database (www.eco.rug.nl/ggdc), University of Groningen, and the Conference Board. Data on fixed capital stock for most European

243

countries and the United States are from the GGDC Total Economy Database; capital stock data for Australia, Canada, Japan, Norway, and Switzerland are from Kamps (2004). Data on the standardized unemployment rate, the employment rate, investment growth, and TFP growth are from the OECD Economic Outlook Database. Real wage growth is the average annual growth rate of real compensation per employee per hour worked; data on real compensation per employee are from the OECD Economic Outlook Database. Data on job security are from Sousa-Poza (2004).

Notes

Preface

1. As Karl Marx wrote to Friedrich Engels in July 1865, "Whatever shortcomings they may have, the advantage of my writings is that they are an artistic whole." The quote is from Wheen (2006), 5.
2. In a letter to George Bainton, October 15, 1888, reprinted in Bainton (1890), 87–88.
3. Judt (2010a) laments the mental captivity of our times, approvingly quoting Czeslaw Milosz's indictment of the ubiquitous servile intellectual: "His chief characteristic is his fear of thinking for himself."

1. The Power of Ideas

1. The influence is clear from a perusal of leading macroeconomics texts, not only in what might be termed a conservative text (Mankiw and Taylor 2010) but also in more liberal ones, including Blanchard (2000), Baumol and Blinder (2008), and Carlin and Soskice (2007). Note that the NAIRU first appeared in the 1980 edition of Paul Samuelson's seminal textbook.
2. Our analysis concerns the twenty high-income OECD countries of Western Europe and North America, Japan, and Australia, as listed in the Appendix. We do not consider in our book the "developing" OECD members (Turkey, South Korea, and Mexico) or its more recent East European members.
3. Friedman (1968); Phelps (1968). Friedman and Phelps developed the idea of a natural rate of unemployment, below which the actual unemployment rate could not be sustained. Friedman (1968, 8) wrote: "The 'natural rate of unemployment' . . . is the [real wage] level that would be ground out by the Walrasian system of general equilibrium equations, provided there is embedded in them the actual structural characteristics of the labor and commodity markets." Friedman's story is pre-Keynesian in all its essentials. The label "natural" is also a gross misnomer, as Blanchard (2000, 117) points out; the equilibrium unemployment rate is anything but natural, as it depends on institutions and policies.
4. We use the terms "equilibrium unemployment," "NAIRU," "structural unemployment," and "steady-inflation unemployment" interchangeably, skipping over

the many nuances in their definitions, so fondly discussed and debated by mainstream economists.

5. For interested readers, the microeconomic foundations are provided in Forslund, Gottfries, and Westermark (2008). They derive equation (1.1) from a strategic Nash bargaining model with unions and firms bargaining over the "scope" for wage increases, that is, the sum of productivity growth and price increases. See also Manning (2005), Carlin and Soskice (2006), and Hatton (2007) for alternative microeconomic underpinnings of equation (1.1).

6. That faster productivity growth leads to lower steady-inflation unemployment has been empirically documented by Ball and Mankiw (2002) for the United States, by Hatton (2007) for Britain, and by Nymoen and Rødseth (2003) for the Scandinavian countries.

7. See Taylor (2010) for a critique of the Pigou effect. Remarkably, Arthur Cecil Pigou himself, according to Baumol (2000, 1n), was in some doubt about the Pigou effect. "Dennis Robertson repeatedly told [Baumol] how on passing Pigou's lair, the great man would regularly emerge, demanding 'Robertson—tell me, what is the Pigou effect?'"

8. We note that in the latter case, actual unemployment is determined by how large the central bank *thinks* the NAIRU is. See Rowthorn (1995); Nickell, Nunziata, and Ochel (2005); Carlin and Soskice (2006).

9. The classic paper here is Calmfors and Driffill (1988), which argues that there is a nonlinear relationship between the degree of collective (wage) bargaining in an economy and the level of unemployment. The idea is that extremes work best: either highly centralized systems with national bargaining or highly decentralized systems with wage setting at the level of the firm produce the best outcomes in terms of employment; systems with an intermediate degree of centralization generate the worst employment outcomes. The reason that highly centralized systems do well is that the bargaining process then takes into account both the inflationary and unemployment effects of wage increases. More recent investigations of labor markets include Auer (2007); Freeman (2005); Manning (2005); and Howell (2005).

10. We note that the United States could not be used as the base norm for labor market deregulation today (2011), because more than 9.6 percent of its labor force has been unemployed during 2009–2010, compared (for example) to 7.5 percent in Germany, 8.2 percent in Italy, and 4.3 percent in the Netherlands. The European unemployment rates mentioned have been adjusted to U.S. concepts.

11. Nickell, Nunziata, and Ochel (2005), 22. Another prominent example is Botero et al. (2004), which celebrates the inefficiencies associated with more extensive labor market regulation, concluding that "heavier regulation of labor has adverse consequences for labor force participation and unemployment, especially of the young."

12. As Rowthorn (1999) explains, assuming that $\alpha_2 = 1$ would mean that the elasticity of capital-labor substitution (in a neoclassical production function) equals unity. Empirical evidence indicates that this elasticity takes a value of about 0.5.

13. Here we assume that capacity utilization and labor productivity are constants.

14. Some mainstream economists accept the possibility that the long-run effects of fiscal policy can be positive, pointing out that fiscal contraction may undermine potential growth by reducing plant and equipment investment, R&D, and public investment in crucial areas such as transportation infrastructure and energy technologies. The IMF (2009) recognizes that a banking crisis makes it more difficult for firms to invest and that the deeper and longer the crisis, the greater the negative permanent impact on investment and growth. In these circumstances, fiscal expansion may pay off by shortening the downturn (or recession). A similar argument has been made by Aghion, Hemous, and Kharroubi (2009), who emphasize that credit constraints on R&D investment become tighter in a recession because profits (internal financing) are reduced. This, in turn, depresses long-run growth.

15. James Galbraith (2009) presents a survey of nonmainstream Cassandras who got it right, including South African economist Patrick Bond, U.S. economists Dean Baker and Gary Dymski, and British economist Wynne Godley. Prominent contributors to the Real World Economics blog (http://rwer.wordpress.com), the International Development Economics Associates network (www.networkideas.org), and the Triple Real Crisis blog (http://triplecrisis.com/tag/financial-crisis) have been questioning mainstream narratives for a long time; they anticipated the financial collapse and issued public warnings of the looming crisis.

16. See the important contributions of Lucio Baccaro (2010), Robert Boyer (2010), and Colin Crouch (2010), who argue that the entrenchment of financial capitalism is so deep and social-democratic thinking is in such disarray as to rule out credible alternatives. See also Judt (2010b).

17. Krugman seems oblivious of his own contributions to mainstream macroeconomics, based on a relentless faith in NAIRU economics (see Baker 2002) and a very strong (but naive) opposition to higher minimum wages in the United States. "Wages are a market price—determined by supply and demand, the same as the price for apples or coal. And it is for this reason . . . that the broader political movement of which the demand for a living wage is the leading edge is ultimately doomed to failure: For the amorality of the market economy is part of its essence, and cannot be legislated away," writes Krugman (1998). For more on the amorality of markets, see Chapter 8.

18. This work was published as a comment on Martin Wolf's "The Economists' Forum" column in *The Financial Times*, 14 February 2007.

2. The Weakness of the Evidence

1. These words are David Howell's (2005). We can only add that the editorial boards of many mainstream economics journals often exhibit a similar kind of confirmation bias.

2. Among the critics, Robert Eisner, former president of the American Economic Association, stands out for being a consistently staunch advocate of the view that the NAIRU does not exist. Eisner (1997) found an asymmetric relationship, where high rates of unemployment led to lower rates of inflation but low rates of

unemployment did not necessarily lead to higher rates of inflation. See also Mishel, Bernstein, and Shierholz (2009) of the Economic Policy Institute (www.epi.org) for early critiques of NAIRU theory.

3. Real wages declined between 1979 and 1995, then showed six years of real wage growth, but wage levels fell back to 1979 levels after 2001.

4. After 2000, the ratio declined to 149:1 following the collapse of the dot-com boom, but it rose back to 275:1 in 2007 (Mishel, Bernstein, and Shierholz 2009).

5. Sociologist Richard Sennett (1998, 2005) makes a similar argument about the social and psychological costs for workers of labor market flexibility in the "New Capitalism."

6. In this section, we draw heavily on Baker et al. (2005b) and Howell et al. (2007).

7. We are not convinced that there is a meaningful direct union density effect on unemployment. Five of the sixteen studies covered in OECD 2006 (see table 3.9) show unemployment-increasing effects of union density; Baker et al. (2005b) have shown that for two of these five studies, these effects disappear in replication tests.

8. This goes back (at least) to the 1950s model of solidaristic wage bargaining in Sweden. See Rehn (1952); Bowles (2002); Haucap and Wey (2004).

9. Our approach is "structuralist," as defined by Lance Taylor because it is "based on social relations among broad groups of actors" and assumes that "an economy's institutions and distributional relationships across its productive sectors and social groups play essential roles in determining its macro behavior" (Taylor 2004, 1).

3. A Growth Model

1. For a useful theoretical exposition of cyclical growth in line with our approach, see Taylor (2010). For recent empirical work on cycles, see Tavani, Flaschel, and Taylor (2011). One finding from these studies is that cyclical growth (à la Richard Goodwin) is well defined in a profit-led economy but more difficult to explain in a purely wage-led system. In a wage-led system, there could be no demand growth to pull output up from the recession trough *if* productivity growth starts to rise more strongly than real wage growth as the economy emerges from a recession. However, falling interest rates and a rising fiscal deficit could offset this wage-led output drag.

2. This rule is dubbed "Einstein's razor," probably because it is a paraphrase of the following statement by Albert Einstein: "The supreme goal of all theory is to make the irreducible basic elements as simple and as few as possible without having to surrender the adequate representation of a single datum of experience" (Einstein 1934, 165).

3. Naastepad (2006) provides a useful detailed classification of OECD growth trajectories, which we do not reproduce here for reasons of space.

4. It follows that if $\beta_2 > 1$, $(d\hat{x}/d\hat{w}) < 0$, that is, a decline in real wage growth leads to a rise in output growth notwithstanding the wage-led nature of the demand regime. The productivity regime in this case dominates the demand regime.

5. It follows that if $\beta_2 > 1$, $(d\hat{x}/d\hat{w}) > 0$, that is, a fall in wage growth leads to a fall in profit-led output growth, because the productivity regime dominates the demand regime.

6. Only when $1 - \beta_1 - \beta_2 < 0$ may it occur that

$$C > \frac{\beta_2}{1 - \beta_1 - \beta_2},$$

in which case lower real wage growth would reduce employment growth in a profit-led economy.

7. Note again that these are not long-run equilibrium values (in a classical sense), because the model is predicated on $\hat{w} \neq \hat{\lambda}$, which is not sustainable in the limit. Hence, $\hat{\lambda}_0$, $\hat{x}_0$ must be regarded as a conditional or provisional equilibrium, as defined by Mark Setterfield (2002).

8. Gordon's argument is consistent with observed (profit-led) U.S. productivity dynamics (Taylor 2010), but it cannot be generalized to the EU economies. The (wage-led) EU economies are governed by the Carrot Strategy (rather than the Stick Strategy), and unemployment is therefore not so much a disciplining device.

9. If $\alpha_1 \neq 0$ in equation (3.24), the model may become unstable in the wage-led case. If a reduction of z leads to higher unemployment, the upward blip in unemployment will make wage growth decline further, and so cause a further decline in the wage share. But then output will go down more, and so on. This destabilizing spiral could be braked by a countercyclical fiscal deficit (as we observe in the data; see Chapter 7) and/or falling interest rates (or movements in the exchange rate that could have feedback with the interest rate).

4. The OECD Productivity Regime

1. Robert Solow wrote, "There is no doubt that they are stylized, though it is possible to question whether they are facts" (1970, 2).

2. Aggregate labor productivity growth is our core supply-side variable. Labor productivity is a comprehensive output measure of technological change and reflects the joint influence of many factors, including embodied and disembodied technological progress, changes in the sectoral employment structure, organizational reform, and human capital formation. It is defined as gross value added (at constant prices) per hour worked. The value-added data and the data on hours worked are internationally comparable. The main problem in aggregate productivity measurement concerns the price index used to convert nominal value added into value added at constant prices, especially in a context in which prices of new information, communication, technology (ICT) goods change at a different rate than do prices of goods included in the index, or if the prices in the index are not adjusted to remove the effect of changes in product quality. Andrew Wyckoff (1995) shows that international differences in price measurement do have significant effects on the estimated growth rates of labor productivity for the office and computer sector, nonelectrical equipment, and metals and machinery, but also finds that differences were marginal at the level of aggregate

manufacturing. The aggregate value-added data we use (provided by the Groningen Growth and Development Centre) have been deflated in a uniform manner.

3. Our productivity growth equation (4.1) may appear not quite consistent with David Gordon's (1996, 151) observation for the United States that when unemployment is high (meaning output growth is low), productivity growth may increase, as the worker discipline threat is strong. We note that in our complete model, if unemployment is high, real wage growth will be low; in a profit-led economy (such as that of the United States), this will raise the profit share and stimulate both output and labor productivity growth. Hence, high unemployment and accelerating productivity growth can occur in tandem within our framework as well, provided the system is profit-led.

4. We note here that, for Marx, technological progress is an instrument to create additional unemployment, whereas NAIRU theory generally assumes that faster (exogenous) technological change reduces the inflation-safe unemployment rate (because it reduces wage-push inflationary pressure).

5. The debate was initiated by Salter (1960), who rejected the idea, arguing that when labor costs rise, any advance that reduces total cost is welcome, irrespective of whether this is achieved by saving labor or saving capital. Useful reviews of this debate, with important contributions by Von Weiszäcker (1966), Kennedy (1964), Samuelson (1965), and Nordhaus (1973), are Ruttan (1997) and Funk (2002).

6. See the major surveys on this issue by Levine and Tyson (1990), Gordon (1996), and Appelbaum et al. (2000). See also work by Bewley (1995, 1999), Huselid (1995), Ichniowski, Shaw, and Prennushi (1995), Buchele and Christiansen (1999), Michie and Sheehan (2003), and Kleinknecht et al. (2006).

7. There is no question that Marx gave primacy to technology over social relations in the long sweep of history, as is exemplified by his famous aphorism "The hand-mill gives you society with the feudal lord; the steam-mill, society with the industrial capitalist" (Marx 1846–1847, 49). But, as Harry Braverman (1974) explains, Marx held that within a given historical period, social relations determine technology.

8. A recent econometric study using firm-level data for the United States finds that innovation and growth are fostered by more stringent labor laws, especially in the more innovation-intensive sectors, because these laws encourage otherwise risk-averse workers and firms to engage in risky innovative pursuits. See Acharya, Baghai, and Subramanian (2010).

9. We do not include a variable for technology diffusion or technological catching up, because this has become of minor (or no) importance among the OECD countries after 1980. Ireland is the exception.

10. The EPL index reflects (1) procedural inconveniences the employer faces when trying to dismiss employees, (2) notice and severance pay provisions, and (3) prevailing standards of and penalties for unfair dismissal. See OECD (1999).

11. We follow Hall and Soskice (2001): two regulatory institutions can be said to be complementary if the presence (or efficiency) of one increases the returns from (or efficiency of) the other. This suggests that nations with a particular type of

regulation in one dimension of the labor market should tend to develop complementary practices in other dimensions as well. If this is correct, regulatory practices should not be distributed randomly across nations, but instead we should see some clustering along the dimensions that divide coordinated (rigid) economies from liberal (flexible) ones.

12. We note that equation (4.2) is close to an identity (in growth rates).

13. Japan is excluded from our categorization. Japan's industrial relations system does not easily fit into our classification (see Dore, Lazonick, and O'Sullivan 1999).

14. Ireland is excluded because its high rate of real GDP growth (labor productivity growth), which during 1984–2004 exceeded average OECD growth by more than 2.8 (2.5) standard deviations, is almost completely due to a process of technological catching up, which has been extremely dependent on foreign direct investment by large multinational high-technology and financial services companies. This catching-up process is not representative of the factors governing growth in the other Anglo-Saxon countries.

5. OECD Demand Regimes

1. This is particularly true for the United Kingdom and the United States, where conflict was endemic and where the tendency for labor to gain a greater share of GDP (at the expense of profits) was most marked. See Dore, Lazonick, and O'Sullivan (1999).

2. Key writings on the profit squeeze are Marglin and Schor (1990); Epstein and Gintis (1995); Cornwall and Cornwall (2001); and Glyn (2006).

3. Quoted in Glyn (2006), 27 (emphasis added). The use of cancer in economic discourse is never innocent, as Klein (2007) argues: it encourages fatalism and justifies drastic measures, as well as reinforcing the widespread notion that the disease is necessarily fatal.

4. These policies resulted in recessionary periods, such as the British and U.S. manufacturing shake-outs of 1980.

5. Major disputes involved air traffic controllers in the United States and steelworkers, railway workers, and coal miners in the United Kingdom. As Klein (2007, 173) documents:

> The Thatcher government considered the union to be its enemy. "It was just like arming to face the threat of Hitler in the 1930s," [U.K. chancellor of the exchequer Nigel] Lawson said a decade later. "One had to prepare." . . . By 1985, Thatcher had won this war too: workers were going hungry and couldn't hold out. . . . It was a devastating setback for Britain's most powerful union, and it sent a clear message to the others: if Thatcher was willing to go to the wall to break the coal miners, on whom the country depended for its lights and warmth, it would be suicide for weaker unions producing less crucial products and services to take on her new economic order. Better just to accept whatever was on offer. It was a message very similar to the one Ronald Reagan had sent a few months after he took office with his response

to a strike by the air-traffic controllers. By not showing up to work, they had "forfeited their jobs and will be terminated," Reagan said. Then he fired 11,400 of the country's most essential workers in a single blow—a shock from which the U.S. labor movement has yet to fully recover.

6. The data are from Naastepad (2006).
7. We must note in this context that both Bowles and Boyer (1995) and Hein and Vogel (2008) find surprisingly limited profit-investment sensitivities for the United Kingdom and the United States. However, as will be clear from the main text, these findings do not appear to be plausible, as they are not in line with major investment studies including Gordon (1995), Glyn (1997), Pugh (1998), Alesina et al. (2002), and Bond et al. (2003).
8. A most striking recent example of Kaldor's paradox is France: in spite of an improvement in price competitiveness (due to a euro depreciation) comparable to that of Germany, French export market shares declined on average by 3 percent annually over the period 1999–2008 (European Commission 2010, 24). Contrariwise, Switzerland saw its exports jump at the same time as its exchange rate appreciated massively.
9. Key studies of the Kaldor paradox include Magnier and Toujas-Bernate (1994); Amable and Verspagen (1995); Fagerberg (1996); Carlin, Glyn, and van Reenen (2001); and Milberg and Houston (2005).
10. Our findings of the long-run elasticity of exports to changes in world demand are comparable to recent econometric findings by the European Commission (2010, 25–27).
11. Hein and Vogel's (2008) estimate for the Netherlands is much larger (−0.20) in absolute terms than our finding, but it is also not consistent with findings of the other studies.
12. All this does *not* mean that export growth, as a source of overall demand growth, is unimportant; what it means is that export growth in the OECD countries is based not on price or labor costs but on embodied technology, quality, and so on. Our analysis in the Appendix to this chapter shows that world trade growth is of overriding importance to OECD output growth and employment. But the OECD economies compete in world markets not on labor costs and prices but rather on high quality and innovativeness.
13. This is captured by the positive fraction ξ ($=v/\mu$), which is smaller in Italy than in the other OECD countries in the sample.
14. These values for coefficient $\beta_1 = 0.45$ and coefficient $\beta_2 = 0.29$ are taken from Chapter 4. For Sweden $C = 1.04$, and for Finland $C = 0.72$.
15. In the Red Queen's race, the Red Queen and Alice keep running but remain in the same spot.

> "Well, in our country," said Alice, still panting a little, "you'd generally get to somewhere else—if you run very fast for a long time, as we've been doing."
> "A slow sort of country!" said the Queen. "Now, here, you see, it takes all the running you can do, to keep in the same place. If you want to get somewhere else, you must run at least twice as fast as that!" (Carroll 2001, 42)

16. Likewise, Austrian economists Stefan Ederer and Engelbert Stockhammer (2007, 134) conclude, based on their econometric investigation for France, that "indeed, the key factor that makes the French economy profit-led is the foreign sector."

17. Germany, where productivity increases are not passed on to workers in the form of higher wages, is often mentioned as the prime European example of this beggar-thy-neighbor strategy. But the example is wrong: Germany's exports are not very sensitive to costs and prices, as we saw before, so lower labor cost and lower prices would have made only a small impact on the demand for Germany's exports. Instead, German export growth is caused by stronger demand for German-type (high-quality) products, while German firms have been boosting profit margins while squeezing wages; as a result, their profit share in gross value added increased from 36.3 percent in 2000 to 41.4 percent in 2008 (Janssen 2011).

18. The source of this quote is Dirda (2009). Dirda reviews the biography by Michael Slater, *Charles Dickens: A Life Defined by Writing* (New Haven: Yale University Press, 2009).

19. This and the following paragraph draw on Dore, Lazonick, and O'Sullivan (1999); Hall and Soskice (2001); Vitols (2001); Bond, Harhoff and Van Reenen (2003); Bond et al. (2003); Gugler, Mueller, and Yurtoglu (2004); Amable, Ernst, and Palombarini (2005); and Höpner (2005).

20. Obviously, this would not be true in a Miller-Modigliani world in which capital markets operate perfectly and there is no uncertainty or informational asymmetry. In markets that correctly value the expected present discounted value of certain future returns, it makes no difference what the horizon of the individual investor is. With perfect information, internal and external funds are perfect substitutes and firm investment decisions are independent of its financing decisions. But capital markets are far from perfect, and fundamental uncertainty (à la Keynes) is a fact of life. See Taylor (2010) for a lucid exposition of why this is the case.

21. See Aoki (2001); Hall and Soskice (2001); Amable, Ernst, and Palombarini (2005); and especially Höpner (2005) for discussion of the theory of institutional complementarities. We emphasize that the concept of complementarity does not imply a grand design or a master designer—it is observed only ex post as the outcome of gradual institutional change.

22. This story has been told in much more detail by Hall and Soskice (2001); Amable (2003); and Hall and Gingerich (2004).

23. Amable, Ernst, and Palombarini (2005) provide a formal (prisoner's dilemma game) model with a noncooperative equilibrium in which the time horizon of financial investors and of unions determine whether the outcome is (1) patient capital combined with highly organized labor or (2) high capital market pressures combined with weak labor.

24. According to estimates by William Lazonick (2009), the Standard & Poor's 500 companies expended $2.4 trillion on stock repurchases during 1997–2008, an average of $5.4 billion per company, and expended a total of $1.6 trillion in cash dividends, an average of $3.8 billion per firm.

25. Financial sector reform to make the United States wage-led will require that the excessive shareholder value orientation of firms' management be curbed. This could be done by imposing various legal restrictions. First, the scope for incentive pay systems for management (bonuses, share options, etc.), which led to short-termist biases in management decisions, must be reduced. Second, a system of worker representation in management and worker co-determination (as in Germany and other countries of the European Union) should be introduced. According to German and EU corporate law, 50 percent of a large company's management board has to be employee representatives (often via trade unions); employees are thus involved in strategic decision making, which will be helpful to the firm because the employees not only possess important (tacit) knowledge of the actual production and technological processes but also have a longer-term orientation (because they are interested in keeping the firm in business to maintain their jobs). Third, fiscal or other restrictions should be imposed on the cross-border activities of private equity (hedge funds, etc.), which are also often based on extremely short-term profitability considerations; hedge funds should be obliged to invest in firms for a longer period (say, for a minimum period of five to seven years), thus restricting speculative behavior.

6. The Generalization of the NAIRU Theory

1. Note that equation (3.23) is not relevant here.
2. To define a full steady state we need to impose one more condition in addition to condition (6.1), namely, that capital stock growth equals output growth. Not doing this, we are working here with a quasi-steady state, but note that our results can be generalized for the rich OECD countries, because their capital-output ratios are pretty stable. We thank Lance Taylor for pointing this out.
3. This is also the point made in Rowthorn (1999).
4. We acknowledge that the measurement of unemployment and its cross-country comparison is problematic over a long period, because unemployment rates, even the ILO standardized one, are not good measures of unused labor supply, since in many countries some unemployed people are hidden in other categories (e.g., disability, early retirement, subsidized employment, prison). This may potentially be a serious limitation of our analysis as well as of earlier studies, but "in the absence of any serious discussion of the relevant numbers in all the countries" (Nickell, Nunziata, and Ochel 2005, 2), we proceed by assuming that its impact on the conclusions is limited.
5. Their preferred approach is a static fixed effects model in first differences with data averaged over five-year periods during 1960–1998 for eighteen OECD countries; these results appear in their table 11. We have rescaled their coefficient estimate to fit the scale of our EPL measure (0–4).
6. According to estimates in Baker et al. (2005a), the average rate of unemployment in nineteen OECD countries increased from 2.8 percent during 1960–1980 to 7.9 percent during 1980–2000.

7. Europe's Nordic Model

1. Maverick evolutionary geneticist Richard Lewontin (1998) emphasizes the importance of cooperation for population survival. One more of Kropotkin's intellectual heirs is Dutch primatologist and ethologist Frans de Waal (2009), who has long been a critic of the notion that the evolution is driven more by the struggle for existence rather than by the need for cooperation and accommodation among interdependent animals that live in groups. De Waal argues instead that, as empathy has deep evolutionary roots, biology offers a giant helping hand to those striving for a just society. But more mainstream biologists argue that when no one is minding the common good, the whole system can collapse; as evolutionary biologist David Sloan Wilson and entomologist Edward O. Wilson (2007, 345) famously wrote, "Selfishness beats altruism within groups. Altruistic groups beat selfish groups. Everything else is commentary."

2. Charles Darwin expressed his view in the metaphor of the wedge. As Stephen Jay Gould (1997, 13–14) explains: "Nature, Darwin writes, is like a surface with 10,000 wedges hammered tightly in and filling all available space. A new species (represented as a wedge) can only gain entry into a community by driving itself into a tiny chink and forcing another wedge out. Success, in this vision, can only be achieved by direct takeover in overt competition."

3. The idea was to oblige profit-making firms to issue new share every year equivalent to 20 percent of their profits. The newly issued shares, which could not be sold, were to be given to the wage earners' fund. Workers would hold the shares and reinvest the income they obtained from dividends in order to finance future social expenditure. As the wage earners' funds grew, they would be able to play an increasing part in directing the corporations which they owned. The crux of the idea was that it would give workers an effective say in how their firms are run without weakening the corporation as a productive concern.

4. Useful assessments of Swedish macro performance under the Rehn-Meidner model are Standing (1988); Meidner (1993); Freeman, Topel, and Swedenborg (1997); Ploughmann and Madsen (2005); and Erixon (2008). Edin and Topel (1997) provide evidence that the policy of equal wages for similar work in Sweden accelerated structural change and productivity growth.

5. The handshake approach has to be contrasted to the "invisible hand" operating in deregulated, uncoordinated markets. According to Bowles, Edwards, and Roosevelt (2005, 473), the "invisible hand approach does not solve the [unemployment] problem," as it needs equilibrium unemployment to stabilize inflation.

6. The main beneficiaries of Nordic solidaristic bargaining are to be found in the tails of the income distribution: low-paid workers on one hand and capitalist employers on the other. The losers are high-skilled middle-class workers. See Moene and Wallerstein (1997).

7. Real wage growth has a much larger impact on GDP growth in Sweden than the Netherlands, because of (1) a smaller import leakage (from the circular flow of income) and (2) bigger income-demand accelerator effects on investment in Sweden.

8. We note that this finding is different from our conclusion in Chapter 5 that a change in real wage growth has no impact on Swedish employment growth and unemployment. The main reason for this difference concerns coefficient β_2 which for the twenty OECD countries takes a value of 0.29 and which for the Nordic countries takes a much higher value of 0.51. This higher value reflects the fact that the process of wage-cost-induced technological progress is stronger in Scandinavia than in the OECD area in general. Due to this, increased real wages do raise productivity growth more strongly than output growth, and hence employment growth is reduced. Using the C coefficient value of 1.04 for Sweden (Chapter 5), a 1 percentage point increase in real wage growth reduces Swedish employment growth by 0.2 percentage points.

9. The Scandinavians, by temperament the most self-lacerating of Europeans (along with the Dutch, we may add), have found much wrong with the way job sharing works, but the principle is accepted and this scheme has provided society with a useful tool for social inclusion.

10. See Lorenz (1992), Moene and Wallerstein (1995, 1997), and Buchele and Christiansen (1999). As Truman Bewley (1999, 1–2) argues, it is important to "take into account the capacity of workers to identify with their firm and to internalize its objectives. This internalization and workers' mood have a strong impact on job performance and call for material, moral, and symbolic reciprocation from company leadership." Likewise, Agell (1999), Akerlof (2007), and Moene (2008) argue that institutions regulating the labor market formalize basic social norms governing exchanges between firms and workers and/or are put in place to solve a number of inherent labor market imperfections—for example, the failure of markets to provide adequate unemployment insurance. In either case, labor market regulation will improve labor productivity by promoting workers' motivation and by stimulating investment in human capital formation.

11. Employers also much preferred to bargain with the "sensible" leadership of the union confederations rather than with the militant leadership of the shop floor union bodies. Moene and Wallerstein (1997) show, in this context, that employers may be able to increase profits by reducing wage inequality relative to the wage schedules associated with decentralized wage bargaining and with a competitive labor market where employers set wages unilaterally.

12. Note that Scandinavian central banks did so following conventional NAIRU logic: reduced public deficits would lower inflationary pressure, because actual unemployment would increase relative to the steady-inflation unemployment rate. In actual fact, reduced deficits (as our estimates show) raise inflationary pressures because lower deficits mean lower productivity growth.

13. Moene (2008, 377) insists that freer trade and higher capital mobility are no threat to the viability of the Nordic model, since the small open economies have long been used to the discipline of international markets. "As long as profits are high enough, capital mobility provides employers with no credible threats." This means that productivity growth has to be sufficiently high (and technological progress sufficiently fast) to offset real wage growth, in which case there is no need for the wage share to fall. Egalitarian growth does not require any protec-

tionist restrictions on foreign trade, or the quasi-imperialist imposition of labor (or other) standards in the developing countries.

14. We note that carefully crafted egalitarian growth in the global North would imply higher import and world trade growth, which benefits the developing countries.

8. Macroeconomics Beyond the NAIRU

1. For a similar early view, see Eisner (1997).
2. Naomi Klein (2007) has called this Friedman's shock doctrine: waiting for a crisis, then implementing reforms and making them permanent.
3. This conclusion is endorsed by Alan Greenspan (2007), who in his memoirs writes that structurally low inflation during the 1990s was mostly due to the collapse of the Soviet Union (leading to a global oversupply of industrial materials and fuels) and the rise of China, which created a labor reserve at low dollar wages.
4. For the *Dogmengeschichte* of the harmonious order based on self-interest, see Hirschman (1977, 1982); Foley (2006).
5. For a Marxian counterargument, see Roemer (1988).
6. This discussion harks back to Kalecki (1943).
7. Compare what Adam Smith (1976, 110) had to say on this point:

> Our merchants and master-manufacturers complain much of the bad effects of high wages in raising the price, and thereby lessening the sale of their goods both at home and abroad. They say nothing concerning the bad effects of high profits. They are silent with regard to the pernicious effects of their own gains. They complain only of those of those of other people.

8. Not everybody will be happy in NAIRU capitalism, of course, but whenever individuals are not happy it is because they have had just bad luck (in a Darwinian sense), have lacked useful skills, or have operated in an institutional setting that has hindered competitive free markets. Arguing thus, the neoliberal ideology associated with NAIRU economics helped create a "spontaneous consensus" that unequal distributional outcomes are the "only game in town." See Palma (2009).
9. Sir Alan Budd, a top U.K. treasury officer in the 1980s, commented that the Thatcher government did see that "raising unemployment was an extremely desirable way of reducing the strength of the working classes . . . What was engineered—in Marxist terms—was a crisis of capitalism which re-created the reserve army of labour, and has allowed the capitalists to make high profits ever since" (Palma 2009, 837).
10. Another interpretation of the monetarist solution to the macroeconomic prisoner's dilemma is to view the authoritarian central bank as an enlightened Platonic guardian who coerces for the common good. But the underlying rationalist attitude is the same as in Hobbes: why should one leave macro policy decisions to the "unwise," who cannot understand their own interests as rational beings? Why should demonstrable error be suffered at the hands of the irrational and

uneducated? See Berlin (1958) for a discussion of the totalitarian undertones in this technocratic-elitist theory of politics.

11. One wonders why, in this view, politicians/policymakers have only a short horizon (the electoral cycle) and limited rationality, as they persist in attempting to temporarily reduce unemployment (and presumably win votes) while creating long-run damage. One equally wonders why rational, self-interested voters would be persuaded by promises of lower unemployment that are known to be ephemeral.

12. See Klein (2007) for an account of how freeing markets has generally relied on political oppression and military dictatorships.

13. In Friedman's words, "The liberal conceives of men as imperfect beings . . . and regards the problem of social organization to be as much a negative problem of preventing bad people from doing harm as of enabling good people to do good" (1962, 12). Economists have focused exclusively on the negative problem.

14. That firms dislike turbulent competition and prefer a cartelized economy had already been noted by Adam Smith (1976, 144):

> People of the same trade seldom meet together, even for merriment and diversion, but the conversation ends in a conspiracy against the public, or in some contrivance to raise prices. It is impossible indeed to prevent such meetings, by any law which either could be executed, or would be consistent with liberty and justice. But though the law cannot hinder people of the same trade from sometimes assembling together, it ought to do nothing to facilitate such assemblies; much less to render them necessary.

Palma (2009, 849n1) adds that when people of the same trade meet together to conspire against the public, "neo-liberal governments not only turned a blind eye, but ended up setting the table, cooking the meal, serving the drinks, and paying the bill."

15. Recognizing this, John Stuart Mill (1998, 46) departed from Benthamist utilitarianism by arguing that utilitarian morality must be founded in "the social feelings of mankind."

16. More evidence on this comes from experimental studies of the ultimatum game, in which one player (the proposer) is given the opportunity to propose a division of a certain sum between herself and the other player (the responder). If the responder accepts the proposal, the sum is divided as proposed. If he rejects the proposal, neither player receives anything. If we assume behavior based on narrow self-interest, the proposer ought to offer only a token sum to the responder (keeping the bulk herself), and the responder ought to accept (since even a token is more than nothing, which is the only alternative open to him). Experimental results show, however, that token offers are hardly made, and even more rarely accepted. Most frequently, proposers propose a 50-50 split, out of a notion of fairness. See Ben-Ner and Putterman (1998).

17. The statement is due to Rapoport and Chammah (1965). We found the citation in Sen (1990, 41).

18. We believe, following Robert Guttmann (2008), Gabriel Palma (2009), and Robert Boyer (2000, 2010), that labor-capital cooperation broke down under pres-

sures of financial markets (the soul of finance, analyzed in Chapter 5). The elimination of cross-border capital controls starting in the 1970s durably increased the bargaining power of financial interests at the expense of the powers of both labor and nonfinancial capital. Phrased in terms of our macro prisoner's dilemma, the deregulation of global financial markets drastically raised the payoffs from noncooperative behavior by firms; witness the fact that reference profitability has increased sharply with financialization (Boyer 2000, table 4). More on this point follows later in the chapter.

19. Unselfishness interpreted as commitment is central to the problem of work motivation: "To run an organization entirely on incentives to personal gain is pretty much a hopeless task," writes Sen (1990, 37). Rebecca M. Blank (2000) observes that there exists a civil service culture in many public agencies, where employees accept lower wages than those found in the private sector because they find the work and the mission of the public agency compelling. Privatization in these cases would demotivate workers, as it would monetize the job, placing greater emphasis on efficiency and price-related aspects of the job. Timothy Besley and Maitreesh Ghatak (2003) have argued likewise: people work harder and are more productive if they work out of commitment for "the benefit of the public." Work to high standards is undermined by the profit-oriented goals of private sector management.

20. We analyze the political fallout of the NAIRU order in the Netherlands in Storm and Naastepad (2003).

21. This title comes from Dawes, van de Kragt, and Orbell (1990).

22. Adolph Lowe's book *Has Freedom a Future?* (1988) is dedicated to this socialization function of education. The tasks involved are huge, given the fact that in liberalism, education narrowly conceived is a function of the dominant power system and education in the broad sense is underemphasized.

23. We could be accused of adhering to a "doctrine of liberation by reason," which assumes that rational people who have been socialized into a common set of norms and values will behave responsibly and not misuse their freedom. This is not the point, however. Following Lowe (1988), we reject mindless conformity and argue that individuals must decide whether or not to follow the social rules. Continuous critical evaluation of social rules is necessary to prevent perpetuating those that are no longer workable or desirable.

24. This view goes back to at least John Stuart Mill (1989), who emphasized liberty as freedom to develop oneself as a human being in the full sense and supported a considerable dose of social legislation to remove obstacles to such self-development.

25. According to French economist Robert Boyer (2010, 351), financial markets boomed after 1990 by selling a dream: "getting rich quickly without understanding why."

26. The halfhearted Swedish attempt to create wage earners' funds floundered in 1992, mainly due to the failure to forge broad interest coalitions behind the scheme. See Lyon (1986) and Meidner (1978, 1993) for evaluations of the idea.

27. Luis Suarez-Villa (2009) presents a profound analysis of the social organization of technological change in contemporary technocapitalism.

28. The savings from the otherwise inescapable public expenditure on unemployment compensation will go a long way toward covering the costs of these public sector jobs.

29. We investigated the issue of aging for the Netherlands. Dutch labor force growth is projected to be −0.5 percent per year during 2010–2045. We find that costs of aging can be financed in a feasible manner only by a significant step-up in labor productivity growth. Labor market deregulation, which reduces productivity growth, is therefore counterproductive in the context of the current demographic shift in the OECD area. See Storm and Naastepad (2008c).

Bibliography

Acharya, Viral V., Ramin P. Baghai, and Krishnamurthy V. Subramanian. 2010. Labor laws and innovation. NBER Working Paper No. 16484. Cambridge, MA: National Bureau of Economic Research.

Addison, John T., and Paulino Teixeira. 2001. The economics of employment protection. IZA Discussion Paper No. 381. Bonn: Institute for the Study of Labor.

Agell, Jonas. 1999. On the benefits from rigid labour markets: Norms, market failures, and social insurance. *Economic Journal* 109: F143–F164.

Aghion, Philippe, David Hemous, and Enisse Kharroubi. 2009. Credit constraints, cyclical fiscal policy and industry growth. NBER Working Paper No. 15119. Cambridge, MA: National Bureau of Economic Research.

Akerlof, George, and Janet Yellen, eds. 1986. *Efficiency wage models of the labor market*. New York: Cambridge University Press.

Akerlof, George A. 1982. Labor contracts as a partial gift exchange. *Quarterly Journal of Economics* 97: 543–569.

Akerlof, George A. 1984. Gift exchange and efficiency wage theory: Four views. *American Economic Review* 74(1): 79–83.

Akerlof, George A. 2007. The missing motivation in macroeconomics. *American Economic Review* 97(1): 5–36.

Akkermans, Dirk, Carolina Castaldi, and Bart Los. 2009. Do "liberal market economies" really innovate more radically than "coordinated market economies"? Hall and Soskice reconsidered. *Research Policy* 38(1): 181–191.

Alesina, Alberto, Silvia Ardagna, Roberto Perotti, and Fabio Schiantarelli. 2002. Fiscal policy, profits and investment. *American Economic Review* 92(3): 571–589.

Alexiadis, Stilianos, and Dimitrios Tsagdis. 2010. Is cumulative growth in manufacturing productivity slowing down in the EU12 regions? *Cambridge Journal of Economics* 34(6): 1001–1017.

Amable, Bruno. 2003. *The diversity of modern capitalism*. Oxford: Oxford University Press.

Amable, Bruno, Ekkehard Ernst, and Stefano Palombarini. 2005. How do financial markets affect industrial relations: An institutional complementarity approach. *Socio-Economic Review* 3: 311–330.

Amable, Bruno, and Bart Verspagen. 1995. The role of technology in market shares. *Applied Economics* 27(2): 197–204.

Angeriz, Alvaro, John S. L. McCombie, and Mark Roberts. 2009. Increasing returns and the growth of industries in the EU regions: Paradoxes and conundrums. *Spatial Economic Analysis* 4(2): 127–148.

Aoki, Masahiko. 2001. *Towards a comparative institutional analysis*. Cambridge, MA: MIT Press.

Appelbaum, Eileen, Thomas Bailey, Peter Berg, and Arne L. Kalleberg. 2000. *Manufacturing advantage: Why high-performance work systems pay off*. Ithaca, NY: Cornell University Press.

Arestis, Philip, Michelle Baddeley, and Malcolm Sawyer. 2007. The relationship between capital stock, unemployment and wages in nine EMU countries. *Bulletin of Economic Research* 59(2): 125–148.

Arestis, Philip, and Iris Biefang-Frisancho Mariscal. 1998. Capital shortages and asymmetries in UK unemployment. *Structural Change and Economic Dynamics* 9(2): 189–204.

Arestis, Philip, and Malcolm Sawyer. 2005. Aggregate demand, conflict and capacity in the inflationary process. *Cambridge Journal of Economics* 29(6): 959–974.

Auer, Peter. 2000. *Employment revival in Europe: Labour market success in Austria, Denmark, Ireland and the Netherlands*. Geneva: International Labour Organization.

Auer, Peter. 2007. In search of optimal labour market institutions. Economic and Labour Market Paper 2007/3. Geneva: International Labour Organization, Employment and Labour Market Analysis Department.

Auer, Peter, Janine Berg, and Ibrahim Coulibaly. 2005. Is a stable workforce good for productivity? *International Labour Review* 144(3): 319–343.

Autor, David H., Lawrence F. Katz, and Melissa S. Kearny. 2006. The polarization of the US labor market. *American Economic Review* 96(2): 190–194.

Autor, David H., William R. Kerr, and Adriana D. Kugler. 2007. Does employment protection reduce productivity? Evidence from US states. *Economic Journal* 117(521): F189–F217.

Axelrod, Robert. 1984. *The evolution of cooperation*. New York: Basic Books.

Baccaro, Lucio. 2010. Does the global crisis mark a turning point for labour? *Socio-Economic Review* 8: 341–348.

Baccaro, Lucio, and Diego Rei. 2005. Institutional determinants of unemployment in OECD countries: A time-series cross-section analysis (1960–1998). International Institute for Labour Studies Discussion Paper No. 160/2005. Geneva: International Labour Organization.

Baccaro, Lucio, and Diego Rei. 2007. Institutional determinants of unemployment in OECD countries: Does the deregulatory view hold water? *International Organization* 61(3): 527–569.

Bainton, George, ed. 1890. *The art of authorship: Literary reminiscences, methods of work, and advice to young beginners*. New York: D. Appleton and Company.

Baker, Dean. 2002. NAIRU: Dangerous dogma at the Fed. CEPR Briefing Paper. Washington, DC: Center for Economic and Policy Research.

Baker, Dean, Andrew Glyn, David Howell, and John Schmitt. 2005a. Unemployment and labor market institutions: The failure of the empirical case for deregulation. Center for Economic Policy Analysis Working Paper. New York: New School for Social Research.

Baker, Dean, Andrew Glyn, David Howell, and John Schmitt. 2005b. Labor market institutions and unemployment: A critical assessment of the cross-country evidence. In David Howell, ed., *Questioning liberalization: Unemployment, labor markets and the welfare state*, 72–118. Oxford: Oxford University Press.

Ball, Lawrence. 1999. Aggregate demand and long-run unemployment. *Brookings Papers on Economic Activity* 1999(2): 189–251.

Ball, Lawrence, and N. Gregory Mankiw. 2002. The NAIRU in theory and practice. *Journal of Economic Perspectives* 16(4): 115–136.

Barbosa-Filho, Nelson H., and Lance Taylor. 2006. Distributive and demand cycles in the US economy: A structuralist Goodwin model. *Metroeconomica* 57(3): 389–411.

Bartelsman, E., A. Bassanini, J. Haltiwanger, R. Jarmin, S. Scarpetta, and T. Schank. 2003. The spread of ICT and productivity growth: Is Europe really lagging behind in the new economy? In D. Cohen, P. Garibaldi, and S. Scarpetta, eds., *The ICT revolution: Productivity differences and the digital divide*, 1–140. Oxford: Oxford University Press.

Bassanini, Andrea, and Romain Duval. 2006. Employment patterns in OECD countries: Reassessing the role of policies and institutions. Social, Employment and Migration Working Paper No. 35. Paris: OECD.

Bassanini, Andrea, and Ekkehard Ernst. 2002. Labour market regulation, industrial relations and technological regimes: A tale of comparative advantage. *Industrial and Corporate Change* 11(3): 391–426.

Baumol, William J. 2000. What Marshall *didn't* know: On the twentieth century's contribution to economics. *Quarterly Journal of Economics* 115(1): 1–44.

Baumol, William J., and Alan S. Blinder. 2008. *Macroeconomics: Principles and Policy*. Mason, Ohio: South-Western College Publishing.

Beck, Thorsten, Asli Demirgüç-Kunt, and Ross Levine. 2000. A new database on financial development and structure. *World Bank Economic Review* 14: 597–605.

Bell, Daniel. 1981. Models and reality in economic discourse. In D. Bell and I. Kristol, eds., *The crisis in economic theory*. New York: Basic Books.

Belot, Michèle, and Jan C. van Ours. 2001. Unemployment and labour market institutions: An empirical analysis. *Journal of the Japanese and International Economies* 15(4): 403–418.

Ben-Ner, Avner, and Louis Putterman, eds. 1998. *Economics, values and organization*. Cambridge: Cambridge University Press.

Berlin, Isaiah. 1969. Two concepts of liberty. In Isaiah Berlin, ed., *Four essays on liberty*. Oxford: Oxford University Press.

Bertola, Giuseppe, Francine D. Blau, and Lawrence M. Kahn. 2001. Comparative analysis of labor market outcomes: Lessons for the US from international long-run evidence. NBER Working Paper No. 8526. Cambridge, MA: National Bureau of Economic Research.

Besley, Timothy, and Maitreesh Ghatak. 2003. Incentives, choice and accountability in the provision of public services. *Oxford Review of Economic Policy* 19(2): 235–249.

Bewley, Truman F. 1995. A depressed labour market index as explained by participants. *American Economic Review* 85 (Papers and Proceedings): 250–254.

Bewley, Truman F. 1999. *Why wages don't fall during a recession.* Cambridge, MA: Harvard University Press.

Bhaduri, Amit. 2006. Endogenous economic growth: A new approach. *Cambridge Journal of Economics* 30(1): 69–83.

Bhaduri, Amit, and Stephen A. Marglin. 1990. Unemployment and the real wage: The economic basis for contesting political ideologies. *Cambridge Journal of Economics* 14(4): 375–393.

Bhaskar, V., and Andrew Glyn. 1995. Investment and profitability: The evidence from the advanced capitalist countries. In Gerald Epstein and Herbert E. Gintis, eds., *Macroeconomic policy after the conservative era: Studies in investment, saving and finance,* 175–196. Cambridge: Cambridge University Press.

Blair, Margaret. 1995. *Ownership and control: Rethinking corporate governance for the twenty-first century.* Washington, DC: Brookings Institution.

Blanchard, Olivier. 2000. *Macroeconomics.* 2nd ed. Upper Saddle River, NJ: Prentice-Hall.

Blanchard, Olivier. 2004. Designing labor market institutions. Mimeo. Available at: http://econ-www.mit.edu/files/687.

Blanchard, Olivier, and Justin Wolfers. 2000. The role of shocks and institutions in the rise of European unemployment: The aggregate evidence. *Economic Journal* 110(462): C1–C33.

Blank, Rebecca M. 2000. When can public policy makers rely on private markets? The effective provision of social services. *Economic Journal* 110(462): C34–C49.

Blau, Francine, and Lawrence Kahn. 2002. *At home and abroad: U.S. labor-market performance in international perspective.* New York: Russell Sage Foundation.

Blecker, Robert A. 2002. Distribution, demand and growth in neo-Kaleckian macromodels. In Mark Setterfield, ed., *The economics of demand-led growth: Challenging the supply-side vision of the long run,* 129–152. Cheltenham: Edward Elgar.

Blinder, Alan S., and Janet Yellen. 2001. *The fabulous decade: Macroeconomic lessons from the 1990s.* New York: Century Foundation Press.

Bluestone, Barry, and Stephen Rose. 1997. Overworked and underemployed: Unravelling an economic enigma. *American Prospect,* March.

Boeri, Tito. 2002. Let social policy models compete and Europe will win. Paper presented at a conference hosted by the Kennedy School of Government, Harvard University, April 11–12.

Boeri, Tito. 2005. Reforming labour and product markets: Some lessons from two decades of experiments in Europe. IMF Working Paper WP/05/97. Washington, DC: International Monetary Fund.

Bond, Stephen, Julie Ann Elston, Jacques Mairesse, and Benoît Mulkay. 2003. Financial factors and investment in Belgium, France, Germany, and the United Kingdom: A comparison using company panel data. *Review of Economics and Statistics* 85(1): 153–165.

Bond, Stephen, Dietmar Harhoff, and John van Reenen. 2003. Investment, R&D and financial constraints in Britain and Germany. Working Paper Series No. W99/5. Oxford: Institute for Fiscal Studies, University of Oxford.

Botero, Juan C., Simeon Djankov, Rafael La Porta, Florencio Lopez-de-Silanes, and Andrei Shleifer. 2004. The regulation of labor. *Quarterly Journal of Economics* 119(4): 1339–1382.

Boushey, Heather, Shawn Fremstad, Rachel Gragg, and Margy Waller. 2006. *Understanding low-wage work in the United States*. Washington, DC: Center for Economic Policy and Research.

Bowles, Samuel. 1985. The production process in a competitive economy: Walrasian, Neo-Hobbesian, and Marxian models. *American Economic Review* 75(1): 16–36.

Bowles, Samuel. 2002. Globalization and redistribution: Feasible egalitarianism in a competitive world. In Richard Freeman, ed., *Inequality around the world*. Basingstoke: Palgrave Macmillan.

Bowles, Samuel, and Robert Boyer. 1995. Wages, aggregate demand, and employment in an open economy: An empirical investigation. In Gerald Epstein and Herbert E. Gintis, eds., *Macroeconomic policy after the conservative era: Studies in investment, saving and finance*, 143–171. Cambridge: Cambridge University Press.

Bowles, Samuel, Richard Edwards, and Frank Roosevelt. 2005. *Understanding capitalism: Competition, command, and change*. Oxford: Oxford University Press.

Bowles, Samuel, and Yongjin Park. 2005. Emulation, inequality and work hours: Was Thorstein Veblen right? *Economic Journal* 115: 397–413.

Boyer, Robert. 2000. Is a finance-led growth regime a viable alternative to Fordism? A preliminary analysis. *Economy and Society* 29(1): 111–145.

Boyer, Robert. 2010. The collapse of finance but labour remains weak. *Socio-Economic Review* 8: 348–353.

Boyer, Robert, and Pascal Petit. 1991. Kaldor's growth theories: Past, present and prospects for the future. In Edward J. Nell and Willi Semmler, eds., *Nicholas Kaldor and mainstream economics: Confrontation or convergence?* New York: St. Martin's Press.

Braverman, Harry. 1974. *Labor and monopoly capitalism: The degradation of work in the twentieth century*. New York: Monthly Review Press.

Bruno, Michael, and Jeffrey Sachs. 1985. *The economics of worldwide stagflation*. Oxford: Blackwell.

Buchele, Robert, and Jens Christiansen. 1999. Labor relations and productivity growth in advanced capitalist economies. *Review of Radical Political Economics* 31(1): 87–110.

Buiter, Willem. 2009. The unfortunate uselessness of most "state of the art" academic monetary economics. *Financial Times*, March 3.

Caballero, Ricardo J., Kevin N. Cowan, Eduardo M. R. A. Engel, and Alejandro Micco. 2006. Effective labor regulation and microeconomic flexibility. Cowles Foundation Discussion Paper No. 1480. New Haven: Yale University.

Calmfors, Lars, and John Driffill. 1988. Bargaining structure, corporatism, and macroeconomic performance. *Economic Policy* 3(6): 13–61.

Calmfors, Lars, and Anders Forslund. 1991. Real-wage determination and labour market policies: The Swedish experience. *Economic Journal* 101(408): 1130–1148.

Calmfors, Lars, Anders Forslund, and Maria Hemström. 2001. Does active labour market policy work? Lessons from Swedish experiences. *Swedish Economic Policy Review* 8(2): 61–124.

Carlin, Wendy, Andrew Glyn, and John van Reenen. 2001. Export market performance of OECD countries: An empirical examination of the role of cost competitiveness. *Economic Journal* 111(468): 128–162.

Carlin, Wendy, and David Soskice. 2006. *Macroeconomics: Imperfections, institutions and policies.* Oxford: Oxford University Press.

Carroll, Lewis. (1871) 2001. *Through the looking-glass.* London: Bloomsbury.

Carruth, Alan, Andy Dickerson, and Andrew Henley. 2000. Econometric modelling of UK aggregate investment: The role of profits and uncertainty. *The Manchester School* 20: 276–300.

Carter, Scott. 2007. Real wage productivity elasticity across advanced economies, 1963–1999. *Journal of Post Keynesian Economics* 29(4): 573–600.

Cornwall, John, and Wendy Cornwall. 2001. *Capitalist development in the twentieth century: An evolutionary-Keynesian analysis.* Cambridge: Cambridge University Press.

Cornwall, John, and Wendy Cornwall. 2002. A demand and supply analysis of productivity growth. *Structural Change and Economic Dynamics* 13(2): 203–229.

Crouch, Collin. 2010. The financial crisis a new chance for labour movements? Not yet. *Socio-Economic Review* 8: 353–356.

Dawes, Robyn M., and Richard H. Thaler. 1988. Anomalies: Cooperation. *Journal of Economic Perspectives* 2(3): 187–197.

Dawes, Robyn M., Alphons J. C. van de Kragt, and John M. Orbell. 1990. Cooperation for the benefit of us—not me, or my conscience. In J. J. Mansbridge, ed., *Beyond self-interest*, 97–110. Chicago: University of Chicago Press.

Dew-Becker, Ian, and Robert J. Gordon. 2008. The role of labor market changes in the slowdown of European productivity growth. NBER Working Paper No. 13840. Cambridge, MA: National Bureau of Economic Research.

Dirda, Michael. 2009. Beneath a host of characters lay a writer akin to Shakespeare, *Washington Post*, November 5.

Dore, Ronald. 2008. Financialization of the global economy. *Industrial and Corporate Change* 17(6): 1097–1112.

Dore, Ronald, William Lazonick, and Mary O'Sullivan. 1999. Varieties of capitalism in the twentieth century. *Oxford Review of Economic Policy* 15(4): 102–120.

Dosi, Giovanni. 1997. Opportunities, incentives and the collective patterns of technological change. *Economic Journal* 107(444): 1530–1547.

Drago, Robert, and Richard Perlman. 1989. Supervision and high wages as competing incentives: A basis for labour segmentation theory. In Robert Drago and Richard Perlman, eds., *Microeconomic issues in labour economics: New approaches.* New York: Harvester Press.

Driver, Ciaran, Paul Temple, and Giovanni Urga. 2005. Profitability, capacity, and uncertainty: A model of UK manufacturing investment. *Oxford Economic Papers* 57(1): 120–141.

Duménil, Gérard, and Dominique Lévy. 2010a. *The crisis of neoliberalism.* Cambridge, MA: Harvard University Press.

Duménil, Gérard, and Dominique Lévy. 2010b. The classical-Marxian evolutionary model of technical change: Application to historical tendencies. In Mark Setterfield, ed., *Handbook of alternative theories of economic growth*, 243–273. Cheltenham: Edward Elgar.

Dutt, Amitava Krishna. 1984. Stagnation, income distribution and monopoly power. *Cambridge Journal of Economics* 11(1): 75–82.

Ederer, Stefan, and Engelbert Stockhammer. 2007. Wages and aggregate demand in France: An empirical investigation. In Eckhard Hein and Achim Trüger, eds., *Money, distribution and economic policy: Alternatives to orthodox macroeconomics*, 119–138. Cheltenham: Edward Elgar.

Edgeworth, Francis Ysidro. 1881. *Mathematical psychics: An essay on the application of mathematics to the moral sciences.* London: C. Kegan Paul.

Edin, Per-Anders, and Robert Topel. 1997. Wage policy and restructuring: The Swedish labor market since 1960. In Richard B. Freeman, Robert Topel, and Birgitta Swedenborg, eds., *The welfare state in transition: Reforming the Swedish model.* Chicago: University of Chicago Press.

Ehrenreich, Barbara. 2001. *Nickel and dimed: On (not) getting by in America.* New York: Holt.

Einstein, Albert. 1934. On the method of theoretical physics. *Philosophy of Science* 1(2): 163–169.

Eisner, Robert. 1995. On NAIRU limit: The governing myth of economic policy. *American Prospect* (Spring): 58–63.

Eisner, Robert. 1997. A new view of the NAIRU. In Paul Davidson and Jan A. Kregel, eds., *Improving the global economy.* Cheltenham: Edward Elgar.

Elmeskov, Jörgen, John Martin, and Stefano Scarpetta. 1998. Key lessons for labor market reforms: Evidence from OECD countries' experiences. *Swedish Economic Policy Review* 5(2): 205–252.

Elster, Jon. 1990. Selfishness and altruism. In J. J. Mansbridge, ed., *Beyond self-interest*, 44–52. Chicago: University of Chicago Press.

Elster, Jon. 2009. Excessive ambitions. *Capitalism and Society* 4(2): article 1, DOI: 10.2202/1932-0213.1055.

Epstein, Gerald, and Herbert E. Gintis, eds. 1995. *Macroeconomic policy after the conservative era: Studies in investment, saving and finance.* Cambridge: Cambridge University Press.

Eriksson, Åsa. 2005. Wage formation and the relation between real wages and unemployment in Sweden. Mimeo. Department of Economics, Lund University, Sweden.

Erixon, Lennart. 2008. The Swedish third way: An assessment of the performance and validity of the Rehn-Meidner model. *Cambridge Journal of Economics* 32(3): 367–393.

Esping-Andersen, Gøsta. 1990. *Three worlds of welfare capitalism.* Princeton: Princeton University Press.

Etzioni, Amitai. 1988. *The moral dimension: Toward a new economics.* New York: Free Press.

European Commission. 2010. The impact of the global crisis on competitiveness and current account divergences in the euro area. *Quarterly Report on the Euro Area* 9(1). Brussels: European Commission.

Fagerberg, Jan. 1996. Technology and competitiveness. *Oxford Review of Economic Policy* 12(3): 39–51.

Faggio, Giulia, and Stephen Nickell. 2007. Patterns of work across the OECD. *Economic Journal* 117(521): F416–F440.

Fitoussi, Jean-Paul, and Francesco Saraceno. 2010. Europe: How deep is a crisis? Policy responses and structural factors behind diverging performances. *Journal of Globalization and Development* 1(1): article 17, DOI: 10.2202/1948-1837.1053.

Foley, Duncan K. 2006. *Adam's fallacy: A guide to economic theology.* Cambridge, MA: Belknap Press of Harvard University Press.

Foley, Duncan K., and Thomas R. Michl. 1999. *Growth and distribution.* Cambridge, MA: Harvard University Press.

Forslund, Anders, Nils Gottfries, and Andreas Westermark. 2008. Prices, productivity and wage bargaining in open economies. *Scandinavian Journal of Economics* 110(1): 169–195.

Forslund, Anders, and Ann-Sofie Kolm. 2004. Active labour market policies and real wage determination. In S. Polachek, ed., *Accounting for worker well-being.* Research in Labor Economics 23. Amsterdam: JAI.

Forslund, Anders, and Alan B. Krueger. 1997. An evaluation of the Swedish active labour market policy: New and received wisdom. In R. B. Freeman et al., eds., *The welfare state in transition: Reforming the Swedish model.* Chicago: University of Chicago Press.

Forstater, Mathew. 2000. Adolph Lowe on freedom, education and socialization. *Review of Social Economy* 58(2): 225–239.

France, Anatole. (1894) 2010. *The Red Lily.* N.p.: FQ Books.

Frank, R. H. 1990. A theory of moral sentiments. In J. J. Mansbridge, ed., *Beyond self-interest,* 71–96. Chicago: University of Chicago Press.

Frank, Robert H. 1988. *Passions within reason: The strategic role of emotions.* New York: W. W. Norton.

Freeman, Richard B. 2005. Labor market institutions without blinders: The debate over flexibility and labor market performance. NBER Working Paper No. 11286. Cambridge, MA: National Bureau of Economic Research.

Freeman, Richard B., Robert Topel, and Birgitta Swedenborg, eds. 1997. *The welfare state in transition: Reforming the Swedish model.* Chicago: University of Chicago Press.

Friedman, Milton. 1962. *Capitalism and freedom.* Chicago: University of Chicago Press.

Friedman, Milton. 1968. The role of monetary policy. *American Economic Review* 58(1): 1–17.

Friedman, Milton, and Rose Friedman. 1980. *Free to choose: A personal statement.* New York: Harcourt.

Fromm, Erich. (1941) 2001. *The fear of freedom.* London: Routledge.

Fromm, Erich. 1977. *To have or to be.* London: Continuum.

Funk, Peter. 2002. Induced innovation revisited. *Economica* 69(273): 155–171.

Galbraith, James K. 1997. Time to ditch the NAIRU. *Journal of Economic Perspectives* 11(1): 93–108.

Galbraith, James K. 2008. *The predator state: How conservatives abandoned the free market and why liberals should too.* New York: Free Press.

Galbraith, James K. 2009. Who are these economists, anyway? *Thought and Action* (Fall): 85–97.

Galbraith, James K., and Enrico Garcilazo. 2004. Unemployment, inequality and the policy of Europe: 1984–2000. *Banco Nazionale del Lavoro Quarterly Review* 228: 3–28.

Galbraith, John Kenneth. 1973. Power and the useful economist. *American Economic Review* 63(1): 1–11.

Garrone, Giovanna, and Roberto Marchionatti. 2004. Keynes on econometric method: A reassessment of his debate with Tinbergen and other econometricians, 1938–1943. Working Paper No. 01/2004. Torino: Dipartimento di Economia "S. Cognetti de Martiis," University of Torino.

Gerschenkron, Alexander. (1968) 2000. The modernization of entrepreneurship. In Richard Swedberg, ed., *Entrepreneurship: The social sciences view*, 129–138. Oxford: Oxford University Press.

Ghoshal, Sumantra. 2005. Bad management theories are destroying good management practice. *Academy of Management Learning and Education* 4(1): 75–91.

Glyn, Andrew. 1997. Does aggregate profitability *really* matter? *Cambridge Journal of Economics* 21(5): 593–619.

Glyn, Andrew. 2006. *Capitalism unleashed: Finance, globalization and welfare.* Oxford: Oxford University Press.

Gordon, David M. 1994. Bosses of different stripes: A cross-national perspective on monitoring and supervision. *American Economic Review* 84(2): 375–379.

Gordon, David M. 1995. Putting the horse (back) before the cart: Disentangling the macro relationship between investment and saving. In Gerald Epstein and Herbert E. Gintis, eds., *Macroeconomic policy after the conservative era: Studies in investment, saving and finance*, 57–108. Cambridge: Cambridge University Press.

Gordon, David M. 1996. *Fat and mean: The corporate squeeze of working Americans and the myth of managerial "downsizing."* New York: Free Press.

Gordon, Robert. 1999. The aftermath of the 1992 ERM breakup: Was there a macroeconomic free lunch? NBER Working Paper No. 6964. Cambridge, MA: National Bureau of Economic Research.

Gordon, Robert J. 1997. The time-varying NAIRU and its implications for economic policy. *Journal of Economic Perspectives* 11(1): 11–32.

Gould, Stephen Jay. 1997. Kropotkin was no crackpot. *Natural History* 106 (June): 12–21.

Greenspan, Alan. 2007. *The age of turbulence: Adventures in a new world.* New York: Penguin.

Gregg, Paul, and Alan Manning. 1997. Labour market regulation and unemployment. In Dennis J. Snower and Guillermo de la Dehesa, eds., *Unemployment policy: Government options for the labour market.* Cambridge: Cambridge University Press.

Gugler, Klaus, Dennis C. Mueller, and B. Burcin Yurtoglu. 2004. Corporate governance and globalisation. *Oxford Review of Economic Policy* 20(1): 129–156.

Guttmann, Robert. 2008. A primer on finance-led capitalism and its crisis. *Revue de la Régulation* 3/4.

Hall, Bronwyn H., Jacques Mairesse, Lee Branstetter, and Bruno Crepon. 1998. Does cash flow cause investment and R&D? An exploration using panel data for French, Japanese and United States scientific firms. Mimeo. Department of Economics, University of California, Berkeley.

Hall, Peter A., and Daniel W. Gingerich. 2004. Varieties of capitalism and institutional complementarities in the macroeconomy: An empirical analysis. MPIfG Discussion Paper 2004-5. Cologne: Max Planck Institute for the Study of Societies.

Hall, Peter A., and David Soskice, eds. 2001. *Varieties of capitalism: The institutional foundations of comparative advantage.* Oxford: Oxford University Press.

Hargreaves Heap, Shawn P. 1980. Choosing the wrong "natural rate": accelerating inflation or decelerating employment and growth. *Economic Journal* 90(359): 611–620.

Hassel, Anke. 1999. The erosion of the German system of industrial relations. *British Journal of Industrial Relations* 37(3): 483–505.

Hatton, Timothy J. 2007. Can productivity growth explain the NAIRU? Long-run evidence from Britain, 1871–1999. *Economica* 74: 475–491.

Haucap, Justus, and Christian Wey. 2004. Unionisation structures and innovation incentives. *Economic Journal* 114: C149–C165.

Hein, Eckhard, and Artur Tarassow. 2010. Distribution, aggregate demand and productivity growth: Theory and empirical results for six OECD countries based on a post-Kaleckian model. *Cambridge Journal of Economics* 34(4): 727–754.

Hein, Eckhard, and Lena Vogel. 2008. Distribution and growth reconsidered: Empirical results for six OECD countries. *Cambridge Journal of Economics* 32(3): 479–511.

Hibbs, Douglas A., and Hakan Locking. 2000. Wage dispersion and productive efficiency: Evidence for Sweden. *Journal of Labor Economics* 18(4): 755–782.

Hicks, John R. 1932. *The theory of wages.* London: Macmillan.

Himmelweit, Susan, Roberto Simonetti, and Andrew Trigg. 2001. *Microeconomics: Neoclassical and institutionalist perspectives on economic behaviour.* London: Thomson Learning.

Hirschman, Albert O. 1970. The search for paradigms as a hindrance to understanding. *World Politics* 22(3): 329–343.

Hirschman, Albert O. 1977. *The passions and the interests: Political arguments for capitalism before its triumph.* Princeton: Princeton University Press.

Hirschman, Albert O. 1982. *Shifting involvements: Private interest and public action.* Princeton: Princeton University Press.

Hirshleifer, Jack. 1985. The expanding domain of economics. *American Economic Review* 75(6): 53–70.

Hobbes, Thomas. 1651. *Leviathan.* Available at: http://oregonstate.edu/instruct/phl302/texts/hobbes/leviathan-contents.html.

Holden, Steinar, and Ragnar Nymoen. 2002. Measuring structural unemployment: NAWRU estimates in the Nordic countries. *Scandinavian Journal of Economics* 104(1): 87–104.

Holmlund, Bertil. 2009. The Swedish unemployment experience. *Oxford Review of Economic Policy* 25(1): 109–125.

Höpner, Martin. 2005. What connects industrial relations and coporate governance? Explaining institutional complementarity. *Socio-Economic Review* 3: 331–358.

Howell, Chris. 2003. Review: Varieties of capitalism: And then there was one? *Comparative Politics* 36(1): 103–124.

Howell, David R. 2005. *Fighting unemployment: The limits of free market orthodoxy.* Oxford: Oxford University Press.

Howell, David R. 2006. Comments on Heckman et al.: "What are the key employment challenges and policy priorities for OECD countries?" Paper presented at the conference "Boosting Jobs and Incomes: Lessons from OECD Country Experiences," Toronto, June 15.

Howell, David R., Dean Baker, Andrew Glyn, and John Schmitt. 2007. Are protective labor market institutions really at the root of unemployment? A critical perspective on the statistical evidence. *Capitalism and Society* 2(1): 1–71.

Howell, David R., and Mamadou Diallo. 2007. Charting US economic performance with alternative labor market indicators: The importance of accounting for job quality. SCEPA Working Paper 2007-6. New York: Schwartz Center for Economic Policy Analysis, New School for Social Research.

Huselid, Mark A. 1995. The impact of human resource management practices on turnover, productivity, and corporate financial performance. *Academy of Management Journal* 38(3): 635–672.

Ichniowski, C., K. Shaw, and G. Prennushi. 1997. The effects of human resource management practices on productivity: A study of steel finishing lines. *American Economic Review* 87(3): 291–313.

IMF. 2003. Unemployment and labour market institutions: Why reforms pay off. In *World Economic Outlook 2003.* Washington, DC: IMF, 129–150.

IMF. 2009. Sustaining the recovery. In *World Economic Outlook 2009.* Washington, DC: IMF.

International Labour Organization. Various years. *Yearbook of labour statistics.* Geneva: ILO. Available at: http://laborsta.ilo.org/.

Irvin, George. 2011. Inequality and recession in Britain and the US. *Development and Change* 42(1): 154–182.

Jacoby, S. 2007. Finance and labor: Perspectives on risk, inequality and democracy. Available at: http://papers.ssrn.com/sol3/papers.cfm?abstract_id=1020843 (accessed January 11, 2011).

Janssen, Ronald. 2011. European economic governance: The next big holdup on wages. Global Labour Column Number 45. Global Labour University Network. Available at: http://column.global-labour-university.org/2010/01/european-economic-governance-next-big.html (accessed January 20, 2011).

Jensen, Michael C. 1986. Agency costs of free cash flow, corporate finance, and takeovers. *American Economic Review* 76(2): 323–329.

Judt, Tony. 2010a. Captive minds, then and now. *New York Review of Books*, July 13.

Judt, Tony. 2010b. *Ill fares the land: A treatise on our present discontents.* London: Penguin.

Kaldor, Nicholas. 1957. A model of economic growth. *Economic Journal* 67(268): 591–624.

Kaldor, Nicholas. 1965. Capital accumulation and economic growth. In F. A. Lutz and D. C. Hague, eds., *The theory of capital.* London: Macmillan.

Kaldor, Nicholas. 1966. *Causes of the slow growth in the United Kingdom.* Cambridge: Cambridge University Press. Reprinted in Ferdinando Targetti and Anthony P. Thirlwall, eds., *The essential Kaldor.* London: Duckworth, 1989.

Kaldor, Nicholas. 1972. The irrelevance of equilibrium economics. *Economic Journal* 82(328): 1237–1255.

Kaldor, Nicholas. 1978. The effect of devaluations on trade in manufactures. In Nicholas Kaldor, *Further essays on applied economics.* London: Duckworth, 99–118.

Kalecki, Michał. 1943. Political aspects of full employment. *Political Quarterly* 14(3): 322–330.

Kamps, Christophe. 2004. New estimates of government net capital stocks for 22 OECD countries 1960–2001. IMF Working Paper 04/67. Washington, DC: IMF.

Kapur, Ajay. 2005. Plutonomy: Buying luxury, explaining global imbalances. *Global Investigator*, Citigroup Research, October 14.

Karanassou, Marika, Hector Sala, and Pablo F. Salvador. 2009. Capital accumulation and unemployment: New insights on the Nordic experience. *Cambridge Journal of Economics* 32(6): 977–1002.

Karanassou, Marika, and Dennis Snower. 2004. Unemployment invariance. *German Economic Review* 5(3): 297–317.

Kennedy, Charles. 1964. Induced bias in innovation and the theory of distribution. *Economic Journal* 74: 541–547.

Keynes, John Maynard. 1931a. The great slump of 1930. In *Essays in persuasion.* New York: W. W. Norton.

Keynes, John Maynard. 1931b. Economic possibilities for our grandchildren. In *Essays in persuasion.* New York: W. W. Norton.

Keynes, John Maynard. 1933. National self-sufficiency. *New Statesman and Nation*, July 15.

Keynes, John Maynard. (1936) 1973. *The general theory of employment, interest and money.* London: Macmillan.

Keynes, John Maynard. 1940. Comment. *Economic Journal* (March). In *The collected writings of J. M. Keynes*, vol. 14: *The general theory and after*, Part II: *Defence and development.* London: Macmillan for the Royal Economic Society, 1973.

Klein, Naomi. 2007. *The shock doctrine: The rise of disaster capitalism.* New York: Picador.

Kleinknecht, Alfred, Remco Oostendorp, Menno Pradhan, and C. W. M. Naastepad. 2006. Flexible labour, firm performance and the Dutch job creation miracle. *International Review of Applied Economics* 20(2): 171–187.

Kropotkin, Pyotr Alexeyevich. (1902) 2005. *Mutual aid: A factor of evolution*. Boston: Porter Sargent.

Krugman, Paul. 1998. Review of *Living wage: What it is and why we need it. Washington Monthly*, September 1.

Krugman, Paul. 2009. *The return of depression economics*. Lionel Robbins Memorial Lecture. London School of Economics.

Layard, Richard, Stephen Nickell, and Richard Jackman. 1991. *Unemployment, macroeconomic performance and the labour market*. Oxford: Oxford University Press.

Lazonick, William. 2009. The new economy business model and the crisis of US capitalism. *Capitalism and Society* 4(2): online article 4. Available at: http://www.bepress.com/cas/vol4/iss2/art4.

Leon-Ledesma, Miguel. 2002. Accumulation, innovation and catching-up: An extended cumulative growth model. *Cambridge Journal of Economics* 25(2): 201–216.

Levine, David I. 1993. Demand variability and work organization. In Samuel Bowles, Herbert Gintis, and Bo Gustafsson, eds., *Markets and democracy: Participation, accountability and efficiency*. New York: Cambridge University Press, 159–175.

Levine, David I., and Laura D'Andrea Tyson. 1990. Participation, productivity and the firm's environment. In Alan S. Blinder, ed., *Paying for productivity: A look at the evidence*. Washington, DC: Brookings Institution.

Lewontin, Richard C. 1998. The survival of the nicest. *New York Review of Books*, October 22.

Ljungqvist, Lars, and Thomas J. Sargent. 1995. The Swedish unemployment experience. *European Economic Review* 39: 1043–1070.

Lorenz, Edward H. 1992. Trust and the flexible firm: International comparisons. *Industrial Relations* 31(3): 455–472.

Lowe, Adolph. 1988. *Has freedom a future?* New York: Praeger.

Lucas, Robert E., Jr. 1981. Tobin and monetarism: A review article. *Journal of Economic Literature* 29(2): 558–567.

Lucas, Robert E., Jr., and Thomas J. Sargent. 1978. After Keynesian macroeconomics. In Federal Reserve Bank of Boston, ed., *After the Phillips curve: Persistence of high inflation and high unemployment*. Conference Series No. 19. Boston: Federal Reserve Bank of Boston.

Lyon, Vaughan. 1986. Swedish wage earner funds: A glimpse of our future? *Canadian Journal of Political Science* 19(3): 573–583.

Lysandrou, Photis. 2009. The root cause of the financial crisis: A demand-side view. Economists' Forum. *Financial Times*, March 24.

Lysandrou, Photis. 2011. Global inequality, wealth concentration and the subprime crisis: A Marxian commodity theory analysis. *Development and Change* 42(1): 183–208.

Magnier, Antoine, and Joël Toujas-Bernate. 1994. Technology and trade: Empirical evidence for the major five industrialized countries. *Weltwirtschaftliches Archiv* 130(3): 495–520.

Malcomson, James M. 1997. Contracts, hold-up and labour markets. *Journal of Economic Literature* 35: 1917–1957.

Mankiw, N. Gregory, and Mark P. Taylor. 2010. *Economics*. London: Cengage Learning.

Manning, Alan. 2005. *Monopsony in motion: Imperfect competition in labor markets.* Princeton: Princeton University Press.

Mansbridge, Jane J., ed. 1990a. *Beyond self-interest.* Chicago: University of Chicago Press.

Mansbridge, Jane J. 1990b. The rise and fall of self-interest in the explanation of political life. In Jane J. Mansbridge, ed., *Beyond self-interest*, 3–22. Chicago: University of Chicago Press.

Mansbridge, Jane J. 1990c. On the relation of altruism and self-interest. In Jane J. Mansbridge, ed., *Beyond self-interest*, 133–143. Chicago: University of Chicago Press.

Marglin, Stephen A. 2008. *The dismal science: How thinking like an economist undermines community.* Cambridge, MA: Harvard University Press.

Marglin, Stephen A., and Juliet B. Schor, eds. 1990. *The golden age of capitalism: Reinterpreting the postwar experience.* Oxford: Oxford University Press.

Marquetti, Adalmir A. 2004. Do rising real wages increase the rate of labor-saving technical change? Some econometric evidence. *Metroeconomica* 55(4): 432–441.

Marshall, Alfred. (1892) 1928. *Elements of economics of industry.* London: Macmillan.

Marx, Karl. 1844. Estranged labour. Manuscript I, *Economic and philosophical manuscripts.* Available at: http://www.marxists.org/archive/marx/works/download /pdf/Economic-Philosophic-Manuscripts-1844.pdf.

Marx, Karl. 1846–47. *The poverty of philosophy.* Available at: http://www.marxists .org/archive/marx/works/download/pdf/Poverty-Philosophy.pdf.

Marx, Karl (1867) 1987. *Capital: A critique of political economy*, vol. 1: *The process of capitalist development.* New York: International Publishers.

McCombie, John S. L. 2002. Increasing returns and the Verdoorn law from a Kaldorian perspective. In John S. L. McCombie, Maurizio Pugno, and Bruno Soro, eds., *Productivity growth and economic performance: Essays on Verdoorn's law.* London: Macmillan.

McCombie, John S. L., Maurizio Pugno, and Bruno Soro, eds. 2002. *Productivity growth and economic performance: Essays on Verdoorn's law.* London: Macmillan.

Meidner, Rudolf. 1978. *Employee investment funds: An approach to collective capital formation.* London: George Allen and Unwin.

Meidner, Rudolf. 1993. Why did the Swedish model fail? *Socialist Register* 29: 211–228.

Meidner, Rudolf, and Gøsta Rehn 1953. *Trade unions and full employment.* Report to the LO Congress 1951. Stockholm: Swedish Confederation of Trade Unions (LO).

Michie, Jonathan, and Maureen Sheehan. 2003. Labour market deregulation, "flexibility" and innovation. *Cambridge Journal of Economics* 27(1): 123–143.

Milberg, William, and Eileen Houston. 2005. The high road and the low road to international competitiveness: Extending the neo-Schumpeterian trade model beyond technology. *International Review of Applied Economics* 19(2): 137–162.

Mill, John Stuart. (1859) 1989. *On liberty.* Cambridge: Cambridge University Press.

Mill, John Stuart. (1863) 1998. *Utilitarianism.* Oxford: Oxford University Press.

Mills, Charles Wright. 1959. *The sociological imagination.* New York: Oxford University Press.

Mishel, Lawrence, Jared Bernstein, and Heidi Shierholz. 2009. *The state of working America.* Ithaca, NY: Cornell University Press.

Mjøset, Lars. 2004. Nordic economic policies in the 1980s and 1990s. Working Paper 07/04. Oslo: Centre for Technology, Innovation and Culture, University of Oslo.

Moene, Karl Oeve. 2008. Labor and the Nordic model of social democracy: Introduction. In David Austen-Smith et al., eds., *Selected Works of Michael Wallerstein: The Political Economy of Inequality, Unions and Social Democracy.* Cambridge: Cambridge University Press.

Moene, Karl Ove, and Michael Wallerstein. 1995. Solidaristic wage bargaining. *Nordic Journal of Political Economy* 22: 79–94.

Moene, Karl Ove, and Michael Wallerstein. 1997. Pay inequality. *Journal of Labor Economics* 15(3): 403–430.

Naastepad, C. W. M. 2006. Technology, demand and distribution: A cumulative growth model with an application to the Dutch productivity growth slowdown. *Cambridge Journal of Economics* 30(3): 403–434.

Naastepad, C. W. M., and Alfred Kleinknecht. 2004. The Dutch productivity slowdown: The culprit at last. *Structural Change and Economic Dynamics* 15(1): 137–163.

Naastepad, C. W. M., and Servaas Storm. 2006. The innovating firm in a societal context: Labour-management relations and labour productivity. In R. M. Verburg, J. R. Ortt, and W. M. Dicke, eds., *Managing technology and innovation.* London: Routledge.

Naastepad, C. W. M., and Servaas Storm. 2007. OECD demand regimes (1960–2000). *Journal of Post Keynesian Economics* 29(2): 211–246.

Naastepad, C. W. M., and Servaas Storm. 2010. Feasible egalitarianism: Demand-led growth, labour and technology. In Mark Setterfield, ed., *Handbook of alternative theories of economic growth,* 311–330. Cheltenham: Edward Elgar.

Nickell, Stephen. 1997. Unemployment and labor market rigidities: Europe versus North America. *Journal of Economic Perspectives* 11(3): 55–74.

Nickell, Stephen. 1998. Unemployment: Questions and some answers. *Economic Journal* 108 (May): 802–816.

Nickell, Stephen, and Richard Layard. 1999. Labor market institutions and economic performance. In Orley Ashenfelter and David Card, eds., *Handbook of labor economics,* vol. 3, 3029–3066. Amsterdam: Elsevier Science.

Nickell, Stephen, Luca Nunziata, and Wolfgang Ochel. 2005. Unemployment in the OECD since the 1960s: What do we know? *Economic Journal* 111: 1–27.

Nicoletti, Giuseppe, and Stefano Scarpetta. 2003. Regulation, productivity and growth: OECD evidence. *Economic Policy* 18: 9–72.

Nicoletti, Giuseppe, Stefano Scarpetta, and Olivier Boyland. 2000. Summary indicators of product market regulation with an extension to employment protection legislation. Economics Department Working Paper No. 226. Paris: OECD.

Nordhaus, William D. 1973. Some sceptical thoughts on the theory of induced innovation. *Quarterly Journal of Economics* 87: 208–219.

Nunziata, Luca. 2005. Institutions and wage determination: A multi-country approach. *Oxford Bulletin of Economics and Statistics* 67(4): 435–466.

Nymoen, Ragnar, and Asbjørn Rødseth. 2003. Explaining unemployment: Some lessons from Nordic wage formation. *Labour Economics* 10(1): 1–29.

OECD. 1994. *The OECD jobs study.* Paris: OECD. Available at: http://www.oecd .org/dataoecd/42/51/1941679.pdf.

OECD. 1997. Is job insecurity on the increase in OECD countries? In *OECD employment outlook 1997*, chapter 5. Paris: OECD.

OECD. 1999. Employment protection and labour market performance. In *OECD employment outlook 1999*, chapter 2. Paris: OECD.

OECD. 2003. *The sources of economic growth in OECD countries.* Paris: OECD.

OECD. 2006. Reassessing the role of policies and institutions for labor market performance: A quantitative analysis. In *OECD employment outlook 2006*, chapter 7. Paris: OECD.

OECD. 2007. More jobs but less productive? The impact of labour market policies on productivity. In *OECD employment outlook 2007*, chapter 2. Paris: OECD.

Olson, Mancur. 1965. *The logic of collective action.* Cambridge, MA: Harvard University Press.

Orwell, George. 1946. Politics and the English language. *Horizon* (April). Available at: http://www.mtholyoke.edu/acad/intrel/orwell46.htm.

Palley, Thomas. 2006. Milton Friedman: The great laissez-faire partisan. Available at: www.thomaspalley.com/docs/articles/macro_policy/milton_friedman.pdf.

Palley, Thomas. 2009. *America's exhausted paradigm: Macroeconomic causes of the financial crisis and the great recession.* New American Contract Policy Paper. Washington, DC: New America Foundation.

Palma, José Gabriel. 2009. The revenge of the market on the rentiers: Why neo-liberal reports of the end of history turned out to be premature. *Cambridge Journal of Economics* 33(4): 829–869.

Parsons, Talcott. 1937. *The structure of social action.* New York: McGraw-Hill.

Patinkin, Don. 1981. *Essays on and in the Chicago tradition.* Durham, NC: Duke University Press.

Phelps, Edmund S. 1968. Money-wage dynamics and labor-market equilibrium. *Journal of Political Economy* 76(2): 678–711.

Phelps, Edmund S. 1994. *Structural slumps: The modern equilibrium theory of unemployment, interest, and assets.* Cambridge, MA: Harvard University Press.

Piketty, Thomas, and Emmanuel Sáez. 2003. Income inequality in the United States 1913–1998. *Quarterly Journal of Economics* 118(1): 1–39 (data updated to 2006 at http://elsa.berkeley.edu/~saez/TabFig2006.xls).

Ploughmann, Peter, and Per Kongshøj Madsen. 2005. Labor market policy, flexibility, and employment performance in Denmark and Sweden in the 1990s. In David Howell, ed., *Questioning liberalization: Unemployment, labor markets and the welfare state*, 284–309. Oxford: Oxford University Press.

Polanyi, Karl. (1944) 2001. *The great transformation.* Boston: Beacon Press.

Pollin, Robert. 2003. *Contours of descent: US economic fractures and the landscape of global austerity*. London: Verso.

Pugh, Geoffrey. 1998. The profit elasticity of investment in West Germany and the investment diversion effects of unification. *Applied Economics Letters* 5(2): 97–99.

Putnam, Robert D. 2000. *Bowling alone: The collapse and revival of American community*. New York: Simon and Schuster.

Ramirez, Anthony. 2006. A job prospect lures, then frustrates, thousands. *New York Times*, November 4, B1.

Rapoport, A., and A. M. Chammah. 1965. *Prisoner's dilemma*. Ann Arbor: University of Michigan Press.

Rehn, Gøsta. 1952. The problem of stability: An analysis of some policy proposals. In R. Turvey, ed., *Wages policy under full employment*. London: W. Hodge.

Robinson, Joan. 1962. *Economic philosophy*. London: Penguin Books.

Robinson, Joan. 1979. *The generalisation of the general theory and other essays*. London: Macmillan.

Robinson, Joan. 1980. Time in economic history. *Kyklos* 33(2): 219–229.

Roemer, John E. 1988. *Free to lose: An introduction to Marxist economic philosophy*. Cambridge, MA: Harvard University Press.

Roemer, John E. 2010. Kantian equilibrium. *Scandinavian Journal of Economics* 112(1): 1–24.

Rowthorn, Robert E. 1977. Conflict, inflation and money. *Cambridge Journal of Economics* 1(2): 215–239.

Rowthorn, Robert E. 1995. Capital formation and unemployment. *Oxford Review of Economic Policy* 11(1): 26–39.

Rowthorn, Robert E. 1999. Unemployment, wage bargaining and capital-labour substitution. *Cambridge Journal of Economics* 23(4): 413–425.

Ruttan, Vernon W. 1997. Induced innovation, evolutionary theory and path dependence: Sources of technical change. *Economic Journal* 107(444): 1520–1529.

Sachs, Jeffrey D. 2006a. Revisiting the Nordic model: Evidence on recent macroeconomic performance. Paper prepared for the CESifo/Center for Capitalism and Society Venice Summer Institute, July 21–22.

Sachs, Jeffrey D. 2006b. The social welfare state, beyond ideology. *Scientific American*, October 16.

Saint Paul, Gilles. 2004. Why are European countries diverging in their unemployment experience? *Journal of Economic Perspectives* 18(4): 49–68.

Salter, W. E. G. 1960. *Productivity and technical change*. Cambridge: Cambridge University Press.

Samuelson, Paul A. 1965. A theory of induced innovation along Kennedy-Weizsacker lines. *Review of Economics and Statistics* 47: 343–356.

Samuelson, Paul A. 1980. *Economics*. 11th ed. New York: McGraw-Hill.

Sapir, André. 2005. Globalisation and the reform of European social models. Background document for the presentation at ECOFIN Informal Meeting in Manchester, September 9. Available at: http://www.bruegel.org.

Sapir, André, et al. 2003. *An agenda for a growing Europe: Making the EU system deliver.* Brussels: European Commission.

Scarpetta, Stefano. 1996. Assessing the role of labor market policies and institutional settings on unemployment: A cross country study. *OECD Economic Studies* 26: 43–98.

Scarpetta, Stefano, and Thierry Tressel. 2004. Boosting productivity via innovation and adoption of new technologies: Any role for labor market institutions? World Bank Research Working Paper 3273. Washington, DC: World Bank.

Schor, Juliet B. 1992. *The overworked American: The unexpected decline in leisure.* Cambridge, MA: Harvard University Press.

Sen, Amartya Kumar. (1977) 1990. Rational fools: A critique of the behavioral foundations of economic theory. In Jane J. Mansbridge, ed., *Beyond self-interest*, 25–43. Chicago: University of Chicago Press.

Sennett, Richard. 1998. *The corrosion of character: The personal consequences of work in the new capitalism.* New York: W. W. Norton.

Sennett, Richard. 2005. *The culture of the new capitalism.* New Haven: Yale University Press.

Setterfield, Mark, ed. 2002. *The economics of demand-led growth. Challenging the supply-side vision of the long run.* Cheltenham: Edward Elgar.

Setterfield, Mark, ed. 2010. *Handbook of alternative theories of economic growth.* Cheltenham: Edward Elgar.

Setterfield, Mark, and John Cornwall. 2002. A neo-Kaldorian perspective on the rise and decline of the Golden Age. In M. Setterfield, ed., *Handbook of alternative theories of economic growth*, 67–86. Cheltenham: Edward Elgar.

Shaw, George Bernard. (1905) 2010. *Man and superman: A comedy and a philosophy.* Los Angeles: Indo-European Publishing.

Siebert, Horst. 1997. Labor market rigidities: At the root of unemployment in Europe. *Journal of Economic Perspectives* 11(3): 37–54.

Singh, Ajit. 1998. Saving, investment and the corporation in the East Asian miracle. *Journal of Development Studies* 34(6): 112–137.

Skidelsky, Robert. 2009. The myth of the business cycle. Available at: http://www.realclearmarkets.com/articles/2009/01/the_myth_of_the_business_cycle.html.

Slater, Michael. 2009. *Charles Dickens: A life defined by writing.* New Haven: Yale University Press.

Smith, Adam. (1776) 1976. *An inquiry into the nature and causes of the wealth of nations.* Edwin Cannan, ed. Chicago: University of Chicago Press.

Solow, Robert. 1970. *Growth theory: An exposition.* New York: Oxford University Press.

Sousa-Poza, Alfonso. 2004. Job stability and job security: A comparative perspective on Switzerland's experience in the 1990s. *European Journal of Industrial Relations* 10(1): 31–49.

Staiger, Douglas, James Stock, and Mark Watson. 1997. The NAIRU, unemployment and monetary policy. *Journal of Economic Perspectives* 11(1): 33–50.

Staiger, Douglas, James Stock, and Mark Watson. 2001. Prices, wages, and the NAIRU in the US in the 1990s. NBER Working Paper No. 8320. Cambridge, MA: National Bureau of Economic Research.

Standing, Guy. 1988. *Unemployment and labour market flexibility: Sweden*. ILO: Geneva.

Stockhammer, Engelbert. 2004. *The rise of unemployment in Europe: A Keynesian approach*. Cheltenham: Edward Elgar.

Stockhammer, Engelbert, Echard Hein, and Lucas Grafl. 2011. Globalization and the effects of changes in functional income distribution on aggregate demand in Germany. *International Review of Applied Economics* 25(1): 1–23.

Stockhammer, Engelbert, Özlem Onaran, and Stefan Ederer. 2009. Functional income distribution and aggregate demand in the Euro area. *Cambridge Journal of Economics* 33(1): 139–159.

Storm, Servaas, and C. W. M. Naastepad. 2003. The Dutch distress. *New Left Review* 20: 131–151.

Storm, Servaas, and C. W. M. Naastepad. 2005a. Strategic factors in economic development: East Asian industrialization 1950–2003. *Development and Change* 36(6): 1059–1094.

Storm, Servaas, and C. W. M. Naastepad. 2005b. De schaduwzijde van arbeidsmarktderegulering. *Economisch-Statistische Berichten* 90(4454): 86–89.

Storm, Servaas, and C. W. M. Naastepad. 2007. It is high time to ditch the NAIRU. *Journal of Post Keynesian Economics* 29(4): 531–554.

Storm, Servaas, and C. W. M. Naastepad. 2008a. Why labour market regulation may pay off: Worker motivation, co-ordination and productivity growth. Economics and Labour Market Paper 2007/4. Geneva: International Labour Organization.

Storm, Servaas, and C. W. M. Naastepad. 2008b. The NAIRU reconsidered: Why labour market deregulation may raise unemployment. *International Review of Applied Economics* 22(5): 527–544.

Storm, Servaas, and C. W. M. Naastepad. 2008c. Wat de commissie Bakker weten moet. *Economisch Statistische Berichten* 93(4534): 260–263.

Storm, Servaas, and C. W. M. Naastepad. 2009a. The NAIRU, demand and technology. *Eastern Economic Journal* 35(3): 309–337.

Storm, Servaas, and C. W. M. Naastepad. 2009b. Labour market regulation and labour productivity growth: Evidence for 20 OECD countries 1984–2004. *Industrial Relations* 48(4): 629–654.

Storm, Servaas, and C. W. M. Naastepad. 2009c. The costs of NAIRUvianism. *Challenge* 52(5): 55–76.

Suarez-Villa, Luis. 2009. *Technocapitalism: A critical perspective on technological innovation and corporatism*. Philadelphia: Temple University Press.

Sveriges Riksbank. 2007. *Penningpolitisk rapport, 2007/3*. Stockholm: Sveriges Riksbank.

Swenson, Peter A. 2002. *Capitalists against markets: The making of labor markets and welfare states in the United States and Sweden*. Oxford: Oxford University Press.

Swenson, Peter A. 2004. Varieties of capitalist interests: Power, institutions, and the regulatory welfare state in the United States and Sweden. *Studies in American Political Development* 18 (Spring): 1–29.

Tavani, Daniele. 2009. Wage bargaining and induced technical change in a linear economy: Model and application to the US (1963–2003). MPRA Paper No. 14635. Munich: Münich Personal RePec Archive.

Tavani, Daniele, Peter Flaschel, and Lance Taylor. 2011. Estimated non-linearities and multiple equilibria in a model of distributive-demand cycles. *International Review of Applied Economics* 25.

Taylor, Lance. 1990. Real and money wages, output and inflation in the semi-industrialized world. *Economica* 57(227): 329–353.

Taylor, Lance. 1991. *Income distribution, inflation and growth. Lectures on structuralist macroeconomic theory.* Cambridge, MA: MIT Press.

Taylor, Lance. 2004. *Reconstructing macroeconomics: Structuralist proposals and critiques of the mainstream.* Cambridge. MA: Harvard University Press.

Taylor, Lance. 2010. *Maynard's revenge: Keynesianism and the collapse of free market macroeconomics.* Cambridge, MA: Harvard University Press.

Thirlwall, Anthony P. 2002. *The nature of economic growth: An alternative framework for understanding the performance of nations.* Cheltenham: Edward Elgar.

Tsakalotos, Euclid. 2006. Social conflict and the effectiveness of aggregate demand management policies. *Review of Radical Political Economics* 38(2): 214–242.

Uchitelle, Louis. 2006. *The disposable American: Layoffs and their consequences.* New York: Alfred A. Knopf.

Verdoorn, P. J. 1949. Fattori che regolano lo sviluppo della produttività del lavaro. *L'Industria* 1: 45–53. Reprinted in English as: On the factors determining the growth of labor productivity, in Luigi L. Pasinetti, ed., *Italian Economic Papers,* vol. 2, 59–68. Oxford: Oxford University Press, 1993.

Vitols, Sigurt. 2001. Varieties of corporate governance: Comparing Germany and the UK. In Peter A. Hall and David Soskice, eds., *Varieties of capitalism: The institutional foundations of comparative advantage,* 337–360. Oxford: Oxford University Press.

Waal, Frans de. 2009. *The age of empathy: Nature's lessons for a kinder society.* New York: Crown.

Wade, Robert. 2009. On the global financial crisis. Interview by Alex Izurieta. *Development and Change* 40(6): 1153–1190.

Weitzman, Martin L. 1984. *The share economy: Conquering stagflation.* Cambridge, MA: Harvard University Press.

Weizsacker, Von C. C. 1966. Tentative notes on a two-sector model with induced technical progress. *Review of Economic Studies* 33(3): 245–251.

Wheen, Francis. 2006. *Marx's Das Kapital: A biography.* London: Atlantic Books.

Wilkinson, Richard G. 1996. *Unhealthy societies: The afflictions of inequality.* London: Routledge.

Wilkinson, Richard G., and Kate Pickett. 2009. *The spirit level: Why more equal societies almost always do better.* London: Penguin Books.

Williams, Howard. 2003. *Kant's critique of Hobbes.* Cardiff: University of Wales Press.

Wilson, David Sloan, and Edward O. Wilson. 2007. Rethinking the theoretical foundation of sociobiology. *Quarterly Review of Biology* 82(4): 327–348.

Wyckoff, Andrew W. 1995. The impact of computer prices on international comparisons of labour productivity. *Economics of Innovation and New Technology* 3(3): 277–293.

Young, Allyn Abbott. 1928. Increasing returns and economic progress. *Economic Journal* 38(152): 527–542.

Index

equilibrium unemployment. *See* NAIRU
European continental (EC) countries,
46–53, 72, 77, 98, 104–107, 125, 144,
165, 191, 198, 205–206, 210
European Mediterranean (EM) countries,
46–52, 191, 204
European Union (EU), 1, 30, 44, 254n25;
Economic and Monetary Union (EMU),
165, 185
exchange rates, 164, 195, 231, 249n9,
252n8; and Bretton Woods, 115, 164
exhilarationism, 67. *See also* profit-led
demand
export growth, 58, 60; and unit labor costs,
137–142, 145

fallacy of composition, 137, 147
financial system, 151–159, 254n25; bank-
based, 21–22, 144, 152–158; stock-
market-based, 21, 144, 152–161
fiscal policy, 3, 8, 17, 22–23, 169–174, 177,
182, 189–190, 197–201, 208, 212, 239;
ineffectiveness of, 8–9; permanent effects
of, 181–184, 206–208; and productivity
growth, 22–23; and unemployment,
181–186, 206–208
"flexicurity" or protected mobility, 98, 105,
198
Foley, Duncan K., 15, 56, 57, 85, 115, 220,
257n4
Forslund, Anders, 194, 198, 200, 201, 202,
209, 246n5
Forstater, Mathew, 241
foundational critique, of NAIRU, 9, 12, 18,
226–229
France, 21, 46, 83, 98, 100, 110–111, 113,
118, 124–129, 130–140, 198, 206, 210,
243, 252n8, 253n16; and earnings
inequality, 30; and financial sector,
153–155; and weakly wage-led demand,
72, 77, 142–147, 163–166
freedom: economic, 220–224, 228–230,
233, 235, 236, 241, 259nn22–23;
freedom to shop, 224; and negative
liberty, 219, 223, 229–230, 240, 258n14;
personal, 219, 220, 229; and positive
liberty, 223, 224, 230–235, 236, 239,
241, 259n24
Freeman, Richard B., 28, 44, 45, 53, 54,
246n9, 255n4
Friedman, Milton, ix, 9, 10, 22, 72, 115,
181, 184, 186, 194, 212, 216, 219–222,
241, 245n3 (chap. 1), 257n2, 258n13

Fromm, Erich, 219, 234
full employment, 3, 33, 74, 113, 114, 126,
188, 189, 190, 213, 215, 217, 218, 238, 239

Galbraith, James K., 2, 3, 12, 24, 25, 27, 29,
32, 43, 113, 166, 181, 182, 185, 186,
212, 213, 214, 215, 217, 218, 219, 220,
221, 224, 235, 241, 247n15
Galbraith, John Kenneth, 234
Germany, 21, 44, 46, 52, 83, 98, 101, 109,
110, 111, 113, 116, 119, 124–127, 129,
130–145, 149, 198, 206, 210, 243,
246n10, 252n8, 253n17, 254n25; and
financial sector, 151–155; and weakly
wage-led demand, 72, 77, 142–147,
162–166
Gerschenkron, Alexander, 152
Ghoshal, Sumantra, 224, 238
globalization, x, 3, 8, 23, 46, 151, 210, 217
Glyn, Andrew, 3, 25, 27, 46, 112, 116, 123,
133, 134, 138, 139, 140, 141, 142, 143,
158, 161, 164, 239, 251nn2–3, 252n7,
252n9
"golden age" of capitalism, 112–116, 126,
161; and social compromise, 114–116,
206, 219
Goethe, Johann Wolfgang von, 112, 151, 240
Gordon, David M., 19, 35, 36, 37, 54, 57,
74, 88, 93, 103, 107, 108, 109, 133, 137,
143, 233, 236, 249n8, 250n3, 250n6,
252n7
Gordon, Robert J., 25, 71, 90, 92, 103, 182,
200
Gould, Stephen Jay, 187–188, 255n2
government: role of, 3, 10–11, 22, 34,
114–115, 123, 158–161, 189–192,
208–211, 217, 219, 220–224, 230–233;
deficit, 59, 61, 159, 160, 164, 219;
spending, 59, 100, 102, 165, 177–178,
182, 197, 199, 207, 208
Greenspan, Alan, 30, 64, 65, 68, 116, 125,
218, 257n3
growth-equity trade-off, conflict between
growth and equality, 3, 23, 46–47, 53,
56, 188, 192, 203, 235
growth model, 20, 53–54, 55–79, 160,
169–174, 195–196

Hall, Peter A., 48, 54, 103, 144, 153, 155,
156, 161, 205, 250n11, 253n19,
253nn21–22
Hein, Eckhard, 83, 103, 129, 130, 134, 137,
138, 142, 143, 151, 252n7, 252n11

Harvard University Press is a member of Green Press Initiative
(greenpressinitiative.org), a nonprofit organization working to
help publishers and printers increase their use of recycled paper
and decrease their use of fiber derived from endangered forests.
This book was printed on recycled paper containing 30%
post-consumer waste and processed chlorine free.